A MISUNDERSTOOD FRIENDSHIP

Studies of the Weatherhead East Asian Institute, Columbia University

STUDIES OF THE WEATHERHEAD EAST ASIAN INSTITUTE,
COLUMBIA UNIVERSITY

The Studies of the Weatherhead East Asian Institute of Columbia University were inaugurated in 1962 to bring to a wider public the results of significant new research on modern and contemporary East Asia.

A Misunderstood Friendship

MAO ZEDONG, KIM IL-SUNG, AND
SINO–NORTH KOREAN RELATIONS,
1949–1976

Zhihua Shen and Yafeng Xia

Revised and Corrected Edition

Columbia University Press
New York

All figures and maps are from Shen Zhihua, *Zuihou de "tianchao": Mao Zedong, Jin Richeng yu Zhong Chao guanxi* [The Last "Celestial Empire": Mao Zedong, Kim Il-sung, and Sino–North Korean Relations] (expanded edition, in Chinese) (Hong Kong: The Chinese University Press, 2018).

Columbia University Press
Publishers Since 1893
New York   Chichester, West Sussex
cup.columbia.edu
Copyright © 2020 Columbia University Press
All rights reserved

Cataloging-in-Publication data available from the Library of Congress.

ISBN 978-0-231-20055-4 (trade paperback)
ISBN 978-0-231-55367-4 (ebook)

For our students

Contents

Acknowledgments

M any individuals and institutions helped in the research and writing of this book. We wish to acknowledge and thank Christian Ostermann and the Cold War International History Project at the Woodrow Wilson International Center for Scholars for permission to use in whole or in part their translations of Russian documents that have been published in their numerous publications or posted on the project's digital archive Web site. For comments and research assistance, we are grateful to the following Chinese friends and scholars: Chen Jian, Fang Xiuyu, Zhu Liang, Jin Chenggao, Jin Chongji, Jin Guantao, Li Sheng, Liu Xiaoyuan, Ma Yuan, Shi Yuanhua, Yang Xiyu, Yang Zhaoquan, Yu Weimin, Zhang Liankui, Zhu Jianrong, Yao Yu, Xu Xianfen, Deng Feng, Xiao Yu, Lü Xuefeng, Dong Jie, Cui Haizhi, Bai Lin, Gao Xiaochuan, Jin Quan, Li Rui, Lin Yizhen, Liu Tong, Liu Yong, Sun Yanshu, Xu Xiangmei, You Lan, Zhang Tingting, Zhao Qingfeng, Gu Jikun, Ge Jun, Shi Jianjun, Zhao Jike, Jiang Huajie, Liang Zhi, Chen Ming, Chen Ningchuan, Qian Xiaohua, Wang Jianhe, Wu Kegang, Xie Li, Yang Lichuan, Yu Jiandong, and Zhang Jianqiang. We also thank foreign scholars, including Gregg Brazinsky, Thomas J. Christensen, Kim Dong-gil, Sergey Radchenko, Avram Agov, Erez Manela, Ria Chae, Jeehye Kim, Carla Freeman, Nobuo Shimotomai, Alsu Tagirova, James Person, Charles Kraus, Bernd Schaefer, Mitchell Lerner, Andrei Lankov, Chris Tudda, Anastasiya Bayok, Priscilla

Roberts, Deborah Kaple, Mark L. Haas, Yuree Kim, Heejae Park, and Miriam Wishnick. We also owe an intellectual debt to the many scholars from whose works we have drawn. We will let our notes and bibliography serve as partial acknowledgment of these invaluable contributions.

While preparing the manuscript, Yafeng Xia was very fortunate to have received two research grants from the Woodrow Wilson International Center for Scholars, a ten-month fellowship (2011/2012) and a six-month public policy fellowship (June–December 2016), and a number of travel grants from Long Island University. Over the years, Nancy Hearst and Neil Silver have served faithfully and diligently as readers and editorial advisors. The editors at Columbia University Press and the Weatherhead East Asian Institute, Columbia University, especially Caelyn Cobb, Kenneth Ross Yelsey, and Miriam Grossman, deserve great credit for making the entire publication process go extremely smoothly. Todd Manza did a great job of copyediting, saving us from many inaccuracies and making this a much better book.

Early versions of chapters 2, 3, and 7 appeared in Shen Zhihua, "Sino–North Korean Conflict and Its Resolution During the Korean War," *Cold War International History Project Bulletin* 14/15 (Winter 2003/Spring 2004); Zhihua Shen and Yafeng Xia, "China and the Post-War Reconstruction of North Korea, 1953–1961," *North Korea International Documentation Project Working Paper* 4 (Washington DC: Woodrow Wilson International Center for Scholars, May 2012); and Yafeng Xia and Zhihua Shen, "China's Last Ally: Beijing's Policy Toward North Korea During U.S.–China Rapprochement, 1970–1975," *Diplomatic History* 38, no. 5 (2014). These have all been substantially revised and are included in this volume with permission from the original publishers.

Chinese names and places are rendered throughout this work in the Hanyu Pinyin system of transliteration. Some names are familiar to the Western readers in their traditional Wade–Giles form. In such cases, the Wade–Giles is given in parentheses after the first use of the Pinyin transliteration, e.g., Jiang Jieshi (Chiang Kai-shek) and Zhou Enlai (Chou Enlai). Korean terms have been transliterated according to the McCune–Reischauer romanization system, except for words with commonly accepted alternative spellings (e.g., Kim Il-sung, *Juche*, Pyongyang). We are extremely grateful to Haeyoung Kim, a PhD candidate at the University of Chicago, who carefully read the entire manuscript in its final stage and fixed many problems with

Korean names and saved us from many errors. Any remaining errors are, of course, the responsibility of the authors.

The earlier version of this work used Dr. James F. Person's working paper "New Evidence on the 1956 September Plenum of the Korean Worker's Party," presented at an April 2016 workshop at the Woodrow Wilson International Center for Scholars, without fair attribution in multiple places in Chapter 3. We sincerely apologize to Dr. Person for not giving his excellent work proper credit. Yafeng Xia, as the main writer of the English version of the book, accepts full responsibility and has revised it so that Dr. Person's influence on the chapter is more properly reflected.

Zhihua Shen

Yafeng Xia

Abbreviations

APRF	Arkhiv Prezidenta Rossiiskoi Federatsii [Archive of the President of the Russian Federation]
AVPRF	Arkhiv Vneshnei Politiki Rossiiskoi Federatsii [Archive of Foreign Policy of the Russian Federation]
CC	Central Committee
CCP	Chinese Communist Party
CFMA	Chinese Foreign Ministry Archives
CPSU	Communist Party of the Soviet Union
CPVA	Chinese People's Volunteer Army
CREST	CIA Records Search Tool
DNSA	Digital National Security Archive
DPRK	Democratic People's Republic of Korea
FRUS	*Foreign Relations of the United States*
GARF	Gosudarstvennyi Arkhiv Rossiiskpi Federatsii [State Archive of the Russian Federation]
GDR	German Democratic Republic
ILD	International Liaison Department
JCP	Japanese Communist Party
JYLSW	*Jianguo yilai Liu Shaoqi wengao* [Liu Shaoqi's Manuscripts Since the Founding of the State]
JYMJW	*Jianguo yilai Mao Zedong junshi wengao* [Mao Zedong's Military Writings Since the Founding of the State]

JYMWG	*Jianguo yilai Mao Zedong wengao* [Mao Zedong's Manuscripts Since the Founding of the State]
KIL	Korean Independence League
KPA	Korean People's Army
KWP	Korean Workers' Party
NA	National Archives
NPMP	Nixon Presidential Materials Project
NSC	National Security Council
PLA	People's Liberation Army
PolAAA	Politisches Archiv des Auswärtigen Amtes [Political Archive of the German Foreign Ministry]
PRC	People's Republic of China
RGANI	Rossiiskii Gosudarstvennyi Arkhiv Noveishii Istorii [Russian State Archive of Contemporary History]
ROK	Republic of Korea
TsAMORF	Tsentral'nyi Arkhiv Ministerstva Oborony Rossiiskoi Federatsii [Central Archive of the Ministry of Defense, Russian Federation]
TsKhSD	Tsentr Khraneniia Sovremennoi Dokumentatsii [Center for the Preservation of Contemporary Documentation]
UNC	United Nations Command
UNCURK	United Nations Commission for the Unification and Rehabilitation of Korea
UNGA	United Nations General Assembly
USSR	Union of Soviet Socialist Republics

Introduction

Refuting a Historical Myth

A fictitious legend about Sino-North Korean relations has spread far and wide in both China and North Korea.[1]

Since the founding of the People's Republic of China (PRC) in 1949, the official newspaper of the Chinese Communist Party (CCP), *Renmin ribao* (People's Daily), and the official newspaper of the Korean Workers' Party (KWP), *Rodong sinmun* (Workers' Newspaper), have frequently carried lengthy articles lauding Sino-North Korean relations, using expressions such as "close as lips are to teeth," "brotherly affection," "sharing weal and woe," "friendship forged with fresh blood and tested in war," and "the traditional friendship between the two peoples will be handed down from generation to generation." One of the two authors of the present volume was born and raised in Mainland China and is the same age as the People's Republic. Like most ordinary Chinese, he grew up hearing such excessive praise of North Korea and Sino-North Korean relations, even during periods of heightened tensions. According to a Chinese idiom, "It takes only three people to spread a rumor about a tiger to make one believe that there really is a tiger." A story, if it is repeated enough times, regardless of whether it is true or not, will become a legend. When you have been told something for sixty years, you naturally tend to believe it.

In fact, North Korea is an extremely secretive country. Even among the Chinese it is completely closed both in terms of media reports and in terms of contacts with foreigners. When we traveled to North Korea in 2006 and

2014, we were, like many other travelers from abroad, constantly followed, and North Korean security personnel strictly controlled all our activities. We felt that we were completely sealed off from any contact with ordinary people. Nonetheless, since the period of China's reform and opening, the mainstream media have continued to toe the same line.[2] The topic of North Korea is so sensitive in China that even the leadership dares not to expose the truth, and Chinese political figures, diplomats, and academics dare not wander into this forbidden area.[3] According to Professor Yang Zhaoquan, a renowned scholar of Sino-Korean relations, in 2012 "there was not one academic book [in China] on the history of Sino-North Korean relations."[4] As a result, China's decision makers and researchers lack a comprehensive, objective, and accurate understanding of the history of Sino-North Korean relations.

Furthermore, in recent years many Chinese have suggested that Sino-North Korean relations have become even more complicated and confusing today than they were in the past. Chinese policy toward North Korea is trapped in a dilemma. But the history of North Korea and the history of Sino-North Korean relations remain a deep secret. The basis for this secret originated during the Cold War, when the respective leaders of the two countries attempted to defend the Sino-North Korean alliance. Special set phrases that were created to describe the history of Sino-North Korean relations, such as "traditional revolutionary friendship," were universally accepted, thus rendering it impossible to understand the true nature of the relationship or to escape the contradictions between history and reality.[5]

In order to comprehend trends in Sino-North Korean relations, to accurately situate the position of the Sino-North Korean relationship, and to formulate current policy toward North Korea, it is of paramount importance that both China and the United States accurately understand the true history of the relationship. To achieve this purpose, it is necessary to refute the historical myth, to tear off the veil, and to eliminate the special set phrases that have been used to describe the history of the relationship. At the very least—even if not for political or diplomatic reasons but only out of scholarly concern—it is the obligation and responsibility of Chinese historians to restore the historical truth.

This book traces the high-level diplomacy between the People's Republic of China and its Communist neighbor North Korea from the late 1940s to the death of CCP leader Mao Zedong in 1976. It provides a realistic and accurate account of the formation, evolution, and gradual decline of the

Chinese–North Korean special relationship during the Cold War. In particular, it reveals many unknown episodes in the interactions between the top leaders of the two countries. We analyze the historical process of relations between the PRC and the Democratic People's Republic of Korea (DPRK) during their first thirty years, to clarify the historical facts and to refute the historical myth.

For a long time, the history of Sino-North Korean relations received very little scholarly attention. It was only during the later years of the Cold War that scholars began to study the history of Sino-North Korean relations from the 1940s to the 1980s. Many of these scholars were South Korean scholars, and they used political science methodology to analyze and predict contemporaneous Sino-North Korean relations and future trends.[6] Works in the former Soviet Union, though stronger in terms of relying upon historical documentation, were more political than academic.[7]

Since the end of the Cold War, and especially with the emergence of the Korean nuclear crisis, Northeast Asia has become much more prominent on the international stage, and thus North Korea has attracted increased scholarly attention. But such studies mainly deal with the nuclear crisis, the famine of the late 1990s, and society and everyday life. They rely primarily on published documents and secondary sources. In contrast, there have been few attempts to reconstruct the historical process.[8] According to Charles Armstrong, very few of the existing studies "can be considered 'scholarship.'" In 2011, Armstrong wrote that "the number of high-quality English-language scholarly books on North Korea published in the last ten years can easily be counted on the fingers of two hands, if not one."[9]

The most important work on Sino–North Korean relations is Yi Chong-sŏk's *The Sino–North Korean Relationship, 1945–2000*, published in 2000 (in Korean). Yi, a former minister of unification in South Korea, later became a research fellow at the Sejong Institute. In light of new historical documents, he traces the history of Sino–North Korean relations from the end of World War II to the end of the twentieth century.[10] However, because the book was published a decade ago, it does not use the more recently available materials from the Chinese, Russian, and Eastern European archives. Yi provides a meaningful analysis of the Sino-North Korean relationship prior to the end of the Korean War, but the remainder of the book is rather weak. Charles Armstrong's 2013 book refers to Chinese intervention in the Korean War, China's economic aid to North Korea's postwar reconstruction, and North Korea during the Sino–Soviet split and the Sino–American rapprochement.[11] Nonetheless, Armstrong does not present a comprehensive overview of the history of Sino–North Korean relations during the Cold War period.

Against a background in which both China and North Korea were socialist countries and members of the International Communist Movement and the United States was their common enemy, China provided unconditional support to North Korea, while Pyongyang generally supported Beijing both politically and diplomatically. North Korea provided a "strategic shield" for China, and China served as North Korea's "great hinterland." However, such a superficial description is too simplistic and overlooks many of the problems and contradictions in the relationship.

Research Questions and Questions of Interpretation

In light of new documentation and studies by other scholars, this book raises straightforward yet important questions. Did China and North Korea have a special relationship during the Maoist era? If so, when did it begin? What was the essence of this special relationship? We argue that the Sino–North Korean special relationship can be traced to 1958, when the Chinese People's Volunteer Army withdrew from North Korea.

Our study highlights the basic features in Sino-North Korean relations. First, after the end of World War II, North Korea was a satellite state, dependent on the Soviet Union, and the Soviet leader Joseph Stalin was instrumental in Kim Il-sung's rise to power. However, following the death of Stalin and the end of the Korean War, North Korea gradually began to develop independent relations with China. Second, after its entry into the Korean War, China had a greater influence in North Korea. Nevertheless, there were major differences between Chinese and North Korean leaders regarding how to fight the war and how to achieve peace. Third, even though North Korea usually took the initiative in its relations with China, when there were conflicts, it was China that generally adopted the more conciliatory policy. Mao played a crucial role in helping Kim Il-sung reach the pinnacle of his power in the late 1950s. Fourth, the Sino–Soviet split in the early 1960s provided North Korea with greater political and diplomatic leverage, allowing Kim Il-sung to navigate between Moscow and Beijing and to greatly enhance North Korea's status in the International Communist Movement. Fifth, after the Sino–Soviet border clashes on

Zhenbao Island in March 1969, Mao attempted to improve relations with the United States. Although China still intended to consider the interests of its smaller allies, such as North Korea, it no longer supported Pyongyang's aggressive foreign policy. The Sino–American rapprochement thus dealt a serious blow to the strategic foundation of the Sino–North Korean special relationship. By 1975, China and North Korea differed fundamentally in terms of their foreign policy postures. As China's revolutionary will waned, Kim Il-sung attempted to assume leadership of the world revolution.

The present study also addresses the following specific questions. When the CCP organized a training institute for representatives from the Asian Communist parties in Beijing in 1949, why did the KWP not send any personnel? Was Mao's decision to dispatch Chinese troops to North Korea based on his fear that "if the lips are gone, then the teeth will be left cold"? Why did Mao intervene in the internal affairs of the KWP in the wake of the August 1956 incident? Why was the 1961 Sino-North Korean Treaty of Friendship, Cooperation, and Mutual Assistance signed only five days after the signing of the Soviet-North Korean Treaty of Friendship, Cooperation, and Mutual Assistance? How were China and North Korea able to resolve the centuries-long Sino–Korean border disputes over Changbai Mountain (长白山; Paektu Mountain in Korean) and Tianchi (天池, Heaven Lake; Ch'ŏnji Lake in Korean) within a matter of only several months? Why did Mao repeatedly refer to Northeast China as Korea's great hinterland? How did Chinese and American leaders deal with the Korean issue during the U.S.–China rapprochement negotiations? In Mao's later years, what were Kim Il-sung's intentions in peddling his *Juche* idea throughout the world, and how did China react?

New Archival Documents

To reconstruct an accurate account of Sino-North Korean relations, it is important to discard the prevailing linguistic constraints as exemplified by the constant repetition of set phrases, and scholars must read the original documents. Although the accessibility of such documentation in both countries is far from adequate, a sizable number of documents exist to provide a good foundation for this study. In terms of the Chinese archives, between 2004 and 2008 the Chinese Ministry of Foreign Affairs declassified three large batches of PRC diplomatic folders dating from 1949 to 1965, among which were 2,424 folders related to North Korea. These include minutes of conversations between Chinese and North Korean leaders, cable communications between the Chinese Embassy in North Korea and the ministry in Beijing, intelligence and research reports by the ministry and related organizations, rules and regulations on how to handle Sino-North Korean relations, and work reports and chronologies compiled by the Chinese Embassy in Pyongyang.[12] These constitute one type of essential documents that have been utilized in this study. Nonetheless, there are two drawbacks in the declassification of the Ministry of Foreign Affairs archives. First, the ministry only declassified files covering the period until 1965. Second, there were too many government restrictions regarding what could be declassified. In principle, none of the documents regarding Sino-North Korean conflicts were declassified, and thus the currently available documents reflect only the cordial and friendly relations between the two countries.

To compensate for the shortcomings of the ministry's files, we have explored archives at the provincial, municipal, and autonomous region levels, all of which have been declassified up to at least the period of the 1980s, and in some cases even to the 1990s. These documents include CCP Central Committee and State Council policies and regulations that were distributed to provincial and municipal governments; large holdings of related reports, circulars, or summaries by those provincial and municipal governments that provided economic and technical aid to North Korea or that hosted North Korean delegations; and letters and cable communications between central government organizations and provincial/municipal governments on specific issues regarding North Korea. For example, the Sichuan and Shanxi provincial archives hold documents regarding the living conditions of the exiled Yan'an faction of North Korean cadres. The present study thus utilizes documents from the Hebei, Hubei, Jiangsu, Jilin, Shaanxi, Shanghai, Shanxi, and Sichuan provincial archives. Additionally, we were fortunate to have had access to internal reference materials and collections compiled by CCP organizations such as the International Liaison Department of the CCP Central Committee. These unpublished materials include, for example, transcripts of Mao Zedong's conversations with Kim Il-sung and other senior North Korean leaders.[13]

Scholars still do not have access to the North Korean archives. Nevertheless, we do have some published materials from North Korea, such as speeches and writings by North Korean leaders, documents from various congresses of the KWP, and issues of the KWP organ *Rodong sinmun* and its theoretical journal, *Kulloja*. We have also relied on archival documents from those countries that maintained relations with North Korea during the Cold War. In the past decade, the North Korea International Documentation Project at the Woodrow Wilson International Center for Scholars has made a concerted effort to mine the archives of North Korea's former allies, particularly those in Eastern Europe and Russia, for insights into DPRK policy making. The Eastern European archives (for example, from Albania, Czechoslovakia, East Germany, and Hungary) contain transcripts of numerous high-level internal meetings at which Kim Il-sung, among others, conveyed opinions about China and PRC-DPRK relations. For example, without the declassified Russian documents we would never have known that the Sino-North Korean relationship was on the verge of collapse after the August 1956 incident. The Eastern European archives also shed much light on Sino-North Korean relations during the period of the Chinese Cultural Revolution, from 1966 to 1969.[14]

Documents from the other side of the "iron curtain" have also been indispensable to this project. Declassified documents from the Republic of Korea offer new perspectives on the study of North Korean foreign policy and Sino-North Korean relations. These include many documents on North Korean diplomacy and North Korean relations with China from the late 1960s. Relations between North and South Korea also affected Sino-North Korean relations. These are a unique source for studying North-South contacts, communications, and negotiations. Although there is no direct documentation in the U.S. archives, intelligence estimates and analytical reports by the Central Intelligence Agency and by the State Department's Bureau of Intelligence and Research provide valuable historical background.[15] We also examined the China volumes of *Foreign Relations of the United States, 1969–1976*, from the Department of State's Office of the Historian, and other China-related documents from the Nixon and Ford administrations that analyze how the United States and China dealt with the Korean issue during the period of the Sino–U.S. rapprochement negotiations, and thereafter at the United Nations.[16]

Oral histories have also played an important role in our research. One of the main features of the studies carried out by South Korean scholars is the use of oral histories and reminiscences by defectors from the North. In addition to interviewing several senior Chinese diplomats who were involved in China's diplomacy with North Korea from the 1950s to the 1970s, we also interviewed numerous former high-ranking KWP officials who fled to China after the fallout with Kim Il-sung in the 1950s, including Kim Kang, deputy head of the Cultural Department of the DPRK government, and Kim Ch'ung-sik, head of the Organization Department of the Pyongyang Municipal Committee of the KWP.[17]

Outline of the Book

This book analyzes the relationship between the People's Republic of China and North Korea in chronological order. Chapter 1 (1945-1950) discusses how the CCP and the KWP assisted each other during their respective seizures of political power and establishment of their revolutionary regimes. They both had close relations with Moscow and became members of the socialist bloc. Nonetheless, prior to China's entry into the Korean War in October 1950, the DPRK was a Soviet satellite state and the CCP and the KWP did not have formal relations. The Soviet Union essentially dominated North Korea during this period, whereas the CCP did not have any influence in North Korea. The CCP Central Committee was very concerned about Kim Il-sung's close association with Chinese members of the No. 88 Independent Infantry Brigade, such as its CCP commander, Zhou Baozhong.[18] Although Mao Zedong was unhappy with Kim Il-sung, as well as with Stalin's decision to launch the Korean War, he prevailed over the dissenting views of his colleagues and decided to send Chinese troops to aid Korea. Mao's decision was based on two priorities: to save and consolidate the Sino–Soviet alliance, and to help Kim Il-sung and assume personal responsibility as the leader of the Asian Revolution.

Chapter 2 (1950-1953) explores high-level PRC–DPRK tensions during the Korean War, as revealed in recently released Chinese sources. It demonstrates that there were actually serious conflicts between the two Communist states with regard to their respective national interests, even though at the same time they were allies fighting a common enemy. For example, when China first entered the war, the two sides had difficulties creating a unified command. After the Chinese army pushed the front toward the 38th parallel, the two countries clashed over the timing of an advance across the parallel and into South Korea. They also disagreed over how to best manage the railway system in order to guarantee a supply line for the Communist army. In early 1952, Kim Il-sung told Mao that he had no desire to continue the war, but Mao insisted on continuing to fight. China's influence and role in North Korea thereby increased dramatically. Prior to the war, Kim had relied on Soviet aid and support, but during the war Stalin stood by Mao and, accordingly, Kim had to suffer the humiliation of becoming completely dependent on both China and the Soviet Union for the survival of his regime. This experience left Kim with deep psychological wounds. Although the Chinese shed much blood during the course of the war, the war failed to create a true friendship between the leaders of the two countries.

Chapter 3 (1953-1956) examines China's comprehensive aid to North Korea after the end of the war. It analyzes Kim Il-sung's strategy of privately acknowledging Chinese aid but publicly emphasizing Korea's "self-reliance." To maintain a semblance of independence, Kim proposed the *Juche* idea and opposed insubordination. The chapter also discusses Kim's purge of the "Moscow faction" (Koreans who had returned from the Soviet Union) and of the "Yan'an faction" (Koreans who had returned from China). New documents reveal that Mao was both shocked and angered by these purges, and a joint Sino–Soviet delegation was dispatched to Pyongyang to intervene. Under pressure, Kim was forced to "admit his mistakes," but he did so only halfheartedly. Ultimately refusing to yield to Soviet and Chinese pressures, he soon resumed the purge. Mao felt that China had lost control over North Korea, and he proposed to the Soviets that they both should take drastic measures to resolve the Korean issue. Sino-North Korean relations thus faced a serious crisis. Ultimately, this led to a major contradiction between Mao's idea of treating states along China's periphery as vassals and protectorates and Kim's *Juche* idea, which opposed "flunkyism" (*shidazhuyi*, 事大主义).[19]

Chapter 4 traces PRC–DPRK relations between 1957 and 1960. After the Polish and Hungarian crises in October 1956, the Soviet Union and China both turned their attention to Eastern Europe. At the same time, Kim continued to purge his potential rivals and to establish his personal dictatorship in North Korea. But with China's growing influence and prestige in the socialist bloc, Mao modified his policy toward North Korea. In order to avoid further alienating Kim, in 1958 Mao withdrew all Chinese troops from Korea. Beijing also no longer provided protection for the exiled Yan'an faction cadres who had fled to China after the August 1956 incident. In turn, when Mao launched the Great Leap Forward in 1958, Kim emulated China by accelerating the Ch'ŏllima movement in North Korea. Based on the slogan "going forward hand in hand," Mao and Kim discussed how the two countries would together enter Communist society. During this period, after the withdrawal of the Chinese People's Volunteer Army from Korea in 1958, Mao helped Kim consolidate his personal dictatorship, and Sino-North Korean relations entered a new phase—the beginning of their "special relationship." As part of this special relationship, China made great efforts to meet Pyongyang's security and economic needs, while North Korea supported Beijing both politically and diplomatically.

Chapter 5 covers PRC–DPRK relations from 1961 to 1965. New documents show that when the Sino–Soviet disagreement erupted in the late 1950s, Kim was adept at balancing between China and the Soviet Union and extracting considerable economic aid from each. The most salient example of this was Kim's ability to secure, almost simultaneously, alliance treaties with both the Soviet Union and China in July 1961. In 1962, when Khrushchev decided to suspend all Soviet aid to North Korea, Kim sided with Beijing in the struggle against "Soviet revisionism." China actually needed the DPRK's political support at this time, as Mao was competing with Moscow for leadership of the International Communist Movement. In return, Beijing intensified its economic aid to Pyongyang and made major concessions on several issues, such as the fate of the more than seventy thousand Korean nationals (*Chaoxianzu*, 朝鲜族) who had illegally crossed the Sino–North Korean border and had fled to North Korea in 1961 and 1962. In addition, the PRC–DPRK border treaty, signed in 1962, gave North Korea a large portion of Tianchi, on the peak of Changbai Mountain, which had previously belonged to China. It was during these years that the Sino-North Korean special relationship reached a new high. On numerous occasions, Mao told Kim Il-sung that Northeast China was the DPRK's great hinterland and that if war were to break out, he would transfer the Northeast Chinese provinces to Kim's command. The Sino-North Korean special relationship was thus further consolidated.

Chapter 6 outlines how Pyongyang handled the very difficult relationship with Beijing when Chinese foreign policy descended into its radical self-imposed isolationist phase during the Cultural Revolution. The Chinese "radicals" accused the KWP of being revisionist and Red Guards engineered a series of incidents along the border. As a result, Sino–North Korean relations reached their lowest ebb and the special relationship faced a severe test. From 1965 to 1969, North Korea was clearly closer to

Moscow than it was to Beijing, but it still made efforts to avoid openly offending Beijing. Neither Kim nor Mao attacked the other publicly, and they each attempted to allow the other some leeway. Meanwhile, between 1967 and 1969, without support from the Soviet Union, Kim launched a series of surprise attacks against the United States and South Korea. The March 1969 Sino–Soviet border clashes and China and North Korea's shared hostility toward Japan, accompanied by their mutual fear of a revival of Japanese militarism, contributed to a sense of urgency to improve relations.

Chapter 7 examines the evolution of Sino-North Korean relations during the process of the U.S.–China rapprochement negotiations from 1970 to 1976. Kim decided to mend the damage to Sino-North Korean relations in order to exploit the profound changes in Sino–U.S. relations. He also began to pursue a radically different reunification strategy—embracing South Korean nationalist calls in the hopes of driving the Americans off the peninsula. Meanwhile, the Sino–U.S. rapprochement alienated China's erstwhile allies Albania and Vietnam. To draw North Korea closer to China, China made a point of defending North Korea's security interests during its negotiations with the United States as well as during the UN deliberations on the Korean issue. In their talks with the Americans, Chinese leaders were not hesitant about admitting China's special relationship with North Korea. Meanwhile, Beijing also provided Pyongyang with massive economic and military aid.

Nevertheless, because of China's strategy of "aligning with the U.S. to oppose the Soviet Union," there were major differences in the respective foreign policies of China and North Korea at this time. At an April 1975 meeting in Beijing, in the wake of the sudden collapse of South Vietnam, Kim made an overture to attack South Korea, but Mao remained noncommittal. The Sino–American rapprochement revealed the growing cracks in the Sino-North Korean special relationship during Mao's later years. Kim firmly believed that the revolutionary nature of both China and the Soviet Union was in the process of weakening and that his *Juche* idea, with Kim Il-sung–ism rather than Maoism at the helm, should guide the world revolution.

This book makes an important contribution to the current literature on alliances. It helps answer several key questions. Why do states form alliances? What factors result in cooperation and under what conditions does such cooperation occur? According to scholars of international relations, alliances can be a means of obtaining or freeing up resources to deal with pressing domestic threats.[20] Alliances also can be a means of providing and promoting ideological support, if they are tied to the advancement of certain governing principles in other countries.[21] However, the main reason why states form alliances is to acquire additional military capabilities so as to better deal with external threats to their interests.[22] In other words, states most often form alliances in order to pool military power to deter or to defeat common enemies. This understanding of alliance formation is at the heart of realist scholarship.[23]

Where does the PRC–DPRK alliance fit into this categorization? In this book, we repeatedly refer to China and North Korea's shared material interests (common threats to their power, chiefly from the United States) and their shared ideological interests (the desire to raise their status in the International Communist Movement and the desire to spread and solidify fellow Communist states). At what times, and under what conditions, did one of these factors matter more than the other? For instance, at some times Kim Il-sung focused on "isms," whereas at other times he did not.

This book also contributes to the literature on the maintenance of alliances. Scholars have argued that, paradoxically, small states often have a disproportionate influence on much stronger partners—the so-called alliance entrapment, or "chain-ganging."[24] North Korea was able to manipulate its giant Communist neighbors for its own benefit, and to balance its two neighbors against each other.[25]

Additionally, the present volume supplements existing Chinese scholarship on Chinese foreign relations and foreign policy making during the Cold War. Since the early 1990s, Chinese scholars have made important strides in the study of China's foreign relations and have published a number of highly influential works on nearly every aspect of Chinese diplomacy of the past sixty-plus years.[26] But studies on Sino-North Korean relations remain an exception to this general trend.

The present study fully demonstrates that the Sino–North Korean relationship was not merely a bilateral issue. The relationship directly affected China's national security strategy as well as the making and evolution of its international strategy. During certain periods, the relationship even had a major effect on the global Cold War. If we accept the premise that the main content of China's foreign relations during the Cold War was how to deal with the Soviet–U.S. confrontation and how to manage its neighbors, then the Sino-North Korean relationship was a key link. Without a better understanding of the true nature of the Sino–North Korean relationship and its unique and important position in the thinking of the Chinese leadership, it is impossible to comprehend the overall diplomatic thinking and behavior of the Chinese leadership during particular historical periods.

One of the key objectives of this study is to remind scholars who seriously study China's foreign relations of the major flaws in present scholarship. It is thus necessary to reconsider the cause-and-effect linkages of many major events. Likewise, it is necessary to revisit current thinking regarding Korea-related issues, which are premised on very limited documentation. The rich historical sources in this book provide concrete evidence that our past understanding of Sino–North Korean relations is, at best, rather superficial. Such an account of the history of Sino–North Korean interactions, detailing the ups and downs in the relationship over the years, not only reveals what was special about the relationship but also dispels many of our former misunderstandings about the relationship between the two countries.

CHAPTER 1

Victory and Expansion of the Revolution in China and North Korea, 1945–1950

M ao Zedong, the leader of Chinese Communist Revolution, and his colleagues had long paid attention to the revolutionary movement in China's neighboring countries, especially in East Asia. Due to historical, geographic, and shared tragic experiences in dealing with the imperialist countries, Chinese Communist Party (CCP) leaders regarded East Asia as a "revolutionary community."[1] On the eve of the establishment of the People's Republic of China (PRC) in 1949, Mao began to deliberate the role of the new China in guiding the revolution in East Asia.

Modern Sino–North Korean relations originated from the fact that revolutionaries in both countries had fought side by side against common enemies and had formed revolutionary friendships. During the Chinese Civil War in the late 1940s, the Democratic People's Republic of Korea (DPRK) generously helped the Chinese Communists by offering shelter for the sick and wounded, providing material aid, and accommodating the Chinese Communists passing through North Korea en route to Mainland China. When U.S.-UN forces pushed north of the 38th parallel and the DPRK was on the verge of total collapse, Mao, against all odds, prevailed over the dissenting voices among his colleagues and resolutely sent the Chinese People's Volunteer Army to fight in Korea.

Nonetheless, the DPRK had been a Soviet satellite state from 1945 up until China's October 1950 entry into the war, during which time China had no influence. Although the Soviet leader Joseph Stalin agreed that the CCP should lead the revolution in Asia, he had no intention of relinquishing his control over North Korea. When Kim Il-sung initiated a scheme to attack the South, Stalin approved of the move. Mao was consulted and reluctantly agreed to accept Kim's plan. But Mao was unaware of the actual planning for the assault and was only informed of the outbreak of war three days after the fact. Before the entry of the U.S.–UN forces into the war, Kim did not believe that China's help was necessary. Although China had prepared to enter the war in August, Kim rejected China's offer on the grounds that Stalin did not approve, as the entry of Chinese troops to the Korean Peninsula would restore China's traditional influence in Korea, which China had lost in 1895 after the First Sino–Japanese War.

Mutual Support in the Course of Seizing and Consolidating Political Power

Throughout their modern histories, China and Korea both suffered from Japanese militarism and expansionism. Beginning with the Russo–Japanese War of 1904, and especially after Japan's annexation of Korea in 1910, large numbers of ethnic Koreans moved to Northeast China, where many of them took part in anti-Japanese activities.[2] During their early histories, Chinese and Korean Communists had relatively few contacts with one another. Nevertheless, similar fates brought them together. After a futile effort to establish a Communist Party in Korea, under extremely difficult circumstances, the various factions of the Korean Communist organizations disbanded, either voluntarily or under pressure. The Korean Communists then shifted their attention to Manchuria in China's northeast. A substantial number of Korean Communists in China, with support from the Communist International, or Comintern, then voluntarily joined the Chinese Communist Party. Thus, within a short period of time the CCP in Manchuria grew stronger and became a force to be reckoned with. In return, the CCP assumed responsibility for assisting the Korean Communists in their efforts to establish their own party. In the aftermath of the Mukden incident, in 1931, the CCP Central Committee (CC) called for an armed struggle against the Japanese invaders.[3] As the CCP gradually shifted its focus to the Second Sino–Japanese War (known in China as the

War of Resistance Against Japan), the Korean Communists in China became integrated into the CCP army.[4]

After the 1937 outbreak of the war, various ethnic Korean anti-Japanese forces in North China united and accepted the leadership of China's Eighth Route Army and the CCP. In January 1941, the North China Korean Youth Association was founded in Tongyu, Shanxi province, at the site of the headquarters of the Eighth Route Army in the Taihang Mountains. The first president of this association was Mu Chŏng. In June 1941, the North China Branch of the Korean Volunteer Corps was established, under the leadership of the Eighth Route Army. In July 1942, with the support of the CCP, the North China Korean Youth Association, led by Kim Tu-bong and Ch'oe Ch'ang-ik, was renamed the Korean Independence League (KIL). Meanwhile, the North China Branch of the Korean Volunteer Corps was expanded and reorganized into the Korean Volunteer Army, with Mu Chŏng as commander in chief and Pak Hyo-sam and Pak Il-u as his deputies. Toward the end of World War II, the leadership of the KIL moved to Yan'an, the site of the headquarters of the CCP CC. In Yan'an, young Koreans such as Sŏ Hwi and Yun Kong-hŭm joined the leadership of the KIL.[5] These Koreans would later be branded as part of the "Yan'an faction" after they returned to North Korea.

In addition to the Yan'an faction, Kim Il-sung's "Guerrilla faction" also returned to Korea, after World War II. According to Russian documents, in the early 1930s the CCP CC in Northeast China entrusted Kim with the task of organizing an anti-Japanese guerrilla campaign in Jilin province. After serving as political commissar at the regiment and division levels, Kim became a commanding officer on the southeast front.[6] In repeated encirclement operations by the Japanese Kwantung Army, many of Kim's guerrillas lost their lives. The few survivors eventually retreated to the Soviet Far East, where they received military training as well as arms and equipment.

In July 1942, the Soviet Far Eastern Front organized the No. 88 Independent Infantry Brigade in the area east of Khabarovsk. The commander of the brigade was CCP member Zhou Baozhong. In the same year, Kim Il-sung and his guerrillas joined the brigade's First Battalion, which mainly consisted of ethnic Koreans. According to Russian records, Kim Il-sung excelled in the military and was making progress in studying Russian language. Receiving much praise, he was quickly promoted to lead the First Battalion.

After the Japanese surrender, on September 19, 1945, the Soviets sent Kim Il-sung and his comrades—including Kim Il, Kang Kŏn, and Ch'oe Yong-gŏn—back to Korea. Kim Il-sung became an assistant to the representative of the Soviet occupation authorities in Pyongyang.[7] As Soviet–American relations deteriorated, so too did the political situation on the Korean Peninsula, which was divided along the 38th parallel by the American and Soviet occupation forces. After the Moscow Conference of December 1945, the Soviets ousted the local nationalists led by Cho Man-sik and installed Kim Il-sung in a leading position. With Soviet endorsement, between July and September 1946, Kim established a pro-Soviet regime allied with the ethnic Koreans from the Soviet Union, such as Hŏ Ka-i, and representatives of the Korean Communist Party in the South, such as Pak Hŏn-yŏng and Pak Chŏng-ae.[8]

During the tide of decolonization after World War II, Communist-led revolutions were on the rise in Asia. Revolutionaries looked toward Moscow for both ideology and material aid. With the outbreak of the Cold War and the formation of the socialist bloc, the Asian Communist parties set as their ultimate goal the establishment of socialist systems in their respective countries, based on their ongoing national liberation movements. In this context, the Chinese and Korean Communists established a close relationship, due to their common revolutionary ideals and mutual aid. This revolutionary (that is, political) factor gave new life to the "lips and teeth" relationship between China and Korea that traditionally had been based solely on geography.

On August 11, 1945, in Yan'an Zhu De, commander in chief of the Eighth Route Army, issued Order No. 6, instructing that the Korean Volunteer Army should march with the Eighth Route Army to Northeast China. The mission was to participate in the annihilation of the Japanese and their puppet troops and to make preparations for the liberation of Korea.[9] On August 12, 15, and 18, the KIL issued three successive proclamations appealing to the ethnic Korean soldiers in the Japanese army to surrender to the CCP's Eighth Route Army and New Fourth Army. It also called on local ethnic Koreans to join the Korean Volunteer Army to fight on behalf of a new Korean republic.[10]

In order to take over Northeast China, the CCP CC dispatched to the region an advance team under the leadership of Chen Yun. According to Chen Yun's report of October 27, the CCP Municipal Committee of Changchun sent a large group of cadres to the area west of Changchun.

The goal was "to expand the army, mobilize the masses, and take over political power."[11] At the same time, advance troops of the Korean Volunteer Army arrived in Andong (now Dandong), but the Soviet army prevented them from entering Korea, invoking the allies' agreement regarding the 38th parallel. In early November, Mu Chŏng led the main force of the Korean Volunteer Army, consisting of more than three thousand soldiers, to Shenyang. Following instructions from the CCP CC, most of the Korean Volunteer Army remained in Northeast China. On December 13, only about seventy of the cadres in this army, including Mu Chŏng, KIL chairman Kim Tu-bong, and KIL deputy chairman Ch'oe Ch'ang-ik, returned to Pyongyang via a Soviet-provided train.[12]

The ethnic Korean officers who remained in Northeast China were reorganized into units 1, 3, 5, and 7 and began to carry out political activities among the ethnic Koreans in the area in order to expand their units and to provide momentum for the Chinese and Korean revolutions. These units were later integrated into the Northeast Democratic United Army under the CCP (the predecessor of the Northeast People's Liberation Army, or PLA), and they would eventually play an important role in the CCP's military campaigns in Northeast China. During the Chinese Civil War, 34,855 ethnic Koreans in the five counties of Yanbian, Jilin province, fought on behalf of the CCP. In addition, more than 100,000 ethnic Koreans joined local Communist-led military organizations, such as the public security forces and the militia.[13]

Before 1949, the CCP CC did not have direct contact with North Korea, being preoccupied with the Chinese Civil War.[14] Its former contacts, and the leading figures in the Korean Volunteer Army, had already left China for Korea, leading to the dismantling of the Korean Volunteer Army. But at the beginning of the Chinese Civil War, in 1946, the CCP faced enormous difficulties in Northeast China, especially in South Manchuria, because the Nationalist army had cut off connections with North Manchuria. Because North Korea was located across the river from South Manchuria and shared an 800-kilometer border with China, the CCP turned to Korea as an alternative source of supplies. In July 1946, the CCP Northeast Bureau opened an office in Pyongyang and appointed Zhu Lizhi as plenipotentiary, thus resuming CCP contacts with Korean leaders. Zhu Lizhi established close relations with Kim Il-sung and Ch'oe Yong-gŏn, and he frequently partied with the Korean leaders who had returned from Yan'an, including Pak Il-u, Mu Chŏng, and Kang Kŏn. They would engage in heavy drinking as they recalled their shared past experiences. On the pretense of establishing friendly contacts, even the Soviet officers stationed in Pyongyang enjoyed visiting Zhu's residence to eat and drink.[15]

According to Zhu Lizhi's June 27, 1947, report to the CCP Northeast Bureau, the North Koreans had generously helped the Northeast Bureau through his office. First, many Korean families offered shelter to fifteen thousand sick and wounded Chinese Communist soldiers and their families who had retreated to North Korea after the fall of Tonghua and Andong. Second, by June 1947 the Koreans had supplied the Northeast Bureau with four batches of between eight hundred and one thousand shipments of supplies, some of which had been obtained through bartering. Kim Il-sung requested that the Soviets transfer supplies to the CCP military, including weaponry that the Soviets had captured from the defeated Japanese army and that had been stored in North Korea. Third, during a period of nine months, Pyongyang accommodated an estimated twenty thousand Chinese Communists, including the staff of the Northeast Bureau and Chinese Communist army troops who were passing through Korean territory. Fourth, when the CCP was forced to retreat, it entrusted 20,000 tons of goods to the Koreans. The Koreans helped enormously in terms of shipping these goods back and forth, for which the Northeast Bureau paid less than 1 percent of the transit duties. Additionally, the shipping costs, from which the CCP was sometimes exempt, were also very low. During periods of emergency, North Korea even suspended passenger transportation to guarantee the transport of shipments to the CCP. In short, Kim Il-sung did exactly what he had promised in a letter to Lin Biao, the commander of the Fourth Field Army: he would do everything possible to help the CCP. Zhu Lizhi commented that North Korea served as a bridge that kept the supply lines open to the Chinese Communists. In particular, in the case of South Manchuria, North Korea was inscrutable, but, consistent with the goals of the Northeast Bureau, it was an absolutely critical rear-guard base that provided tremendous support to the PLA.[16]

From the second half of 1947 to early 1948, more than 520,000 tons of goods belonging to the CCP was transshipped or exchanged via North Korea. In addition, 8,685 Chinese passengers passed through the Tumen-Namyang port in 1948. Chen Yun, Zhu Rui, Liu Yalou, Xiao Hua, Zhang Aiping, and many other leaders of the Northeast Bureau all crossed Korean territory on numerous occasions. Later, many influential democratic personages and overseas Chinese representatives, including Li Jishen, Shen

Junru, Zhang Lan, Ma Xulun, and Cai Tingkai, en route to attend the meetings of the Chinese People's Consultative Conference, traveled from Hong Kong to the Mainland via North Korea.[17] South Korean scholar Hongkoo Han argues that North Korea's help to the CCP "had influence over the War in a decisive manner."[18] But it should be noted that Kim Il-sung did not send North Korean soldiers to China to fight with Mao's troops during the Chinese Civil War.[19]

The CCP reciprocated Kim Il-sung's aid by supplying him with grain and soldiers. In late summer and early fall of 1946, via Ding Xuesong, who had just returned to North Korea from Yan'an, Kim Il-sung asked the Northeast Bureau for grain aid. According to Zhu Lizhi, by the summer of 1947 the Northeast Bureau had sent 10,000 tons of grain to Kim via Liu Yalou, chief of staff of the Northeast Democratic United Army. The Northeast Bureau later sent Kim 2,000 additional tons of grain. Including the grain it exchanged for Korean goods, the CCP provided Kim with a total of some 30,000 tons of grain.[20]

Moreover, the CCP helped Kim build an army, consisting primarily of those ethnic Koreans who had served in the former Korean Volunteer Army and the Northeast Democratic United Army. The transfer of the ethnic Korean soldiers in the PLA to Kim Il-sung was arguably the CCP's greatest help to Kim. After August 1946, Kim Kwang-hyŏp, Kang Kŏn, and Ch'oe Kwang, with guidance from Soviet military advisers, began to lead groups of ethnic Korean PLA soldiers in the Northeast back to Korea. By the time of the establishment of the Korean People's Army (KPA) on February 8, 1947, the returnees from China were part of the KPA's First Division, with Kim Ung as division commander and Kang Kŏn as chief of staff. In addition to this first group of returnees, incomplete statistics reveal that between 1946 and March 1949 another eight hundred ethnic Korean military cadres and military school students returned to Korea from the liberated areas of Northeast China. These experienced ethnic Korean officers had survived the test of war in China and soon would become the backbone of the KPA.[21]

Both Kim Il-sung and Mao Zedong understood the importance of their mutual help in their respective struggles to establish political regimes. Kim Il-sung once stated, "It is the lofty, internationalist obligation of the Korean Communists and people to aid the revolutionary cause of the Chinese people."[22] Moreover, he believed that the victory of the Chinese Revolution would benefit Korea's security and development. Mao Zedong also firmly believed in the unity of the Asian anti-imperialist forces. He said, "It is impossible for any true people's revolution to succeed or to consolidate its success in one country without various forms of support from the inter-national revolutionary forces."[23] Such revolutionary internationalism explains the readiness on the part of both Mao and Kim to help each other in times of need.[24] When the CCP was on the verge of victory, there was even talk about the possibility of establishing an alliance among all Asian Communist parties.[25] The time seemed ripe for Mao Zedong's China and Kim Il-sung's Korea to enter into a formal alliance. Unfortunately, this process was disrupted by additional revolutionary moves by Kim.

Mao's Design for an Asian Cominform

In July 1948 Mao Zedong proposed to Ivan Kovalev, representative of the All-Union Communist Party (Bolsheviks) to the CCP, that Mao should visit Moscow as early as possible to consult with Stalin regarding coordi-nation of policies between the party and the CCP.[26] Among the issues to be discussed were unification of the revolutionary forces and the estab-lishment of relations with other Communist parties in the East.[27] After a period of hesitation, Stalin rejected Mao's request. By early 1949, Stalin had changed his wait-and-see approach toward China. Mao's tough stand against Soviet intervention in the Chinese Civil War made Stalin realize that he did not fully understand the CCP.[28] He had to determine the true nature of the political doctrine of the CCP if he really intended to establish friendly relations with a future Chinese regime. Thus Politburo member Anastas Mikoyan was sent to Xibaipo, the headquarters of the CCP CC.[29]

During conversations with Mikoyan on February 3, 1949, Mao formally brought up the issue of establishing an Asian Cominform (Communist Information Bureau). When Mikoyan asked him about joint actions by the Asian Communist parties, Mao responded that the CCP did not yet have a clear view, but in general it was in favor of establishing relations with the Communist parties of Indochina, Siam (Thailand), the Philippines, Indo-nesia, Burma, India, Malaya, and Korea. At that time, the CCP already had close ties with the Communist parties in Indochina and Korea, but less close ties with the parties in the other countries, with which it main-tained contacts mainly via liaisons in Hong Kong. Also, the CCP had few connections with the Japanese Communist Party (JCP).

Mao thus proposed establishing an Asian Cominform similar to the Cominform in Europe, once the situation had stabilized in China. After discussing the issue of the JCP, Mao said that the Communist parties in Siam and Indochina had already expressed support for such an organization. The CCP proposed that the Communist parties in China, Korea, Indochina, and the Philippines take the lead in establishing a Cominform bureau in Asia. Mikoyan immediately expressed the view that the Central Committee of the Communist Party of the Soviet Union (CPSU) did not believe that the CCP had to join the Cominform; rather, it should establish and lead an Asian Cominform, which initially could be composed of the CCP, the JCP, and the Korean Workers' Party (KWP), and then later could be expanded to other parties. Mao proposed that the CPSU and the CCP establish direct connections and that the CCP would then contact the JCP and the KWP, to which Mikoyan replied positively.[30] Although Mao, at first, had suggested this proposal only tentatively, after Mikoyan's positive reply, he seemed eager to move ahead. Mikoyan's visit aroused a latent ambition among CCP leaders that China should play a leading role in guiding the Asian Revolution. This ultimately had important and long-term effects on China's policy toward East Asia.

No historical record has come to light revealing any communications between the CCP and the other Communist parties in Asia at the time. However, in May 1949, in a conversation with Kim Il, representative of the KWP, Mao spoke about an Asian Cominform. Both North Korea and the CCP made reports to the Soviet Union about this conversation. North Korea's version was that Mao had inquired about Kim Il-sung's March visit to Moscow, specifically asking about the position of the KWP and whether Kim had discussed the issue of an Asian Cominform with Stalin. Mao said the CCP had already heard from the Communist parties in Burma, Malaya, Indochina, and four other countries, and that they had suggested that an Asian Cominform be created. Mao contended that, from the CCP's point of view, "it is premature to create a Cominform" since China and Indochina were still at war and the situation in North Korea remained tense. If a Cominform were to be created, it would be considered a military alliance.[31] The Chinese version of the report was relatively brief. Mao Zedong believed that "it is too early to create an Asian Cominform" because among the twelve countries in the East, the CCP only maintained contacts with the parties in Mongolia, Thailand, Indochina, the Philippines, and Korea, and it knew little about the parties in the other countries and had relatively few contacts with the parties in Japan and Indonesia. Therefore, the CCP should first carry out research and only later establish relations with the parties in those countries.[32]

Mao's eagerness can be seen in the different nuances in the two versions of the reports to the Soviet Union. But Mao did not want Stalin to be aware of his impatience. The wording "too early" and "premature" was his way of putting out feelers. After all, Mao was worried that Stalin might come to regard him as a Tito of the East.[33] He was not sure whether Stalin agreed wholeheartedly with the establishment of an Asian Cominform and he did not want Stalin to think that the CCP was attempting to "set up a separate kitchen" before its actual seizure of political power in China.

Mao's concerns turned out to be correct. In his response on May 26, Stalin warned Mao that once the PLA approached the borders of Indochina and Burma, it would lead to a revolutionary situation in those countries, as well as in Indonesia and the Philippines. This could result in a loss of control by the imperialists. Therefore, the imperialists would blockade or initiate armed conflicts with the PLA in order to consolidate southern China within their sphere of influence. Moreover, the British and U.S. armed forces might land in Qingdao to attack from the rear as the major PLA military force pressed south. This would pose a serious danger to the PLA. It was also likely that Britain and the United States would take advantage of other ports, such as Tanggu in Tianjin, to land behind PLA lines. Thus, Stalin suggested that the CCP should not be in any rush to prepare a southern invasion near the borders with Indochina, Burma, and India. Rather, it should dispatch two elite forces, one to Tianjin and one to Qingdao, to prevent the enemy from landing there. Soon thereafter, Stalin clearly expressed his approval of Mao's opinions regarding postponing the creation of an Asian Cominform.[34]

Obviously, Mao was very disappointed with Stalin's response. In fact, Mao's true intention was to create a supreme headquarters within China for the Asian Revolution. He sought to ascertain Stalin's attitude during Liu Shaoqi's secret visit to the Soviet Union. On July 27, 1949, during a meeting of the CPSU and CCP delegations, Stalin apologized for his mistake in urging Mao to enter into negotiations with Jiang Jieshi (Chiang Kai-shek) in Chongqing in 1945. He declared that the CCP was already a mature party and he expressed his desire that the CCP play a leading role in the International Communist Movement. Stalin suggested that the CCP and the CPSU should each take on additional responsibilities, while playing different roles and sharing the burden in the international revolutionary movement. He hoped that China would take responsibility for the colonial and semicolonial countries in the East, whereas the Soviet Union would take responsibility for the countries in the West. Since the center of the revolution had shifted to China and East Asia, China should fulfill its obligations in leading the revolution in the East Asian countries and should establish closer ties with the countries in Southeast Asia.

Gao Gang, a member of Liu Shaoqi's delegation and the party boss of the CCP Northeast Bureau, suddenly posed a disingenuous question: "Can the CCP join the Cominform?" Stalin caught the undertone of this comment and replied that this would be inappropriate because the situation in China was completely different from that in Europe. Since conditions in China and the other East Asian countries were quite similar, Stalin responded that China could consider establishing a "League of Communist Parties in East Asia." He added that the Soviet Union was both a European and an Asian country, so in the future it might also join an East Asian Cominform.[35] Although Stalin spoke about transferring leadership of the Asian Revolution to the CCP, apparently he did not really trust the CCP. Hence, Stalin insisted it was still too early to establish an Asian Cominform.

Nevertheless, from Mao's point of view the real problem had actually been resolved. Years later, on May 25, 1957, Mao told K. E. Voroshilov, visiting president of the Supreme Presidium of the USSR, that China was a big country in Asia and its primary interest was in Asia. In 1949, he had already reached an agreement with Stalin that China should focus on Asian issues.[36] Mao had found it sufficient that Stalin had suggested that the CCP should lead the Communist parties in the Asian countries. An Asian Cominform was merely a matter of formality. With these comments by Stalin, Mao attempted to put his plan into action.

The CCP CC was relocated from Xibaipo village to Peiping (later Beijing) in March 1949. One of the first tasks for the Central Committee was to establish contacts with the other Communist parties in Asia and to provide guidance for their revolutionary activities. By early July, the United Front Work Department of the CCP CC had begun to prepare to mobilize the leaders of the Communist parties in Asia to learn from the revolutionary experiences of the CCP. Following Stalin's suggestion that the CPSU and the CCP divide responsibilities in leading the revolutions in Europe and Asia, respectively, at the end of July China offered a one-year first "study group" for Asian Communist leaders, to be held in Zhong-nanhai. The study group was headed by then secretary-general of the United Front Work Department Lian Guan. It was divided into seven small country teams, including high-ranking Communist party members from Vietnam, Thailand, the Philippines, Indonesia, Burma, Malaysia, and India. But the KWP did not send any delegates. This clearly indicates that Moscow had no plan to shift its control of North Korea over to Beijing. The key study materials consisted of the *Selected Works of Mao Zedong*, and the teams were led by leaders of the CCP CC and the heads of the related departments, including senior CCP leaders Zhu De, Chen Yi, Liu Bocheng, Deng Xiaoping, Li Tao, Li Weihan, Peng Zhen, Zhang Wentian, Luo Ruiqing, Chen Boda, An Ziwen, Liu Ningyi, and Liao Luyan, among others. The content of the lectures included armed struggle, the united front, party building, mass movements, theoretical issues, and the experience of the Chinese Revolution.[37]

After the founding of the People's Republic of China, and especially after Stalin's apparent recognition of the Chinese revolutionary experience in seizing military power, China's role as a leader of the Asian Revolution became increasingly pronounced and enthusiasm in the CCP boomed. The CCP CC believed it was not only its responsibility but also in its own security interests to support the revolutions in East Asia. On October 7, 1949, an editorial in the official newspaper of the Cominform stated that the victory of the Chinese Revolution was a milestone in human history and was of worldwide historical significance. It not only affected the fate of the Chinese people but also would determine the fate of people in both the East and the West. The PRC was a "faithful friend and a reliable fortress" for people in the colonial and dependent countries. The Chinese Revolution would further "accelerate the final victory of workers in all countries and the advent of a Communist victory."[38] The editorial's congratulatory message was sufficient to excite the Chinese Communists.

The Trade Union Conference of Asian and Australasian countries further highlighted the experience and standing of the CCP in the Chinese Revolution. On November 6, only fifteen days after the founding of the PRC, the conference was convened in Beijing. The CCP openly declared its willingness to assume responsibility for leading the Asian Revolution. As chairman of the conference, Liu Shaoqi, in his opening remarks, vigorously touted the experience of the Chinese Revolution, concluding that armed struggle was the basic route for the success of the Chinese people.

"This is the path of Mao Zedong," which was the "inevitable path toward the liberation of other people in colonial and semicolonial countries."[39]

The conference passed many resolutions, the most important of which was to create the Asian Liaison Bureau of the World Federation of Trade Unions. Liu Shaoqi later said that the executive committee of the federation recognized that leadership of the Asian Liaison Bureau belonged to those Chinese comrades who best understood the situation in the Asian countries.[40] On November 23, Liu Shaoqi spoke highly of the success of the conference. He said that the victory of the Chinese working classes meant they "should bear more obligations. . . . They have the onerous responsibility of assisting the working classes and laborers in the capitalist countries, especially those in the colonial and semicolonial countries of Asia and Australasia. . . . This is their honorable obligation."[41] Liu's speech clearly revealed the CCP leaders' sense of responsibility toward the revolution in East Asia. This would have important implications for New China's diplomacy. The first test would be for the CCP to assist the revolutionary activities in Indochina and on the Korean Peninsula.

Mao's trip to Moscow, from late 1949 to early 1950, and the establishment of the Sino–Soviet alliance prompted Chinese leaders to promote a more active East Asian policy. During his visit, Mao broached with Stalin the topic of the revolutionary movement in Indochina and the situation on the Korean Peninsula. In order to improve its understanding and strengthen its leadership of the Communist parties in Asia, in February 1950 the CCP CC created a committee under the United Front Work Department, with Li Weihan as secretary, to conduct research on the Asian countries.[42] On March 14, only ten days after Mao and Chinese Premier and Foreign Minister Zhou Enlai had returned from Moscow, Liu Shaoqi drafted an inner-party instruction, elaborating on the CCP's decision to provide all-out support for the Asian Revolution. This would be the CCP's guiding principle for assisting Vietnam and resisting France. Liu wrote, "After the victory of the revolution, the CCP should use all available means to help the Communist parties and those among the oppressed peoples of Asia to fight for liberation. This is the unshakable obligation of the CCP and the Chinese people, and it is also one of the most important means to consolidate the worldwide victory of the Chinese Revolution." Therefore, "we should provide fraternal assistance and warm hospitality to Communist parties and revolutionaries from all countries, encourage them and modestly listen to their opinions, introduce them to details about the experience of the Chinese Revolution, answer their questions carefully, and not behave in any way that appears to be indifferent or arrogant."[43] This shows that the CCP leaders were already determined to shoulder the responsibility of leading the Asian Revolution.

The Origins of the Korean War

In the second half of 1949, Mao Zedong and Kim Il-sung were both eager to reunify their countries. Mao wanted to liberate Tibet and Taiwan, and Kim wanted to reunify Korea. To realize these goals, they competed for help from Moscow. In the end, the outbreak of the Korean War indicated that Moscow had favored Pyongyang over Beijing in this regard. The theory of "collusion among the three countries," specifically that the Korean War was cooked up among North Korea, China, and the Soviet Union, used to be quite popular among scholars.[44] However, newly declassified documents reveal a far more complicated story. Initially, Stalin and Mao were both opposed to Kim Il-sung's premature plan to use force to reunify the Korean Peninsula. For some reason, Stalin later changed his mind, gave Kim a green light, and forced the war on Mao. With respect to this issue, relations among China, the Soviet Union, and North Korea were both delicate and complex. Although the CCP did not agree with Kim Il-sung's "adventurism," Mao decided to support Kim after he took action.

In April 1949, the CCP realized that Kim Il-sung was planning to attack the South. At the time, it was rumored that the United States would soon withdraw its troops from South Korea and that the Syngman Rhee regime was busy preparing for a major offensive against the North.[45] In response, Kim Il-sung secretly sent Kim Il, head of the Political Department of the KPA, as an envoy to China to seek help. Kim Il met with Mao Zedong, Zhu De, and Zhou Enlai. Mao was worried that Rhee could launch a military offensive against the North at any time, and he therefore advised Kim Il-sung to be thoroughly prepared for such a scenario. Mao promised to send Chinese troops to North Korea to help, if Rhee did indeed attack or if Japan intervened on Rhee's behalf. Conversely, Mao made it clear that Kim Il-sung should not be tempted to launch the first strike, even if the Americans departed and Japan intervened. If Kim were to attack the South, Mao warned, in no time General Douglas MacArthur would transfer the American occupation forces from Japan to Korea. Under such circumstances, the CCP would be unable to provide timely help to Kim Il-sung, because the main PLA forces were still south of the Yangtze River.

In response to Kim's request for more ethnic Korean soldiers from the PLA, Mao pointed out that the PLA had three divisions consisting of ethnic Koreans; two were stationed in Shenyang and Changchun and one was stationed in South China. Mao promised that the two divisions in the Northeast, including their arms and equipment, could return to Korea at any time. However, the third division had to complete its operations in southern China before returning to Korea. Kim's envoy also raised the issue of the establishment of a Cominform in the East. Mao responded that it was still too early. He explained that, given the fact that China and Indochina were still at war and that the Korean situation was deteriorating, people might mistake a Cominform in the East for a military alliance.[46] It was obvious that Mao did not want Kim to take any military action before the CCP had liberated Tibet and Taiwan. This is the main reason why Mao was not interested in Kim's proposal to form an Asian Cominform. For Mao, the purpose of CCP aid to Kim, including the return of the ethnic Korean troops, was to help Kim defend the North, not to assist him in launching an attack against the South.

The two Korean divisions in Changchun and Shenyang to which Mao had referred were the 164th Division (stationed in Changchun) under Yi Tok-san and the 166th Division (stationed in Shenyang) under Pang Ho-san, both of which were part of the Northeast Military Region of the PLA. After the Soviet troops withdrew from the Korean Peninsula, Kim Il-sung was so afraid of an attack by the South that, in early July 1949, he requested that the two divisions immediately be returned to North Korea. Upon their return, the 164th Division was reorganized into the Fifth Division of the KPA, stationed in Raman, and the 166th Division was reorganized into the Sixth Division of the KPA, stationed in Sinŭiju. At the time of their return, the 164th Division comprised 10,821 troops and the 166th Division comprised 10,320. Both divisions were fully equipped with both heavy and light arms. As suggested by Terentii Shtykov, Soviet ambassador and chief military adviser to Kim Il-sung in Pyongyang, the purpose of the two divisions was to defend North Korea against any possible attack from South Korea.[47]

The issue of sending a second group of Korean officers and soldiers back to Korea was raised during Mao's visit to Moscow. On December 25, 1949, Lin Biao and other PLA commanders reported that there still were about six thousand ethnic Korean soldiers scattered among various PLA units. Some of these Korean soldiers had been reluctant to cross the Yangtze River and had asked to be returned to Korea. Since the Chinese Civil War had already come to an end, Lin Biao and other PLA commanders suggested, "On behalf of the interests of the Korean people, these seasoned Korean troops should be sent back to Korea." Their report continued that, with North Korea's agreement, the PLA would be happy to reorganize all its Korean soldiers into a formal division, or four to five formal regiments, and to provide them with short-term training before sending them back to Korea. Four days later, Nie Rongzhen, acting chief of the PLA General Staff, transmitted this report to Mao Zedong, who was in Moscow at the time, and asked for instructions.[48]

Mao consulted with the Soviets about this matter. On January 8, 1950, Stalin instructed Shtykov to find out what Kim Il-sung thought about it. Meeting with Kim the next day, Kim told Shtykov that he had received a letter from China's trade representative on behalf of the Chinese government. The letter had stated, "With the end of the Chinese Civil War, the Korean soldiers in the PLA are now idle; therefore, the Chinese government is willing to transfer them to Korea if the DPRK government so wants." Kim asked for Soviet advice as to how to reply to this letter. Kim told Shtykov that he did want to take over these troops and that he would dispatch three representatives to China to negotiate the issue with the Chinese government. For the time being, North Korea would have trouble accommodating them, so Kim wanted the Chinese government to allow them to remain in China until April 1950.[49]

After receiving Kim's reply, in mid-January 1950 Liu Shaoqi, vice chairman of the CCP and Mao's second in command, instructed Wen Shizhen, director of the Trade Representative Office of the Northeast People's Government in Pyongyang, to inform Kim that the Chinese government was willing to accommodate his requests. The CCP agreed to receive three Korean representatives in China to prepare for the transfer of the Korean troops. Beijing also agreed to reorganize the troops in China and not to return them to Korea until April, after they had received their summer uniforms. Liu Shaoqi informed Lin Biao of this plan.[50] The Korean delegation, which included Kim Kwang-hyŏp, chief of combat operations of the KPA, arrived in Beijing on January 14 to begin negotiations with Nie Rongzhen on the transfer of the ethnic Korean troops.[51]

On January 22, Liu Shaoqi sent a telegram to Mao informing him that Kim Il-sung had sent a delegation to China to take over the more than fourteen thousand ethnic Korean officers and men in Lin Biao's army, and that Kim had also requested that these men be fully equipped when they were returned to Korea. Mao instructed his staff to do as Kim requested. Liu passed Mao's instructions to Lin Biao on January 28.[52] Between March and April, two groups of ethnic Korean soldiers who were assembled in Zhengzhou were returned to Korea. Once in Korea, they were reorganized into the Fourth and Seventh regiments of the KPA.[53] Before departing China for Korea, they sent telegrams to Mao Zedong, Zhu De, and Lin Biao to express their gratitude. They wrote that the Chinese Revolution not only represented the best model for the oppressed people in the East but also established a solid foundation for the victory of the Korean Revolution.[54] By June 1950, 47,764 ethnic Korean officers and soldiers who had formerly served in the PLA had returned to North Korea (21,141 in 1949 and 26,623 in 1950).[55]

Having endured the test of a large-scale war in China before joining the KPA, the returned Korean troops undoubtedly greatly enhanced the KPA's fighting capacity. Nevertheless, a careful examination of this historical process reveals that neither Beijing nor Moscow was plotting an offensive against South Korea by returning the troops to North Korea. In fact, both Moscow's and Beijing's motivations were based purely on moral grounds. The CCP in particular felt a deep sense of obligation to help the Korean Communists. As noted, in the summer of 1949, during Liu Shaoqi's secret trip to Moscow, the Chinese and Soviet Communist parties had already discussed a division of labor in the International Communist Movement.[56] Hence, it was the responsibility of the CCP to aid the Korean Communists. At the time, however, any assistance to North Korea was to be for defensive purposes only. Both Mao and Stalin were opposed to the idea of reunifying Korea by force. Kim Il-sung also was in no hurry for these troops to return to North Korea. It is quite possible that launching a war against the South was not yet high on his agenda.

However, as revealed in the Russian archival documents, soon after the U.S. troops left the Korean Peninsula, in June 1949, Kim Il-sung became increasingly eager to launch a first strike against the South. On September 3, Kim submitted a proposal to Moscow via the Soviet Embassy in Pyongyang, suggesting the launching of an offensive to seize the Ongjin Peninsula and the area between the peninsula and Kaesŏng.[57] In late

September, in a discussion about Kim's proposal, the Politburo of the CPSU Central Committee decided to oppose it. In its reply to Kim, Moscow explained that attacking the South would mean starting a war, for which North Korea was not yet ready, either militarily or politically. Moreover, if a military conflict initiated by the North evolved into a lasting war, it would give the Americans a good excuse for resorting to any means of interfering in Korean affairs.[58] On this issue, Beijing and Moscow were in agreement.

After the founding of the PRC, Kim once again raised the issue of Korean reunification. On October 21, 1949, Mao Zedong sent a telegram to Stalin, telling him that the Korean comrades wanted to reunify Korea by force but that the CCP leaders had advised them not to do so.[59] On October 26, Vyacheslav Molotov, first deputy prime minister of the Soviet Union, drafted a reply on behalf of Stalin: "We agree with you that the KPA should not attack the South (yet). We have also pointed out to our Korean friends that the KPA is not prepared either politically or militarily for such a proposed attack."[60] Andrei Gromyko, first deputy foreign minister, felt that Molotov's draft was too direct, so he sent a revised version on November 5: "We believe that we must inform you that we support your opinion on the issue under discussion, but we would advise our Korean friends to act according to the spirit [of our response]."[61] Apparently, on this point Stalin continued to share Mao's objections.

During the latter half of 1949, several factors convinced Stalin that the situation favored a North Korean attack on the South, with minimal cost to the USSR. These factors included the Soviet Union's successful test of an atomic bomb in August; the Communist victory in China in October 1949; the signing of the Sino–Soviet Treaty of Friendship, Alliance, and Mutual Assistance in February 1950; the exclusion of the USSR from the postwar Japanese settlement; the rearmament of Germany; and the establishment of the North Atlantic Treaty Organization and the clear American commitment to defend Western Europe, in contrast to what appeared to be a weakening American defense in East Asia.[62] Chinese historian Yang Kuisong argues that, by this time, Stalin not only was ready to cede to China a leadership role in Asia but also had basically accepted Mao Zedong's revolutionary outlook on "armed seizures of power and war to resolve problems," and he had urged the Japanese, Indian, and other Asian Communist parties to follow China on the path to armed revolution.[63] Additionally, Zhihua Shen has long argued, "It would be obvious to Stalin that if war broke out on the Korean peninsula, whatever the result, the Soviet strategic goal in the Far East—acquisition of an out-let on the ocean and an ice-free port—would be guaranteed."[64]

Given this situation, when he learned that Kim Il-sung had once again proposed reunifying Korea by military means, Stalin was inclined to change his formerly negative attitude and agree to Kim's request. At a January 17, 1950, luncheon, an agitated and excited Kim first told two Soviet Embassy counselors and then the Soviet ambassador that, following China's success-ful liberation, the next issue would be to liberate the people of South Korea. He said he could hardly sleep at night when he thought about reunifying Korea. But the last time he had visited Moscow and raised this issue, Stalin had told him that he could counterattack South Korea only if Syngman Rhee's forces were to attack the North. The problem was that Rhee had not launched an offensive and thus the issue of Korean national reunification dragged on without resolution. Kim wanted to meet with Stalin again to seek his guidance on the liberation of the South by the KPA. In line with instruc-tions from Moscow, Ambassador Shtykov responded cautiously to Kim.[65]

But, to Shtykov's surprise, on January 30, 1950, Stalin responded that he supported Kim's plan, and he summoned Kim to Moscow for secret talks. Stalin did not tell Mao about this, even though Mao happened to be in Moscow at the same time. Because Mao had asked Stalin to assist in the liberation of Taiwan and Stalin had turned him down, it would have been difficult for Stalin to convince Mao to support military action in Korea. After Mao left Moscow, Stalin and Kim held extensive talks, between April 10 and April 25, regarding plans to launch a war on the Korean Peninsula. However, Stalin instructed that Kim should first obtain Mao's endorsement before launching the war. This might be because Stalin wanted to respect the divi-sion of labor between the Chinese and Soviet Communist parties so that he would not be cornered on the Korean question in the future.[66]

On May 12, as Stalin had instructed, Kim decided to make a secret trip to Beijing to inform the CCP leaders of his "intention to reunify the coun-try by military means and to report on the results of discussions on this issue with Moscow." In fact, Kim was reluctant to visit Mao. He told Shtykov that he "did not have any more requests for assistance from Mao, since all of his requests had been satisfied in Moscow, and he had already been provided with necessary and sufficient assistance."[67] Nonetheless, Kim flew to Beijing on May 13.

On that same day, Kim and Chinese leaders held their first meeting, about which, unfortunately, no records are yet available. But the Soviet ambassador to Beijing, N. V. Roshchin, filed a report indicating that this first meeting between Kim and the Chinese leaders did not go well and in fact was drawn to a close late that night. According to Roshchin's telegram to Moscow, Zhou Enlai had called on the Soviet Embassy at 11:30 that night and had asked the embassy to immediately send a telegram to Stalin. Zhou's message read, "The Korean comrades notified us of Comrade Filippov's instructions as the following: The situation has changed, and it is now acceptable for the DPRK to make a move; but North Korea must discuss this issue with the Chinese comrades and Mao Zedong himself. . . . Comrade Mao Zedong would appreciate Comrade Filippov's personal explanation about this." At the end of the telegram, he stressed that the Chinese comrades demanded an immediate reply.[68]

Stalin now had to explain to Mao that the Soviet government had changed its position on the Korean question. Stalin sent a telegram to Mao on May 14 to confirm what Kim had told Mao. But in his telegram Stalin also emphasized that the Korean question would eventually have to be resolved by joint Chinese–Korean efforts. Stalin wrote that if the Chinese comrades opposed Kim's plan, then the issue would be reconsidered. Stalin suggested that Mao obtain from Kim details about his April meetings with Stalin.[69] At this point, Stalin was giving Mao an opportunity to reconsider and reject North Korea's plan to attack. But Mao was eager to assume a leadership role in the Asian Revolution and to expand the Chinese revolutionary experience. As noted, after Mao's trip to Moscow, Liu Shaoqi had, on March 14, drafted an inner-party instruction elaborating on the CCP's decision to provide all-out support for the Asian Revolution.

Although Kim's attack would disrupt China's unification plans (involving Taiwan, and probably also Tibet), Mao did not make any attempt to stop Kim. Nonetheless, Mao cautiously proposed a postponement of the signing of the Sino-DPRK alliance treaty until after Korean reunification, and Stalin agreed with this.[70] Due to a lack of information, it is not yet clear when and how the issue of the Sino–DPRK alliance treaty was initially raised. Nevertheless, the fact that Mao delayed the treaty seems to indicate his reservations about the scheme concocted by Stalin and Kim.

When meeting with Kim on May 15, Mao explained that he hoped that Kim could wait until the CCP took over Taiwan before launching an attack against the South, so that China would be able to provide sufficient assistance to North Korea. But Kim had already made up his mind to take action, so Mao expressed respect for his decision. Mao stated that China was prepared to provide necessary assistance to North Korea because the reunification of Korea was a common goal of the people of both Korea and China. Mao announced that he would dispatch Chinese troops to Korea if the United States were to intervene in the war. He also offered to transfer Chinese troops closer to the Chinese–Korean border and to provide some arms and equipment to the KPA if Kim thought they were needed. Kim thanked Mao but rejected his offer. As soon as the meeting was adjourned, Kim declared, in front of the Soviet ambassador, that China and North Korea had reached agreement on all of the issues discussed during their meeting.[71] One can only imagine Kim's satisfaction and Mao's embarrassment at the time.

By then, ill feelings had already grown between the North Korean and Chinese leaders. Kim resented the fact that Mao had been reluctant to support his proposal for immediate reunification of Korea by military means, despite all the things that he and his people had done to help the CCP during the Chinese Civil War. In principle, Mao was not opposed to national reunification by military means, and he understood that Kim was attempting to follow China's example. However, Mao believed that Chinese reunification should have priority over Korean reunification. So the impatient Kim turned to Moscow for help, thereby displeasing Mao.

Because Kim was distrustful of the Chinese, after he returned to Korea, he did not inform the Chinese government of the progress in North Korea's war mobilization efforts.[72] It was not until three days after the outbreak of the war that Kim finally sent a military attaché to notify the Chinese leaders of the war situation on the Korean Peninsula. Mao was understandably outraged. He told Shi Zhe, his Russian interpreter, "They are our next-door neighbors, but they did not even consult with us before they started the war. They have not notified us until now."[73] This disturbing episode, however, did not undermine Mao's determination to dispatch Chinese troops to aid the North Koreans.

Mao's Deliberations on Sending Troops to Korea

After studying Chinese and Russian archival materials for more than two decades, scholars have reached a consensus on the reasons behind China's decision to enter the Korean War.[74] However, recently declassified documents add rich details to this piece of history, revealing, in particular, the discord that existed among Mao, Stalin, and Kim on the issue of China's entry into the war before UN troops had crossed the 38th parallel.

Although Mao had misgivings about the timing of North Korea's attack on the South, he still attempted to aid North Korea after the United States entered the war. In early July, the Chinese government agreed to return to Korea the two hundred ethnic Korean cadres stationed with the Chinese troops in the Northeast Military Region. Moreover, between late June and early September the Chinese government made great efforts to mobilize 347 ethnic Korean doctors, nurses, drivers, and engineers to return to Korea to serve their motherland. Meanwhile, Zhou Enlai informed Roshchin of China's approval of Moscow's request to use the Changchun Railway and Chinese territorial airspace to transport military supplies to North Korea.[75]

The Chinese leaders also informed the Soviets that China was willing to offer military aid to North Korea. On July 2, Zhou Enlai met with Ambassador Roshchin and discussed China's thinking on the war situation. Zhou said that it was likely that the United States would dispatch more troops to Korea, landing in southern ports and then directing them to move northward along the railway. Zhou advised that the KPA should advance southward as soon as possible in order to take over these ports. Zhou stated that the North Koreans should build an especially strong line of defense around Inch'ŏn to protect Seoul and to prevent the landing of American reinforcements. Although Zhou complained that Kim had ignored Mao's repeated warnings about America's intervention, he made it clear that if American troops were to cross the 38th parallel, Chinese soldiers would put on KPA uniforms and fight against the Americans as volunteers. Zhou told Roshchin that China had amassed three armies in the Northeast, totaling 120,000 soldiers, and he asked whether the Soviet Union could provide air cover for these forces.[76] On July 4, Zou Dapeng, director of China's Intelligence Administration, described to Roshchin China's plan to transport North Korean troops to South Korea via China's Shandong Peninsula and to send Chinese military experts to South Korea to help the KPA.[77] Mao was most likely eager to bring the Korean War to a rapid end so that he could resume an attack on Taiwan.[78]

Although the KPA was making favorable progress in the war, Stalin was preparing for unforeseen events, in light of the U.S. intervention. Stalin immediately gave his blessing to Zhou's plan. He said that it was the right time for China to assemble nine military divisions along the Chinese–Korean border so that China could take immediate action if the Americans were to cross the 38th parallel. Stalin also promised to do his best to provide air cover for these troops.[79] He urged China to send representatives to Korea to enhance Sino–Korean communications and to deal with any potential problems.[80]

At the time, Ni Zhiliang, Chinese ambassador to North Korea, was still on sick leave in China. To continue contacts with North Korea, as early as June 30 Zhou Enlai decided to send Chai Junwu (who later changed his name to Chai Chengwen), initially assigned to work in the Chinese Embassy in East Germany, to North Korea as political counselor. Before Chai left for Pyongyang, Zhou commented that the Korean people were now situated on the very first front of the Communist struggle. Zhou instructed Chai to express China's support for the Korean people, to ask them what China could do for them, and to tell them that China would do its best to help them.[81] On July 12, Zhou told Kim Il-sung that China would not tolerate any American interference in Korean affairs and that the Chinese government was prepared to help North Korea as much as it could. At the same time, China asked North Korea to provide Chinese troops with five hundred Korean maps on the scale of 1:100,000, 1:200,000, and 1:500,000 and to send to China sample KPA uniforms. Kim Il-sung immediately informed the Soviet Embassy of Zhou's comments. Kim stated, "Because the United States and some other countries have openly intervened on behalf of Syngman Rhee, it is now justified for countries such as Czechoslovakia and China to commit troops to help the DPRK." But Shtykov deliberately ignored Kim's remarks.[82]

On July 19, Kim Il-sung once again informed the Soviet Embassy of a conversation between Kim's envoy in Beijing and Mao. Mao believed that the Americans were prepared to fight a prolonged war and might escalate their troop levels in Korea. He suggested that Kim should temporarily halt the offensive against the enemy, for the sake of preserving the main KPA forces. Mao also promised to provide the KPA with arms and equipment, and he said that, if necessary, China would be willing to dispatch its own troops to Korea. For that purpose, China had already organized four armies totaling 320,000 men. Mao expected a reply from Kim by August 10. When Kim asked where Moscow stood on the issue of China's entry into the war, Shtykov replied that he did not know. Kim then said that he did not realize that Mao had not yet consulted with Stalin regarding China's entry into the war. Shtykov once again said that he did not know anything about this. The Soviet ambassador then sent a telegram to Moscow to inquire about Stalin's stance on the issue so that he would be prepared to answer Kim's questions.[83] However, Stalin never responded. It seems that Stalin did not really want China to send its troops to Korea unless a more urgent situation were to occur. After several probes, Kim came to understand Stalin's hesitations.

Perhaps because of Stalin's position, the Korean government cut the Chinese Embassy out of the loop. As Chai Chengwen has recalled, Kim received him with great courtesy when he first arrived in Pyongyang, telling him that he would have direct access to Kim at any time. Kim also appointed Sŏ Hwi, deputy chief of the General Political Bureau of the KPA, to provide daily briefings to the Chinese military attachés on the status of the war. But the Chinese soon realized that Sŏ Hwi's briefings were not very different from the evening propaganda broadcasts and that Chai did not really have easy access to the core North Korean leaders. The North Koreans always delayed responding when the Chinese Embassy requested that they arrange for Chinese vice military attachés to visit the KPA. After many contacts with Korean officials at different levels, Chai came to the conclusion that the North Koreans were prohibited from providing any military intelligence to the Chinese. Even those Korean cadres in the Yan'an faction, with whom Chai had fought side by side during World War II, never mentioned to him what was occurring on the front. Chai was convinced that these cadres were strictly prohibited from revealing any information.[84] Meanwhile, the North Korean government refused to receive a Chinese military staff team that the PLA had planned to send to North Korea on a fact-finding mission.[85]

By August the war had reached a stalemate along the Naktong River and Chinese leaders felt it was urgent to be prepared to enter the war. On August 11, in accordance with Mao's instructions, the Thirteenth Army Group held a general meeting of officers at the army and division levels to educate and prepare Chinese officers. Gao Gang, commander and political commissar of the Northeast Military Region, explained the purpose of making preparations for China's entry into the war. He said that China must volunteer to actively aid the Koreans. He instructed that the Chinese troops "will be entering Korea under the name of a volunteer army. The troops will wear Korean uniforms, use Korean designations, and fly the KPA flag." Gao Gang even instructed the core officers and cadres to use Korean names, and he ordered that each preparatory task be assigned to a special responsible person, be strictly carried out, and be completed on time.[86]

On August 19 and August 28, Mao spoke about the Korean War with Soviet philosopher-academician Pavel Yudin, who was then in Beijing to help edit the *Selected Works of Mao Zedong*. Mao worriedly pointed out that the most recent intelligence had revealed that the United States was determined to escalate the war by committing more troops to Korea.[87] If this turned out to be the case, then the North Koreans would be unable to deal with the situation on their own and they would need direct assistance from China. Meanwhile, the Chinese government warned the North Korean government to be prepared for the worst. Although China did not explicitly propose sending troops to Korea, China's intention was obvious to the Koreans.

In August and early September, Mao held two meetings with North Korean representative Yi Sang-jo to discuss the war situation. Mao contended that the KPA had made several mistakes: it had not established a sufficient reserve army, it had distributed its forces evenly along the front line, and it had focused on seizing territory rather than on annihilating the enemy. Mao pointed out that Inch'ŏn–Seoul and Namp'o–Pyongyang were strategic points and easy targets for an attack by the enemy. Therefore, said Mao, the KPA had to consider whether to retreat and to redeploy in advance of U.S. attacks. Liu Shaoqi also noted that the North Korean government should prepare the people psychologically for a prolonged war.[88] In early September, after Mao's repeated requests, the Chinese military decided to expand the Northeast Border Defense Army to 700,000 men by adding 200,000 replacement troops and to update the army's equipment.[89] China obviously was doing this in preparation for a possible American attack that could draw China into the war.

Kim certainly understood Mao's intentions regarding entering the war, but he first had to consult with Moscow. On August 26, Kim telephoned the Soviet ambassador to inform him of intercepted intelligence indicating that the Americans were planning to land in the area around Inch'ŏn and Suwŏn. Kim stated that he would take necessary measures to fortify defense of the area. That evening, on orders from Kim, his secretary, Mun Il, told Shtykov that Kim was still thinking about asking the Chinese comrades to send troops to aid Korea, due to the difficult conditions facing the

KPA on the front. Mun Il said that Kim wanted to know Moscow's opinion about this. Mun Il also mentioned that, on several occasions, Kim had wanted to write to Stalin about this and had also wanted to submit this question for discussion before the Politburo of the Korean Workers' Party. After realizing that Shtykov had no intention of discussing it, Mun Il quickly explained that he was raising all these issues on his own initiative and that Kim had not asked him to do so. Shtykov noted that Kim had lost confidence in the KPA's ability to win the war, which explains his several attempts to win the support of the Soviet Embassy in terms of permitting the entry of Chinese troops into the war. But after sounding out the Soviets through Mun Il, Kim never again referred to this issue.[90]

Stalin was concerned that China's entry into the Korean War would greatly complicate the East Asian situation. Although he had said that China should play a leading role in supporting the revolution in Asia, in 1950 he was not yet ready to abandon the Soviet Union's exclusive control over North Korea. Therefore, he hoped to keep Chinese troops out of Korea unless he had no other choice. In response to Kim Il-sung's repeated inquiries, Stalin explicitly dismissed Kim's request for international assistance. On August 28, Stalin sent a telegram to Kim stating, "CC VKP (b) [All-Union Communist Party (Bolsheviks)] has no doubt that the interventionists will soon be driven out of Korea with ignominy. Comrade Kim Il-sung should not feel uneasy because of the fact that he has not won successive victories in the war against the interventionists. Sometimes victory may be accompanied by setbacks and even by local failures." Finally, Stalin promised, "If necessary, we can provide additional assault and fighter aircraft for the Korean Air Force."[91] On August 31, Soviet Ambassador Shtykov reported to Stalin, "Kim Il-sung was very pleased to receive your letter and thanked you several times." Kim understood the importance of the letter and asked if he could "bring it to the attention of the members of the Politburo of the KWP." Obviously to protect himself, Kim explained that "some members of the Politburo do not understand the situation. It will be useful for them to know the content of this letter."[92] Now Kim was quite clear about Stalin's negative opinion about China's entry into the war. Instead, he placed all his hopes on Moscow.

Kim seemed to regain confidence because of Moscow's promise. Because he could not secure support from the Chinese forces, Kim decided to end the battle in the South. When, on September 4, Chai Chengwen mentioned to Kim that the war had reached a stalemate, Kim replied optimistically that the battle of Pusan had already begun and that the crack shock brigade would soon break the deadlock. When asked about the possibility of an American landing behind the backs of the KPA, Kim asserted that, for the time being, the American troops would not be able to launch a counteroffensive. He insisted that the American troops were not expecting significant reinforcements and that it would be very difficult for them to land at those ports in the rear.

Kim's adventurism was becoming increasingly obvious. As Chai reported, Kim did not at first take into account the possibility of an American intervention, and he anticipated ending the war within one month. After the American intervention, Kim boasted that all the problems would be resolved before August 15 and that victory would be achieved by the end of August. His subsequent total mobilization of manpower and materials, including technicians and students, indicated that Kim intended to place all his hopes on a single throw. These efforts ended up being an enormous waste of both manpower and materials. On September 10, Chai returned to Pyongyang from Beijing with a message for Kim from Zhou Enlai. Zhou was asking Kim to consider a strategic retreat. "I will never consider a retreat," replied Kim.[93]

After the successful landing of the U.S.–UN forces in Inch'ŏn, on September 15, the situation on the Korean Peninsula deteriorated drastically. The KPA was clearly fighting a losing battle, and Chinese leaders felt that China was already being dragged into the war. On September 18, Zhou Enlai summoned Roshchin and the Soviet military advisers to complain that the North Koreans shared very little military intelligence with the Chinese. China had notified North Korea that it wanted to send some military-technical cadres to Korea to investigate the battlefields, but North Korea had never responded. Zhou believed that North Korea should withdraw its main forces to the North if it lacked a reserve army of 100,000 men, as indicated by the official statistics. Zhou deliberately pointed out that the Western countries were now very worried that the Soviet Union and China might intervene in the war, even though they were not prepared for a long, large-scale war. Zhou told the Soviets, "We should take advantage of the fear on the part of the Western countries and take action to demonstrate our intentions. From this perspective, China's transfer of troops from the South to the Northeast was sufficient to upset the British and American governments."[94] In the end, Zhou asked Roshchin and the Soviet military advisers to inform the Soviet government of China's position as soon as possible, and he expressed his wish for a speedy reply from Moscow.

Moscow replied on September 20, criticizing the North Koreans for not furnishing the Chinese government with updated military intelligence but explaining that this was because the North Korean leaders were young and inexperienced. Moscow agreed with Beijing that the main forces of the KPA should immediately withdraw to the North and build a line of defense around Seoul. However, Stalin did not respond regarding the issue of China's entry into the war, as raised by Zhou.[95] Zhou had no choice but to advise Kim to concentrate on protecting the 38th parallel, to uphold a spirit of self-reliance, and to prepare for a long war.[96] On September 21, Liu Shaoqi told Roshchin that if the Americans had the upper hand in Korea, "China will feel obligated to help the Korean comrades."[97]

While proposing to Moscow that China would enter the war, Zhou Enlai directly inquired about the North Korean opinion on this issue. On September 19, Zhou called in North Korean Ambassador Yi Chu-yŏn to inform him of his conversation with Roshchin on the previous day. Zhou asked him what China could do to help North Korea after the Inch'ŏn landing.[98] On the following day, Kim informed the Soviet ambassador of Zhou's inquiry. Kim explained to Shtykov that the Chinese and North Korean governments had an agreement that if the enemy were to land in the rear-guard area, China would send troops to Korea to provide assistance. Kim then asked Shtykov how he should reply to the Chinese inquiry. After the Soviet ambassador replied with a "No comment," Kim immediately said that the Chinese army was excellent and had much combat experience but that it was still an open question how it would perform in the face of intensive, ongoing U.S. bombing. Almost all the North Koreans present echoed, "If [we] let the Chinese army enter the war without proper air cover, the serious situation on the front will not improve very much." Only the foreign minister, Pak Hŏn-yŏng, explicitly expressed the hope that China would enter the war. Without instructions from Moscow, Shtykov "avoided responding to this question."[99]

On September 21, the Politburo of the KWP held a meeting to discuss how to respond to China's proposal to send troops to Korea. Pak Hŏn-yŏng, Kim Tu-bong, and Pak Il-u all believed that North Korea obviously could not rely on its own forces to defeat the Americans, and therefore North Korea had no choice but to request that the Chinese government send troops to Korea. But Kim Il-sung stated, "Given the fact that the

Soviets gave us all the weapons that we asked for, on what basis should we ask for Chinese help?" Kim believed that "the Soviets and the Chinese will not allow the Americans to seize Korea." Finally, Kim suggested that, for the time being, a resolution requesting Chinese assistance not be passed. Instead, he suggested that they first write to Stalin to seek his advice. Kim emphasized that "if [we] ask for Chinese military assistance without referring [the question] to the Soviet Union, the Soviets might complain, 'Isn't it enough that we sent over all these advisers and weapons?'" Kim also said that if North Korea accelerated the building of its army, it would not be necessary to seek assistance from the Chinese. Therefore, no resolution was passed at this meeting.[100]

On September 30, Moscow received a report from Shtykov that Seoul was probably already lost, the road for the KPA to retreat northward was blocked, and communications had been cut off. Kim worried that the enemy would cross the 38th parallel and North Korea would be unable to build its army to provide effective defense. The members of the Politburo discussed the situation and drafted a letter to Stalin appealing for air support. Meanwhile, the Koreans also drafted a letter to Mao, hinting at a request for help. Panicking and lacking in confidence, they did not know what to do. That same night, Kim sent a personal letter to Stalin asking for "direct military assistance." If that were not possible, Kim asked for "international volunteers from China and other people's democratic countries."[101] Due to this unprecedented emergency, Stalin finally ceded. On October 1, Stalin sent a telegram to Mao, requesting that Chinese troops enter North Korea as volunteers and organize defense in the area north of the 38th parallel. Stalin stated disingenuously, "I have not mentioned this to the Korean comrades and am not intending to do so. But I have no doubt that they will be very happy to hear this news."[102]

From October 1, when Mao received Stalin's telegram, to October 19, when the Chinese People's Volunteer Army finally crossed the Yalu River, Mao managed to override all dissenting voices among the Chinese leadership, and his motion to send troops to Korea was passed. The Soviets had explicitly told the Chinese not to expect Soviet air cover for the time being, but Mao was determined to enter the war regardless. As an ally and the leader of the Asian Revolution, Mao believed that China was committed to helping North Korea, even though there was no official alliance treaty requiring it to do so.[103]

On the issue of China's entry into the war, Pyongyang generally took its cues from Moscow. No evidence has come to light to show that Kim Il-sung was reluctant to welcome Chinese troops to Korea because of the existence of a Yan'an faction in North Korea. What is apparent is that, in 1950 Kim, situated between his two giant socialist neighbors, valued and trusted the Soviets more than he trusted the Chinese. From Stalin's perspective, after the United States intervened in Korea and threatened the 38th parallel, it was up to China to take responsibility for the security of North Korea and the socialist east front. After China's entry into the war, Moscow adjusted its position to be consistent with that of Beijing, and it supported China whenever there were disagreements between China and North Korea on war-related issues.

With support from Moscow, Kim Il-sung strengthened his control over North Korea, while the CCP seized political power in Mainland China. Both had close relations with Moscow and became members of the socialist bloc. During the Chinese Civil War, North Korea provided the CCP Northeast Bureau with humanitarian and material aid, and the DPRK hoped to benefit from this in the future. Revolutionary and ideological factors thus joined the traditional "lips and teeth" relationship premised on geopolitical proximity. Kim Il-sung and Mao Zedong both understood the importance of mutual help in their respective struggles to establish political regimes. This revolutionary internationalism explains their readiness to lend a hand to each other in times of need.

CHAPTER II

Sharp Contradictions Among the Leadership, 1950–1953

R egardless of Mao Zedong's motives, China's decision to send troops to Korea ultimately saved Kim Il-sung and his regime. For a long time, the socialist bloc consistently boasted that Chinese and Korean troops fought side by side against the U.S. imperialists. Chinese and North Korean media repeatedly claimed, "Sino–Korean friendship was forged with fresh blood and tested in war." However, with the declassification of Chinese and Russian sources, we now know that there were many disagreements between the Chinese and the North Koreans regarding how to fight the war and how to make peace. Superficially, they were close allies. But in actuality they had very different concerns regarding a series of strategic and tactical issues.

Difficulties in Creating a Unified Command

The first urgent question raised by China's entry into the war was who should command the joint army. Throughout the war, the two countries continued to remain at odds over this issue.

At the same time that Chinese Premier and Foreign Minister Zhou Enlai was in Moscow negotiating for Soviet assistance, such as air cover and military equipment, the Chinese and North Koreans had already begun to map the deployment of the Chinese troops in Korea. A series of differences surfaced, such as questions about command, communications, supplies, and transportation. Due to a lack of time, they did not reach any agreement. On October 8, 1950, Mao informed Kim Il-sung that China had decided to send troops to Korea and that he had requested Pak Il-u to proceed to Shenyang for further discussions.

Pak arrived that very evening, but he did not go into detail about the arrangements for the entry of the Chinese troops. He confirmed that the United States was sending more troops to Korea, so he urged that China immediately dispatch its troops. With respect to logistics, Pak only mentioned currency and supplies of firewood. He advised that the Chinese People's Volunteer Army (CPVA) should use North Korean currency and then later repay the North Korean government at a proper exchange rate. He also stated that the local North Korean government would purchase firewood from local markets and then resell it to the CPVA at market prices. Because Kim had already retreated from Pyongyang to Tŏkch'ŏn, Pak reported that Kim wanted CPVA headquarters to be located in Tŏkch'ŏn. This indicates that Kim was contemplating unifying the two commands. Chai Chengwen, then political counselor at the Chinese Embassy in Pyongyang, speculated that Kim initially thought that the CPVA would only be used in cases of emergencies and thus would be subject to his command. When it became apparent that China's intention was to dispatch several hundred thousand volunteer soldiers, Kim realized that he could not suggest putting the CPVA under his command. This is why he proposed a combination of Chinese and Korean command posts.[1]

However, the commander in chief of the CPVA, Peng Dehuai, had different ideas about this. First, in his telegram to Beijing on October 1, Stalin had explicitly stated that the Chinese commander should control the CPVA.[2] In addition, Peng's observations in Korea had led him to doubt the ability of the North Korean commanders. In telegrams to the Central Military Commission of the Chinese Communist Party (CCP), Peng pointed out numerous concerns about the North Korean army. For instance, he referred to serious problems with the North Korean recruitment policy. The North Korean government had ordered that all male citizens between the ages of sixteen and forty-five should join the army, but it did not provide assistance to their families, thus leaving the families to face serious livelihood problems. Furthermore, Peng felt that the North Korean commanders were amateurs, noting that on October 19 they had ordered the army to defend Pyongyang to the death, thereby trapping some thirty thousand men. Peng also noted that the North Koreans did not want to establish a political commissar system, although they had agreed to carry out party and political work in the Korean People's Army (KPA). Peng later told Chai Chengwen, "I had to be responsible for both the Chinese and the Korean people, as well as for several hundred thousand soldiers!"[3]

In short, Peng never considered it an option for the North Koreans to command the Chinese troops. However, for a number of reasons he never raised the issue of unifying command. First, it was not clear where the North Korean government stood on this issue. Moreover, the KPA "had virtually disintegrated as a fighting force. Remnants of military units that had escaped encirclement were . . . [still] regrouping in China."[4] Because the North Korean troops could not join in the fighting for the time being, China did not want to deal with the issue of who would lead the troops. When Kim and Peng met for the first time at Dayudong, on October 21, neither of them raised the issue of unifying the military command of the two armies. When the issue of coordination between the troops came up, Kim agreed to appoint Pak Il-u as liaison officer to Peng's headquarters. On October 25, the CCP Central Committee officially appointed Pak as deputy commander, vice political commissar, and deputy secretary of the CPVA Party Committee.[5]

However, with the expansion of CPVA operations, it became increasingly urgent that the military leadership of the Chinese and Korean forces be unified. During the first campaign, Peng Dehuai had on a number of occasions reported that the lack of coordination between the troops had caused many problems for CPVA operations. The CPVA faced language barriers, an unfamiliar terrain, and road blockades by the retreating North Korean government, army, and civilians.[6] Moreover, the KPA units had more than once mistakenly attacked the CPVA. For instance, on November 4, when the Thirty-Ninth Army of the CPVA encircled the U.S. Twenty-Fourth Division southeast of Pakch'ŏn, the CPVA was attacked by a KPA tank division that was proceeding toward Sunch'ŏn. As a result, the enemy was able to escape.

The supply and transportation situations were also chaotic, due to little or no coordination.[7] In response, Peng urged that Beijing raise the issue of military coordination with Kim Il-sung. Peng wanted KPA headquarters to be situated closer to CPVA headquarters. Beijing entrusted the Chinese Embassy in Pyongyang to transmit Peng's message to Kim, and on

November 7 Pak Il-u, on behalf of Peng, visited Kim to discuss this issue. But the results of their three-day meeting were disappointing. First, Kim only reluctantly accepted Peng's proposal to open new fronts in the enemy's rear—after Terentii Shtykov, then Soviet ambassador to North Korea, expressed unreserved support. Second, Kim insisted on relying on his liaison staff for communications and the exchange of intelligence. He refused to relocate KPA headquarters closer to CPVA headquarters, to say nothing of unifying their military commands. Third, Peng subtly criticized North Korea's practice of mistreating prisoners of war, noting that North Korea had tortured staff at the U.S. and UK embassies. Fourth, Kim insisted on the use of force to encircle and suppress KPA deserters, and he charged them with treason, even though he had accepted the offer by the CPVA to recall such deserters to service.[8]

Via the CCP Central Military Commission, Peng also requested that Kim allow the 6,200 survivors of the KPA's Sixth Division, who had joined the CPVA's 125th Division, to remain with the CPVA division. But Kim insisted on transferring the KPA's Sixth Division elsewhere. Later, more than five thousand men from the KPA's Seventh Division joined the CPVA's 125th Division. Peng again requested that these troops remain with the CPVA division, but he never received a response from Kim. Also, to Peng's frustration, the North Korean leaders and their Soviet military advisers opposed Peng's plan for a second campaign, to retreat several hundred miles so as to arrange for an ambush. Instead, the North Koreans and their Soviet advisers insisted that the CPVA should cross the Ch'ŏngch'ŏn River and continue to pursue the enemy.[9]

It is understandable that Kim Il-sung did not want to cede control over the KPA. This was an issue of national sovereignty and pride. But it is puzzling that Kim still wanted several hundred thousand Chinese troops to be under his command, even though he had just experienced the loss of control over several hundred thousand Korean troops. The available documents indicate that Kim had been deluded by misreading the thinking in Moscow and Beijing. To minimize any effects from the United States as a result of China's entry into the war, the Chinese government took pains to emphasize the unofficial nature of the CPVA. This explains the extreme caution on the part of the Chinese government when speaking publicly about the CPVA military command. When news spread that Chinese troops had entered Korea and had confronted UN troops on October 25, Kim asked Beijing for permission to issue an official confirmation of this news so as to boost North Korean morale. On November 7, Mao responded that Kim could note in his speech that the CPVA, under the unified leadership of the KPA, had provided aid to resist the aggressors. However, Mao advised Kim not to say anything further. Zhou Enlai emphasized that it was not the "Chinese Volunteer Army" that had entered Korea but rather the "Chinese People's Volunteer Army." On November 12, Zhou urged Kim to use the following phrase to refer to China's entry into the war: "the entry of the Chinese People's Volunteer Army into the war under the command of the KPA headquarters."[10] Such rhetoric was only for public consumption. The truth was that China never considered ceding military leadership of the CPVA to the North Koreans. On the contrary, Mao specifically advised that Kim should meet Peng Dehuai and Gao Gang face-to-face as early as possible to discuss the coordination of Chinese and Korean forces.[11] The essential question to be decided was which side would control the troops.

Given the importance of a united command, Mao took the initiative to ask Moscow for an explicit reply. On November 13, Mao sent a telegram to Stalin relaying Peng's proposal. In his telegram, Mao wrote that he hoped that comrades Kim Il-sung and Shtykov would permanently stay on the front so that Kim, Shtykov, and Peng could form a three-man team jointly responsible for issuing military policy. He advised that, in order for the war to proceed smoothly, the three men should consult with one another to formulate unified policies regarding recruitment, combat strategy, the rearguard and frontline battlefields, and other war-related issues. Noting that Beijing supported Peng's proposal, Mao wished to know whether Moscow also endorsed it. If so, Mao asked that Stalin inform Shtykov and Kim of his approval. Mao reiterated the importance of unity among the leading North Korean, Soviet, and Chinese comrades by asserting that victory would only be possible if the leaders of the three countries could work out unified military and political policies, if the KPA and the CPVA could coordinate their activities, and if, as Stalin suggested, many of the Chinese and North Korean troops could be merged (with the KPA units remaining intact).[12]

On November 15, Kim and Shtykov were invited to CPVA headquarters, and Gao Gang joined them from Shenyang. As soon as the meeting began, Peng stated frankly that command of the two armies must be united. Gao explained that because the Korean Peninsula was so narrow, a unified command was absolutely necessary to win the war. Shtykov clearly stated that the Chinese should direct both the Chinese and the Korean troops, reinforcing his point by criticizing the KPA for losing so many battles and wasting Soviet military aid, including some of the best equipment from the Soviet Union. Conversely, he praised the CPVA for annihilating a large number of enemy troops despite its inferior arms and equipment. However, when it was Kim's turn to speak, he merely introduced the circumstances facing the KPA and referred to a united command.

Given the urgency of the situation, Peng took the initiative to propose a specific plan for uniting command: Kim, Shtykov, and Peng would form a three-man team to jointly direct and coordinate all the troops. However, Kim remained silent, and Shtykov had to await instructions from Moscow before he could make any comments. In the end, the issue was deferred until the end of the second campaign.[13] On the same day, Stalin cabled Shtykov to have him inform Kim Il-sung that the Soviet Union agreed to the establishment of a unified command under Chinese leadership.[14] But it was not easy for Kim to hand over military power to the

Figure 2.1 Gao Gang, Kim Il-sung, and Peng Dehuai discuss the issue of the Sino–Korean Joint Command at the Chinese People's Volunteer Army headquarters, November 15, 1950.

Chinese. Not only did this represent a loss of face for Korea, but also Kim feared that it might undermine his control over North Korea. Therefore, Kim did not take any actions to carry out Stalin's instructions.

On November 17, Mao told Peng and Gao Gang that Stalin had expressed unreserved support for Peng's proposal and had promised to immediately notify Kim and Shtykov of his opinion. In addition, M. V. Zakharov, chief military adviser of the USSR to China, supported unifying the command of the CPVA and the KPA. Mao instructed that Peng should pay attention to Kim's reactions to this development.[15]

To further pressure Kim, on November 21 Shtykov met with Kim and Pak Hŏn-yŏng, the North Korean foreign minister, to inform them that Moscow was sending General V. N. Razuvayev to replace General N. A. Vasil'yev as chief military adviser for the commander in chief of the Korean People's Army. Shtykov noted that, from then on, according to an order by the Soviet defense minister, Razuvayev was to be responsible for all military-related issues. Kim, understanding his meaning, noted, "I should also resign from the position of commander in chief."[16]

After the Soviet Union had clarified its position, Kim asked for a meeting with Mao. On December 3, Kim arrived in Beijing and told Mao that Stalin had instructed him by telegram to establish a joint CPVA and KPA command. According to Kim, Stalin had said that, because the Chinese command was more experienced than the Korean command, a Chinese should be the chief commander and Koreans should be the deputy commanders. Kim reported that the Politburo of the Korean Workers' Party (KWP) had already approved this arrangement. Mao then recommended that Peng Dehuai be made chief commander and political commissar of the joint forces, and Kim recommended that Kim Ung be made deputy commander and Pak Il-u be made deputy political commissar. It was agreed that any order issued to the joint forces should be signed by all three men— Peng Dehuai, Kim Ung, and Pak Il-u—but orders issued to the CPVA would be signed as before, only by the Chinese. The Joint Command was to be responsible for issues on the front line, such as military combat, whereas the North Korean government was to be responsible for mobilization, training, military administration, policing, and other issues in the rear. The Joint Command, however, was also to make suggestions about rear-guard affairs. Sharing one office, the CPVA headquarters and the KPA General Staff remained under the Joint Command. It was decided that the Joint Command would not be publicized and its existence would only

Figure 2.2 Kim Il-sung with senior generals from both China and North Korea at the time of the formation of the Sino–Korean Joint Command, December 1950.

appear in internal papers. Jurisdiction of the Joint Command was also to include railway transportation and maintenance.[17]

After Kim Il-sung returned to Korea, he and Peng Dehuai held friendly discussions, on December 7. The two men agreed to set up the Joint Command within the next several days. To Peng's satisfaction, Kim promised that, from then on, he would not directly interfere in military affairs. He also accepted China's suggestion that deployment of the Third Army of the KPA would be canceled and it would be placed under the command of Song Shilun, who was the commander of the nearby Ninth Army of the CPVA.[18] To pacify Kim, Peng repeatedly said, "The courage and perseverance of the KPA and its strict Soviet-style military management are worthy of emulation." He ordered that the officers of the Ninth Army learn from the Third Army Corps of the KPA. He also instructed that Chinese officers should use every opportunity to introduce to the North Korean officers the Chinese experiences in local political and military organizational work. At the same time, Peng was worried that the Chinese officers might offend the North Koreans, so he warned the Chinese officers not to be dogmatic when the Chinese experiences contradicted the established North Korean practices.[19]

For the same reason, Mao ordered that CPVA headquarters not draft a regulation for the jurisdiction of the Joint Command. He believed that such a regulation would be detrimental to both bilateral and international relations. Mao stressed that the Sino–Korean Joint Command should remain secret. Only officers at the army or independent division level were allowed to be aware of its existence. But in practice, Mao emphasized, the Joint Command was to be in charge of all combat-related issues.[20] On December 8, Zhou Enlai drafted the Sino–Korean Agreement on the Establishment of the Sino–Korean Joint Command, noting "after receiving consent from Comrade Kim Il-sung . . . please send us a telegram for approval. It will then be regarded as a done deal, and you can then implement it." In mid-December, the Joint Command of the Chinese People's Volunteer Army and the Korean People's Army was established.[21]

A joint command was also needed for the air war. Having witnessed the CPVA's initial success in the war, Stalin decided to allow the Soviet Air Force to join the war as well.[22] On October 29, 1950, Soviet advisers told Zhou Enlai that Moscow had agreed to provide air cover in the Andong area, even flying across the Sino–Korean border. Moscow promised to move its air base from Shenyang to Andong within ten days.[23] On November 1, the Soviet Air Force moved above the Yalu River for the first time.[24] In early January 1951, Zakharov notified China that two divisions of the Soviet Air Force would soon enter Korea to provide air cover for the lines from Ji'an to Kanggye and from Andong to Anju. In addition, by early April, five Chinese air divisions and three North Korean air divisions would enter the war. In response to these developments and encouraged by the Soviet advisers, China proposed creating a Joint Air Command. After consultations, in March the Sino–Korean Joint Air Command was established, based on the model of the joint ground command. For political reasons and due to language barriers, the Soviet Air Force did not take part in this Joint Air Command.[25]

But not all of the KPA was under the Sino–Korean Joint Command. By April 15, 1951, the Korean troops trained in China had returned to Korea. As a result, the KPA was expanded to include seven army groups. Four of the seven groups were under the control of the Joint Command

and the remainder were under the direct command of the commander in chief of the KPA.[26] The Korean cadres in the Joint Command, appointed by the KWP, were Kim Ung and Pak Il-u, Yan'an faction cadres who had been with the CCP and the Eighth Route Army during the War of Resistance Against Japan. Although the Chinese leaders knew them well and trusted them, Kim Il-sung did not trust them. On July 6, Kim informed the Sino–Korean Joint Command that Ch'oe Yong-gŏn would replace Kim Ung, who was to become deputy minister of national defense. On February 5, Pak Il-u was also recalled.[27] Kim was basically reluctant to forgo his power to command the troops.

As a result of Moscow's intervention, the problem of unifying military command of the CPVA and the KPA was finally resolved by the institutionalization of the Joint Command. It was only natural that the United States had assumed command of the UN troops. But the issue of a unified military leadership for North Korea and China was problematic. For the North Koreans, giving up command over their own troops was a question of national pride. For the Chinese, the main concern was to win the war. Thus, because the Chinese troops were superior to those of their North Korean counterparts in terms of both military power and battle experience, the Chinese believed that they should lead the Joint Command. From a practical point of view, it was necessary that military leadership be under the CPVA, which was a reality that Kim Il-sung had to face when he entered into the alliance with China.

Disagreements Over the Southward Strategy

While the KPA was successfully pushing toward the South, Mao Zedong had a long conversation with Yi Sang-jo, Kim Il-sung's personal representative. Mao stressed that the Korean leaders should remember that they were facing a very strong enemy. The KPA was moving forward but was neglecting its rear defense. It was possible that the enemy would land in the rear and cut off the KPA's transportation lines. Mao warned that the Korean leaders, mindful of this danger, should carry out a strategic retreat. However, Kim would not tolerate such a warning, and he told Yi not to convey Mao's opinion to anyone else.[28]

After the CPVA's second campaign successfully pushed the front line to near the 38th parallel, Peng Dehuai, as the commanding officer on the battlefield, sought to allow his troops some time to rest and regroup. In a report to Beijing, he pointed out that the recent victories had significantly enhanced the spirit of the North Korean government, army, and civilians but had also given rise to unfounded optimism about a quick victory. The Soviet ambassador had said that the American troops would be able to escape if the Sino–Korean Joint Command did not advance quickly. This view was broadly shared by the North Korean comrades in the KWP Central Committee.

Peng, however, believed that the Joint Command still had a long way to go before it could win the war. He pointed out that as the enemy's position changed from offensive to defensive, its front line became shorter and its strength became more concentrated, which in fact was advantageous to the UN forces. Peng also noted that although the enemy's morale was very low, it still had approximately 260,000 troops and would not quickly leave Korea. For these reasons, Peng urged that the CPVA adopt a policy of gradual advance.[29] Zhou Enlai agreed with Peng, proposing that if there was no chance for the CPVA to annihilate the enemy near Seoul, then the CPVA should be given a period of time to regroup, regardless of whether the enemy decided to defend or to abandon Seoul.[30] For political reasons, however, Mao overruled these suggestions and ordered that the CPVA immediately launch a third campaign and cross the 38th parallel.[31]

From a military perspective and in terms of the long-term situation, Mao believed in Peng's strategy of gradual advance. He also agreed that after crossing the 38th parallel, all of the main forces (including those of the KPA) should withdraw several dozen miles in order to allow the troops to rest and regroup.[32] The result of the third campaign confirmed Peng's prediction. Although the KPA-CPVA forces crossed the 38th parallel and captured Seoul and some other territory, they did not inflict heavy casualties on the enemy because the UN forces retreated strategically in an orderly manner.

On January 3, 1951, Peng sent a telegram to Kim Il-sung to inform him that the enemy had retreated in a timely fashion after its defensive line had been broken; therefore, only three thousand enemy soldiers had been captured. If the enemy continued to escape southward, Peng told Kim, the KPA-CPVA troops would follow them to Suwŏn and then remain there until receiving further orders. After Seoul, Inch'ŏn, Suwŏn, and Ich'ŏn were seized, Peng said, the third campaign should immediately pause so that the troops would have time to regroup and be replenished. If the enemy mounted a heavy defense around Seoul, said Peng, the CPVA should not try to launch a fierce attack, due to the unfavorable conditions.[33] Mao relayed Peng's decisions to Stalin.[34] Based on the assessment that the enemy was trying to induce the already exhausted Chinese troops to move deep into the Naktong River area to attack its well-defended base,[35] on January 8 Peng ordered that his troops stop.[36] This decision left the North Koreans deeply disappointed.

Even before the Sino–Korean Joint Army had crossed the 38th parallel, Kim Il-sung was already very dissatisfied with the "slow advance" of the Chinese army. He complained about the Chinese army to the chief Soviet military adviser, noting that "they receive their instructions from Beijing."[37] One day prior to the third campaign, on December 30, 1950, Kim passed on the contents of Mao and Peng's letter to Razuvayev (who had also replaced Shtykov as Soviet ambassador to North Korea, on December 14, 1950), stating that, according to the Chinese battle plan, the campaign had not been carried out in depth and two KPA corps would have to withdraw to north of the 38th parallel.[38] Thus, the chief Soviet military adviser asked Peng Dehuai whether Beijing had announced that the 38th parallel no longer existed. The Chinese army had advanced south of the 38th parallel but then retreated north of the line. How could the Chinese explain this politically?[39]

The North Koreans were very excited when the third campaign first began. On January 2, 1951, *Rodong sinmun* (Workers' Newspaper) published Kim Il-sung's report, a few days earlier, to the third meeting of the Standing Committee of the KWP. The report stated that, with respect to the 38th parallel, the KWP and the people "cannot tolerate [it], and cannot sit by and watch." Thus, the current military task was to cross the 38th parallel and "to chase the enemy and to launch a decisive battle."[40] Kim seemed to have learned a lesson from the previous setbacks, and thus he agreed to allow the troops to rest and regroup for two months after crossing the 38th parallel. But in his heart he still expected a quick victory. He cleverly used Pak Hŏn-yŏng and newly appointed Soviet Ambassador Razuvayev to deal with the Chinese. On the day that Peng ordered the troops to halt their advance, Kim told Chai Chengwen that the troops should not rest for longer than one month. If too much time were to pass, he explained, the rivers and rice paddies would begin to thaw, thereby hampering troop movements. Furthermore, the enemy was also using the time to rest, said Kim. Kim also planned to talk in person with Peng, who immediately conveyed Kim's message to Mao, and at the same time insisted that his army must have some time to rest and regroup.[41]

On the morning of January 9, when he heard that the CPVA and KPA had already stopped their advance, Zakharov expressed his disapproval. He said that he had never heard of any victorious army not pursuing the enemy or advancing toward victory. He said this pause would allow the enemy a chance to catch its breath and thus it would squander the advantage that the CPVA had gained. Even after Nie Rongzhen's patient explanation, Zakharov firmly insisted on his opinion.[42] At this point, Stalin sent a telegram to suggest that, to avoid international blame being placed on China, the CPVA should remain north of the 38th parallel, including in the coastal regions, while the KPA should be allowed to continue its southward advance. Mao immediately relayed this message to Peng.[43]

On the evening of January 10, Kim Il-sung, together with Chai Cheng-wen, called on Peng Dehuai's headquarters. During the meeting, Peng analyzed their own and the enemy's situations and stressed that their forces definitely needed time to rest and regroup. After a proper rest, the troops would be able to annihilate more of the enemy during the next campaign, said Peng. Kim agreed to allow the troops some time to rest, but he proposed that it be for a shorter period. He suggested first dispatching three armies to advance southward, while allowing the remaining troops to rest for one month. Peng explained that resuming military operations might force the enemy to abandon several more areas, but it would also push the enemy's main forces into a narrow region around Pusan. Such a concentration of UN troops would not help Peng's strategy of dividing and conquering the enemy. Kim argued that, in addition to annihilating the enemy, it was also important to seize other areas. Peng explained that, after the enemy's forces had been destroyed, more territory could easily be taken. Kim, however, pursued a different logic, contending that it would be beneficial to conquer more territory and to increase the population for the sake of postwar elections after a peace settlement. For Peng, such considerations were unnecessary for the time being because the most important thing at that point was to defeat the enemy. Sensing the impasse at the meeting, Peng showed Kim the telegram from Mao that conveyed Stalin's opinion. Kim still refused to budge, claiming that he was not expressing his personal opinion but the collective opinion of the Politburo of the KWP. To reinforce his point, Kim phoned Pak Hŏn-yŏng and asked him to immediately join the meeting.[44]

On the following day, Peng received an urgent telegram from Mao. Mao had accepted Stalin's suggestion and proposed that the First, Second, Third, and Fifth armies of the KPA be deployed south of the Han River, while the CPVA would withdraw to Inch'ŏn and north of the Han River to rest and regroup for two or three months. The CPVA would be responsible for the defense of Inch'ŏn, Seoul, and the areas north of the 38th parallel. The troops that were being trained in Northeast China would provide reinforcement for the KPA. But if Kim felt that it was unnecessary to resupply and reorganize the KPA troops, the KPA could continue its advance under the direct command of the North Korean government.

Peng, Kim, and Pak Hŏn-yŏng engaged in a heated debate that evening. Kim and Pak believed that Stalin's suggestion that the KPA advance on its own indicated Stalin's belief that the conditions were favorable for North Korea and that the American troops would soon leave Korea. Pak referred to several recent news and intelligence reports provided by the Soviet Union to argue that the United States had already made up its mind to leave Korea and was looking for an excuse to withdraw its troops. Pak argued that the Sino–Korean forces should continue to pursue the enemy because it would give the United States a perfect excuse to withdraw. Otherwise, the American forces would remain in Korea even longer.

Peng rejected this idea, arguing that if the Chinese and Koreans did not advance, the Americans could still withdraw on their own with a perfectly good excuse. Pak responded that military pressure should be applied to intensify internal conflicts among the American capitalist class. To this, Peng replied that only by destroying more U.S. divisions could China and Korea deepen American domestic conflicts, and only after regrouping could the CPVA destroy more enemy troops. At this point, Kim interrupted to repeat his idea about sending three CPVA army groups farther south and allowing the remaining forces to rest for one month before advancing forward.[45]

Peng began to lose his patience. Raising his voice, he told Kim and Pak that their mistaken views were based on good but unrealistic intentions. He said:

In the past, you assumed that the United States would never send troops to Korea. You never thought about what to do if they did send troops. Now you say that the American troops will definitely withdraw from Korea, but you are not considering what you will do if the American troops do not withdraw. You are hoping for a quick victory, but you are not making concrete preparations and this will only prolong the war. You are hoping to end this war by luck. You are gambling with the fate of the people, and this will lead to disaster. The CPVA needs two months to rest and regroup—not one day less. It may even require three months. Without considerable preparation, not a single division is going to advance south. Your underestimation of the enemy is a serious mistake and I will not tolerate it. If you think I am not doing my job, you can fire me, court-martial me, or even kill me.[46]

Then Peng repeated Mao's opinion: the CPVA would be responsible for defending all of the coast and inland territory north of the Inch'ŏn–Yangyang line. Four army groups of North Koreans, consisting of about 120,000 men, had already rested for approximately two months. Peng said that the North Koreans had the final say about these troops and they could allow these troops to advance southward if they so wished. Peng said that if the American troops did indeed withdraw from Korea, he would certainly congratulate and celebrate Korea's liberation. But if the American army did not withdraw, the CPVA would advance southward as planned. Under these circumstances, Kim had no choice but to admit that the KPA was not prepared and had not completely recovered, so it could not advance on its own. Kim reluctantly agreed that the CPVA should have two months to rest and regroup. In the end, the two sides decided to hold a joint meeting of senior officers and staff to exchange experiences and unify thoughts.[47]

When Stalin learned about the Peng-Kim dispute, he took the Chinese side. He composed a telegram stating that the leadership of the CPVA was correct. He also wrote that the truth undoubtedly rested with Commander Peng Dehuai. Referring to Peng as a military genius of his times, he praised him for leading the poorly equipped troops to defeat the most powerful imperialist country in the world. Stalin also criticized the Soviet ambassador for being an amateur when it came to military matters, and he forbade him from interfering with Peng's command in the future.[48]

At this point, Mao stepped in to press Kim. On January 14, he sent a telegram to Kim, stating:

In the next two to three months, the Chinese volunteers and the Korean troops must carry out some serious major tasks, including replenishing the troops with newly trained soldiers, making sure that the newly trained soldiers learn from the experience of the veterans, upgrading the troops' arms and equipment, rebuilding the railways, storing food and ammunition, and improving the transportation lines and rear services. Completing these jobs can secure the final victory.... If the enemy continues its stubborn resistance ... we must be sufficiently prepared for a prolonged war. Otherwise we will repeat the mistake that the KPA made between June and September of 1950.[49]

Mao also sent a copy of this telegram to Stalin.

During meetings with Peng from January 16 to January 18, Kim admitted that it would be risky for the KPA to advance southward on its own. He also told Peng that the KWP Politburo had discussed this matter and had concluded that the Chinese were correct about insisting that the troops should be allowed to rest for two months.[50] However, Kim certainly was not happy. Later, Ambassador Razuvayev reported that when the Americans were about to withdraw, the Chinese left Suwŏn and retreated to the 38th parallel. The Chinese halted their large-scale offensive and sent unprepared troops to attack the enemy. This seemed to indicate that the Chinese wanted to end the war at the 38th parallel, thus seriously harming the prestige of the Chinese among the North Korean leaders, even though the North Koreans were aware of the difficulties with which the Chinese troops were dealing.[51] Long after the end of the Korean War, it was still rumored within the KWP that the CPVA had been reluctant to pursue the total liberation of Korea when the American aggressors were losing the war in early 1951.[52] One can only imagine Kim's disillusionment with the CPVA.

From a military perspective, Peng's plan was well thought out and well founded. Conversely, the North Korean leaders were inflated with unrealistic enthusiasm because they evidently looked at the war not merely through military lenses but also through political lenses. It is worth noting, however, that such Sino–North Korean disagreements were only tactical. In terms of overall strategy, Beijing was generally in agreement with Pyongyang and Moscow. All three sought to use military means to force the UN troops to leave the Korean Peninsula, thereby completely resolving the Korean problem. It was in this spirit that Mao and Kim ignored the UN call for a cease-fire in January 1951, thus losing a perfect opportunity to bring the war to an early end.[53]

The Struggle Over Railway Management

The supply line for the CPVA and the KPA was greatly extended as a result of the three successful campaigns and the shift of the front line toward the south. However, this new development caused new logistics problems. The North Korean economy had collapsed under the pressure of the war, and by the end of 1950 industrial production had come to a complete standstill. After the Chinese and North Korean troops crossed the 38th parallel, the North Korean government made great efforts to rebuild the economy, including drafting the Plan for the Recovery and Development of the National Economy for the First Season of 1951. On February 22, 1951, the North Korean government passed a resolution to improve wartime railway transportation, stressing the importance of the railways for the recovery of industry and agriculture and for the healthy functioning of the national economy.[54] China and North Korea soon found themselves in disagreement over control of railway transportation.

The CPVA faced a serious supply problem. It could not obtain supplies from local Koreans because the war-torn country was already facing a serious shortage of resources. It could not seize supplies from the enemy because the well-equipped American troops were highly mobile. The only option left for the CPVA was to ship supplies from China. However, transportation from China to Korea was not easy, due to the mountainous terrain, long distance, and poor road conditions. Additionally, the CPVA owned very few trucks and many had already been destroyed by America's endless air bombing.[55] In short, road transportation was severely strained. This increased the importance of railway transportation. As early as late October 1950, Peng Dehuai asked the CCP Northeast Bureau to take measures to improve railway transportation by arranging joint management with the North Koreans. Peng also asked Beijing to dispatch a Railway Engineering Corps to North Korea to help with maintenance. A large group of railway engineering troops and workers arrived in North Korea on November 6 to work side by side with the KPA railway construction forces and the North Korean railway workers.[56]

When he met with Gao Gang on November 16, Peng proposed establishing a Sino–Korean joint railway command for the purpose of improving railroad management, coordinating Sino–North Korean transportation, improving supply lines, and facilitating the transfer of wounded soldiers.[57]

Subsequently, Chinese representatives were sent to North Korea to discuss this issue with the relevant North Korean officials. But little came of these efforts. Only after Kim visited Beijing on December 3 to negotiate establishment of the Sino–Korean Joint Command did China and North Korea reach a preliminary agreement regarding a joint railway command. During a talk with Peng Dehuai on November 7, after his return to North Korea, Kim agreed that Gao Gang should appoint a railway management team.[58] In late December, the Chinese side established the Northeast Military District Railroad Transportation Command (later renamed the Northeast Military District Transportation Command). China appointed Liu Juying as commander, Yu Guangsheng as political commissar, and Ye Lin as deputy commander of this newly created transportation command, which was responsible for shipping supplies to the front and constructing and repairing the railroads. At the same time, a temporary North Korean Railroad Military Management Bureau was jointly managed by China and North Korea.[59]

From January 22 to January 30, 1951, the Northeast Military District held a conference in Shenyang to study logistics problems facing the CPVA. Zhou Enlai and Nie Rongzhen, acting chief of staff of the People's Revolutionary Military Commission of the Central People's Government of the PRC, led a team of military leaders to attend the conference. Zhou expressed his hopes of building an unbeatable steel supply line for the CPVA.[60] These efforts resulted in the resumption of railway transportation in northern Kujang and Chŏngju and the building of a 384-kilometer railway extension. A total of 2,944 shipments were received in January 1951, 44 percent more than had been received during the previous month. By April, in the area under the control of the military transportation command, 1,321 kilometers of the 1,391-kilometer-long railway were back in operation.[61]

Although the railway was largely restored, several basic logistics problems remained unresolved. China and North Korea independently managed the railways within their respective borders, but a lack of coordination caused serious security problems. For instance, the North Korean railway sector used plain codes for communications, despite the active espionage activities by the enemy, thus leading to a constant leaking of transportation intelligence and causing serious damage to railway operations and transportation of military stocks. As a result, only 60 to 70 percent of the total supplies sent from the rear could reach the front and the remainder was lost en route.[62]

Aside from the U.S.-UN bombing, the most serious problem was inadequate management and lack of coordination among the railway agencies. The poor communications and selfish competition for vehicles, rails, and schedules contributed to a disastrous transportation system. What often occurred was that less-needed material was shipped before the most-needed material, and when the less-needed material reached the front, people were in no hurry to unload it. Consequently, the trains with the most-needed material had to wait for the tunnels to be cleared. Thus, it often took longer than it should have for a train to pass through. Tunnel traffic north of Hŭich'ŏn was so bad that in late December 1950, 329 freight trains were waiting in line to enter the tunnel.[63]

China and North Korea had many disagreements about the newly organized, supposedly jointly managed Railroad Military Management Bureau. The two sides could not agree on whether the military should establish direct control over this bureau or should manage it via a military representative system. They also could not agree on whether military supplies or materials for civilian use and construction should be given higher priority. Moreover, because organization of the bureau had yet to be completed, morale among railway personnel was low. Peng complained to Mao about the transportation problems and warned, "If we do not find a quick solution, the war will be prolonged."[64] A coordinated or unified system was urgently needed to guarantee safe and smooth transportation.

China and North Korea had reached agreement in principle regarding joint railway command during Kim's visit to Beijing in December. After Kim's return to North Korea, he told Chai Chengwen, "On several occasions, the Chinese comrades discussed with us the issue of military control of the railway, but some of our people were too foolish to understand that nothing can be done without a military victory." He asked Chai to tell Gao Gang to entrust the railway personnel to work out the details, because the general policy on this issue had already been settled in Beijing.[65] But the agreed-upon general policy did not prevent the two sides from disagreeing with each other during negotiations on the specifics.

On February 19, 1951, the following was reported by Chinese negotiators Ye Lin, minister of transportation of the Northeast People's Government of China; Zhang Mingyuan, deputy commander of the Northeast Logistics Command; and Peng Min, staff member of the Railway Engineering Corps. The North Koreans did not thoroughly consider many of the issues under discussion, and their opinions often contradicted one another. But their main ideas were clear. First, the North Koreans objected to the principle that transportation for military use should take priority over that for North Korea's economic reconstruction. According to Pak Hŏn-yŏng, the economy was politics, and this disagreement would be better resolved between Kim Il-sung and Gao Gang. Second, the North Koreans requested that the North Korean Ministry of Transportation participate in management of the railway. Although they agreed to establish a joint military transportation command headed by the Chinese under the Sino–Korean Joint Command, they insisted that this new agency should work together with the Korean Ministry of Transportation. The North Koreans suggested that China establish a new bureau similar to the North Korean Military Transportation Management Bureau. Third, the North Koreans were opposed to the idea of military control of the railroad. Instead, Pak Hŏn-yŏng suggested restoring the former railway administrative bureaus and replacing the provisional military railway bureau with the Chŏngju Railroad Administrative Bureau.[66]

By mid-March, the two sides still could not agree on the basic principles regarding railway management. The North Korean leaders understood that a military takeover of the railways during wartime could maximize the efficiency of railway transportation. They also understood that military control of the railway bureau was a way to solidify Sino–North Korean joint military control. Therefore, in theory the North Koreans could not oppose this formula. In practice, however, they established their own military transportation bureau to control the railways. With Order No. 21 of the Ministry of Transportation, they restored the jurisdiction and some of the tasks of the former administrative bureaus, thus undercutting and restricting the activities of the Joint Railroad Military Management Bureau.

To resolve this problem as quickly as possible, Zhou Enlai was willing to compromise. Although he insisted on establishing a joint military control commission under the Joint Command to unify railroad maintenance and the dispatch of vehicles, he conceded that the North Korean Ministry of Transportation could be responsible for administration of the North Korean railways. Kim supported this formula, but Minister of Transportation Pak Ŭi-wan made additional demands. According to Pak, the joint military control commission was only to be responsible for making plans and for inspecting and supervising railway transportation, whereas railroad maintenance was to be assigned to a separate agency entrusted to the leadership of the Ministry of Transportation. What the North Koreans were demanding in fact nullified joint Sino–North Korean military control of the railway agency.

Due to North Korean inconsistencies and the deep rift between the two sides on this issue, the Chinese representatives felt that in reality nothing would change, even if they reached an agreement on paper. They believed that the issue was too complicated and too important to be settled on their own, so they requested that Beijing send higher-level officials to continue the negotiations. Peng had no choice but to suggest that Kim Il-sung be informed of Pak Ŭi-wan's opinions and to leave the problems to be resolved between the Chinese and North Korean governments. His hope was that the North Korean government would make sure that all military supplies were properly shipped and that specific regulations regarding railway administration and transportation would be worked out.[67]

In general, the North Koreans proposed three principles: the North Korean Ministry of Transportation should control the North Korean railway administration; a joint command of military transportation should be established, with a Chinese as the chief and a Korean as the deputy; and joint command of the Railway Engineering Corps should be established, also with a Chinese as the chief and a Korean as the deputy. In response to these proposals, Gao Gang suggested a five-point outline to elaborate China's position. First, China insisted on military control of the railway, but it could be embodied in a military representative system. Military representatives at all levels would exist under a Joint Command of Transportation, with the Chinese taking the lead over the Koreans. The military representatives would have the final say on military transportation-related issues. Second, the Joint Command of Transportation would be located in Shenyang. It would dispatch a general representative to the North Korean Ministry of Transportation to supervise enforcement of military transportation plans. Third, North Korea would guarantee uninterrupted telephone service among the Joint Command of Transportation, its general representative to the Ministry of Transportation, and military representatives at all levels. Fourth, a joint railroad maintenance command would be established, directed by the Joint Command of Transportation and advised by the Ministry of Transportation. Fifth, the Chinese railway staff in North Korea would be under the leadership of the North Korean railway agencies, but their political work would be under the direct leadership of the Chinese military representatives.

The Chinese representatives resumed negotiations with the North Koreans on the basis of Gao Gang's five points. The North Koreans basically accepted Gao's five points, except the issue of who would have authority over the Joint Railway Maintenance Command, about which the North Koreans did not take a clear position. The North Koreans agreed in principle to open up the entire railway network, and they were willing to allow the Joint Command of Transportation to determine the ratio of transportation for military use to transportation for economic reconstruction. The North Koreans also invited Beijing to send representatives to the North Korean Ministry of Transportation and other railway administrative agencies under this ministry to assume deputy posts. The negotiators agreed to sign the accords so that they could submit them to their respective governments for ratification. Zhou Enlai instructed the Chinese negotiators to try their best to include in the accords the issue of leadership of the Joint Railway Maintenance Command, but eventually he asked that the negotiators simply sign the accords and send them back to Beijing.[68] It was at this time, however, that Moscow made its opinion known, thus changing the situation.

Zhang Mingyuan, one of the Chinese negotiators, recalled that at the heart of the Sino–North Korean disagreement over the railway issue was the question of who should control the Joint Command of Transportation. By that time, most North Korean rails and locomotives had been destroyed, and the majority of trains running in North Korea were from China. In addition, it was primarily the Chinese who were actually repairing the rails, transporting the goods, and conducting the trains. China provided the equipment and materials for railway maintenance and even supplied personnel for the North Korean railway administration. Thus, from a practical point of view, the Chinese negotiators argued that the North Koreans were not capable of directing railway transportation and therefore the Chinese should be in charge of wartime transportation in North Korea. But due to the important issue of national sovereignty, the North Koreans and their Soviet advisers insisted that Pyongyang should control the North Korean railways. Zhou Enlai pointed out that the source of this problem was not in Pyongyang but in Moscow, and he indicated that China would consult with Moscow for an appropriate solution.[69]

When the Chinese negotiators were about to sign the accords, in accordance with Zhou Enlai's instructions of March 25, Stalin sent a telegram to clarify the Soviet position: The consul in Shenyang, Andrei Ledovskii, had just sent the Soviet leadership a telegram explaining Comrade Gao Gang's view that, for effective transportation of military materials to the front, the Korean railways should be managed by the Chinese. From the consul's report, it is clear that Kim Il-sung supported this view, but the Korean ministers seemed to oppose it because it affected North Korean sovereignty. Stalin and the Communist Party of the Soviet Union Central Committee supported Comrade Gao Gang's opinion without reservations. For the sake of winning the war, it was absolutely necessary to accept this plan. In terms of Korea's own interests, it was necessary that Korea and China establish closer relations.[70]

Zhou immediately forwarded this telegram to Gao Gang and Peng Dehuai, instructing them to "continue to insist that the unified railway maintenance command be placed under direction of the Joint Command or the Joint Command of Transportation, or even to place the North Korean railway administrative agencies under direct military control." Therefore, the Chinese representatives postponed the signing of the negotiation accords. The Chinese government invited the North Korean minister of transportation to Shenyang for further discussions.[71]

In accordance with Stalin's opinion, during the subsequent negotiations the Chinese negotiators took a tougher stance and presented a new proposal. On April 16, Zhou Enlai sent a message to Kim Il-sung via Ni Zhiliang, the Chinese ambassador in Pyongyang, demanding military control of the North Korean railways and the establishment of a Sino–North Korean joint military transportation headquarters under the Joint Command to unify administration, transportation, maintenance, and protection of the North Korean railways.[72] After Stalin's view became clear, Kim was forced to make concessions and accept Zhou's new proposal. On May 4, 1951, the two sides in Beijing concluded the Agreement on Military Control of Korean Railways During the War, which clarified policy on management of the transportation system and the allocation of transportation resources.

In accordance with the spirit of this agreement, in July the Central Bureau for Military Control of the Korean Railways, responsible for railway transportation in the war zone, was officially opened in Anju. Leadership of this bureau consisted of Liu Juying, director and political commissar, and two deputy directors, one of whom was Chinese and the other Korean. Under the Central Bureau were five branch bureaus, located in Hŭich'ŏn, Chŏngju, New Sŏngch'ŏn, Pyongyang, and Kowŏn and staffed by a total of twelve thousand Chinese volunteers. On August 1, the Sino–Korean Joint Railroad Transportation Command was established in Shenyang, with He Jinnian as commander and Zhang Mingyuan as political commissar. Both He Jinnian and Zhang Mingyuan were also deputy commanders of the Northeast Military District. The Sino–Korean Joint Railroad Transportation Command was under the direct control of the Sino–Korean Joint Command. In November, the Joint Command of Transportation appointed Liu Juying to set up the Frontline Railway Transportation Command in Anju, responsible for interagency coordination among the Central Bureau for Military Control of the Korean Railways, the Railway Engineering Corps, and the Railway Artillery Group. The expanded Railway Engineering Corps consisted of a total of fifty-two thousand men, or four divisions, three regiments, and a volunteer engineering brigade. Thereafter, under the unified leadership, the railway transportation troops, engineering corps, and artillery groups cooperated to adopt the strategy of responding to concentration with concentration and responding to mobility with mobility to fight the enemy. These efforts resulted in a major improvement in the efficiency of railway transportation.[73]

Among all the issues on which China and North Korea disagreed, the issue of control of the railways was the only one that affected North Korean domestic affairs and touched on the issue of national sovereignty. Peng Dehuai did not ignore this issue, even when he was purged and harshly criticized in 1959. He emphasized that the military takeover of the railways was necessary due to the unavoidable exigencies under wartime conditions, and authority over the railways would be restored to the North Korean government immediately after a cease-fire agreement had been signed.[74] Nonetheless, this issue left Kim Il-sung disappointed that, with help from Moscow, China had imposed its own opinions on him.

Differences Over How to End the War

The Korean armistice negotiations, conducted between U.S. military officers representing the UN Command and Chinese and North Korean military personnel, were held from July 10, 1951, to July 27, 1953, thus lasting more than two years. It took a total of 575 meetings before an agreement was reached. During this period, ground actions continued, although they were more limited in scale than during the first year of the conflict. On the other hand, the U.S.-UN bombing entered its most destructive phase. About 45 percent of American casualties occurred during these two years,[75] and Chinese, North Korean, and South Korean forces suffered massive losses as well.

The failure of a major Communist offensive in late April 1951 (the fifth campaign) "demonstrated once and for all the inability of the CPVA's assault to push the well-equipped UN forces off the peninsula." Beijing evidently expected not only to reach a cease-fire but also to settle the conflict. After the CPVA secured a foothold near the 38th parallel, a peace agreement for the restoration of the status quo seemed advisable to Beijing. A policy of "continuing to fight while negotiating peace" (*biantan bianda*, 边谈边打) was thus agreed upon by the central leadership in Beijing in late May 1951.[76]

Figure 2.3 Kim Il-sung meets with Mao Zedong in Beijing to discuss issues relating to armistice negotiations, June 3, 1951.

But Kim Il-sung was against any plan for a prolonged war and demanded that the Sino-Korean Joint Command launch a general attack in late June and mid-July. Mao thus invited Kim to Beijing for consultations.

On June 3, 1951, Mao and Zhou Enlai persuaded Kim to accept "restoration of the 38th parallel [as a short-term objective] and phased withdrawal of all foreign troops [from Korea] through negotiations and a political settlement on Korea's future by peaceful means [as long-term goals]." But Kim insisted on postponing a general attack to August.[77] Unable to convince Kim to accept the armistice negotiations, Mao requested assistance from Stalin. Kim and Gao Gang thus flew to Moscow and met with Stalin on June 10. Stalin told Kim that he believed that "a cease-fire is a good thing."[78] Because North Korea was dependent on the Chinese and the Soviets, Kim eventually had no choice but to agree to negotiations based on an armistice along the 38th parallel.

According to Ambassador Razuvayev, "The Korean leaders were a bit wary of the armistice negotiations, although they did not openly spell out their reservations." After returning to North Korea, Kim was depressed. He believed that Soviet Ambassador Jacob Malik's June 23 UN speech appealing for armistice negotiations was "a clear indication of China's attempt to end the war and to be relieved of providing aid to North Korea." But the North Korean media did not publish any comments on the speech. Although the North Korean leaders came to understand "the military and political necessity of reaching an armistice," they also complained that the Chinese negotiators (mainly Li Kenong) had made undue compromises with the Americans and had failed to consult the North Korean negotiators in a timely and adequate fashion. In particular, when Mao notified Kim that if the Americans accepted the line of contact at the battlefront as the line of demarcation, the Chinese were ready to pass on this issue, Kim strongly protested, responding immediately by stating, "This concession is impossible because it represents a serious political setback" for North Korea. He told Pak Hŏn-yŏng, "I prefer to continue the war without the Chinese than to make such a concession." Razuvayev noted that "in recent months, the Koreans have obviously been cold toward the Chinese. They are leaning more toward the Soviet Union."[79] Due to the alleged U.S.-UN bombing near the negotiating area in Kaesŏng, the Chinese suspended the talks from August 22 to October 24, 1951.[80]

During the second half of 1952, as the two sides in the Korean War achieved a balance of power on the battlefield, the armistice negotiations at Panmunjom reached a deadlock. The major obstacle was the prisoner of war question.[81] In concert with his global strategy of confronting the United States, Stalin supported Mao in continuing the war and not making any concessions during the peace talks. Until Stalin's death, the two Communist governments generally followed a common strategy in dealing with the Korean question.

However, Kim Il-sung had different ideas about the armistice. In February 1952, the negotiations at Panmunjom produced a decision that, ninety days after an armistice was signed, a political conference would be held to resolve issues related to Korea. At the time, Kim wanted to conclude the negotiations as quickly as possible. Soviet Ambassador Razuvayev told Moscow that Kim was inclined to sign the armistice and to leave all unsettled questions to the political conference. According to Razuvayev, "Kim Il-sung does not see any benefit in prolonging the negotiations because the American air force is causing horrendous losses to the Democratic People's Republic of Korea." Nor did Kim see any reason for arguing over the POW question during the negotiations. In his view, many of the Chinese POWs had previously been members of Jiang Jieshi's troops and thus were politically unreliable. So what was the point of negotiating on their behalf? Kim therefore suggested that the Chinese side make concessions on the POW issue during the negotiations.[82] Kim also told Mao that he was unwilling to continue the war.[83]

The POW issue was, however, not the sole factor affecting Beijing's decision making. As is revealed in Razuvayev's report, the Chinese leadership was concerned that "once the Korean War is over, Soviet military supplies will be reduced or even terminated." In addition, a rush to reach an armistice might result in a weakening of the Chinese-North Korean alliance. Li Kenong, the chief Chinese official directing the negotiations at Panmunjom, believed that, without mobilizing international public opinion and making preparations for a long-term struggle, the Sino–North Korean side would not be able to force the Americans to make any concessions. In agreement, Mao thus instructed Li, "You must take a firm and steadfast stand. Only with such a stand will you seize the initiative and force the enemy to back down. To achieve such a goal, however, you should be prepared to continue to maneuver with the enemy for several more months."[84] Kim and his associates initially hoped to conclude an armistice agreement with the Americans no later than May. They even began to use this timetable to arrange for the political and economic work. But when the armistice negotiations stalled due to the POW controversy, Razuvayev reported that "the Korean leaders are enormously disappointed. Kim Il-sung has urged the Chinese comrades to conclude an armistice agreement by making concessions on the POW question."[85]

In his response to Kim, Mao spared no effort to convince the Korean leader that it would be harmful to the Chinese-North Korean side both politically and militarily if the enemy's deceptive proposal were to be accepted, especially at a time when the enemy was applying military pressure through indiscriminate bombing. Indeed, the Korean people and the CPVA would end up making more sacrifices by continuing the war, but they "will also be able to strengthen themselves, inspire the peace-loving people of the world to oppose aggressive wars, and promote the world movement to protect peace." In Mao's opinion, the main U.S. forces that had been drawn to the East had suffered greatly. But this situation had been advantageous to construction in the Soviet Union and to the worldwide national revolutionary movement. Hence, a world war had been postponed. Mao vowed to Kim that China would do its best to help the Korean people overcome all their difficulties, pledging that "if our ability is inadequate, I will join you in requesting Filippov's [Stalin's] assistance." Mao also informed Kim that the Chinese leaders would inform Stalin of their position and seek his opinion.[86] In his next message to Stalin, Mao stated that the Chinese "resolutely refuse this provocative and seductive plan of the enemy and [we] are prepared to expand the war. Kim Il-sung does not agree with this proposal."[87]

Although in agreement when corresponding with Mao, Kim still insisted to the Soviet ambassador that an armistice agreement should be concluded and exchange of the POWs should take place as soon as possible to win international support.[88] As revealed by recently declassified archives, Kim was willing to concede on the POW issue and to discard the principle of "complete repatriation." Aside from his concern about war casualties and economic damages, Kim also had another reason: he planned to detain the South Korean POWs. According to a report by the Soviet ambassador, "The Korean comrades believe that a large number of South Korean POWs should be detained and assigned to heavy manual labor in the North. There is no need to consider their desire to return home." Consequently, Pyongyang detained 13,094 South Korean POWs, 6,430 of whom served in the North Korean army, while the remainder served under the Ministry of the Interior and the Ministry of Railways. In addition, North Korea refused to affirm as POWs the 42,262 troops from the South who had been forcibly enlisted during the early stages of the war.[89] Under such circumstances, it was impossible for North Korea to support the "all-for-all formula" in terms of repatriation.

By March 1, 1952, negotiations on Gao Gang's fourth point had been narrowed to one issue—voluntary or forced repatriation. The details of the exchange could be easily settled as soon as this principle had been decided upon. But the Chinese-North Korean side gave no sign of weakening in terms of its adamant opposition to any form of voluntary repatriation, regardless of how it was disguised. When the UN side proposed on July 13 to return eighty-three thousand Communist POWs instead of seventy thousand, which was the number that had been proposed in April, the Chinese "negotiation steering group" intended to accept this number and reported it to Mao.[90]

As the fighting dragged on through 1952, the North Koreans increasingly desired to end the war, and they appeared to be more malleable on the POW issue than the Chinese. Nevertheless, Mao was clearly anxious to avoid undermining the prestige of the PRC by accepting unfavorable armistice terms.[91] In his July 15 telegram to Stalin, Mao contended that "in the American plan [about the POW issue], the proportions for the two sides are extremely unequal. The enemy is attempting to use this issue to break the wartime unity of the Korean and Chinese people. It would be extremely disadvantageous for us to submit to such pressure from the enemy." Mao declared that even if the talks were to break down, he still would not concede: "Because this is a political matter, and not only for Korea and China, it will also have repercussions for the entire revolutionary camp."[92] The following day, Stalin replied, "Your position regarding the peace negotiations is completely correct."[93] When Beijing and Moscow agreed with each other, Kim had no choice but to fall in line.

A tripartite consensus was worked out in Moscow in August 1952, while Zhou Enlai was in the Soviet Union holding talks with Stalin. Later, Kim Il-sung, Pak Hŏn-yŏng, and Peng Dehuai joined these talks. The Zhou–Stalin conversations dealt with economic work, but the focus was on Korea. Zhou described for Stalin the situation on the battlefield, asserting that the enemy's offensive could be overcome. He claimed that the Chinese–North Korean troops not only were able to hold the current line but also would be able to launch a counteroffensive. In Zhou's words, "We are quite certain that we can endure an even longer war."

As for the POW issue, Stalin pointed out that the Americans would want to resolve the issue on their own terms but that international law provided for repatriation of all POWs except criminals. Stalin asked what Mao's attitude was on this issue. Would he remain steadfast or would he make concessions? At this point, Zhou informed Stalin of the Chinese–North Korean disagreements about continuation of the war and about Mao's insistence on "repatriation of all POWs." Stalin immediately responded, "Mao Zedong is right. This war is causing considerable harm to the United States. The North Koreans have sacrificed their lives, but they have not lost anything. The Americans are aware that this war is not to their advantage and thus they want to end it right away, especially after they learned that our troops are stationed in China. What we need now is both willpower and patience." As if he feared a policy vacillation on the part of the Chinese leadership, Stalin brought up yet another issue. He reminded Zhou, "You must be firm in dealing with the Americans. The Chinese comrades must realize that China will never be able to regain Taiwan if the United States does not lose this war."

Zhou certainly did not go to Moscow to retreat from Mao's stance. He thus proposed three alternative steps to deal with the POW question, making it clear that the Chinese side would soften its attitude only in reaction to concessions initiated by the Americans. First, if the Americans still insisted on partial repatriation, the Chinese side would announce the detention of the same percentage of American and South Korean POWs; second, the POW issue could be solved via mediation by a neutral country (such as India); and third, an armistice agreement could be signed first, leaving the POW issue to be settled later. In their ensuing discussions, Stalin appeared to favor the first option, whereas Zhou spent some time on the second. Nevertheless, they both agreed that the negotiations should insist on all-for-all repatriation; there would be no retreat due to American intimidation, and the American side had to make the first move in terms of concessions.[94] At a banquet after their meetings, Stalin said, "China should become the arsenal of the East. . . . The East depends on China . . . China is the core of Asia."[95] This, without a doubt, enhanced China's right to speak on the Korean issue.

To persuade Kim to accept the Chinese position, Stalin invited him to Moscow for consultations. At a meeting on September 4, Kim told Stalin that there was no fundamental difference between the Chinese and the North Koreans on the issue of negotiations. Kim said, "We agree with the Chinese proposal. But we would like to sign an armistice agreement because the Korean people are suffering." Stalin told Kim that he supported Mao's position—"repatriation of all POWs."[96] On November 10, 1952, the Soviet representative to the UN proposed a new formula for resolution of the Korean question: cease-fire first, then all-for-all repatriation of the POWs. On November 28, Zhou Enlai issued a Chinese government statement in support of the Soviet proposal.[97]

After the Kim–Stalin talks, Kim no longer requested a cease-fire and instead focused on how to secure more material support from the Soviet Union.[98] However, before the war finally ended, Sino–North Korean conflicts once again emerged over the question of whether to immediately sign a cease-fire. This was the final difference between the two sides during the war. At the time of Stalin's death on March 5, 1953, Beijing seemed willing to bring the war to an end. Furthermore, the post-Stalin Soviet leadership, under Georgi Malenkov, was interested in improving relations with the West. Pursuing what some political observers have called a Soviet "peace offensive," fearful that a continuation of the war might escalate into a global conflict, and more confident about its own military capability since they already had their own nuclear arsenal, the new Soviet leaders were eager to end the war in Korea.[99]

However, Syngman Rhee, leader of South Korea, did not want to end the war, and he tried to sabotage an agreement by releasing prisoners without authorization from the UN command. In response, the Chinese side insisted on launching a new offensive in order to secure more advantageous cease-fire terms. The North Koreans demanded that an armistice be signed immediately, but Peng Dehuai, acting with support from Mao, overruled Kim Il-sung and began a final successful military campaign.[100]

On the cease-fire issue, Kim Il-sung had North Korea's practical interests in mind. Because it was impossible for North Korea to emerge victorious, Kim believed it would be best to end the war as quickly as possible and to promote domestic economic reconstruction in order to consolidate his rule. But Mao shouldered responsibility for leading the Asian Revolution. Hence, he favored continuation of the war with an eye to the general situation in the confrontation between the two blocs and to the security interests of the socialist bloc in Northeast Asia and elsewhere in Asia. It is for this reason that Stalin always supported Mao when China and North Korea disagreed.

Although he remained behind the scenes, Stalin certainly was the flag-bearer of the socialist bloc. The fact that Mao made the decision to send Chinese troops to Korea under an extremely difficult situation is indicative of CCP loyalty to the socialist bloc. By earning the trust of Stalin, Mao was thus able to consolidate the Sino–Soviet alliance. During the war, Moscow agreed with Beijing on all major issues, thus further strengthening the Sino–Soviet alliance.

Because China had sent massive numbers of troops to North Korea, Beijing gradually came to dominate Korean affairs and to have a say in war strategies and tactics. Kim Il-sung was forced to endure humiliation by deferring to Chinese decisions. Although Pyongyang dared not show any disrespect for Moscow, it still felt a bitter grudge against Beijing, and Kim was not particularly grateful that the Chinese had saved his regime. South Korean scholar Hongkoo Han has pointed out that the North Korean leaders believed that China's entry into the Korean War, in addition to the geopolitical considerations, simply represented repayment for the decisive role the Koreans had played during the anti-Japanese struggle in the 1930s and during the Chinese Civil War in the late 1940s. In the North Korean leaders' calculations, because Korea was much smaller than China, the thousands of Korean souls who had "sacrificed for the Chinese Revolution [were] . . . commensurate with" the tens of thousands of Chinese troops who had been sent to the Korean War.[101]

Despite his strong sense of national independence and his intention to be absolute ruler over North Korea, Kim faced many challengers, such as the Southern faction (the South KWP faction), the Moscow faction, and the Yan'an faction.[102] During the war, many of the Yan'an faction cadres became military leaders, and they maintained close contacts with the CPVA. This made Kim quite uneasy. In addition to the psychological issues, the CPVA leaders were often contemptuous of the command and fighting abilities of the North Koreans. Furthermore, Beijing used Moscow to keep Pyongyang in line. Thus, although the Chinese paid a huge amount in terms of blood and resources to win the Korean War, the Chinese and the

North Koreans failed to establish a sincere and trusting friendship based on a common ideology. This proved to be troublesome for their future relations.

During the Korean War, conflicts and disagreements between China and North Korea were solely related to war—how to fight the war and how to win peace. But Mao Zedong insisted on not interfering with North Korea's domestic affairs. For instance, when the Yan'an faction's high-level North Korean officials were purged by Kim Il-sung during the war, China kept aloof from it. Mao never thought of deposing Kim Il-sung. Mao emphasized unity and friendship with Kim Il-sung and North Korea. This was a special feature of Sino–North Korean relations, which was very different from how the United States handled its relations with South Korea.

CHAPTER III

Chinese Economic Aid and Kim's *Juche* Idea, 1953–1956

A fter the death of Stalin and the end of the Korean War, both Soviet–North Korean relations and Sino–North Korean relations gradually began to change. The new leaders of the Soviet Union were more willing to allow China to lead and organize the revolutions in Asia, and Mao happily accepted this challenge. To pacify Kim Il-sung and to maintain China's dominant voice in Korean affairs after the war, Mao decided to provide Pyongyang with a massive amount of economic aid. North Korea achieved its postwar economic reconstruction by primarily relying on aid from China, the Soviet Union, and the Eastern European Communist countries. Although China was economically much weaker than the Soviet Union and had suffered immense losses during the war, it in fact provided much more economic aid to Pyongyang than did the Soviet Union. Kim Il-sung was satisfied with the Chinese aid, even though he seldom spoke in public about the aid that he had received from either China or the Soviet Union. Instead, he began to publicly stress Korean "self-reliance."

To establish his personal dictatorship, Kim eliminated the cadres from the Southern faction (those from the South Korean Workers' Party) and he sidelined the cadres from the Moscow faction (those from the Soviet Union) and the Yan'an faction (those from China).[1] Meanwhile, he proposed an antiformalist and antidogmatist ideology and proclaimed his *"Juche"* (*Chuch'e*) idea, thus taking the moral high ground.[2] According to Dae-Sook Suh, *Juche* "signified the end of political dependence and subservience to the Soviet Union and China and the promotion of Kim himself as a leader and thinker to the nonaligned nations."[3]

After the Twentieth Congress of the Communist Party of the Soviet Union (CPSU), Kim was unwilling to accept the CPSU's new program. The Yan'an faction cadres, united with the Moscow faction cadres, attempted to make use of Moscow's dissatisfaction with Kim by criticizing him and attempting to force him to change course. At the August 1956 plenum of the Korean Workers' Party (KWP), Kim's Guerrilla faction carried the day, and many Yan'an faction cadres who were purged as members of an antiparty clique fled to China. Mao Zedong was shocked at this and, after consultation with the CPSU, Chinese Defense Minister Peng Dehuai and Soviet Deputy Chairman of the Council of Ministers Anastas Mikoyan led a joint Chinese Communist Party (CCP)–CPSU delegation to Pyongyang to force Kim Il-sung to reverse this verdict. Due to the pressure from both Beijing and Moscow, Kim issued a self-criticism and reinstated some of the purged cadres. After the Polish and Hungarian crises, however, he continued his purge of cadres in North Korea and attempted to bring the Korean issue before the UN. Realizing that both China and the Soviet Union had lost control over North Korea, Mao stressed the importance of blocking the breach on the Eastern front of the socialist bloc, even discussing the possibility of using extreme measures to resolve the issue. Thus began a period of serious crisis in Sino-North Korean relations.

Although the Chinese and the North Koreans frequently disagreed and had conflicts with each other during the Korean War, Stalin's intervention generally forced the North Koreans to defer to the Chinese position. Unlike Stalin, however, Mao had no intention of interfering with Korea's sovereignty or its internal affairs, nor did he seek to directly control North Korea. Conversant in Chinese history and knowledgeable about the Chinese classics, Mao naturally, or at least subconsciously, accepted the idea that China was the "Celestial Empire." Throughout history, China and Korea had maintained a suzerain–vassal relationship (*zongfan guanxi*, 宗藩关系).[4] One characteristic of these relations was that China required submission but did not seek to deprive the vassal state of its sovereignty. As the historian Chen Jian aptly puts it, "Mao believed that to send Chinese troops to Korea was not for such an 'inferior' purpose as pursuing China's direct political and economic control over North Korea but was for the purpose of, among other aims, achieving the Korean Communists' inner acceptance of China's morally superior position in directing the 'revolutions in the East.'"[5]

To strengthen Sino–North Korean relations, Mao insisted that the Chinese army and government respect the Korean people and treat them as equals, both politically and diplomatically. On December 18, 1950, Mao revised the "Directive Regarding the Establishment of the Chinese People's Volunteer Army" by adding "Our Chinese People's Volunteer Army must show friendship and respect for the Korean people, the Korean People's Army, the Korean People's Democratic Republic, the Korean Workers' Party, other democratic parties, and Comrade Kim Il-sung, the leader of the Korean people."[6] In economic and military affairs, China was willing to provide North Korea with all-out support. This policy extended to North Korea's postwar reconstruction period.

Chinese Economic Aid to North Korea

By the time the fighting ended, in July 1953, the northern half of the Korean Peninsula had been completely destroyed. Industrial output, which had endured three years of ongoing bombing, had declined by nearly 40 percent since 1949.[7] Production of consumer goods was reduced and agricultural production had dropped by 24 percent.[8] Hundreds of thousands of acres of farmland had been destroyed, along with nearly three-quarters of the homes. Electricity production was down to 26 percent of its prewar level, chemical production was down to 22 percent, fuel production was down to 11 percent, and metallurgical production was down to 10 percent of their prewar levels. The transportation infrastructure had been devastated, with 70 percent of trains and 85 percent of ships destroyed, and much of the railway system was not operational.[9] The Democratic People's Republic of Korea (DPRK) estimated that war-related damages amounted to 420 billion won, or nearly $170 million at the contemporary exchange rate.[10]

Nevertheless, North Korea was highly successful in securing foreign aid for its postwar reconstruction. In the immediate postwar period, the Soviet Union, China, and the other Communist countries provided substantial aid to North Korea, totaling some one-third of North Korea's 1954 financial budget. Coming in the form of labor, material supplies and goods, the reconstruction and building of plants, civil construction work, technology transfers, and the education of specialists and students, the aid played a vital role in North Korea's economic recovery. In his article "Fraternal Socialism," Charles Armstrong documents the contributions of the Soviet and

Eastern European countries, but he neglects the tremendous role that China played in North Korea's reconstruction.[11] Although China was also facing a dire economic crisis at the time, the assistance Beijing provided to North Korea was comparable to or even surpassed that provided by Moscow. In particular, at the war's end a peak of thirty-four divisions of the Chinese People's Volunteer Army (CPVA) were stationed in North Korea, providing free labor—an indispensable contribution—until the last fifteen divisions were withdrawn in 1958.[12]

This first section examines North Korea's postwar reconstruction, paying particular attention to Chinese economic aid. It analyzes how this aid affected Sino–North Korean political and diplomatic relations as well as Sino–North Korean–Soviet triangular relations during the "honeymoon" phase of the Sino–Soviet alliance, from 1953 to 1957.

During the war, Kim Il-sung was already very concerned about postwar reconstruction. Within days of the signing of the armistice, Kim approached the Soviet Union, a backstage player during the war, to request economic aid. On July 31, 1953, Kim sent to the Soviet Embassy in Pyongyang a report describing the extent of the war damage and the need for Soviet assistance to rebuild the economy.[13] After receiving the report from its embassy in Pyongyang, the CPSU Presidium on August 3 passed a resolution to provide North Korea with 1 billion rubles for economic reconstruction.[14] At the Sixth Plenum of the Central Committee (CC) of the KWP, on August 5, Kim outlined North Korea's economic recovery plans. The new economic program would consist of three stages: a preparatory period of about six months to one year to assess needs and to make plans, a Three-Year Plan (1954–1956) to bring the economy back to its pre-1950 level, and a Five-Year Plan (1957–1961) for general industrialization of the country.[15]

In the end, the Soviet Union, China, East Germany, Poland, Czechoslovakia, Hungary, and other "fraternal countries" all contributed to North Korea's reconstruction.[16] The postwar reconstruction of North Korea represented a true division of labor in the socialist camp, wholly consistent with the renewed interest in coordinating intrabloc investments and trade policies. According to documents from the Soviet Ministry of Trade, nearly one-third (33.3 percent) of the reconstruction aid came from the Soviet Union, 29.4 percent came from China, and 37.3 percent came from the Eastern European Communist countries, Mongolia, and North Vietnam.[17] To paraphrase Karl Marx: "From each according to its ability, to North Korea according to its need."

China's influence and role in North Korea increased dramatically during the Korean War period. Kim Il-sung had relied on Soviet aid and support from 1945 to 1950, prior to the war. After the CPVA was dispatched to Korea, following the collapse of the North Korean offensive in the fall of 1950, Stalin stood firmly on the side of Mao Zedong whenever Kim clashed with the Chinese over how to fight the war or how to achieve peace. Kim thus suffered the humiliation of becoming completely dependent on China and, to a lesser extent, on the Soviet Union for the survival of both his regime and North Korea. This experience undoubtedly had a deep psychological impact and probably explains why North Korean leaders were hesitant to seek economic aid from China immediately after the end of the war. Instead, Kim led a delegation to Moscow in September 1953 to settle the terms of Soviet aid, which amounted to 1 billion rubles ($250 million). It was decided that these funds would primarily be used to rebuild major factories and institutions.[18]

In November 1953, Kim then dispatched Minister of Commerce Yi Chu-yŏn to Poland, Czechoslovakia, Hungary, Romania, Bulgaria, Albania, and East Germany to request economic aid. Each of these Eastern European Communist countries agreed to participate in some reconstruction projects as part of their contribution to North Korea's economic recovery. The total commitment from the Eastern European countries for the next ten years amounted to 1.147 billion rubles ($286.75 million), of which nearly one-half came from East Germany. By the end of 1954, total aid from the Eastern European countries totaled 202 million rubles ($50.5 million).[19]

Also in November, two months after his trip to the Soviet Union, Kim Il-sung visited China for two weeks. Despite their wartime clashes, Beijing was ready to make an initial commitment, which in fact turned out to be much more generous than that from Moscow. During their first meeting, on November 16, Zhou Enlai proposed the signing of a secret Sino–Korean technology cooperation agreement. Then, on November 23, China and North Korea signed the Sino–Korean Economic and Cultural Cooperation Agreement.[20] Chinese aid would include cancellation of North Korea's wartime debt, which amounted to 729 million Chinese yuan ($364.5 million) and a gift of 800 million Chinese yuan ($400 million) in aid for the 1954-1957 period, of which 300 million Chinese yuan ($150 million) would be made available during the first year.[21] These funds were to be used to purchase industrial and construction materials, machinery, and grain, and to repair the railways and bridges. From 1954 to 1956, China also supported 22,735 Korean refugee children.

Additionally, it offered very favorable terms in other areas. According to the Sino-North Korean agreement, the North Korean government would pay Chinese experts dispatched to Korea the same salaries as they earned in China (plus a travel allowance, health-care costs, and lodging and transportation). In contrast, the DPRK government had to offer the Soviet experts dispatched to Korea much higher living allowances. Korean trainees (mechanics and technicians) sent to China enjoyed the same treatment as their Chinese counterparts in Korea, and Pyongyang was only required to pay their travel and lodging expenses. However, Pyongyang had to pay much more for the Korean trainees in the Soviet Union, including an average monthly instruction fee of 100 to 150 rubles ($25 to $37.50). The Chinese government provided free lodging and tuition, whereas the Soviet government charged 50 percent of the total costs for the Korean students in the USSR, including lodging and tuition.[22] In 1954, the first year of the reconstruction, China made a commitment to provide the equivalent of more than 3 billion rubles ($750 million) in free economic aid to North Korea, which was much more than the 2.2 billion rubles ($550 million) in aid from the Soviet Union and the Eastern European countries. China's aid to North Korea in 1954 was equal to 3.4 percent of China's total budget in that year.

In view of the losses that China had suffered during the war, why did China make such an enormous commitment to North Korea? Some scholars argue that it reflected "in part the Chinese government's interest in competing with the USSR for influence in North Korea."[23] We disagree with this interpretation. It is unlikely that China sought to compete with the Soviet Union in the immediate aftermath of the Korean War. At the time, China was dependent on the Soviet Union for its own economic reconstruction, and the Sino–Soviet alliance was still in its honeymoon stage. A more plausible explanation is that Mao knew that China had alienated the North Koreans during the war. Due to the historical legacy that affected Sino–Korean relations and Mao's aspiration to be the leader of the Asian Revolution, Beijing had no choice but to pay a high price to maintain its influence in North Korea. Recognizing the damage to Sino–DPRK relations during the war, on November 23 Zhou Enlai told a DPRK delegation that Chinese assistance and the Sino–Korean Economic and

Cultural Cooperation Agreement would "regularize the traditional friendship and cooperation" between the two countries.[24]

Fraternal aid played a crucial role during the early stages of Korea's reconstruction. In 1954, such funds constituted 31.6 percent of the North Korean budget.[25] Although the Soviet Union and the Eastern European countries provided industrial projects, especially in heavy industry, China provided 130,000 tons of grain, 40 million meters of cotton cloth, 600,000 pairs of shoes, and 300,000 suits of winter clothing. In addition, nearly 500,000 Chinese People's Volunteers in Korea provided much-needed labor. By the time of their withdrawal from Korea in October 1958, they had repaired 881 public spaces and 45,412 rooms in private homes, and they had restored or built 4,263 bridges, 429,220 meters of dams, and 1,218.71 kilometers of ditches and canals, as well as providing many other services.[26]

On March 11, 1954, the DPRK cabinet passed a resolution stating, "We have successfully completed the 1953 plan, which is the preparation for recovering and developing the people's economy."[27] The DPRK then began to implement its Three-Year Plan for economic recovery. During this period, the Soviet Union continued to provide industrial equipment and China continued to supply daily necessities and industrial raw materials.[28] From 1954 to 1957, the total amount of Chinese exports to North Korea amounted to 922 million Chinese yuan ($461 million) and imports totaled 127 million Chinese yuan ($63.5 million). In addition, China canceled North Korea's trade deficit. Among its exports, China provided 449,000 tons of grain, 178,000 tons of soybeans, 3,950 tons of cotton yarn, 35,590 tons of cotton, 88.476 million meters of cotton cloth, 3.456 million tons of coal, 260,000 tons of coke, and 11,200 tons of rubber. The imports included seafood, iron, raw materials for the chemical industry, and apples.[29] Additionally, in 1954 alone, China accepted more than three thousand North Korean trainees, who were assigned to work in Shanghai, Shenyang, and other cities.[30] The Soviet Union, China, and the Eastern European countries built 20 percent of the new factories completely on their own.[31]

Taking advantage of the massive amounts of foreign aid that it received, the DPRK accomplished its Three-Year Plan by 1955, one year ahead of schedule. According to official North Korean sources, industrial investments in capital construction in 1955 totaled more than three times the amount of capital construction investments during the five prewar years. Furthermore, total industrial output in 1955 was 56 percent higher than that in 1949.[32] But the excessive investments in infrastructure caused huge deficits, the dislocations in industrial development led to shortages of consumer goods, the rapid rate of agricultural collectivization generated serious resentment among the peasants, and many urban residents lost their jobs due to the rapid nationalization and the elimination of private trade and cottage industries.[33]

During reconstruction, the Moscow and Yan'an faction cadres cited the experiences in the Soviet Union and China to criticize the KWP's economic policies and Kim Il-sung's eagerness for rapid success and instant benefits. To suppress such criticisms, Kim launched an intraparty struggle to place the blame on other leaders. At the Tenth Session of the KWP Central Committee in April 1955, Kim Il-sung criticized the sectarianism of Pak Il-u, Kim Ung, and Bang Ho-san, all of whom were members of the so-called Yan'an faction. He also blamed Pak Ch'ang-ok of the Moscow faction and Kim Il of the Guerrilla faction for the spring 1955 grain crisis. Kim pointed out, "Neither the Soviet Union nor China will help us forever. We must be prepared to deal with our difficulties."[34] Kim Il-sung felt threatened by the cadres in the Moscow and Yan'an factions, citing their practice of criticizing KWP mistakes.[35]

To suppress the differing views within the party, Kim Il-sung proposed his idea of *Juche*. On December 28, 1955, he delivered to Propaganda Department staff a speech entitled "On Eliminating Formalism and Dogmatism and Establishing *Juche* in Ideological Work," in which he criticized Hŏ Ka-i, Pak Ch'ang-ok, Pak Yŏng-bin, and Pak Il-u, stating, "Those who returned from the Soviet Union advocate the Soviet method and those who returned from China advocate the Chinese method. This is a meaningless debate. . . . We are carrying out the Korean Revolution. . . . The Korean Revolution is the *Juche* of our party's ideological work. Thus, all our ideological work should serve the interests of the Korean Revolution."[36] Japanese historian Nobuo Shimotomai notes, "What eventually became the famous ideology of *Juche* started as a tool used to eliminate Soviet influence on DPRK ideology and education, although the term *Juche* itself was not clearly defined until the end of the 1950s."[37]

In order to promote the *Juche* idea, Korean leaders seldom mentioned the massive economic aid the country had received from fraternal countries.[38] Kim's intention was not to offend the Soviet Union and China but rather to promote his authority and leadership. In fact, Kim knew quite well that North Korea's economic reconstruction had critically depended on both the Soviet Union and China. The purpose of his *Juche* idea was to maintain political and diplomatic independence. This did not exclude seeking economic aid, as long as North Korea did not become overly dependent economically or lose its freedom of action. Although he vehemently advocated *Juche* within party circles, in formulating the Five-Year Plan Kim continued to seek foreign aid, especially from Moscow and Beijing.

While criticizing formalism and dogmatism, Kim raised important questions about "autonomy" and "independence." According to the Marxism and Leninism advocated by Stalin, "internationalism" was a classic term accepted by all Communists. In the International Communist Movement, the interests of the Soviet Union and of the Soviet Communist Party corresponded to the interests of all international proletarians. The antithesis of internationalism was nationalism, and anyone who defied Moscow and conflicted with Soviet interests would be accused of advocating nationalism. For this reason, Yugoslav leader Josip B. Tito was denounced as a nationalist and was excommunicated from the socialist bloc in 1948. Additionally, between 1949 and 1952 many Eastern European Communist leaders were accused of nationalism and were purged. To demonstrate its support for the Stalinist line, the Chinese Communist Party published an article entitled "On Internationalism and Nationalism."[39]

After the death of Stalin, the new Soviet leaders censured Stalin's personality cult, advocated equality among fraternal parties, and loosened their grip over Eastern Europe. The most conspicuous case occurred in May to June 1955, when Soviet leader Nikita Khrushchev personally traveled to Belgrade to offer his humble apologies to Tito and to mend fences with Yugoslavia.[40] Demonstrating his political acumen, Kim Il-sung seized this historic opportunity to propose his idea of *Juche*, or self-reliance. The essence of the concept was nationalism, highlighting Korean cultural traits, historical features, and national interests. From this high ground, it was easy for Kim Il-sung to attack the Moscow and Yan'an faction cadres, who frequently extolled the experiences and practices of the Soviet Union and China.

While attending the Twentieth Congress of the CPSU, in February 1956, DPRK Vice Premier Ch'oe Yong-gŏn asked Soviet leaders for a moratorium on the Soviet loan to North Korea and on remittance of the matured debt. Pak Ch'ang-ok later revealed that North Korea had hoped to receive from the Soviet Union additional goods and material aid equal to some 1 billion rubles ($250 million). It also expected to receive the same amount from China. In May 1956, one month before departing for Moscow, Kim repeated this request to the Soviet ambassador but reduced the amount to 500 million rubles ($125 million). He hoped that the Eastern European countries (primarily East Germany, Hungary, and Czechoslovakia) would also agree to a moratorium on remittance of the matured debt. Additionally, he planned to request another loan from East Germany.[41]

In June and July 1956, Kim Il-sung led a delegation to the Soviet Union and Eastern Europe. East Germany agreed to donate 18 million rubles ($4.5 million), which was left over from the fund for the reconstruction of Hamhŭng, in the form of daily necessities.[42] The Soviet Union agreed to give an additional 300 million rubles ($75 million) of free economic aid and to cancel the 570 million rubles ($142.5 million) of debt.[43] However, the amount of aid Kim received was far less than what he had hoped for. The Soviet Union and the Eastern European countries had their own economic concerns, and they were offended by North Korea's pretensions. According to Soviet Ambassador V. I. Ivanov's cable to Moscow during the Third Congress of the KWP, in April 1956, Korea "has not given up on establishing a closed-door economy and pays little attention to strengthening connections among the socialist bloc countries and forming a division of labor."[44] In his lengthy report to the Congress, Kim never acknowledged the massive aid that North Korea had received from the Soviet Union, China, and other fraternal countries.

With the shortfall in aid from the Soviet Union and its Eastern European fraternal allies, Kim once again turned to China for the additional aid required to launch the Five-Year Plan. After speaking with Chinese diplomats in Pyongyang in August, the DPRK State Planning Commission drafted a proposal requesting that China provide economic aid. Chinese Ambassador Qiao Xiaoguang assumed that Kim Il-sung would lead a delegation to attend the Eighth Congress of the CCP to discuss the aid issue. Meanwhile, in 1957 the DPRK Embassy in Beijing submitted a draft agreement on the exchange of commodities between the two countries. According to the agreement, China would provide North Korea with 200 million Chinese yuan ($100 million) in commodities, and the DPRK would export to China 40 million Chinese yuan ($20 million) in goods. The North Korean draft agreement did not mention how it would make up for this difference. In his meeting with Qiao Xiaoguang, on August 21, Kim Il-sung noted that North Korea could not satisfy the material needs of its own people and thus he needed China's help.[45] But only several days later, at a plenary session of the KWP CC, Kim Il-sung purged longtime challengers of his development strategy, during the KWP "August incident," thereby straining Sino–North Korean relations.

The August Incident

From 1954 to 1956, the foreign and domestic policies of the CCP and the CPSU were consistent. Internationally, they both emphasized peaceful coexistence, and domestically, they both focused on economic restructuring. Although Moscow and Beijing hoped that the other Communist parties in power would follow their examples, North Korea resisted.[46] Soviet officials in North Korea noted that, in terms of foreign policy, the North Korean government placed priority on military strength and, in terms of economic planning, it stressed heavy industry. The Soviet Foreign Ministry observed that, with respect to both foreign relations and economic development, their Korean comrades overestimated their own capacity and underestimated that of the democratic camp. Furthermore, they did not acknowledge the aid given to them by the Soviets, the Chinese, and other countries.[47]

Another report from the Soviet Foreign Ministry referred to the awkward relationship between China and North Korea. For instance, CPVA headquarters was located many miles away from Pyongyang. Living conditions there were poor, and the North Korean leaders rarely visited. In the War Museum in Pyongyang, only one of the twelve exhibition rooms extolling North Korean military achievements was dedicated to the CPVA. All of the other exhibition rooms praised the military actions by the Korean People's Army and made no mention of the CPVA. The report also mentioned that Kim Il-sung planned to gradually remove from their official posts all those cadres who had lived in China. I. F. Kurdiukov, vice foreign minister of the Soviet Union, noted that after China recalled its ambassador from North Korea, in 1952, a new Chinese ambassador did not arrive in Pyongyang until January 1955. At receptions hosted by the North Korean Embassy in Beijing, Zhou Enlai rarely chatted with the North Koreans. Kurdiukov concluded that the Chinese comrades were not happy with the North Koreans, but they never expressed their unhappiness in public and they exercised great restraint when interacting with the North Koreans.[48] These observations by the Soviets are generally accurate.[49] But the

Soviets overstated Kim Il-sung's intention to remove the Yan'an faction cadres from their posts. Given the scale and the results of the several rounds of inner-party political struggles during the previous years, Kim's struggles at the time were not focused on or limited to the Yan'an faction.

The KWP had been founded in 1949.[50] When the Soviet troops withdrew from North Korea in 1948, the KWP's predecessor had consisted of several factions. Under Kim Il-sung, the members of the Guerrilla faction were uneducated, poor peasants. Although they did not represent a majority, they dominated the KWP because they controlled the military and the police. The Yan'an faction, including many political figures and military leaders, would play an important role during the war. The Moscow faction included ethnic Koreans from the Soviet Union. Finally, there was also a Southern faction. The Moscow faction and the Southern faction were less influential in the KWP, but they did contribute several important party leaders.

During the war years, Kim began to purge those who had the potential to challenge his power and prestige. His first targets were the Yan'an faction cadres who were in charge of the military. In December 1950, after the fall of Pyongyang, Mu Chŏng was removed from his post. Soon thereafter, Pak Il-u was also removed from his post and Bang Ho-san was arrested. The next targets were members of the Moscow faction. In November 1951, Hŏ Ka-i, the most famous figure in the Moscow faction, was expelled from the KWP Standing Committee because of differences of opinion with Kim. It was only due to intervention by Moscow that he was able to retain his position as vice premier. But ultimately, on July 2, 1953, he committed suicide.[51]

In August 1953, Yi Sŭng-yŏp and other cadres in the Southern faction were tried as American spies, for sabotaging the Southern revolution, and for attempting to overthrow the DPRK.[52] These cases were essentially a preview for the trial of Pak Hŏn-yŏng, who had been arrested six months earlier. Pak was a leading figure in the Southern faction, whose members mainly consisted of professional revolutionaries. During the period of the Japanese Occupation, which began in 1910, they had remained in Korea to struggle against Japanese imperial rule. In December 1955, Pak was charged with three counts of spying for the Americans, destruction of the democratic forces in the South, and the overthrow of the government in the North. He was sentenced to death.[53]

After several rounds of such purges, Kim Il-sung was successful in establishing his personal authority over all the factions in the KWP.

However, the dissenting voices within the KWP were not completely eliminated; rather, they were only temporarily suppressed. The postwar leadership of North Korea included Kim Il from the Guerrilla faction, Kim Tu-bong and Kim Ch'ang-man from the Yan'an faction, Pak Ch'ang-ok and Pak Yŏng-bin from the Moscow faction, and Pak Chŏng-ae from the Southern faction.[54]

Some scholars argue that *Juche*, which Kim Il-sung put forward for the first time in December 1955, was intended to eliminate the Soviet influence in the KWP while strengthening North Korean ties with China. One piece of evidence supporting this argument is the fact that Kim began a new round of political purges against Pak Ch'ang-ok, Pak Yŏng-bin, and other ethnic Korean cadres from the Soviet Union not long after he proposed his *Juche* idea. Additionally, Kim mentioned that, in order to purify the party spirit, KWP members should learn from the CCP rectification movement.[55] Given Moscow's far-reaching influence in the socialist world, it is a legitimate argument that the *Juche* idea was aimed at eliminating Soviet influence from North Korea. But it is less convincing that this ideology sought to strengthen North Korea's ties with China. Kim would typically change sides, from time to time, from Moscow to Beijing. Because North Korea was situated between two powerful neighbors, he had no choice but to do this in order to survive. But he would never tolerate it if either one of these great powers dared to threaten his position as leader of his country. The events of August 1956 and the aftermath provide solid evidence of this point.

At the February 1956 Twentieth Party Congress, First Secretary of the CPSU Nikita Khrushchev proposed a series of guiding programs with respect to international, domestic, and intraparty affairs. Khrushchev's proposals represented a dramatic departure from the policies advocated by his predecessor Joseph Stalin at the 1952 Nineteenth Party Congress. In terms of international affairs, Khrushchev proposed "peaceful coexistence, peaceful transition, and peaceful competition" as "the guiding principles and general line."[56] Domestically, he introduced policies to adjust economic development and planning priorities. Apart from a general call for improving organizational and ideological work, with respect to intraparty affairs he raised the issue of strengthening collective leadership and opposing the cult of personality.[57] In the wake of the congress and inspired by the new trends in the socialist bloc, there were dissenting voices in the KWP, mainly among the ethnic Koreans who prior to 1945 had lived in either the Soviet Union or China but by the late 1940s had already returned to North Korea. They questioned Kim Il-sung's domestic and foreign policies, and they called for more "intraparty democracy and collective leadership." But Kim was not receptive to this criticism.[58] As historian James Person points out, Kim "viewed his critics as conduits of outside influence who served the interests of Moscow and Beijing by mechanically replicating Soviet and Chinese economic, political, and cultural practices. Kim was not just intolerant of different opinions, he was also a megalomaniac who believed that only he knew what was best for Korea."[59]

On March 19, via Ambassador Ivanov, Kim Il-sung received a written version of Khrushchev's "secret" speech entitled "The Personality Cult and Its Consequences." Kim indicated that the KWP would respond in the spirit of the speech. But Ivanov learned that, in addition to Ch'oe Yong-gŏn, who had just returned from Moscow and had given an oral report on his visit, only three people, including Kim, spoke at the KWP CC plenum on the following day, which was intended to be devoted to studying the materials on the Twentieth Congress of the CPSU. When Kim spoke about the personality cult, he focused on how the Southerners in the KWP worshipped Pak Hŏn-yŏng, but he did not mention that many party members worshipped Kim. Kim did instruct that the press and other propaganda agencies should no longer mention contributions by individuals. Khrushchev's secret speech was read to the plenum in Korean, but it was not discussed, and the plenum did not pass any resolution about the speech.[60]

After the plenum, the KWP CC issued a secret document to instruct party agencies at all levels to study the spirit of the Twentieth Congress of the CPSU. This document emphasized that the KWP had always followed Marxism and Leninism in every respect and had never abandoned the most fundamental party principle of collective leadership. In referring to the personality cult, the document stated that a personality cult had previously existed within the party but that its existence was due only to Pak Hŏn-yŏng.[61]

From April 23 to April 29, 1956, the KWP held its Third Party Congress. The main agenda of the Congress included a reshuffling of personnel and further elimination of the opposition. The Congress did not discuss the problem of the personality cult, even though there were many rumors about it circulating among the people. Furthermore, it did not address the dissatisfaction shared by many cadres with regard to the recent personnel changes, nor did it refer to the economic difficulties and the dissatisfaction among the masses about their living conditions. In addition to celebrating the political and economic achievements of North Korea, Kim Il-sung devoted his lengthy report to criticizing the members of the Southern faction, such as Pak Hŏn-yŏng, and the factional activities that sought to split the party. He neither praised nor opposed the spirit of the Twentieth Congress of the CPSU and the principle of collective leadership. Many people wanted to speak at the Congress, but they were not allowed to do so. The reshuffling of personnel was meant to guarantee loyalty to Kim. Among the seventy-one Central Committee members, only twenty-eight had been former members and forty-three were newly elected. Among the forty-five alternate members, only two were former alternates and forty-three were newly elected.[62]

During the Congress, both the speakers and the press excessively praised Kim Il-sung. This was regarded as very abnormal by the representatives of the Soviet Foreign Ministry.[63] In this regard, it is illuminating to consider Kim Ch'ang-man's speech to the meeting held by the Pyongyang Municipal Committee for KWP activists to implement the spirit of the Third Party Congress. Kim Ch'ang-man was a loyal follower of Kim Il-sung and deputy chairman of the KWP. After highly praising the significance of the Third Party Congress, Kim Ch'ang-man turned to the topic of the personality cult. He said that a personality cult did not currently exist in the KWP. However, he said, one had existed in the past—for example, in the cult of Pak Hŏn-yŏng in the South and the cult of Hŏ Ka-i in the North. Kim Ch'ang-man warned activists not to spread rumors that there was a personality cult in the KWP. He stated that anyone who made such comments would be punished, because this would weaken the party.[64]

The reshuffling of personnel at the KWP's Third Party Congress was directed against the Moscow faction. At a meeting to review the candidates for the KWP CC prior to the convening of the Congress, Kim Il-sung pointed out that those cadres who had returned to Korea from the Soviet Union and had retained dual citizenship should not be elected to the Central Committee. Ch'oe Yong-gŏn angrily suggested that they even should be expelled, for straddling two sides. As a result, all of the candidates from the Moscow faction were eliminated as candidates to the KWP CC.

At a Standing Committee meeting after the Third Party Congress, Kim stressed the problem of intelligence security and discipline. These remarks were directed against those Moscow faction cadres who frequented the Soviet Embassy. He demanded that, thereafter, any contacts with foreigners had to be conducted through the Ministry of Foreign Affairs or the Ministry of Foreign Trade. At the time, Kim showed somewhat more tolerance toward the Yan'an faction. At the Standing Committee meeting, he suddenly spoke about the case of Pak Il-u. He said that, after an investigation, it was still unclear how Pak had erred. Kim Tu-bong and Kim Kwang-hyŏp then proposed that Pak Il-u be released immediately. However, Ch'oe Yong-gŏn insisted that he should be executed. Foreign Minister Nam Il argued that he should be disciplined. Finally, Kim Il-sung concluded that Pak Il-u would eventually be released, but not at that time.[65]

Kim did release Yi Sang-jo, who belonged to the Yan'an faction and had, at the beginning of the Korean War, been Kim's envoy to Beijing and, thereafter, North Korean ambassador to the Soviet Union. He had returned from Moscow to attend the Third Party Congress of the KWP. During the Congress, he sent two brief notes to the presidium of the Congress, suggesting that they discuss the problem of a personality cult in the KWP. The presidium ignored his suggestion, but Kim Ch'ang-man summoned Yi and harshly criticized him. Ch'oe Yong-gŏn, Pak Kŭm-ch'ŏl, and others proposed removing him from his ambassadorial post. This episode ended when Kim Tu-bong told Kim Il-sung that he did not agree that Yi should be punished.[66]

Because he knew that a conflict with Moscow was unavoidable, due to his purge of the Moscow faction cadres, Kim Il-sung exercised restraint in dealing with the members of Yan'an faction. Even before the Twentieth Congress of the CPSU, the Soviet Foreign Ministry had taken note of the rising personality cult of Kim Il-sung within the KWP and had suggested that the CPSU CC warn Kim about it.[67] Now the Intelligence Committee, under the Ministry of Foreign Affairs of the Soviet Union, was noting the connection between the fall of the Moscow faction comrades and their repeated warnings to Kim about the danger of a personality cult. Based on this observation, the Intelligence Committee suggested that the CPSU CC should help the KWP correct its mistakes.[68]

The Far East Bureau of the Soviet Foreign Ministry wondered whether the political struggles against comrades such as Pak Ch'ang-ok represented the beginning of a movement against ethnic Koreans who held Soviet citizenship.[69] In late 1955, there were 136 such cadres in North Korea. According to a decision by the Supreme Soviet on December 31, 1955, these Soviet Koreans would not be allowed to hold dual citizenship. Many replied that they preferred North Korean citizenship, but twenty-four of them indicated that they wanted to retain their dual citizenship. After Pak Ch'ang-ok and Pak Yŏng-bin were removed from their posts, many of those who had chosen North Korean citizenship regretted their decision because of the purge and the discrimination against those who had returned from the Soviet Union. Some even went to the Soviet Embassy and secretly asked to keep or to regain their Soviet citizenship.[70]

As soon as he returned to Moscow, Yi Sang-jo met with Nikolai Fedorenko, deputy foreign minister of the USSR. Yi first briefed him on Kim Il-sung's plan to visit the Soviet Union and other Eastern European countries in order to seek economic aid. Thereafter, he provided a detailed report on the abnormal phenomena that were occurring within the KWP, such as how the cult of Kim Il-sung had spread throughout the country, how the KWP had not followed the spirit of collective leadership, and how every decision was made personally by Kim. Yi noted that Kim was extolled to the skies: "The Korean People's Revolutionary Museum has been turned into a museum of Kim Il-sung's personal history." He noted that it was even claimed that "during his childhood, Kim Il-sung had led the Korean people in their liberation movement against the Japanese." Yi referred to Kim's mistakes in economic and personnel affairs as well as to his mistakes during the war. He repeated his hope that the CPSU CC would help put the KWP back on track and, in particular, would help Kim overcome his weaknesses as soon as possible.[71] At another meeting, Yi suggested that the Soviet leaders should request that the entire North Korean delegation attend the meeting of Soviet leaders with Kim so that all the members of delegation would hear Moscow's opinions.[72]

After the KWP's Third Party Congress, Kim Il-sung made an extended trip to the Soviet Union and the Eastern European countries, from June 1 to July 17, to seek additional economic aid. According to Russian documents, a group of North Korean leaders had already grown dissatisfied with the KWP's personality cult and its personnel and economic policies. This group included Kim Tu-bong, Ch'oe Ch'ang-ik, Pak Ch'ang-ok, Pak Ŭi-wan, Sŏ Hwi, Yun Kong-hŭm, and Kim Sŭng-hwa. During Kim Il-sung's June 1956 visit to Poznan, Polish workers were protesting against the Communist government, thus further inciting antagonism against Kim. Those who were dissatisfied wished to expose and criticize Kim's mistakes, during the upcoming August plenum of the KWP.

On June 8, Deputy Prime Minister Ch'oe Ch'ang-ik met privately with the Soviet ambassador. He spoke about recent developments in North

Korea, especially the erroneous direction being taken in personnel affairs. Ch'oe referred to the discrimination against those who were not members of the Guerrilla faction, and he lamented that those who were being promoted were uneducated, inexperienced, and only good at flattering their superiors, thereby contributing to the spread of a personality cult. He sought urgent help from the Soviets to correct the KWP's mistakes, and, believing that Kim generally listened to Moscow, he expressed a wish that Moscow would advise Kim.[73] Sŏ Hwi and Yun Kong-hŭm colluded with other Yan'an faction cadres to form an opposition that sought to force Kim Il-sung to step down. They were successful in winning Ch'oe Yong-gŏn and Kim Tu-bong over to their side.[74] Because of the general dissatisfaction with Kim Il-sung, several tens of thousands of workers in Pyongyang began to demonstrate. Four of the five Standing Committee members of the KWP Pyongyang Municipal Committee were sympathetic to the workers.[75]

Detailed information about Kim Il-sung's meetings with Soviet leaders during his trip to the Soviet Union is not yet available. What is known is that Nikita Khrushchev received Kim and offered him advice. In the meantime, Khrushchev admitted that he did not understand the entire situation, so he entrusted the Department for Liaison with Communist and Workers' Parties in Socialist Countries to carry out an investigation. Kim accepted Khrushchev's criticism and stated that he would correct his mistakes. Moscow later notified the CCP CC about the Khrushchev–Kim meeting. Mao Zedong commented positively on the way in which the Soviets had dealt with Kim.[76]

On August 2, 1956, the CPSU Central Committee further expressed its opinion via its embassy: Moscow hoped that Kim would take more of an initiative to criticize and rectify the KWP's mistakes.[77] Thus, Beijing and Moscow both were voicing their opposition to Kim's purge of his opponents.[78] Moscow was obviously unhappy with the KWP because of its purge of the Moscow faction and its continuing encouragement of a personality cult. Beijing's, and especially Moscow's, attitudes emboldened the opposition within the KWP, who thought that external pressures would put Kim on the defensive. In fact, Moscow's attitude encouraged the opposition within the KWP to launch an offensive against Kim during the August plenum of the KWP CC.[79]

When Kim Il-sung returned from his overseas trip, on July 19, Ch'oe Yong-gŏn and Nam Il reported to him on the activities of the opposition as well as on the domestic situation.[80] Kim reacted swiftly. On a number of occasions Kim Il-sung, Nam Il, and Pak Chŏng-ae contacted the Soviet Embassy. On the one hand, they repeated that they accepted Moscow's criticism. On the other hand, however, they argued that the opposition was splitting the party by accusing the officials around Kim Il-sung of incompetence, fawning, and historical problems and asking for their removal on false grounds. Arguing that these dissenters were attempting to stall the party's policy making and to incite dissatisfaction, they concluded that they constituted an antiparty clique that tarnished the party's reputation, harmed the status of the party, and created a dangerous situation.[81]

At the same time, Kim Il-sung and his followers repeatedly spoke individually with some of the dissenters, using both sticks and carrots to divide the opposition. For instance, they successfully won over Kim Tu-bong, they neutralized Pak Ŭi-wan, and they sent Kim Sŭng-hwa to Moscow to study. In addition, Kim Il-sung ordered that the police spy on the dissenters and interrogate their drivers and maids. To take preventive measures, Kim also summoned Interior Minister Pang Hak-se, who was then on a foreign trip, to return immediately to North Korea. As a result of these efforts, Kim gained the upper hand.

He was also satisfied with the attitude of the Soviet Embassy, as Ambassador Ivanov made it clear that the goal of the upcoming plenum should be to consolidate the ruling status of the KWP and to unify the party.[82] Therefore, Kim Il-sung decided to hold a Standing Committee meeting before the plenum, to unify thought. Although, based on Moscow's instructions, Ivanov asked Kim to take an initiative to correct the KWP's mistakes and not to attack the dissenters, he in fact implied that Moscow did not support the dissenters' call for the removal of the officials around Kim. The Soviets explicitly assured Kim that they would not interfere in North Korea's internal affairs, to Kim's great relief.

At the KWP's Standing Committee meeting of August 21 to August 23, despite some dissenting voices, it was concluded that the policy of the Central Committee was generally correct. It was decided that it had mainly been Hŏ Ka-i, Pak Ch'ang-ok, and some other individuals who had made mistakes and that the Standing Committee would take actions to rectify them. When it came to the newly promoted leaders, the investigation found no evidence of wrongdoing and thus there was no reason for their removal. Kim Tu-bong's speech during this meeting was not at all impressive. The fact that he did not speak out was the key reason why Kim Il-sung was able to manipulate the meeting.

On August 28, the Standing Committee of the KWP passed a draft speech that Kim Il-sung would present during the forthcoming plenum. In this speech, Kim was to speak about the achievements of his recent trip, the domestic situation, and the present and future tasks of the KWP. The tone of the draft was precisely the same as that in Kim's previous speeches. The draft did not discuss internal party affairs and it only mentioned in passing that the plenum could discuss these issues. At the end of the draft, Kim suggested that opposition was dying hard, and he called on all party members to be vigilant and to do their part to oppose factionalism.[83]

The plenum of the KWP CC was held on August 30 and August 31. First, Kim Il-sung delivered the draft report that had been approved by the Standing Committee. The next two speakers nodded in acceptance, to flatter everything that Kim said. The third speaker was Minister of Trade Yun Kong-hŭm, who had a Yan'an background. In his speech, Yun angrily exposed the many mistakes that existed in the party. While speaking, he was interrupted several times and his voice was stifled by shouts from the unfriendly audience. Ch'oe Yong-gŏn even stood up from his seat to yell at Yun. The atmosphere in the conference hall suddenly became chaotic.[84] Ch'oe Ch'ang-ik wanted to stand up to speak on behalf of Yun, but he never got a chance. When Yun Kong-hŭm, Deputy Minister of Culture Kim Kang, and Director of the Bureau of Building Materials Yi P'il-gyu returned home during the recess, they found that their telephone lines had been cut. Alarmed by this situation and fearing recrimination and/or arrest, they sought Sŏ Hwi, chairman of the trade unions, and they traveled by military vehicle toward the Yalu River bridge on the Sino–North Korean border.[85]

For the remainder of the day, only Ch'oe Ch'ang-ik and Pak Ch'ang-ok expressed support for Yun Kong-hŭm's speech. All the other speakers condemned Yun and his supporters on the basis that their speeches were antiparty and against the revolution. They accused Ch'oe Ch'ang-ik of being part of an antiparty clique. The next day, the meeting passed a resolution to take action against those people who were devoted to antiparty activities. This included the expulsion of Yun Kong-hŭm, Sŏ Hwi, Kim Kang, and Yi P'il-gyu from the party; the removal of Ch'oe Ch'ang-ik from the Standing Committee; and the removal of Pak Ch'ang-ok from the cabinet and the Central Committee. All of these issues were transferred to a special Central Committee commission for further investigation.[86] Pak Ch'ang-ok was soon sent to the east coast to manage a small sawmill and Ch'oe Ch'ang-ik was assigned to manage a pig farm.

Why did the dissenters fail? The personality cult was initially Kim Il-sung's weakness. The new Soviet leaders were initially unhappy with Kim Il-sung because he was not supportive of the program of the Twentieth Congress of the CPSU. The dissenters might have been encouraged by Moscow's attitude. But Khrushchev's secret speech rocked the socialist bloc and brought turmoil to the Eastern European countries. Therefore, by the summer of 1956 Moscow had become tolerant of Kim's personality cult. This encouraged Kim Il-sung and weakened the strength of the dissenters.

What role did China play in the August 1956 incident? Andrei Lankov claims, "It looks highly probable that the August opposition received some support from the Chinese Embassy even prior to the August plenum itself. Actually, it is possible that the entire affair was instigated by the Chinese."[87] According to the Russian archives, on September 14 Ambassador Ivanov reported to the CPSU CC that Yun Kong-hŭm and three others had fled to China "in accordance with advice from the Chinese Embassy."[88] After Peng Dehuai was purged, in 1959, Kim Il-sung and Mao Zedong both did an about-face. During their meeting on May 21, 1960, Kim told Mao that the reason why the dissenters had "dared to make a fuss was because they had received support from Peng Dehuai."[89]

It seemed that the North Korean "antiparty" incident had indeed been supported by the Chinese. But available documentary evidence at present does not support this argument. According to information currently available, after Kim Il-sung's talk with Soviet leaders in July 1956, the CPSU briefed the CCP. However, as yet, neither the details nor the response of the CCP have surfaced.[90] According to the Russian archives, when Chao Keqiang, counselor at the Chinese Embassy, met Soviet Chargé d'Affaires A. Petrov on August 3, he said, "When a certain Korean comrade asked the embassy staff their view on the issue of the personality cult, they were told to follow the *Renmin ribao*'s formulation."[91] This fits well with what Kim Ch'ung-sik reported to Shen Zhihua in an interview. When asked whether the members of the Yan'an faction ever contacted the Chinese Embassy about this, Kim Ch'ung-sik reported that the Chinese Embassy was indifferent and avoided meeting them. They thus no longer visited the embassy.[92]

The timing of Soviet Ambassador Ivanov's call on the Chinese Embassy on August 17 suggests that the Soviets hoped to sound out the Chinese view on the issue. But Chinese Ambassador Qiao Xiaoguang avoided the topic and instead mentioned only North Korea's request for Chinese aid during the Five-Year Plan period.[93] According to Kim Kang, it was their own decision to flee to China, due to the urgency of the situation, and it had nothing to do with the Chinese Embassy.[94] It appears that the Chinese did not know much about the inner struggle within the KWP and had no intention of interfering.[95] But after the Yan'an faction cadres fled to China, as James Person notes, "A domestic policy dispute—while inspired by development in the socialist camp—officially became an international incident."[96] China was forced to play a major role in the KWP's internal affairs in the wake of the August incident.

Joint Intervention by the CCP and the CPSU

After the plenum, there were numerous searches and arrests throughout North Korea to quell the dissent.[97] The actual situation with regard to many important questions in the party was distorted. Inner-party struggles were presented to the public as a palace coup plotted by a small number of dissenters who disagreed with some party and government leaders. On September 1, Kim Il-sung and Ch'oe Yong-gŏn called on the Soviet and Chinese embassies, respectively, to brief them on the situation at the plenum and its resolutions.[98]

On August 31, 1956, Yun Kong-hŭm, Sŏ Hwi, Kim Kang, and Yi P'il-gyu arrived via military vehicle at China's border checkpoint at Andong (Dandong). After officials learned their identities, they were escorted to Beijing. Once in the capital, Premier Zhou Enlai and Minister of Public Security Luo Ruiqing promptly received them and listened to their report. They were soon provided with salaries and benefits similar to those of Chinese officials at the ministerial/provincial levels and were asked to write detailed accounts of the episode.[99]

On September 3, the North Korean government notified the Chinese Ministry of Foreign Affairs that four Korean citizens had crossed the border at Andong and had been intercepted by the Chinese border patrol. The North Korean government demanded that the Chinese government repatriate them. On receiving this message, Ambassador Qiao Xiaoguang replied that, due to their unusual status, it would be impossible for China to force the four Koreans to return to North Korea. Qiao later asked Soviet Ambassador Ivanov about Moscow's opinion on this issue.[100] Beijing had apparently already made a decision, but Moscow was somewhat more cautious.

On September 5, Sŏ Hwi, Yun Kong-hŭm, Yi P'il-gyu, and Kim Kang submitted a long report to the CCP CC, detailing their views about what had happened in North Korea. They argued that Kim Il-sung had established dictatorial control over the party, the government, the military, and the judiciary, and they highlighted the serious mistakes committed by the KWP, such as inciting the Korean War and then committing major blunders during the course of the war; Kim's suppression of a democratic work style within the party; the creation of factionalism, the imposition of a rash and leftist economic policy, and neglect of the people's livelihood; and fabrication of history and propagation of a personality cult around Kim Il-sung. In propaganda work, the KWP placed too much emphasis on the Korean national spirit and seldom publicized the aid North Korea had received from the Soviet Union, China, and other fraternal countries. They concluded that Kim Il-sung had "started to betray the revolution. . . . Kim Il-sung has become an obstacle to the Korean Revolution. Only after Kim Il-sung is removed can the Korean Revolution develop swiftly and unification of the motherland and socialist reconstruction be promoted."[101] In view of their situation at the time, it is most likely that these four Koreans were not objective when writing their report. For instance, some North Korean books and journals from the period portray Chinese aid in a very positive light.

At the same time, Soviet leaders also received other reports about the August incident. On September 5, the North Korean ambassador to the Soviet Union, Yi Sang-jo, asked to meet with Deputy Foreign Minister Fedorenko, and he submitted a letter addressed to Khrushchev on the August event. Yi criticized Kim for suppressing those who had tried to advise him and asked for intervention by the CPSU CC. Yi also stated that, on two occasions, the Ministry of Foreign Affairs of the DPRK had summoned him to return home. However, he had claimed that he was ill and could not travel.[102]

On September 6, the Presidium of the CPSU CC held a meeting to discuss the Korean issue. The Presidium decided to entrust Boris Ponomarev, head of the CPSU CC Department for Relations with Foreign Communist Parties, to receive Yi Sang-jo but to think carefully before meeting him, and via the Chinese ambassador it replied that the CPSU CC would entrust members of a Soviet delegation that was then in China attending the CCP's Eighth Party Congress to consult with the CCP CC on the Korean problem.[103]

At a meeting on September 10, Ponomarev told Yi Sang-jo that the CPSU was concerned about what was occurring in North Korea. He said that the CPSU delegation in Beijing would consult with both the KWP delegation, which also was in Beijing, and the CCP, but that the CPSU would not interfere in KWP internal affairs. Ponomarev rejected the idea of discussing Yi's suggestion that the CPSU publicize its criticism of the KWP.[104] In fact, this cautious attitude on the part of the Soviet Union had been in place even prior to the revelation about the KWP's inner-party struggle. Khrushchev's de-Stalinization speech had caused an earthquake that affected not only the Soviet Union but also the entire socialist camp. On April 15, the CCP CC had published an article in *Renmin ribao* (People's Daily) entitled "On the Historical Experience of the Dictatorship of the Proletariat," explaining its opinion on the issue of personality cults. This "generated a huge response in the Soviet Union, Eastern Europe, and the world Communist movement."[105] These developments made the CPSU more circumspect about the issue of de-Stalinization, and it even suppressed some anti-Stalin rhetoric that it considered to be too radical. A June 20 resolution passed by the CPSU CC illustrates the shift in attitude on the part of the CPSU.[106] In later conversations and correspondence with Kim Il-sung, the Soviet leaders revealed their new caution about continuing the struggle against the personality cult. Kim immediately passed this information on to the members of the KWP.[107] It is fair to say that this shift in the attitude of the Soviets was a factor that emboldened Kim to take more extreme measures to deal with the problems in the KWP.

To ease the tensions in the KWP and to win support from Moscow, after the August plenum Kim Il-sung adopted a policy of conciliation toward the formerly purged or suppressed Moscow faction cadres. On the afternoon of September 14, Pak Chŏng-ae assembled some two-thirds of the Moscow faction cadres, a total of about one hundred people. The purpose of this meeting was to announce that the KWP CC had changed its policy toward those cadres with a Moscow background and that they would be rehabilitated.[108] The reason for this change was simple: the main target of Kim Il-sung's political struggle had shifted to the Yan'an faction. According to Kim's report to Moscow, it had primarily been the Yan'an faction cadres who were involved in the August antiparty conspiracy. For instance, the chief instigators of the factionalism were Ch'oe Ch'ang-ik and Kim Tu-bong. Among the dissenting returnees from China, Kim Tu-bong was most senior and held the highest position in the government.

Kim Il-sung had allegedly said that everyone involved in the political coup was from the Yan'an faction.[109] Kim changed his attitude toward the Moscow faction so as to focus on the mounting pressures from Beijing.

Politburo member and Deputy Chairman of the Council of Ministers Anastas Mikoyan led a CPSU delegation to the September 1956 Eighth Congress of the CCP in Beijing. Mikoyan was a confidante of Nikita Khrushchev and arguably the second most powerful player in Soviet politics in the late 1950s and early 1960s. On September 13, the Presidium of the CPSU CC instructed the CPSU delegation to consult with their Chinese colleagues and with the North Korean delegation regarding the situation in the KWP.[110] During the Congress, on September 16 Mikoyan met with the KWP delegation headed by Ch'oe Yong-gŏn. But this meeting did not go well. Mikoyan scolded the North Koreans for not earlier sharing more information about the August plenum. Ch'oe even refused a toast with Mikoyan.[111]

On September 17, Mikoyan reported to the CPSU CC that a meeting with the North Koreans had been proposed by the Soviet delegation. But the North Koreans were not prepared to meet their Soviet counterparts. Thus, their response was very brief, and they offered excuses for what they did at the August plenum. Therefore, Mikoyan complained that the North Koreans had "limited themselves to several previously memorized phrases to explain what had happened at the KWP August plenum . . . [and] avoided going beyond the bounds of the instructions they received."[112] Mikoyan reported, "We cannot accomplish the task the Central Committee entrusts us with because Kim Il-sung actually has not planned to come [to Beijing to meet with us]."[113] Mikoyan then proposed that "the only way for a discussion with the North Koreans would be to first exchange opinions with Chinese comrades and then go to Pyongyang for one or two days, together with representatives of the CCP, to discuss the issue there."[114]

On the evening of September 18, Mao Zedong, Zhou Enlai, and Peng Dehuai discussed the Korean problem with the Soviet delegation. Mikoyan said that he had spoken with the members of the Korean delegation and had criticized them. He also reported that Ch'oe Yong-gŏn had not taken this criticism well. Mikoyan noted that the CPSU did not really understand what was occurring and had not yet formed a final opinion.[115] Mao expressed his deep concern that many North Korean comrades had been arrested, expelled from the party, and removed from their positions for no good reason. Mao stated directly that Kim Il-sung was following Stalin's example—he could not tolerate any dissenting voices and he tried to kill anyone who disagreed with him. Mao also noted that the purpose of sending Chinese and Soviet delegations to Pyongyang was not to "discover the truth" but to advise Kim on how to unite the comrades, to reverse the current course in the political struggle, and to rehabilitate those who had been expelled and removed from their positions.

Mikoyan responded, "Our two parties should help the KWP leader correct his mistakes. . . . We trust Kim Il-sung, but we cannot tolerate what he has been doing as the leader of the KWP."[116] Mikoyan then proposed that the CPSU and the CCP send a joint delegation to North Korea. Mao agreed, but warned that Kim Il-sung would likely regard the visit as an act of foreign interference in the KWP politics.[117] Mao warned, "It is very likely that Kim will say that in the past you interfered in Yugoslavia and now you want to interfere with North Korea. During the Yugoslav intervention, there was only the Soviet Union, but now there is also China."[118] Mao warned, "Kim is afraid that our two parties are digging at his wall."[119] But, Mao pointed out, "Kim Il-sung knows that we do not intend to overthrow him and that we only want to help him. At the same time, it is necessary to let Kim Il-sung know that he cannot preserve his leadership without correcting his mistakes."[120] Mao further said: "We will also advise those who were subjected to these struggles to adopt a conciliatory attitude and we will advise that the two sides reach a reconciliation."[121] Mikoyan did not reply directly to Mao's comments. Instead, he said that he would talk to Kim, but that he had a lot of work to do back home and he could not remain in Korea for a long time.[122]

The memorandum of conversation between the Chinese and Soviet leaders demonstrates that Mao Zedong had many grievances with Kim Il-sung and had little trust in him.[123] Mao proposed, "It is advisable to adopt a resolution while the delegation is there. Otherwise, in the future words alone will be of no use. Once the delegation leaves, they will start to fight again."[124] After adoption, the resolution "should be published in the press."[125] Mao suggested that the delegation should also invite the Soviet and Chinese ambassadors to North Korea to participate in the discussion so that they could monitor North Korea's implementation of the resolution after the departure of the delegation.[126] Nevertheless, Mao had doubts about whether Kim would pay heed to the delegation.[127] He told Mikoyan that the success of the trip to Pyongyang rested mainly with the Soviets because the Koreans would not listen to the Chinese. Mikoyan responded, "They may listen to us, but they will do whatever they want."[128] Mao then reiterated, "The KWP leadership does not listen to any of the CCP's advice but at the same time it does not listen to 70 percent of the advice from the CPSU."[129]

CCP leaders then met with the members of the Korean delegation. Mao had already pointed out that there were serious problems in North Korea's economic and personnel policies. He told the members of the delegation that the next morning the CCP and the CPSU would send a joint delegation to Pyongyang, and he asked that Ch'oe Yong-gŏn accompany the delegation. Mao noted that the purpose of the delegation was to help North Korea solve its problems, not to jeopardize its interests. Mao admitted that he had already had problems with the KWP. For instance, before the outbreak of the Korean War, he had warned Kim Il-sung not to start the war. After its outbreak, he had warned Kim that the enemy might land in the rear. Peng Dehuai and Li Kenong asked the Korean delegation, "Who started the Korean War, the American imperialists or the Koreans?" Mao further said that he would ask the Koreans to allow those who had fled to China to return to North Korea, but Kim would have to reinstate them in the party and allow them to return to their former positions. Mao advised the North Koreans to solve these problems rationally during party meetings.[130] In short, the CCP's attitude was clearer than that of the CPSU. But the CCP did not have any agenda other than to demand that Kim correct his mistakes.

Before the declassification of the documents, one scholar had argued that "the purpose of this mission was not only to study the situation in the DPRK after the August Plenum and to stop the purges but also possibly to replace Kim Il Song with another person considered more suitable by China and the USSR . . . the initial thrust came from the Chinese side."[131] However, newly available Chinese and Russian documents reveal that neither China nor the USSR had any intention of replacing Kim Il-sung. In their numerous conversations, the Chinese and Soviet leaders repeatedly said that they wanted to support Kim and to help him correct his mistakes. Their only purpose was to stabilize the situation in North Korea. The harsh words by the Chinese leaders were indicative of their anger with Kim. But Mao said that he did not intend to overthrow Kim and he sought to improve Sino-North Korean relations.[132]

When Mikoyan, Peng Dehuai, and Ch'oe Yong-gŏn arrived in Pyongyang by air on September 19, Kim Il-sung did not show up at the airport to greet them, as normally would have been expected.[133] Kim must have regarded the arrival of the joint Sino-Soviet delegation as a threat to his personal power. After all, three months earlier Mikoyan had played an important role in removing from power the general secretary of the Hungarian Working People's Party, Mátyás Rákosi.[134] Later, in the evening of the arrival of the Sino-Soviet delegation, Kim Il-sung and Foreign Minister Nam Il met with Mikoyan and Peng Dehuai for four hours. In the evening of September 20, the KWP CC Standing Committee met with the delegation leaders. The North Koreans continued to defend what they did at the August plenum, whereupon Mikoyan delivered a lengthy speech in response. He indicated that the purpose of the joint Sino-Soviet delegation was to carry out its internationalist duty and help eliminate any "signs of crisis" in the KWP so as to stabilize the "vanguard of the socialist bloc."[135] He urged the KWP to hold a new plenum, to rectify the mistakes of the August plenum, and to pass a new resolution that would then be published in the press.[136] After extensive and sometimes heated discussions, with Kim generally accepting the opinion of the CCP and the CPSU, the KWP CC Standing Committee decided to hold a plenum on September 22, but later changed to September 23.[137] In advance of the plenum, the KWP CC Standing Committee would meet to draw up a draft resolution. Nam Il asked Mikoyan and Peng Dehuai to participate in the drafting of the draft resolution and they agreed.[138]

In the evening of September 22, upon Kim's request, the Soviet delegation met with Kim Il-sung and Nam Il. During this meeting, Kim showed Mikoyan a copy of the revised draft of the resolution. Mikoyan reiterated that the CPSU and the CCP would continue to support Kim if he agreed to take the initiative to engage in a self-criticism and to assure them that he would correct his mistakes. Kim pledged that "all the suggestions by the CPSU will guide my work. The CPSU has indisputable authority in my heart. . . . The KWP will never commit the kind of mistakes it has made in recent months."[139] He also promised Mikoyan that he would release Pak Il-u.[140] Obviously, Kim was attempting to curry favor with Mikoyan in order to demonstrate that he was closer to Moscow than he was to Beijing. This explains why, in his later report to the CPSU CC, Mikoyan praised Kim.

On September 23, the KWP Central Committee plenum passed a resolution admitting that the August resolution had been premature and agreeing to rehabilitate Ch'oe Ch'ang-ik and Pak Ch'ang-ok to their former positions on the Central Committee, but not to their government posts, and to allow those who had escaped to China to be reinstated in the KWP but not to the KWP CC. Kim also promised to end the purge of high-level officials.[141]

Mao met with the Soviet delegation when it returned to Beijing late on September 23. He argued that the joint Soviet–Chinese delegation had not criticized Kim as strongly as they should have. He said that it had been a serious mistake that Kim Il-sung had started the war and that Kim still refused to admit it. Mao said to Mikoyan, "You promoted Kim Il-sung. Just like a small tree, you planted it. The Americans pulled it up. We planted it in the same place. It is now extremely pompous." But Mikoyan attempted to limit the blame on Kim, claiming that Kim had recently made some progress, such as doing a good job in drafting the resolution for the September KWP plenum. Mikoyan was quite satisfied, declaring that "our mission has been completed."[142] But Mao thought otherwise, noting, "The issue is not at all over; it is only just beginning."[143]

Mao proved to be right. As Soviet ambassador V. I. Ivanov observed, the CCP and CPSU had imposed their own opinions on Kim Il-sung, forcing him to revise the August resolution. To Kim Il-sung, this represented a huge humiliation because within the course of less than one month the KWP had been forced to adopt two contradictory resolutions. This was also an insult to Kim's *Juche* ideology. Thus, after the joint Sino-Soviet delegation departed Pyongyang, despite his promises to Mikoyan and Peng Dehuai, Kim did not publicize the September resolution. He informed party members of the September resolution, but the newspapers only referred to it in passing.[144] According to James Person, "Kim started taking measures to eliminate conduits of Soviet and Chinese influence in the DPRK by purging, over the course of the next two years, most of the remaining Soviet-Koreans and China-returned Koreans."[145] Nor did Kim follow through on his promise to release Pak Il-u and to resume providing food to the families of Yun Kong-hŭm and the other dissidents. Despite China's repeated warnings, Kim continued to delay enforcement of the agreement that had been reached with Mikoyan and Peng.[146] By this time, however, the crises in Poland and Hungary were diverting the attention of Moscow and Beijing, thus pushing the Korean problem to the sidelines.

By the second half of 1956, Sino–North Korean relations had reached their lowest point since the end of the Korean War. Distrusting the Chinese, the DPRK government on November 5 sent a memorandum to the Chinese and Soviet governments, proposing that North Korea attend the Eleventh Session of the UN General Assembly in the hope that the UN would help mediate the situation on the Korean Peninsula, that the foreign troops would withdraw, and that the country would be reunified.[147]

China opposed the DPRK's scheme, stating that the UN was belligerent and thus not qualified to carry out an impartial resolution of the Korean issue. This also would have violated the trilateral agreement among the Soviet Union, China, and North Korea on an unbiased resolution of the Korean issue, which had been reached at the 1954 Geneva Conference. After consulting with Moscow, China replied on December 8 that both de facto and de jure the UN was belligerent. Because the UN recognized only South Korea, it was not qualified to mediate the Korean issue. The Chinese government stated, "At present, it is premature for a comprehensive resolution of the Korean issue." An impartial resolution "will entail a long-term struggle." But North Korea insisted that only fourteen members of the UN participated in the Korean War and that those who were not involved in the war might support Pyongyang's position.[148] It seems that Pyongyang was unaware of the workings of the UN.

Kim Il-sung might also have intended to caution Beijing and Moscow not to apply too much pressure on him. Mao further argued that North Korea's actions had revealed that it might leave the socialist bloc and that Kim Il-sung might defect to the Western bloc. In Mao's view, this was a very serious issue. In his talk with Soviet Ambassador Pavel Yudin on November 30, Mao censured Kim Il-sung, saying, "Kim wants to drive the CPVA out of Korea. He might follow Tito's road, or even that of Nagy." Mao stated that China could take advantage of the CPVA in Korea "to help Kim Il-sung correct his mistakes." It could also adopt a policy of noninterference, withdraw the CPVA from Korea, and let North Korea determine its own affairs. Mao asked Yudin to report his views to Khrushchev and to the CPSU CC.[149] On December 16, the Soviet chargé d'affaires in Beijing, K. A. Krutikov, told Acting Premier Chen Yun that Moscow "pays close attention to the Korean problem as Mao Zedong had mentioned in his talk with Yudin." The Soviet government agreed with the Chinese government position that "it is inappropriate for the Korean government to ask the UN for help to reunify Korea. [The Soviet government] will instruct its ambassador in Pyongyang to dissuade the Korean government from pursuing this."[150]

Despite Mao's earlier sense of obligation to North Korea, because of the strained relations it was no longer possible for China to provide any more aid to North Korea. When the North Korean leadership requested an additional 50 million Chinese yuan ($25 million) in free aid in September 1956, Beijing rejected Pyongyang's request after a period of silence. North Korea thereupon canceled Vice Premier Kim Il's trip to China.[151] Furthermore, in negotiating Sino-North Korean trade for 1957, China did not fulfill North Korea's request for grain. The DPRK had asked China for 200,000 tons of grain, but China only committed to providing 90,000 tons. However, after repeated negotiations, China agreed to give 150,000 tons.[152] On November 28, Kim Il-sung complained to Ambassador Ivanov, "Not long ago, Zhou Enlai called in the ambassadors from the people's democratic countries and briefed them on China's domestic situation. He indicated that China could not provide additional aid to the other socialist countries before the end of the Second Five-Year Plan. Thus, the Korean government will have to reconsider its 1957 plan and reduce its construction fund and purchase less coke and gas from China."[153]

Under these circumstances, North Korea again turned to Moscow, requesting an additional 1,500 tons of cotton in 1957 and subsidies in the amount of 31 million rubles ($7.75 million) to resolve its deficit problem. Kim emphasized that "other than consolidating contacts and friendship with the Soviet Union, Korea has no other political line."[154] Meanwhile, it was announced at the December 1956 KWP CC plenum that the Second Five-Year Plan would primarily be supported by domestic funds.[155]

In terms of Sino-North Korean relations and Soviet-North Korean relations during the 1953-1956 period, Pyongyang was closer to Moscow than it was to Beijing. Though he did not make it immediately clear, Kim Il-sung obviously resented the joint Sino–Soviet intervention in September 1956, perceiving "the visit as meddling in the KWP's internal affairs."[156] But, for a time, he was considering using Moscow to counter Beijing. As for Mao, he had to rely on Moscow's help to resolve the Korean issue and to improve Sino-North Korean relations. It seems that, in this respect, Mao had confidence in Khrushchev. China had assisted Khrushchev in resolving the Polish and Hungarian crises and, in return, Mao expected that Moscow would help Beijing tackle the Korean issue. Unfortunately, Mao's expectations proved to be mistaken.

CHAPTER IV

Mao's Policy of Mollification, 1957–1960

T he Polish and Hungarian crises of October 1956 shook the entire socialist bloc, thus exerting a subtle influence on Sino–Soviet, Soviet–North Korean, and Sino–North Korean relations. To deal with the crises, on October 30, 1956, the Communist Party of the Soviet Union (CPSU) Central Committee (CC) issued a declaration of equality among all Communist countries. As a result, CPSU relations with the Eastern European countries and with North Korea improved. Therefore, Moscow did not support Beijing's proposal to resolve the North Korean issue via strong measures. Meanwhile, after the Polish and Hungarian crises, the Chinese Communist Party (CCP) began to play a greater role in Eastern European affairs. China's influence and prestige grew steadily, both in the Soviet Union and in Eastern Europe. Mao Zedong thus had to reconsider China's policy toward North Korea.

With respect to the Polish and Hungarian crises, CCP leaders strictly adhered to two principles. First, they seized the opportunity to criticize Stalinism and to join hands with the Eastern European countries to address both Soviet "great power chauvinism" and abuses by the CPSU. In this manner, they stressed principles of independence and equality in socialist interstate relations, epitomized especially by China's attitude toward the Polish issue. Second, CCP leaders focused on coordinating relations between the USSR and its satellites. They emphasized that there should be unity and stability in the socialist camp, and they opposed all measures and inclinations that deviated from socialism.[1]

These opinions and principles that the CCP proposed both during the Polish and Hungarian crises, as well as subsequently, helped to resolve the CPSU's problems in its relations with the Eastern European Communist parties. However, at the same time, in handling its relationship with the Korean Workers' Party (KWP), the CCP found itself in an awkward position. In a conversation with Soviet Ambassador Pavel Yudin on November 30, 1956, Mao proposed both "active" and "passive" schemes to resolve the Korean issue. In fact, the CCP was more inclined to take an "active" approach—making use of the Chinese army in North Korea to force Kim Il-sung to alter his policies, similar to what the Soviet Union had done in Hungary in October 1956. Mao believed that Kim Il-sung had already become, or would soon become, a Nagy-type traitor to the revolution and that North Korea would break away from the socialist camp. Thus, he felt that it was necessary to take strong measures to block the Eastern "breach" in the socialist camp.

But Moscow did not support Beijing in this regard because Soviet leaders held a different opinion of the KWP. After the Polish and Hungarian crises, the KWP grew much closer to the Soviet Union. Three days after the Soviet government issued its declaration of equality, the KWP, on November 2, indicated "its full agreement with the declaration." Thereafter, Kim Il-sung told his newly appointed ambassador to the Soviet Union, Li Sin-p'al, "The DPRK has no other political line other than to consolidate contacts and friendship with the Soviet Union."[2] This statement indicated that Kim had not betrayed the revolution and that North Korea had not deviated from the socialist camp.

Mao's Apology

As Sino–North Korean relations grew tense, Kim Il-sung began to lean on Moscow. After the Soviet Union sent its troops to Hungary, Foreign Minister Nam Il of the Democratic People's Republic of Korea (DPRK), on November 2, 1956, told Soviet Ambassador V. I. Ivanov that, thereafter, North Korea would take all necessary measures to strengthen its friendship with the Soviet Union. He further noted that all progressive forces must closely unite around the Soviet Union.[3] The Soviet Union, having weathered the crises in Eastern Europe, began to change its attitude with regard to the provision of economic aid to North Korea. In February 1957, the CPSU CC approved a Soviet–North Korean trade agreement for 1957 as well as an agreement to provide commodities free of charge to North Korea. In addition to providing large quantities of mechanical equipment, industrial materials, and other goods, the Soviet Union decided to provide an additional 40,000 tons of wheat and agreed to import 100,000 tons of zinc, 35,000 tons of calcium carbide (which, in fact, the Soviet Union did not need), and 500 tons of monazite from North Korea. To satisfy the DPRK's request for additional aid, the Soviet government also agreed to import commodities from North Korea at prices that were higher than those on world markets.[4] Furthermore, it accepted Kim Il-sung's special request that the Soviet Union allow North Korea to use 50 million rubles ($12.5 million) in advance credits. In April 1957, Ambassador Ivanov, who had been critical of the North Korean leadership, was recalled and replaced by A. M. Puzanov.[5]

In a measure to further ingratiate North Korea with Moscow, Kim had the North Korean Ministry of Foreign Affairs spread rumors about China to the Soviet Embassy in order to foment Sino–Soviet discord. One example was a rumor about how the Chinese deputy foreign minister had summoned individually the North Korean, Vietnamese, and Mongolian ambassadors to brief them on the Hungarian crisis. Allegedly, the Chinese had said that the Soviets had admitted their mistakes on the Polish issue and that Yi Sang-jo admired China but despised the Soviet Union.[6] Beijing may have heard about these things, but it did not react. Nevertheless, Beijing's perceptions of North Korea were changing.

In early 1957, Sino–North Korean relations were relatively inactive. Newly appointed Ambassador Puzanov reported on April 10 that North Korea would complete formulation of its Five-Year Plan in May and June and would like feedback from both the Soviet Union and China. Ambassador Qiao Xiaoguang promptly responded that China might not be able to offer any additional aid.[7] When Kim Il-sung decided to send a delegation to learn from China's experience in formulating its own Five-Year Plan, China procrastinated in responding and then finally informed Pyongyang that such a visit would only be possible in July. As a result, the North Korean leaders complained to the Soviets that it was difficult to get along with the Chinese ambassador.[8]

However, Mao's attitude toward North Korea began to change in the second half of 1957. After Stalin's death, in 1953, the personal charisma of the new Soviet leader was insufficient to lead the International Communist Movement, thus resulting in a decline in CPSU influence. The Twentieth Congress of the CPSU and the 1956 Polish and Hungarian crises further weakened the leading role of the CPSU. In contrast, the status of both Mao and the CCP improved substantially as CCP influence expanded from Asia to Europe. Mao believed that he was much more sophisticated theoretically than Soviet leader Nikita Khrushchev and that therefore the CCP was quite qualified to be a coleader of the socialist camp.[9] It thus became necessary that China exhibit some magnanimity toward the DPRK.[10]

Kim Il-sung responded swiftly. In early July, while continuing to criticize and expose the "antiparty clique" in the KWP, Kim decided to free Pak Il-u and allow him to depart for China. Kim stated, "The Chinese comrades trust the Korean Workers' Party, not a few dissidents."[11] Shortly thereafter, the DPRK planned to send a delegation to China to negotiate its First Five-Year Plan and bilateral trade. Despite improvements in bilateral relations between Pyongyang and Beijing, Kim was not optimistic about securing additional aid from China, and he had already received a disappointing response from Moscow. When the DPRK delegation visited Moscow in July to discuss the First Five-Year Plan, the delegation asked for an extension of the 240 million ruble loan ($60 million), which would have matured in 1961–1962. However, this request was rejected. The Soviet leaders could not tolerate the DPRK's continuous requests for aid. At a Presidium meeting of the CPSU CC, Anastas Mikoyan pointed out that the DPRK's First Five-Year Plan was unrealistic and not achievable. "We should tell them frankly that they should pay back their debt with interest." Khrushchev also agreed that Kim Il-sung should pay his debts. "Otherwise, we will not give him any new loans. Our principle is 'to calculate the economic accounts.'"[12]

Thus, the North Koreans did not have high hopes about aid from China when its delegation was dispatched to Beijing in September 1957. Kim Il-sung told the Soviet ambassador that, in the past, Pyongyang had asked for too much from China and that this time it would ask for less.[13] Thus, they planned a low-key visit to China and did not intend to ask for aid directly. Furthermore, during the visit the North Koreans attempted to avoid public activities and media reporting.[14]

Contrary to their expectations, however, they received a windfall in China. Led by Kim Il, the delegation visited China from September 13 to October 6, 1957. In general, China endorsed North Korea's First Five-Year Plan. Nevertheless, by elaborating on China's own experience, the Chinese negotiators expressed concerns that Korean growth rates were too high, agricultural investment was too low, and accumulation and investment rates as well as consumption levels were too high. With respect to trade, China agreed to provide aid to Korea to resolve its material difficulties to the extent that it was capable and to do its best to satisfy the DPRK's need for critical materials such as coal, sulfur, rubber, and so forth. China also agreed to import 8,000 tons of calcium carbide from North Korea, even though China already had its own surplus.

North Korea was very satisfied with the negotiations, as they "basically resolved all the major issues."[15] During actual implementation of the trade agreement, China made further concessions and adopted measures to increase bilateral trade. The total volume of China's trade with the DPRK in 1957 was $56.01 million. In 1959, it doubled to $115.84 million, and in 1960 it reached a total of $120.37 million. China enjoyed a favorable trade balance every year from 1957 to 1960, amounting to $62.29 million. China eventually transferred the North Korean trade deficit into loans that it provided to North Korea for free.[16]

By October 25, 1957, the seventh anniversary of the entry of the Chinese People's Volunteer Army (CPVA) into Korea, Sino–North Korean relations had improved considerably. Kim Il-sung sent a letter to Yang Yong, commander of the CPVA, to express North Korea's gratitude. Kim also sent a congratulatory cable to Mao and in response received a personal cable from Mao expressing his thanks. The North Korean government held a commemoration meeting in Pyongyang and organized the masses to express sympathy, to erect statues, and to pay their respects to those who had given their lives during the war. Several days later, on the anniversary of the Russian October Revolution, *Renmin ribao* (People's Daily) reported on the festive atmosphere in the CPVA camp.[17]

To further improve relations, Mao met with Kim Il-sung during the November 1957 Moscow Conference of World Communist and Workers' Parties and apologized to him for interfering in the internal affairs of the KWP in September 1956. To alleviate Kim's fears of interference in the future, Mao took the initiative to propose the withdrawal of all Chinese troops from Korea. Kim later told the Soviet ambassador that Mao's talk was "very cordial, friendly, and candid. We are very satisfied."[18]

The Complete Withdrawal of the Chinese People's Volunteer Army

Mao's decision to withdraw the CPVA from North Korea was yet another measure designed to further placate Kim Il-sung. At the end of the Korean War, about 1.2 million Chinese soldiers still remained in Korea.[19] At the Geneva Conference of 1954, China called for the withdrawal of both Chinese and American forces from the Korean Peninsula by April 1956, and as a result both sides began to withdraw their troops. Seven divisions returned to China in September 1954, and six additional divisions returned in March 1955. By April 1956, there were only about 440,000 Chinese troops remaining in North Korea.[20]

In the opinion of the Chinese and the Soviets, the CPVA was the main socialist bloc force that balanced the American forces in South Korea. China was thus the representative of the socialist bloc in the handling of the Korean issue after the armistice. Although China had voluntarily handed the "affairs of the Military Armistice Commission over to the care of the Korean People's Army [KPA] representatives, who were under Pyongyang's direct supervision by late 1954" and had also scaled down the size of the CPVA delegation in Kaesŏng, Pyongyang still had to consult with Beijing on major decisions.[21] Furthermore, the large number of Chinese troops stationed in Korea allowed China to play a dominant role in Korean affairs. China's call for a withdrawal of troops mainly aimed to divert pressure from the neutral countries. It was a response to the U.S. attempt to disband the Commission of Neutral Countries and in practice it was meaningless.[22]

After the August incident of 1956, China and North Korea began to differ over how to bring about the withdrawal of the U.S. troops from South Korea and how to reunify the Korean Peninsula. Pyongyang did not want Beijing to play any role in these matters. Meanwhile, Mao had to consider whether the CPVA should remain in Korea. As discussed in chapter 3, Mao discussed this issue with Mikoyan on September 18, 1956, and with Yudin on November 30, 1956. He asked the Soviet leaders to consider this matter and to propose a solution.[23]

Mao's hesitation about withdrawal from North Korea had much to do with the Polish and Hungarian crises. During the crises, the masses had stormed party and government office buildings, and on October 24, 1956, a disturbance had occurred in Budapest. As a result, Soviet troops were sent in to suppress the demonstrators. During the crises, Polish and Hungarian leaders had demanded that the Soviet troops be withdrawn. At first, Mao was obviously worried, believing that "this will pose a serious threat to the socialist bloc." But he soon changed his mind. On October 29, Liu Shaoqi transmitted to the Soviet leadership Mao's advice that the Soviet Union should allow the other socialist countries to enjoy greater freedoms in political, economic, and military affairs. The Soviet leaders agreed to draft a declaration of equality among the Soviet Union and the Eastern European countries, and on October 30 the declaration was accepted by the Presidium of the CPSU. Khrushchev recommended that the issue of the withdrawal of Soviet troops stationed in the socialist countries be discussed at the next meeting of the Warsaw Pact member states. But by then Mao's stance toward the Hungarian crisis had changed. He believed that there was a danger of a "capitalist restoration" in Hungary and thus he opposed the withdrawal of Soviet forces.[24] Mao's conversations with Yudin clearly reflected Mao's awkward predicament with regard to stationing troops in foreign countries.

There is very little available archival evidence about how the Soviet Union reacted to Mao's two plans to deal with the North Korean issue. According to Sergey Radchenko, who has conducted extensive research in the Russian Foreign Ministry Archives, Yudin's telegram about his conversation with Mao is available but there are no minutes of the conversation. However, it is likely that Yudin did indeed send the minutes of their conversation to the CPSU CC.[25] In Yudin's view, this conversation was both important and confidential.

On January 4, 1957, prior to Zhou Enlai's trip to the Soviet Union, the Soviet Foreign Ministry worked out its talking points with regard to the Korean problem. These talking points echoed China's opinion that, given the current situation, it was necessary for the CPVA to remain in Korea for the benefit both of the Korean people and of the entire socialist camp.[26] Soviet Foreign Minister Dmitri Shepilov reported to the CPSU CC, "In his conversation with Ambassador Yudin, Mao criticized the North Korean leadership and Kim Il-sung himself." Thus, "the Foreign Ministry hopes to discuss the Korean issue with Zhou Enlai." He stressed, "In view of the current situation on the Korean Peninsula, it is imperative that the CPVA remain in the DPRK."[27]

It seems that the Soviet Foreign Ministry was unaware of the entire content and intention of Mao's conversation with Yudin. From the perspective of the Soviet Foreign Ministry, it hoped that, in deciding whether the CPVA should remain or should withdraw from Korea, China would take the interests of the entire situation into account. From the presently available documentation, we can conclude that the CPSU CC never directly replied to Mao's proposal. This indicates that the Soviet leaders were very cautious about this issue and did not support the CCP's strong measures to remove Kim Il-sung.

There are at least three reasons why the CPSU took a more conservative approach. First, although Kim Il-sung had made many mistakes, in the CPSU's view, Kim had not betrayed the revolution. Second, North Korea was now actively leaning toward Moscow, which was conducive to the consolidation of the CPSU's weakened political position after the Twentieth Congress of the CPSU. Third, although he remained reticent about this, Khrushchev resented Liu Shaoqi's and Zhou Enlai's criticisms of the Soviet Union's great power chauvinism.[28] Even though the CCP had criticized the CPSU for interfering in the internal affairs of other countries, it had committed the same offense with respect to North Korea, Vietnam, and Mongolia.[29] Without support from the Soviet Union, the CCP had to reconsider its policy toward North Korea.

On January 9, 1957, during a trip to the Soviet Union, Zhou Enlai and Khrushchev discussed the issue of the withdrawal of the CPVA troops from North Korea. Zhou also raised the possibility of a Soviet withdrawal from East Germany. Khrushchev indicated that a Soviet withdrawal from East Germany would depend on the timing and the occasion, but nevertheless he advocated a Chinese withdrawal from Korea. It is important to point out that Zhou did not at this time propose a unilateral withdrawal of Chinese troops from Korea, and Khrushchev was only consenting to Zhou's proposal for a simultaneous withdrawal of both Chinese and American troops from the Korean Peninsula.[30]

The January 1957 proposal by the CCP CC to withdraw Chinese forces from Korea had much to do with the international censure that Moscow had incurred after its suppression of the Hungarian uprising, as well as the uneasiness and anxiety that existed in the socialist bloc at the time. Beijing wanted to avoid Moscow's mistakes and to use its withdrawal from North

Korea to encourage a Soviet withdrawal from the German Democratic Republic.[31]

In his January 1957 talk with Zhou Enlai, Khrushchev avoided the main issue in Mao's conversation with Yudin and did not attempt to persuade the CPVA to remain in Korea. This indicated that Moscow was not supportive of Beijing's "active measures" to deal with the North Koreans. Mao thus had to alter his policy toward North Korea accordingly.

The Anti-Rightist Campaign in the summer of 1957 was probably an important factor in forcing both the CCP and Mao to completely alter Chinese policy toward North Korea. When renowned members of the democratic parties and leading intellectuals raised sharp criticisms of "CCP leadership and the socialist road," workers went on strike, peasants left the people's communes, and college students and veterans took to the streets. Mao was thus seriously worried that a Hungarian-type counterrevolutionary incident could occur in China. He suddenly made an abrupt U-turn and called for the entire party to engage in the anti-rightist struggle.[32] Domestic political developments in China required support from the fraternal parties. By this point, Mao was no longer amenable to taking tough measures against North Korea. The clouds over Sino–North Korean relations were dissipating.

When meeting with newly appointed North Korean Ambassador Yi Yŏng-ho on June 21, 1957, Mao said, "Our socialist countries should unite more closely. Socialist countries led by the Soviet Union should unite more closely to fight against our common enemy. . . . We will continue our cooperation with Korea to strengthen our unity." Yi Yŏng-ho reported to Mao that the KWP was studying Mao's report on how to correctly handle contradictions among the people.[33] On August 13, Mao Zedong, Liu Shaoqi, and Zhou Enlai jointly cabled the North Korean leaders, congratulating them on the twelfth anniversary of Korean liberation and expressing their hope that "the indestructible and fraternal Sino–Korean relationship will be consolidated and develop day by day."[34] On August 23, North Korea responded positively. Foreign Minister Nam Il told Soviet Ambassador Puzanov, "I will personally take steps to establish cordial, frank, and comradely relations with Chinese Ambassador Qiao Xiaoguang."[35]

According to internal reports by the Xinhua News Agency, relations between the CPVA and the North Korean government and people were very tense. Some CPVA officers and soldiers behaved rather poorly toward both North Korean officials and ordinary people. There were many cases of illegal CPVA detentions and interrogations of high-ranking Korean officials, including Nam Il, Pang Hak-se, Pak Chŏng-ae, as well as of ordinary people, and Korean women were reportedly raped by CPVA officers and soldiers. The DPRK government and people gradually came to view the CPVA as an occupation force, violating North Korean sovereignty and thus no longer welcome.[36] This definitely undermined China's image and became yet another reason for Mao to withdraw Chinese forces from North Korea.

But Mao waited until he felt that it was necessary to improve relations with North Korea. When he met with Kim Il-sung, Nam Il, and Kim Ch'ang-man on November 9, 1957, at the Moscow Conference, he told Kim Il-sung that he would withdraw all Chinese forces.[37] At first, Kim was taken aback, but at their second meeting he thanked Mao for his decision, stating that this would put pressure on the United States to follow suit in South Korea. China and North Korea then reached an agreement that the North Korean government would first issue a statement demanding that all foreign forces be withdrawn from the Korean Peninsula. China would then unilaterally withdraw its troops.[38]

According to the Russian archives, Mao discussed two issues with Kim Il-sung: the withdrawal of the CPVA and the Korean political refugees in China. In discussing the reasons for withdrawing Chinese troops, Mao referred to the economic issues—that is, the burden of providing logistical support to the CPVA. Mao also stressed that such an action might force the United States to withdraw its two divisions from South Korea. He believed that North Korea was strong enough to defend itself on its own because it "has a stable border and an army of 300,000 strong." Regarding the North Korean political refugees in China, Mao suggested that, during Kim's trip to Vietnam via Beijing, he meet with them in Beijing and "grant them amnesty." Mao promised that China would never use these people to oppose the DPRK. Finally, Mao said that the Chinese government would send Zhou Enlai to visit North Korea, and he asked Kim whether Mao himself might be welcomed to North Korea.[39]

After the North Korean delegation returned home, Korean leaders on numerous occasions reiterated that Mao Zedong had apologized for sending Peng Dehuai and Anastas Mikoyan to interfere in Korea's internal affairs in September 1956. At a meeting of about 150 cadres on November 28, Kim Ch'ang-man said, "Comrade Mao Zedong apologized several times for the CCP's unjustifiable interference in KWP affairs in September 1956."

Kim Ch'ang-man revealed that, after meeting with Mao, Peng Dehuai also visited Kim Il-sung. Peng, too, apologized for the "September affair" and the misconduct by the CPVA.[40] It appears that the essence of Mao's November 1957 talk with Kim Il-sung in Moscow was to apologize to him and to the KWP. The purpose of China's unilateral decision to withdraw was to demonstrate that China would no longer interfere in North Korea's internal affairs. But Mao was unwilling to admit his mistakes in front of the Soviets. Thus, the Chinese excuses for withdrawal included the so-called economic burden, the attempt to force the United States to withdraw from South Korea, and China's trust in North Korea's capacity for self-defense.

In its open announcement, the Chinese government stated that its reason and motivation for withdrawing from North Korea was to force an American withdrawal from South Korea so as to promote peace on the Korean Peninsula and to relax tensions in the Far East and the world.[41] China's decision to withdraw from North Korea surprised even the U.S. government. According to the U.S. State Department's Division of Research and Analysis for the Far East, the purpose of China's withdrawal was to assist Moscow in its propaganda campaign, to demonstrate China's peaceful posture, to influence the elections in South Korea, and to transform China's image from that of an "aggressor."[42] But the State Department failed to consider the Chinese withdrawal from the perspective of Sino-North Korean relations.

South Korean scholars have published widely on China's motives to withdraw in 1957. They offer various perspectives: China withdrew to relieve itself of an economic burden, to respond to Kim Il-sung's persistence in urging a withdrawal, to focus on the Great Leap Forward at home, to provide economic rather than military aid to North Korea, or to pressure the Soviet Union to withdraw from Eastern Europe.[43] The official Chinese history argues that Mao offered to withdraw because the situation in Korea had stabilized and the KPA was already much stronger. Thus, it was no longer necessary for the Chinese troops to remain.[44] One Russian scholar contends that China was unwilling to be "bound hand and foot" by the political responsibility of "jointly fighting against possible U.S. aggression."[45]

By December 1957, North Korea and China had agreed to the "Plan for the CPVA to Withdraw from the DPRK." The withdrawal would take place in a number of steps. First, the North Korean government would issue a statement calling for the withdrawal of the UN forces and the CPVA from Korea. The two Koreas would hold consultations on the basis of equality, and a free election would be held in Korea under the supervision of the neutral countries. Second, the Chinese government would issue a statement supporting the proposal by the North Korean government. The Chinese government would then formally announce that it was willing to negotiate with the North Korean government on the timing and steps for a withdrawal, and it would ask that the UN forces do the same. Third, the Soviet government would issue a declaration in support of the North Korean and Chinese statements and would propose the convening of a conference of the concerned countries to peacefully resolve the issue. According to the Chinese plan, the CPVA would withdraw from Korea in three groups: a first group in March and April 1958; a second group in July, August, and September 1958; and third group by the end of 1958.[46]

The Chinese withdrawal was carried out accordingly. On January 8, 1958, Zhou Enlai notified the Soviet ambassador of China's withdrawal plan.[47] On January 16, the Soviet Foreign Ministry replied that it was a wise plan.[48] Therefore, on February 5 the North Korean government issued a statement calling for the withdrawal of both Chinese and American forces from North and South Korea, the holding of free elections, and the peaceful reunification of North and South Korea. On February 7, the Chinese government issued its own statement in response to the North Korean statement. China stated that it was prepared to negotiate with the Koreans and to withdraw its troops. It also called on the United States and the other countries to withdraw their troops from South Korea. Shortly thereafter, the Soviet Union issued a statement in support of this formula.[49]

On February 14, Zhou Enlai led a Chinese delegation to North Korea to discuss the specifics of the withdrawal. The two sides agreed that, between March 1958 and the end of the year, the remaining Chinese troops would depart from Korea in three groups. They also issued a joint statement emphasizing that the Koreans should resolve the Korean problem on their own, without foreign interference. The first group of six divisions, totaling 80,000 men, departed from Korea between March 15 and April 25; the second group of six divisions and other special troops, totaling 100,000 men, departed between July 11 and August 14; and the third group, totaling 70,000 men, including the headquarters, three divisions, and the logistics troops, departed between September 25 and October 26. Despite its departure, the CPVA left all of its camps, arms and equipment, and other supplies to the KPA.[50]

Figure 4.1 Kim Il-sung at the farewell party for the Chinese People's Volunteers, October 1958.

After eight years in Korea, the CPVA had finally returned home. This undoubtedly boosted Sino–North Korean friendship. At a send-off banquet, Kim Il-sung said, "The Korean people will always side with the Chinese people in the struggle against aggression." Throughout October, North Korea engaged in Korean–Chinese friendship activities, and a North Korean-Chinese Friendship Association was established. During his November visit to China, Kim Il-sung told Mao Zedong that about 6.8 million Koreans had signed a thank-you letter to the CPVA.[51]

The Tragic Fate of the Yan'an Faction Cadres

The main reason for the unexpected deterioration in Sino-North Korean relations in late 1956 was the issue of how to deal with the KWP cadres who had opposed Kim Il-sung and had fled to China. Mao strongly censured Kim and sent Peng Dehuai to Pyongyang in an attempt to force Kim

to revoke his decision against these cadres. But after Mao decided to tolerate Kim and to adopt a friendly policy toward North Korea, his attitude
toward these runaway Korean cadres gradually changed. Scholars of Sino-
North Korean relations have followed their fate after they fled to China.
Due to the scarcity of historical documentation, however, very little is
known about this piece of history. Based on Shen Zhihua's interviews with
three survivors, documents in the Jilin and Sichuan archives,[52] and frag-
ments of information from the Russian archives, we here attempt to provide the contours of the experiences of the Korean cadres who fled to
China.

As reported in chapter 3, on August 30, 1956, Yun Kong-hŭm, Sŏ Hwi,
Yi P'il-gyu, and Kim Kang entered China from Andong (Dandong) in a
military vehicle. The Chinese border guards were suspicious of their identities, and after reporting to the higher authorities, they immediately
escorted the three to Beijing. Zhou Enlai and Minister of Public Security
Luo Ruiqing received them and listened to their account of what had
occurred.

After the August incident, due to pressures from China and the Soviet
Union, Kim Il-sung did not take immediate action against these opposition cadres, but many within the KWP still felt insecure. Some Yan'an faction cadres sought political asylum at the Chinese Embassy in North
Korea. In principle, the Chinese Embassy permitted them to return to
China, but it did not offer them asylum in the embassy compound. Seventeen Yan'an faction cadres escaped to China on their own. This group
included Hong Sun-kwan (deputy chairman of the Pyongyang Municipal
KWP Committee), Kim Ch'ung-sik (director of the Organization Depart-
ment of the Pyongyang Municipal KWP Committee), Hong Kwang
(member of the KWP committee of Kim Il-sung University), Han Kyŏng
(member of the KWP committee of the General Federation of Trade
Unions), Yang Il-p'yŏng (chairman of the KWP committee of the KPA
General Hospital), Yi Khi-sang (chairman of the KWP committee in the
North Korean Embassy in the Soviet Union), and Kim Chun-kŭn and Yi
Hŭi-sang (staff members in the North Korean Embassy in the Soviet
Union).[53] With the exception of a few (such as Kim Kwang-hyŏp and Im
Ch'un-ch'u) who threw themselves into the lap of Kim Il-sung, the Yan'an
faction cadres who remained in North Korea were purged. Pak Il-u and
Kim Ung were placed under house arrest and Bang Ho-san was secretly
executed.

The Chinese government initially provided these cadres with privileged treatment. They were assigned to upscale apartments in Jilin and on October 1, 1956, they were invited to review the annual National Day celebration parade from the gates of the Forbidden City overlooking Tiananmen Square. They each received a monthly stipend of either 200 renminbi (for those who ranked at or above the provincial or ministerial levels) or 150 renminbi (for those who ranked below the provincial or ministerial levels). An additional 50 renminbi was provided to those who were accompanied by family members. These stipends were about five to six times the salary of ordinary Chinese government workers at the time. The CCP did not assign the cadres jobs; instead, they were sent to study at the Central Party School in Beijing. However, these good times ended very quickly.

After the Polish and Hungarian crises, Mao began to have misgivings about the new Soviet policy that downplayed class struggle and emphasized détente with the United States. Mao further questioned the Soviet Union's capability to lead the socialist bloc. Sino–Soviet discord deepened, especially after the November 1957 Moscow Conference.[54] Consequently, in pursuing its own self-interest, the CCP exercised great restraint toward the North Korean government. It therefore became less sympathetic to the Yan'an faction cadres in exile.

According to Chinese local documents, on March 4, 1957, Kim Ch'ung-sik, who was then residing in Jilin, wrote to Wu De, first secretary of the CCP Jilin Provincial Committee, stating that he wanted to submit materials about himself and the KWP to the CCP CC and the CPSU CC. He expressed a wish to go to Beijing to submit these materials in person.[55] Had he made the request several months earlier, the CCP probably would have chauffeured him to Beijing and would have accepted his materials with great interest. But the situation had already changed and the CCP was no longer interested. At a meeting with Fu Zhensheng, a secretary of the CCP Jilin Provincial Committee, Kim Ch'ung-sik was chastised: "The way you came to China was neither legal nor normal. We asked that you return to your own country, but you insisted on remaining here. We had no choice but to allow you to stay. . . . The CCP and the KWP have always been friendly to each other. China refuses to interfere in the internal affairs of its fraternal parties and countries." Finally, Fu Zhensheng conveyed a message from the CCP CC that advised Kim Ch'ung-sik to avoid any contacts with the Koreans in China or with local Chinese-Koreans and not to discuss Korea-related issues with anyone.[56]

On April 26, 1957, the North Korea consulate in Changchun issued the following instructions to the Jilin Provincial Foreign Affairs Office: "Kim Chun-kŭn and Yi Hŭi-sang, both former staff members of the North Korean Embassy in Moscow, have fled to China and now reside in Changchun. They have been stripped of their diplomatic status. The consulate has received instructions from higher authorities to confiscate their passports. Please assist us in accomplishing this task and notify us about their activities after they arrived in Changchun." Jilin province asked for instructions from the International Liaison Department (ILD) of the CCP CC.[57]

We have not found the response from the ILD, but we have found that, on June 28, Kim Chun-kŭn and Yi Hŭi-sang wrote to the CCP CC to express their wish to attend regular party activities and study sessions because they anticipated that they would be remaining in China for an extended period of time. On July 9, the ILD asked the CCP Jilin Provincial Committee to inform them that the CCP did not have any suitable activities for them. As far as self-study was concerned, the ILD entrusted the CCP Jilin Provincial Committee with the task of assigning suitable comrades to assist them.[58]

As the CCP's attitude toward the KWP and the August incident changed and Sino–North Korean relations improved, the fate of these runaway cadres further deteriorated. After returning from a trip to North Korea on February 21, 1958, Zhou Enlai told cadres in Liaoning province, "Sŏ Hwi and Yi P'il-gyu are really bad. Not only do they oppose the KWP but they are opposed to the CCP and the CPSU as well. They consider China, the Soviet Union, and the DPRK to be authoritarian regimes." Zhou also said that those who had fled from North Korea to China were one-sided and the biased information that they had provided had misled the Chinese. Zhou then spoke about Kim Il-sung. He noted that Kim Il-sung had been selected by the Soviets. "Although he is not an ideal leader, he was chosen to be the 'general.' If we do not trust him, it will be detrimental to Sino–North Korean friendship and it will also have a negative effect on Sino–Soviet friendship and solidarity."[59]

The CCP soon decided to banish the runaway North Korean cadres to the southwest provinces, far away from the Sino–North Korean border. On February 12, the ILD cabled the CCP Sichuan Provincial Committee: "The CCP Central Committee has decided to arrange for four senior runaway KWP cadres to settle in Chengdu. The CCP Sichuan Provincial Committee should take care of their daily lives." Sichuan province thereupon located a private residence on Wenmiao Front Street in Chengdu, with quiet and pleasant surroundings and fully furnished rooms. A cook, a waiter, and one or two staff persons were assigned to take care of them.[60] On April 23, the ILD accepted Sichuan's arrangements and noted that the ILD would cover all their expenses. Sichuan province would arrange study sessions for them, but they would not be required to attend. The ILD further instructed, "Do not make any promises regarding their applications to become naturalized Chinese citizens. In principle, they should be treated as foreign guests. They may participate in the celebrations on International Labor Day [May 1] and China's National Day [October 1], but please do not invite them to the VIP observation deck to observe such activities."[61]

In July 1958, Yun Kong-hŭm and three other cadres were resettled in Chengdu. Several other cadres were resettled in Taiyuan, Shanxi province. On September 8, the ILD further instructed, "Those who want to work should be assigned to general clerical posts in state-owned enterprises or administrative units, not in party or government organizations." They should use false names and they must obey the three pledges to which they had signed their names: "Do not get in touch with any Koreans who travel to our country; do not write or send letters to the DPRK; and do not talk to any Chinese about Korean internal affairs." They were not to be granted Chinese citizenship or party membership, but they would be permitted to marry.[62]

The United Front Department of the CCP Sichuan Provincial Committee consulted with the North Korean cadres and on December 7 reported that Yun Kong-hŭm had been assigned to work for a local produce corporation under the provincial commerce department, Kim Kang had been assigned to work at the Sichuan People's Theater under the provincial culture department, and Yi P'il-gyu had been assigned to work at Chengdu Red Flag Iron Works. They all used assumed names, were treated as Chinese-Koreans, and continued to receive a 200 renminbi monthly stipend. Because of poor behavior, Sŏ Hwi was not assigned a job. Whenever Kim Il-sung visited China, the cadres' activities were closely monitored and they were not allowed to leave the city. Sŏ Hwi was extremely unhappy about the improvement in Sino-North Korean relations, whereas Yun Kong-hŭm welcomed the change.[63]

In the early 1960s, as Sino–Soviet relations were on the verge of collapsing, the CCP expressed its friendship with North Korea. When Mao met with Kim Il-sung in July 1961, he blamed Peng Dehuai, who had been purged at the Lushan Conference in August 1959, for China's intervention in the KWP's internal affairs in 1956. Mao attacked the Yan'an faction cadres, stating, "Gao Gang and Peng Dehuai are Khrushchev's men. Peng Dehuai only trusted Pak Il-u. Yi Sang-jo always spoke ill of you to Li Kenong. . . . In 1956, they schemed to split with you."[64] At a June 1962 meeting with Pak Kŭm-ch'ŏl, head of the delegation from the DPRK's Supreme People's Assembly, Mao accused Peng Dehuai of secretly colluding with Kim Tu-bong.[65] Consequently, those North Korean cadres who had opposed Kim Il-sung were subject to even more difficult conditions in China. The Chinese government decided to strip them of their privileged treatment. CCP documents no longer referred to them as "Korean runaway cadres" but rather as "Korean antiparty factionalists."

In April 1962, the ILD proposed new measures for handling these cadres: "It is suggested that the North Korean antiparty factionalists and their family members should be turned over to the jurisdiction of the public security organs." They were divided into several groups. First, since Sŏ Hwi, Hong Sun-kwan, Kim Ch'ung-sik, Yi Kyu-ch'ŏl, Pak Hyŏn, and Kim Chun-kŭn had already committed crimes, their cases were to be decided in accordance with the law. They would be supervised and controlled by the public security organs and sent to state-run farms in outlying provinces to engage in suitable work. They were to be given the same material benefits as other cadres at the state farms, but their family members would not be allowed to accompany them. Second, Yun Kong-hŭm and Kim Chŏng-nyong, who had exhibited better behavior, were to be treated as foreign nationals residing in China. Their living arrangements would be taken care of by the Red Cross, but they would be monitored internally by the public security organs. There were to be no changes to their living benefits. Third, it was necessary to reexamine Yi P'il-gyu and six other people, and their cases were to be handled in accordance with the previous two situations.[66]

In the end, six people, including Sŏ Hwi and Hong Sun-kwan, were arrested and sentenced to prison. Sŏ Hwi, who had attempted to escape to the Soviet Union but was caught in front of the Soviet Embassy in Beijing, was given the longest sentence, of five years.[67] In view of Yun Kong-hŭm's repentance, the CCP Sichuan Provincial Committee suggested that his material benefits and favorable treatment be retained. The ILD instructed, "In view of the KWP's attitude, it is no longer suitable for the CCP to take care of them. Yun Kong-hŭm should be handled in accordance with the new regulations."[68] Yun Kong-hǔm applied to return to North Korea, but in the end he was not able to make the trip. This fact contradicts the claim that the PRC extradited four former KWP CC members in 1962.[69] Chinese leaders promptly relayed to North Korean Ambassador Han Ik-su its new policies toward these North Korean "defectors". Very satisfied, Han stated, "We should deal with these factionalists with a resolute attitude, careful education, and serious punishment." In reference to the CCP's attitude and stance toward the August incident, Han said, "Comrade Kim Il-sung often speaks of it, believing that the CCP did a great job."[70]

The Great Leap Forward and the Ch'ŏllima Movement

After Mao's apology to Kim Il-sung in November 1957, Sino-North Korean relations gradually improved. Mao praised Kim for signing the Moscow Declaration and for insisting on upholding anti-imperialism, socialism, and proletarian internationalism. Mao also said that, despite their good intentions, it had not been a good move for the Soviets and the Chinese to interfere in North Korea's domestic affairs and that this bad move had led to bad results. On March 9, 1958, *Renmin ribao* published excerpts from Pak Kǔm-ch'ŏl's KWP Congress speech, in which one long paragraph was devoted to criticizing Ch'oe Ch'ang-ik and Pak Ch'ang-ok, who were mentioned by name and branded as an "antiparty faction."[71]

Since the CCP was no longer sympathetic to the Yan'an faction, Kim did not hesitate to punish the opposition leaders. After returning to Korea from Moscow, Kim took immediate action to further purge his opponents within the KWP, including those cadres with Yan'an connections as well as other leaders who were dissatisfied with Kim, such as Kim Von-bon and Cho Co-an.[72] The Chinese Embassy in Pyongyang obtained a copy of a speech written for KWP internal use. It read, "By early 1958, the DPRK had completely exposed and smashed those anti–Korea and anti-KWP factionalists and had further eliminated the poisonous legacy of Ch'oe Ch'ang-ik, Pak Ch'ang-ok, Yun Kong-hǔm, Kim Sǔng-hwa, Sǒ Hwi, Yi P'il-gyu, and other anti-KWP factionalists." In referring to international relations, the speech used the phrase "the socialist camp led by the Soviet Union and China," and it praised China for its unmistakable strength and tremendous role in resolving international conflicts.[73]

Kim Il-sung greatly benefited personally from the withdrawal of the CPVA and Mao's policy of mollification. After purging various domestic opponents, Kim reached the pinnacle of power and his personality cult was revived. Unlike Stalin, who was fond of dominating and controlling the countries along the Soviet periphery, Mao believed that winning North Korea's friendship was more important than physically controlling it. He thus granted North Korea full independence and freedom, hoping to make Kim into a true friend through a policy of mollification. Kim was thus able to establish complete control over North Korea. Kim's consolidation of power was also a result of domestic politics in North Korea.

Under such circumstances, China and North Korea began the year of 1958 hand in hand. During this year, China embarked on the Great Leap Forward and the People's Commune movement,[74] and the DPRK accelerated its Ch'ŏllima movement.[75] On June 11, Kim Il-sung asserted, "All of the workers are, upon the call of the Party, riding a flying horse [ch'ŏllima] running forward to socialism."[76] On June 13, *Rodong sinmun* (Workers' Newspaper) published a front-page article entitled "To March Riding a Flying Horse!"[77] Before the Korean government delegation led by Yi Chu-yŏn departed to China on August 3, Kim instructed, "Carefully learn and study the Chinese experiences and bring them back to Korea." While in China, the delegation visited more than one hundred enterprises and work units. They believed that North Korea should imitate many Chinese practices, such as cadres engaging in manual farm labor, work-study programs, school-run factories, and education combined with production and labor. Very impressed, they felt that "China's Great Leap Forward not only will determine China's fate but also the future of the world as well."[78]

North Korean newspapers proposed the slogan "Steel and Machines are the Kings of Industry." Like China, North Korea launched a public hygiene campaign to eliminate four pests (mice, sparrows, flies, and mosquitoes) and schistosomiasis. It also began a small-scale steel-making project. In rural areas, it instituted a policy of merging the cooperatives and operating mess halls. Similar to China's People's Commune movement, the North Korean cooperatives became entities comprising agriculture, industry, commerce, schools, banks, and hospitals. The North Korean media claimed that the rural cooperatives represented the transition from collective ownership to public ownership and constituted the sprouts of communism.[79] During his visit to China in November 1958, Kim told Mao, "We want to consolidate the cooperatives. Although we do not use the term 'people's

Figure 4.2 Zhou Enlai entertains Kim Il-sung during Kim's visit to China in November 1958.

communes,' we have taken measures to merge the cooperatives. . . . We have merged fifteen thousand cooperatives into 3,873 cooperatives. Thus we have achieved the integration of villages and cooperatives." Mao responded approvingly, "This represents the unity of the government and the cooperatives."[80]

To learn from China's practice of "every citizen a soldier," the DPRK established Red Guard units in cities, in factories and mines, and in rural areas. Kim Il-sung called on all people to "continue to work very hard for one to two years. . . . Communist society is not far away. . . . We can achieve it within four or five years."[81] The Great Leap Forward appeared to have had an influence on Kim and his supporters. In the fall of 1958, Kim began to talk about catching up with Japan in industrial production in the same fashion that Mao spoke about overtaking Great Britain.[82] In contrast, the Great Leap Forward and the People's Commune movement did not receive much praise from the socialist bloc. Kim Il-sung was the only one who sang its praises and attempted to imitate Chinese practices.

Mao thus began to view Kim in a new light. On February 13, 1959, Mao added a remark to foreign affairs material prepared by the Foreign Affairs Office of the State Council, "In the past, some comrades paid more attention to the shortcomings, not the achievements, of the Korean comrades. They committed the mistake of taking a one-sided view of things."[83]

As Sino-North Korean relations improved, China greatly increased its aid to the DPRK. During his visit to North Korea in February 1958, Zhou Enlai promised to supply Pyongyang with 10,000 tons of cotton annually, and he inquired about the amount of coke that the DPRK needed. Zhou proposed that the CPVA would help the KPA build fortifications and would jointly build the Yunfeng (Unbong) hydroelectric power station. Kim Il-sung said that, according to Japanese studies, it would be possible to build three hydroelectric power stations along the Yalu River. After returning to China, Zhou instructed the Foreign Ministry to work on these plans.[84] Pyongyang was very encouraged by Zhou's attitude. In early June, the DPRK asked China to build a textile factory and two paper mills. China soon agreed to this new request.[85]

On August 3, a Korean government delegation visited Beijing to negotiate the terms for the provision of industrial equipment and for the signing of a long-term trade agreement. According to the 1959-1962 trade agreement, China would supply North Korea with coal, cotton, tires, cotton yarn, compressed steel, ferromanganese, sulfur, paraffin wax, and gypsum. The negotiations also touched on much wider substantive areas. As a *Renmin ribao* article noted, "The Sino-Korean economic relationship has entered a period of long-term cooperation."[86]

During the period of the DPRK's Three-Year Plan, China mainly supplied consumer goods to North Korea. In contrast, during the period of the DPRK's Five-Year Plan, China provided industrial equipment and materials.[87] On October 18, China and North Korea signed an agreement to establish a science and technology commission, which would include the exchange of blueprints, reference materials, samples, specialists, trainees, and mutual trust for technical appraisals.[88] On October 26, the CCP CC approved a report by Foreign Minister Chen Yi and State Planning Commission Chairman Li Fuchun on strengthening foreign economic aid. The report proposed that the Ministry of Commerce should place priority on the provision of goods and the Ministry of Transportation should make it a priority that such goods be transported. All of the foreign aid projects were to be listed as priority projects in related units and in provincial and municipal governments.[89] Kim Il-sung told the Chinese that he was very grateful.[90]

On November 22, 1958, after a four-year hiatus, Kim Il-sung visited China and received a very warm welcome. A *Renmin ribao* editorial described Sino–DPRK relations "as close as lips to teeth, sharing together danger and safety, brotherly affection, and bound by a common cause."[91] During their conversation, Mao told Kim, "We affirm the correct line of the Korean Workers' Party. Our policy is comprised of three 'respects': to respect the Korean nation, to respect the Korean party, and to respect the Korean leaders." Kim was very pleased and responded, "The Sino–Korean relationship is exceptional. Many Korean cadres have visited China and have grown under the guidance of the CCP." Both sides expressed a hope to enhance mutual visits and within several years to enter Communist society hand in hand. In a discussion of economic issues, Kim noted that Korea was short of raw materials, especially cotton and coke. Mao immediately responded that China would supply as much cotton as the DPRK needed. Zhou Enlai added that China would also provide the 1 million tons of coke that Pyongyang had requested.[92]

The North Korean leaders and media spoke highly of Kim's visit, stating that it elevated Sino–North Korean relations to a new level.[93] Additionally, the visit also consolidated and strengthened Kim's indisputable leadership position at the March 1958 First Party Conference. At the conference, Kim Tu-bong, chairman of the Presidium of the Supreme People's Assembly and nominal head of state of the DPRK, was purged.[94] Balázs Szalontai notes, "His [Kim Tu-bong's] downfall indicated that Kim Il-sung no longer felt constrained by the potential disapproval of Beijing and Moscow."[95] Indeed, by the time the CPVA departed North Korea in October 1958, there was no group of people capable of challenging Kim and his partisans. As Robert Scalapino and Chong-Sik Lee write, "The central trend of the period was the enhancement of Kim, the Leader, to a point beyond the reach of mortal man. The cult of Stalin in its most excessive phases was now equaled."[96]

Meanwhile, North Korea also asked the Soviet Union for additional aid, in particular for the equipment and material that China was unable to provide. When Pyongyang asked Moscow for 5,000-ton-capacity punch presses, 1,300 to 1,400 tons of stainless steel, and parts and material to manufacture heavy-duty trucks, the Soviet ambassador awkwardly responded that the Soviet Union could supply only one-tenth of the stainless steel that Pyongyang had requested. Kim Il-sung then wrote to Khrushchev personally to request help. Kim's letter thanked "the Soviet government for having spared no effort to satisfy Korea's needs." Kim pointed out that the requested products, such as machines, equipment, materials, and, in particular, stainless steel, tractors, bulldozers, excavators, and motor vehicles, were important for the DPRK's national economic development.[97]

In order to receive more aid from the Soviet Union, the DPRK changed its political attitude toward the Soviet Union. At the Twenty-First Congress of the CPSU in January 1959, Khrushchev implicitly criticized China's economic policy.[98] Kim Il-sung, who was present at the Congress, said that Khrushchev's report was profound and that "we find the answers in Khrushchev's report regarding how best and most efficiently to construct socialism and communism in our country." In his remarks to the Congress, Kim stated emphatically that the DPRK had always been learning "from the rich experience of Soviet collectivization."[99] During their conversations, Kim accepted the Soviet leaders' criticism of Korean economic policies. Khrushchev thus agreed to offer the DPRK more aid.[100] On March 17, the Soviet Union and the DPRK signed a new economic cooperation agreement. According to the agreement, the Soviet Union would provide North Korea with industrial equipment and technical aid worth 500 million rubles ($125 million) and would assist North Korea to build a power station, a chemical factory, flax mills, woolen mills, and an expanded Kim Ch'aek iron factory and Pyongyang silk mills.[101]

Because of the intensive domestic mobilization and massive foreign aid, from 1958 to 1959 North Korea was able to achieve a breakthrough in economic development. According to the Korean Central Statistics Bureau, between 1957 and 1958 the total value of industrial output increased by 40 percent. This was twice the value in 1956 and four times the value in 1949. The value of grain output reached 3.7 million tons, which was 12 percent more than planned. Basic construction investment was 34.1 billion won, an increase of 26 percent from the previous year. The total value of industrial output in the first season of 1959 increased 75 percent over that during the same period of 1958, and 7 percent over that during the fourth quarter of 1958. On May 8, 1958, the KWP Standing Committee announced that the Five-Year Plan would be completed by August 15, 1959, two years ahead of schedule.[102] The rejoicing North Korean leaders announced that per capita industrial and grain output would surpass that of socialist

Czechoslovakia and capitalist Japan. North Korea was "mounting a flying horse to march to the socialist pinnacle."[103]

China and North Korea Marching Hand in Hand on the "Communist Road"

During the Great Leap Forward, China's rhetoric and efforts to enter Communist society had important effects on North Korea. At the Second Plenary Session of the Eighth Congress of the CCP on May 17, 1958, Mao said, "We do not raise the slogan of 'cadres decide everything' and 'technology decides everything' that Stalin put forward. Nor do we raise the slogan of 'Soviet power plus electrification equals communism' that Lenin put forward. . . . Our slogan is 'to build socialism in a fuller, quicker, and more effective way.' Is this slogan wiser? I think it is. We are students educated by the masters, and we should be wiser. The latecomers come first! In my view, communism may arrive earlier in China than in the Soviet Union."[104]

On August 29, 1958, the CCP CC passed the Resolution on the Establishment of the People's Communes in the Countryside. It stated, "It seems that the realization of communism will not be something for the remote future. We should actively use the format of the people's communes to find the path to move into communism."[105] At the Zhengzhou Conference in November, after reading Stalin's *Economic Problems of Socialism in the USSR*, Mao, Liu Shaoqi, and Deng Xiaoping discussed the issue of the transition to communist society, comparing the situation in China with that in the Soviet Union. Mao stated, "What is meant by 'completing the construction of socialism'? What is the 'transition to communism'? Definitions are needed." In referring to China, Mao stated resolutely, "Three years of hard struggle, and then twelve more years, fifteen years is the transition to communism. Don't publish that, but it won't be good if we don't do it."[106] At the Wuchang Conference on November 23, an elated Mao announced:

How much time it will take for all of China to enter communism, no one knows that now; it's hard to estimate—ten years? fifteen years?. . . For the Soviet Union forty-one years, plus twelve more . . . and that's just to prepare conditions [for entering communism]. . . . Considering it in terms of benefit to the proletariat of the whole world, perhaps it would be better if the Soviet Union entered [communism] first, . . . [and we] still [should] not enter; at least wait two or three years after the Soviet Union enters, then enter, lest [we] cause Lenin's party, the country of the October Revolution, to lose face.[107]

At the time, North Korean leaders began to imitate Chinese expressions and rhetoric. On October 10, 1958, Ch'ae Hŭi-chong, a secretary of the KWP CC, told a visiting Chinese delegation that, after achieving the grand goal of the Ch'ŏllima movement, "we can march into communism. We believe that communism is not in the distant future. We can reach communism in our generation."[108] On November 20, at a workshop for municipal and county party propagandists, Kim Il-sung pointed out, "In our view, communism is not a thing in the distant future. If we continue to struggle for four to five years, we can reach the goal."[109] On another occasion, Kim Il-sung said that the Soviet Union, China, and North Korea would be the first three countries to enter communism.[110] Kim Ch'angman, vice chairman of the KWP, stated at a meeting, "If we follow the party's instructions and work hard for another one or two years and triumphantly achieve all the tasks set by the party, we will directly enter communist society."[111] It seems that Kim Il-sung was even more anxious than Mao Zedong. Whereas the Chinese talked about the "transition" to communism, the North Koreans talked about the "entry" into communism. Whereas Mao talked about arriving at the gates of communist society ahead of the Soviet Union, Kim Il-sung hoped that North Korea would enter communist society ahead of China.

During Kim Il-sung's visit to China in November to December 1958, he discussed with Mao the issue of entry to communism. Kim told Mao, "Korea will begin its Second Five-Year Plan in 1961, and we expect to accomplish the building of socialism during this period. This is because the value of our industrial output is much greater than that of the Eastern European countries." This time, however, Mao was a bit cooler-headed and stated, "Shouldn't we adopt another method? It is better that we do not declare the building of socialism and instead that we raise the standards. . . . As for the entry to communist society, we should let the Soviet Union enter first. . . . If the Soviet Union enters within fifteen years, we can enter within twenty years or more. This will be beneficial to the unity of the world proletariat. This is an international issue."[112] Realizing his slip of the tongue, after returning home Kim Il-sung ordered

North Korean propaganda departments not to speak lightly about entry into communist society.[113]

By late 1958, Mao had become aware of the tendency to boast and to be impatient during the Great Leap Forward and the People's Commune movement. At an expanded CCP Politburo meeting in Wuchang, on November 21, Mao stated that industrial assignments, irrigation works, and grain production should be reduced appropriately.[114] Mao also said, "We said that we are powerful, but we have no real evidence. We boast too much. This is improper."[115] In reviewing the Resolution on Several Issues Regarding the People's Communes, Mao wrote, "Whether earlier or later, the transition from collective ownership to ownership by the whole people depends on the level of the development of production and the political awakening of the people."[116] Coming from peasant stock, how could Mao believe Chinese media reports that 1 *mu*, which is 1/15 hectare, would produce 10,000 *jin* (more than 11,000 pounds) of grain? Although he was unfamiliar with industry, in view of the criticism by Soviet experts in China, Mao could not turn a blind eye to this. But he trusted the strength of the masses, and reliance on the masses was the magic weapon of the CCP. Thus, when discussing propaganda work with Hu Qiaomu and Wu Lengxi, on December 6, Mao pointed out the importance of opposing boasting and exaggeration. He urged them to pay attention to three things: preventing the spread of negativism, protecting the initiative of the masses, and considering the international repercussions of propaganda work.[117]

North Korea encountered similar problems with its Ch'ŏllima movement. According to a report by the Chinese Embassy in Pyongyang, the tendency to boast and exaggerate, to issue false output reports, and to set unrealistic targets resulted in many difficulties and imbalances. North Korea's trade deficit with China hit a record high of 40 million rubles.[118] According to reports from the Hungarian Embassy in Pyongyang, because male laborers were "mobilized for urban reconstruction," by the mid-1950s "some 70 to 80 percent of the agricultural workforce" consisted of women and children. In addition to their eight-hour workdays, people also had to engage in four to five hours of unpaid work per day, not counting attending political meetings.[119] Although serious problems existed in terms of planning, funding, manpower, and raw materials, at the KWP CC Standing Committee meeting in May 1959, Kim Il-sung urged the North Korean people that "the socialist high tide should not fall . . . speed up . . . aim high . . . tighten your belts and work harder for another year."[120]

During these years, Mao and Kim shared the same ambitions and experienced the same joys, as well as setbacks. When meeting with Deputy Premier Chŏng Il-yong in June 1959, Zhou Enlai said, "We made a Great Leap Forward, and you mounted a flying horse. It is natural that we have encountered new problems with this uncommon speed of development." When Chŏng described to Zhou the difficulties that North Korea had experienced, Zhou felt an irresistible impulse to say, "Your situation is similar to ours. . . . We are fellow sufferers."[121]

As a result, China and North Korea made efforts to help each other. Whereas Beijing provided Pyongyang with all-out economic aid, Pyongyang supported China politically. After Beijing suppressed the uprising in Tibet in March 1959, there was an international anti-China high tide. According to the Chinese Foreign Ministry, by May 1959, newspapers and periodicals in more than thirty countries were vilifying China. Parties in power in the socialist countries and socialist parties in the capitalist countries generally supported Beijing's suppression of the uprising in Tibet, but they were extremely cautious. After the Sino–Indian border clashes in 1959, they avoided criticizing India or its prime minister, Jawaharlal Nehru, with the Soviet government refusing to reprint China's counterattack against India and deleting any references to "Indian expansionism" in published news items. Other parties followed suit. North Korea was the only country that openly supported China, holding India responsible for the conflict and demanding that China and India resolve the problems in accordance with China's proposals.[122]

Peng Dehuai had been commander in chief of the CPVA during the Korean War and China's minister of defense in the 1950s. After he criticized Mao's radical economic policy during the Great Leap Forward, Mao retaliated, at the Eighth Plenary Session of the Eighth CCP CC, held in Lushan in August 1959, by dismissing Peng from office. Several of Peng's sympathizers were also purged. After this session, an anti–rightist opportunist struggle was launched in China. The CPSU and the Eastern European Communist parties published news reports about these political developments in China, but they did not provide any additional commentaries. In contrast, North Korea published the entire contents of the report of the Eighth Plenary Session of the Eighth CCP CC, and *Rodong sinmun* issued a lengthy editorial entitled "Glorious Victory of the CCP's General Line," praising the militant will of the continuous leap of the Chinese people.[123]

According to the Chinese Foreign Ministry, the reports by the Soviet and Eastern European Communist countries on the Eighth Plenary Session had deleted confirmation of the success of the People's Commune movement and the anti–rightist opportunist struggle. Only North Korea, Vietnam, and Czechoslovakia issued full and positive reports. In particular, North Korean newspapers emphasized that "our country will accomplish the Five-Year Plan three years ahead of schedule," praising it as "a great leap forward" and pointing out that a "foundation of people's communes has been consolidated in our country." After receiving the Eighth Plenary Session document, Kim Il-sung told Chinese diplomats that the "anti–rightist opportunist struggle is correct. Without the anti–rightist opportunist struggle, we cannot make good progress."[124]

At a September 21 meeting with Ambassador Qiao Xiaoguang, Kim said that he hoped to visit Beijing and to meet with Chairman Mao and President Liu Shaoqi. Kim assured the ambassador that he fully supported the report of the Eighth Plenary Session of the Eighth CCP CC, the Great Leap Forward, the people's communes, and the General Line, and he opposed the rightist opportunist clique headed by Peng Dehuai. Kim said that the KWP was not surprised that Peng was antiparty. The KWP had long had problems with Peng, but it had never raised them, due to consideration of the unity of the two parties. Kim hoped to discuss this issue with the CCP CC during his trip to Beijing. Mao Zedong paid much attention to Kim's statements, and he immediately instructed that Qiao Xiaoguang's telegram be distributed as a CCP CC document.[125]

Sino-North Korean relations thus reached their first high-water mark in 1958-1959. Mao gave full support to Kim Il-sung both politically and economically, and Kim moved closer to Beijing than he was to Moscow. This was the beginning of the Sino–North Korean "special relationship" during the Cold War. But this was a new era, and Sino-North Korean relations were no longer characterized by the traditional suzerain–vassal relationship. Kim would never bow to the Chinese. As Sino-Soviet relations deteriorated, Kim found an opportunity to assert his independence and to carry out his *Juche* idea.

CHAPTER V

North Korea's Balancing Act, 1961–1965

B y late 1958, Sino–Soviet differences on domestic and foreign policy issues had been revealed in the negative Soviet attitude toward China's Great Leap Forward, the People's Commune movement, and Beijing's shelling of Jinmen. In June 1959, Nikita Khrushchev rescinded the Sino–Soviet agreement intended to assist China's nuclear weapons program. In October 1959, Chinese and Soviet leaders engaged in heated face-to-face disputes in Beijing. At the early June 1960 World Federation of Trade Unions conference in Beijing, the Chinese Communist Party (CCP) openly challenged the theories and policies of the Communist Party of the Soviet Union (CPSU) with respect to major issues in the International Communist Movement. In late June, the CPSU organized a counterattack in Bucharest. In its retaliation against the CCP's uncompromising position, the Soviet Union announced that, by September 1, 1960, it would recall all Soviet experts posted in China. Thereafter, Sino–Soviet relations drastically deteriorated and the Sino–Soviet alliance was on the verge of collapse.[1]

Obviously, in the struggle over the leading role in the International Communist Movement, both the CCP and the CPSU were attempting to win the support of the other Communist parties in the socialist bloc. Under such circumstances, both the CCP and the CPSU were eager to win political support from North Korea. Beijing and Moscow thus competed to provide Pyongyang with military and economic aid. Furthermore, because

North Korea was an Asian country and China's neighbor, it was vitally important for Beijing to have Pyongyang on its side. Kim Il-sung was adept at maintaining a delicate balance between China and the Soviet Union, extracting considerable economic assistance from each.

Sino–Soviet Competition to Win Over North Korea

Like the Three-Year Plan period, the Five-Year Plan period created a number of problems in North Korea. According to Soviet and Hungarian studies, serious economic problems existed in North Korea during the period of high-speed development from 1957 to 1959. These included major imbalances among the various industrial sectors, with electricity and fuel lagging far behind other sectors. The inferior quality of Korean industrial products and the excessive population in the cities were also problematic.[2] In order to complete the Five-Year Plan ahead of schedule, North Korea paid a huge price. As one study has suggested, "The North Koreans in 1958 lived close to a marginal subsistence level." Nonetheless, growth during the reconstruction period (1954-1959) was extremely high—36 percent per annum.[3]

The North Korean leaders were well aware of these difficulties. Before the formal announcement of completion of the Five-Year Plan, in May 1959, and without much explanation, Kim Il-sung designated 1960 as a "buffer year" for adjusting and rectifying North Korea's economic development.[4] This also was to be the year to prepare for the Second Five-Year Plan (later changed to a Seven-Year Plan).[5] North Korea thus began to search for external aid. In June 1959, it requested and received an urgent supply of 30,000 tons of wheat from the Soviet Union and a five-year extension on a 123 million ruble ($30.75 million) loan that was scheduled to mature in 1960. In February 1960, Pyongyang asked for, and received, another 50,000 tons of wheat from the Soviet Union.[6] On May 2, Kim Il-sung told Ambassador A. M. Puzanov that if Khrushchev was unable to visit Pyongyang, then Kim would like to visit Moscow. However, this time when Kim asked Puzanov for additional aid, the Kremlin balked.[7]

Kim was very disappointed when the Soviet Union hesitated to fulfill his wish to visit Moscow and postponed Khrushchev's long-planned trip to North Korea. The Soviet Union was worried that these exchanges might undermine Khrushchev's visit to the United States, scheduled for

September 1959.[8] Furthermore, Kim was extremely resentful that the Soviet Union was reluctant to offer him additional economic aid. In May 1960, when a U.S. U-2 spy plane invaded Soviet airspace and was shot down, a four-power summit of the United States, the Soviet Union, Britain, and France, which Khrushchev had initially eagerly supported, was aborted.

In the CCP's view, the U-2 incident proved that its views were correct. The CCP and Mao Zedong tried to make use of the incident to put pressure on Khrushchev to accept the CCP's worldview. Whereas Khrushchev advocated détente with the United States, Mao emphasized struggle, which was also consistent with Kim's policy toward the United States. During his secret visit to Beijing, in May 1960, Kim Il-sung supported China's political line in the Sino–Soviet polemics. Kim told Mao that the CCP's theoretical article, "Long Live Leninism—In Commemoration of Lenin's Ninetieth Birthday," which was published on April 16, 1960, was very good because it resolved many theoretical issues. The article challenged Khrushchev and the Soviet leaders on the issues of peaceful coexistence, socialist revolution, and the nature of imperialism. Kim stated that, as early as 1955, the Democratic People's Republic of Korea (DPRK) had rejected Khrushchev's suggestion not to oppose the U.S. imperialists.[9]

In a discussion of the joint Sino–Soviet interference in the internal affairs of the Korean Workers' Party (KWP) in the wake of the 1956 August incident, blame was conveniently shifted to Anastas Mikoyan and Peng Dehuai. When Kim met Deng Xiaoping on his May 1960 visit, Deng promised that China would provide North Korea with aid in the amount of 400 million renminbi during its Seven-Year Plan period. Deng also told Kim that, in the future, China would provide Pyongyang with additional cotton, since it was not economical for North Korea to grow its own cotton. In referring to China's economic construction policy, Mao stated, "We will never deviate from the General Line, the Great Leap Forward, and the people's commune." Kim responded, "In 1955, the Soviet Union said that we were moving too rapidly in our agricultural cooperativization campaign. But after reading Chairman Mao's article, we decided to continue."[10]

The Soviet Union was aware of these new developments in Sino-North Korean relations. Two weeks later, Kim was secretly invited to visit Moscow. While in Moscow from June 13 to June 18, CPSU Central Committee (CC) Secretary Frol Kozlov and Deputy Chairman of the Council of Ministers Anastas Mikoyan leaked to Kim details about the 1956

Sino–Soviet joint intervention in the August incident, placing the blame on the CCP.[11] To further upset Kim, Khrushchev ordered that Mikoyan give Kim the minutes of Mao's November 30, 1956, conversation with Ambassador Pavel Yudin. In that conversation Mao had stated that it was possible that Kim might betray the revolution and degenerate into a Tito or Nagy type of traitor.

Enraged by this revelation, Kim declared that the KWP would always stand by the CPSU on major policy issues. After returning to Pyongyang, Kim severely criticized Mao at the July plenum of the KWP. He said that China's policy aimed to "turn Korea into a Chinese colony." He also said that he would never trust the Chinese or visit China again.[12] Nevertheless, Kim did not want a complete rupture with China. In private, the North Korean leaders assured Moscow that they would never repeat China's mistakes and that they would remain on guard against China.[13] But Pyongyang did not publicly censure China.

In July 1960, Moscow rewarded Kim by sending a letter confirming a continuation of the flow of wheat, cotton, and loans to North Korea. Khrushchev also promised to visit North Korea in September. Kim was very excited about this news and seemed to be grateful to the Soviets. When Ambassador Puzanov handed the North Korean leader a copy of the USSR note on the withdrawal of the Soviet experts from China, Kim expressed indignation about China's "unfair treatment" of the Soviet experts. On several occasions, he described the Chinese leaders as a "cabal."[14] In August, a DPRK delegation arrived in Moscow to sign an agreement whereby the Soviet Union would relieve Pyongyang from paying back 760 million rubles ($190 million) in military loans and would allow a moratorium on its economic loan of 140 million rubles ($35 million). Kim excitedly stated, "This is free aid in the amount of 900 million rubles ($225 million)."[15]

Beijing was watching closely. The Chinese Embassy in North Korea reported that the North Korean leaders' recent speeches and media reports "highlighted the Soviet Union and put down China. . . . [They] only mention China's achievements in domestic construction without touching on China's foreign policies and international role. They have even proposed the slogan of 'thoroughly opposing dogmatism.'"[16] This perception was accurate. In a July 2 report, Hungarian Ambassador Karoly Prath noted that with respect to domestic and foreign political issues, "the DPRK completely shares the position of the Soviet Union."[17]

To prevent the DPRK from leaning completely to Moscow, China had to do more. Thus, it voluntarily offered to increase its aid to North Korea, even though it was experiencing its own extremely difficult economic situation in the wake of the Great Leap Forward. A North Korean economic delegation was invited to visit China in October. On September 10, the Chinese Foreign Ministry issued a propaganda notice requesting that *Renmin ribao* (People's Daily) and the Hong Kong-based pro-Communist China newspaper *Ta Kung Pao* publish some welcoming editorials. During the North Koreans' visit to China, newspapers were instructed to publish many news articles and photos on the economic achievements in North Korea.[18] On September 17, the Chinese Embassy in Moscow reported that the Soviet Union had agreed to cancel the military debt North Korea had incurred during the Korean War—a total of 700 million rubles ($175 million).[19] This news further upset Chinese leaders.

After negotiating for more than a month, China and North Korea signed a loan agreement to provide equipment as well as technical aid.[20] On October 5, in a conversation with Yi Chu-yŏn, deputy prime minister and trade minister of the DPRK, Zhou Enlai said that, in 1960, Albania, Cuba, Guinea, and Algeria had all requested aid from China. But China's economy had suffered greatly as a result of the recall of the Soviet experts. China "might face a debt" with the other countries, but it would guarantee its aid to the DPRK. Regarding its loans, Zhou told the North Koreans that they could postpone repayment of matured loans for another ten to twenty years, or even forever.[21] The loan agreement specified that from 1961 to 1964 the Chinese government would provide North Korea with 420 million rubles ($105 million) in long-term loans. According to South Korean sources, this "raised the total of Chinese economic aid to the DPRK since the end of the Korean War to slightly above the level of that granted by the Soviet Union."[22] China would help North Korea build rubber tire plants, wireless communication equipment industrial units, and factories to manufacture daily necessities.[23]

To implement the agreement, on October 18 China and North Korea signed a protocol on science and technology cooperation. China's Ministry of Light Industry would train seventy-six Koreans in China and would also send forty-five to forty-eight Chinese experts to North Korea.[24] Although 1960 was the year of the great famine in China, the People's Republic of China (PRC) provided the DPRK with an additional

230,000 tons of grain.[25] According to CIA intelligence analysis, by that time, China's aid to North Korea already surpassed that of the Soviet Union. Beijing was providing Pyongyang with massive economic aid despite its extremely difficult domestic economic situation in the hopes of maintaining its influence in North Korea. But Pyongyang continued to uphold its neutrality in terms of the Sino–Soviet dispute.[26]

Drawing on their own experiences in dealing with the Soviet leaders, the Chinese leaders paid a great deal of attention to national sentiment in North Korea. On February 13, 1959, Mao noted on a state foreign affairs document, "Some comrades take a one-sided view of the Koreans. They pay more attention to the mistakes rather than to the achievements of the Koreans."[27] During a football game between the Chinese and North Korean teams, in October 1960, the Chinese crowds heckled the Korean referee. This incident attracted the attention of Zhou Enlai, who instructed the State Sports Commission to strengthen the education of the masses.[28] When North Korean newspapers and magazines intentionally tampered with the text of the Chinese National Day report, Beijing "turned a blind eye."[29] These cases further demonstrate that Chinese leaders were paying attention to Sino–North Korean relations and were making great efforts to remain friendly with their North Korean counterparts.

China's economic aid produced some superficial effects. Kim Il-sung adopted an implicit position of supporting China in its disputes with the Soviet Union. North Korea also adopted a positive view of China's Great Leap Forward and its general line for economic reconstruction, crediting China's achievements to the correct leadership of Mao Zedong. Even when China faced serious economic crises in 1961, the North Korean leaders continued to support China's domestic and foreign policies.[30] Although the CCP and the CPSU both intended to improve relations, each persisted in its own opinion and the heated debates continued. At preliminary sessions for drafting declarations, or in speeches at official meetings, the delegates from North Korea, Albania, Vietnam, and Japan openly supported the Chinese position. At the November 1960 Moscow Conference, they criticized the views and practices of the CPSU from their varying perspectives. Such support for the CCP warranted a compromise declaration and a temporary Sino–Soviet détente.[31]

Around the time of the November 1960 Moscow Conference, North Korea adopted a clear policy in line with the Chinese position on the international political struggle. For instance, North Korea initiated a new campaign to oppose flunkeyism and to establish its *Juche* ideology. The main purpose was to oppose blind copying of the Soviet Union and to advocate learning from the Chinese. The North Korean media continuously carried articles that opposed revisionism and leftist opportunism, claiming that revisionism was the main danger in the current international workers' movement.[32] On this basis, China and North Korea further coordinated their foreign policies. In April 1961, the UN General Assembly adopted a resolution to invite North and South Korea to the UN (with no voting rights) in order to participate in a debate on the Korean issue, on the condition that they each acknowledged the right of the UN to resolve the issue. Pyongyang intended to attend the meeting. In view of its differences on this issue with the Chinese in 1956, Pyongyang first asked for the Chinese opinion. In principle, the Chinese government agreed with North Korea's position, but it offered a three-point suggestion for revision. North Korea partially accepted the Chinese suggestion and thus revised its Foreign Ministry statement.[33]

China's aid to North Korea and Kim's leaning toward Beijing prompted the Soviet Union to sign long-term aid and trade agreements with North Korea. When a North Korean delegation visited Moscow in September to negotiate a trade agreement, it made little headway. According to a report by the commercial office of the Chinese Embassy in Moscow, North Korea was unwilling to accept an unfavorable balance of trade by taking a loan; the Soviet Union did not agree to North Korea's request to reduce exports of raw materials and to increase imports of machinery. North Korea wanted to sign a seven-year agreement, but the Soviet Union was only in favor of signing a five-year agreement.[34] At this juncture, "a widening gap between Moscow and Pyongyang was soon revealed when Moscow pushed North Korea to adopt a 'peaceful coexistence' strategy with the South Koreans."[35]

Kim Il-sung felt snubbed when Khrushchev once again canceled his trip to Pyongyang, which had been scheduled for October 8, 1960. Kim thus came to realize that Khrushchev valued relations with Washington more than relations with Pyongyang. To retaliate against Moscow, Kim did not go to Moscow to commemorate the forty-third anniversary of the October Revolution, citing "health reasons." He also did not visit the Soviet Embassy in Pyongyang for the occasion. But the Soviet Embassy reported

that Kim had attended all the activities when a Chinese military delegation, headed by Vice Premier He Long, had visited Pyongyang in October, on the tenth anniversary of Chinese entry in the Korean War.[36]

To prevent Pyongyang from drifting even closer to Beijing,[37] on December 24, 1960, Moscow signed with Pyongyang a technical aid agreement
for 1961-1967 and a long-term loan agreement for 1961-1965. According
to these agreements, the Soviet Union would help expand the annual pro-
ductivity of Kim Ch'aek Iron Factory in Hamhŭng to 2.8 million tons of
steel and 2.3 million tons of steel products. It also would build a
600,000-kilowatt thermal power station at Tŏkch'ŏn, a 400,000-kilowatt
thermal power station in Pyongyang, and an oil refinery with 2 million
tons of crude oil processing capacity, and it would supply the required
amount of crude oil. Additionally, it would help build film studios as well
as flax and woolen mills. According to these agreements, the Soviet Union
would provide North Korea with machinery, equipment, cotton, petro-
leum products, and other goods. Within five years, the amount of bilateral trade was to increase by 80 percent.[38]

The Signing of the Soviet–North Korean and the Sino–North Korean Alliance Treaties

At the end of World War II, Stalin had been able to install "friendly governments" in the countries along the Soviet Union's periphery and had
signed a series of "friendship, cooperation, and mutual assistance treaties"
with these countries.[39] To avoid provoking the West, the Soviet Union
refrained from using the word "alliance." Nevertheless, attentive to Chinese needs, the Soviet Union changed the word "cooperation" to "alliance"
when preparing the Sino–Soviet Treaty of Friendship, Alliance, and Mutual
Assistance in 1950.[40] In contrast, in March 1949 the Soviet Union signed a
cultural, economic, and cooperation agreement with North Korea, not a
bilateral alliance treaty. One Russian scholar argues, "North Korea never
became an area of special concern to Russia."[41] But in fact North Korea
remained a Soviet satellite and Moscow's influence prevailed over Pyongyang. Otherwise, the Soviet Union would not have withdrawn from North
Korea in 1948. When Kim Il-sung visited Beijing to seek Mao's support to
launch an attack on South Korea in May 1950, he proposed signing
with China an alliance treaty patterned after the Sino–Soviet treaty. Mao

prudently advised Kim to wait until the reunification of Korea, and Stalin agreed with Mao's opinion.[42] Nonetheless, it was evident that China, the Soviet Union, and North Korea were allies during the Korean War.

After the withdrawal of the Chinese People's Volunteer Army from North Korea, an imbalance in military strength existed between North and South Korea. When attending the Twenty-First Congress of the CPSU in Moscow in January 1959, Kim proposed to Khrushchev that North Korea and the Soviet Union sign a treaty of friendship, cooperation, and mutual assistance. After a period of preparation, Soviet Chargé d'Affaires Sergei Antonov presented Chinese Foreign Minister Chen Yi with a memorandum regarding the intention of the Soviet Union and North Korea to sign an alliance treaty. The content of the treaty was similar to the treaties signed between the Soviet Union and the other socialist countries. On September 19, China responded by fully agreeing with the signing of such a friendship, cooperation, and mutual assistance treaty.[43]

But from late 1959 to early 1960 Khrushchev was actively promoting Soviet–American détente. Naturally, he was not enthusiastic about signing an alliance treaty with North Korea. It was at this time that China became involved. On March 3, 1960, the Chinese Embassy in Mongolia reported that the Mongolian government indicated that Mongolian leader Yumjaagiin Tsedenbal had expressed interest in visiting Beijing to sign a friendship and mutual assistance treaty and to seek Chinese economic aid. In response, on March 20, Zhou Enlai drafted a telegram inviting Tsedenbal to visit Beijing to sign the Sino–Mongolian Treaty of Friendship and Cooperation. On March 21, Mao Zedong added instructions to Zhou's draft telegram to Xie Pusheng, Chinese ambassador to Mongolia: "If [North] Korea and Vietnam wish to conclude alliance treaties, including an article on Chinese military aid, I think we should agree."[44] Soon, the Chinese Foreign Ministry instructed its ambassadors to the DPRK and Vietnam that "if they voluntarily mention this issue, take a chance and say that we highly approve should the DPRK (and Vietnam) want to sign a treaty, and we will immediately prepare to exchange opinions on it."[45] On May 31, Vice Foreign Minister of China Luo Guibo met with North Korean Ambassador Yi Yŏng-ho, giving him a draft copy of the Sino–Mongolian Treaty of Friendship and Cooperation. Yi promised to report to his government as soon as possible.[46]

As Sino–Soviet relations deteriorated, in June 1960 Khrushchev invited Kim Il-sung to visit the Soviet Union in order to further isolate the

Chinese. At the time, Kim again brought up the issue of Khrushchev's planned visit to the DPRK and Khrushchev promised that he would visit North Korea and sign a Soviet–North Korean alliance treaty in September.[47] However, Khrushchev continued to postpone his visit. Nevertheless, to fulfill his promise of concluding a friendship treaty with North Korea, in June 1961 Khrushchev sent Aleksei Kosygin, first vice chairman of the Council of Ministers, to visit North Korea in his stead, thus moving Soviet-North Korean relations to a higher level.[48] While in North Korea, Kosygin invited Kim to visit Moscow to conclude the alliance treaty. According to Vadim P. Tkachenko, "The Soviet-North Korean treaty represented a long-standing desire on the part of the DPRK. Between 1958 and 1961, Kim Il-sung's three visits to Moscow always preceded a visit to Beijing. Apparently such visits to Moscow were motivated by Kim's calculated behavior to invite Khrushchev to Pyongyang and to sign an alliance treaty with the Soviet Union."[49] Kim thus accepted the invitation for a visit to the Soviet Union, which was scheduled to take place from June 29 to July 12.

On June 16, North Korea's foreign minister, Pak Sŏng-ch'ŏl, met with Ambassador Qiao Xiaoguang to brief him on the forthcoming North Korean–Soviet friendship treaty. Based on earlier instructions from the Chinese Foreign Ministry, Qiao used the occasion to sound out Pyongyang's position with regard to the signing of a Sino–Korean friendship treaty. On June 28, one day prior to his departure for the Soviet Union, Kim Il-sung met with Qiao and proposed that, after his visit to the Soviet Union, he would go directly to Beijing to sign the treaty. On the following day, the Chinese notified the North Koreans that Kim would be welcome to visit China on July 10, after his trip to the Soviet Union, and that the two parties could sign the Sino–Korean Treaty of Friendship, Cooperation, and Mutual Assistance.[50] Soon thereafter, the Korean side gave the Chinese a draft of the Soviet–North Korean treaty, suggesting that the Chinese side review the treaty and the communiqué for further discussion.[51]

Taking the Soviet-North Korean treaty as a model, the Chinese draft stipulated comprehensive political, military, economic, and cultural cooperation and mutual assistance. "The most salient feature of the Sino-Korean treaty is the emphasis on the nature of the military alliance."[52] Whereas the Soviet-North Korean treaty was to enter into effect only if either country were attacked, the Sino-Korean treaty defined their bilateral relations as a military alliance. In addition, whereas the Soviet–North

Figure 5.1 The signing of the Sino–North Korean Treaty of Friendship, Cooperation, and Mutual Assistance by Kim Il-sung and Zhou Enlai, July 11, 1961.

Korean treaty was effective for only ten years, subject to renewal every five years thereafter, the Sino-Korean treaty was effective for an indefinite period. Thus, the Sino-Korean treaty was clearly stronger, in terms of security guarantees, than the Soviet-North Korean treaty.[53] North Korea fully agreed with the Chinese draft.[54] Obviously, the Chinese leaders were offering a more generous commitment to North Korea for the purpose of competing with the Soviet Union.

Kim Il-sung concluded the Soviet-North Korean Treaty of Friendship, Cooperation, and Mutual Assistance on July 6. After visiting Kiev on July 10, he flew directly to Beijing, two days ahead of his scheduled departure from the Soviet Union.[55] In China, from July 10 to July 15, he was accorded a state reception, and the Sino-North Korean Treaty of Friendship, Cooperation, and Mutual Assistance was signed on July 11. Negotiations had been finalized in less than two weeks, after North Korea agreed to the terms, and both sides were very satisfied. Zhou Enlai stated at a return banquet at the North Korean Embassy in Beijing that "the Sino-[North] Korean treaty affirms the militant friendship forged in blood among our two countries and people." Kim Il-sung pointed out that the Sino–Korean treaty "expands the fraternal friendship and alliance between our two people formed and developed over the course of prolonged struggle." It also "establishes a new foundation" for our relations.[56]

We agree with South Korean scholar Dong-jun Lee's view that the Sino-North Korean treaty was a product of China's strategic behavior, based on its national interests rather than on Kim Il-sung's diplomatic skills. When the Chinese learned about the forthcoming Soviet-North Korean treaty, they "hastened to co-opt North Korea" by including more compelling commitments in the treaty. "North Korea tactfully jumped on the Chinese bandwagon."[57]

After signing the treaty with China, North Korean relations with Moscow also improved. At a mass rally in Moscow on July 6, Kim Il-sung stated that the forthcoming Twenty-Second Congress of the CPSU not only "would open a new stage for Communist construction in the Soviet Union; it would also make a great contribution to the International Communist Movement." On July 15, Kim announced at a mass rally in Pyongyang that "the friendship and solidarity between the Korean and Soviet people will be unbending and long-lasting."[58] Regarding the CPSU draft constitution, *Rodong sinmun* (Workers' Newspaper) issued an editorial on August 3, stating, "The new draft constitution of the CPSU scientifically expounds on the basic issues of our era and on the basic issues of construction in Communist society. . . . It is of great significance to the development of the International Communist Movement and the workers' movement."[59]

Kim clearly was a wily politician who was good at praising the Chinese and belittling the Soviets when meeting with the Chinese. Likewise, he was adept at praising the Soviets and deprecating the Chinese when meeting with the Soviets. By maintaining an equidistant policy between Moscow and Beijing, Kim not only consolidated his standing within the party and government but also gradually began to feel that he was an important and indispensable member of the socialist bloc. After his return to Pyongyang, the Fourth Congress of the KWP highlighted the achievements in domestic economic reconstruction and the great prospects for the Seven-Year Plan. The KWP stated that the aim of strengthening friendship and solidarity with the socialist bloc headed by the Soviet Union and China, which had been proposed at the Third Congress of the KWP, had been achieved. The visit of Kim's delegation to both the Soviet Union and China played an epoch-making role in strengthening the unity of the socialist bloc.[60]

North Korea survived the "buffer year" unscathed, thus establishing a good foundation for future economic development. Taking advantage of the confrontation and competition between Moscow and Beijing, it was able to extract the greatest economic benefits from each side. By the beginning of the 1960s, North Korea's economic development was much more impressive than that of South Korea, and this would remain the case until at least the mid-1970s.[61] Fraternal assistance played an important role in the DPRK's successful postwar reconstruction. According to Soviet statistics, by April 1, 1960, North Korea had received a total of 5.5 billion rubles ($1.375 billion) of free economic aid from the socialist countries, of which 1.3 billion rubles ($325 million) came from the Soviet Union and 900 million rubles ($225 million) came from China. In addition, the Soviet Union provided 3.6 billion rubles ($900 million) in low-interest loans, and China gave three batches of no-interest loans.[62] According to South Korean statistics, from the end of the war to the 1970s, total aid to the DPRK from the socialist countries totaled $2.043 billion, $1.653 billion of which was given between 1950 and 1960, and $1.638 billion of this consisted of economic aid (including $340 million that North Korea was exempt from repaying). Of this aid, 43.14 percent came from the Soviet Union and 30.75 percent came from China.[63] As its economy developed, the share of foreign aid that North Korea received dropped from 33.4 percent of its budget in 1954 to 2.6 percent in 1960.[64] This is indicative of the role that foreign aid played in North Korea's economic development. Without the foreign aid, the DPRK could never have achieved its postwar reconstruction.

Toward the end of 1961, Soviet–North Korea relations began to grow tense. When Khrushchev again censured Stalin's personality cult, at the Twenty-Second Congress of the CPSU in October 1961, he was in fact directing his criticism at both Mao Zedong and Kim Il-sung. At an internal party meeting on November 27, Kim stated that the KWP stood resolutely against revisionism, which represented a major threat to the contemporary International Communist Movement.[65] Soon thereafter, Radio Pyongyang suspended broadcasts of Korean-language programs from Radio Moscow and copies of *Pravda* and *Kommunist* were confiscated at the post offices.[66]

Several days later, the ambassadors from Bulgaria, Poland, Hungary, and East Germany met to discuss North Korea's relations with the Soviet Union. They agreed that "the influence of the pro-Chinese forces in the KWP leadership had increased and that Kim Il-sung had made concessions to them." They felt that because of his "personality cult," "Kim naturally viewed the Soviet critique of this phenomenon as a threat and thus shifted to an anti-Soviet, pro-Chinese stance."[67] As a result, Moscow resorted to economic weapons. It suspended its annual supply of 100,000 metric tons of grain, and trade negotiations between the two countries reached an impasse. Furthermore, North Korea's request for forgiveness of cargo that it had owed the Soviet Union in 1961 was rejected. The Soviet Union also asked that North Korea supply all overdue goods during the first season of 1962.

Despite its emphasis on self-reliance, North Korea turned to China for help.[68] In December 1961, Yi Chu-yŏn secretly visited China to request urgent economic aid. But at this time, in the wake of the disastrous Great Leap Forward, China faced its own very difficult economic situation. China tried its best, but it was unable to satisfy North Korea's needs. For instance, North Korea asked for an immediate order of 3,000 tons of steel tubes and 25,000 additional tons of steel tubes in 1962, and 100,000 spindles. Because China could not supply these goods, it allowed the North Koreans to come to China to dismantle and remove spindles from textile mills that had ceased production.[69] After Yi Chu-yŏn left China, the Chinese State Council sent out the following directive: North Korea urgently needs 100,000 spindles but we do not have any reserve supplies. The premier has approved the dismantling of the equipment at the newly built textile factories in Handan, Shijiazhuang, and Zhengzhou.[70] Although in 1960 China still had an outstanding debt to the Soviet Union of 1.2 billion rubles ($300 million), Ye Jizhuang, China's foreign trade minister, agreed to cancel all of North Korea's debt to China. Ye was praised by North Korean Deputy Premier Kim Il, who exclaimed, "This is the act of a brother."[71]

The Chinese leaders went out of their way to provide North Korea with grain, coke, coal, industrial products, and equipment. In terms of foreign relations, Mao ignored the fact that one of the major functions of his diplomats in Pyongyang was to gather intelligence and to carry out research and issue reports on North Korea. During Mao's July 1961 meeting with Kim in China, the issue of the Sino–Soviet intervention in North Korean affairs in September 1956 was again brought up. Mao blamed Qiao Xiaoguang, Chinese ambassador to Pyongyang, for "seeing more shortcomings in the DPRK than he should have." He then pointed to Qiao, who was also present, and said, "I asked you to help the DPRK and to study the

Korean issue. You have not studied [the Korean issue]. This is because you are politically weak."[72] The Chinese Foreign Ministry immediately recalled Qiao Xiaoguang and appointed Hao Deqing, who formerly had been Chinese ambassador to Hungary, as the new ambassador to Pyongyang. In fact, Qiao had been following the instructions of the Chinese Foreign Ministry in carrying out his duties as ambassador. He had doggedly defended China's interests in dealing with the North Korean government. But the North Korean Foreign Ministry did not find him easy to deal with and grew resentful of him.[73]

After Hao Deqing arrived in Pyongyang, Foreign Minister Pak Sŏng-ch'ŏl told him: If you need to know the conditions in Korea, it will suffice to ask me. You do not have to read the newspapers or to analyze information. That will waste a lot of your time and you still will not have a clear idea about the situation. In the past, Qiao Xiaoguang had done such things, and he was later criticized for it by the CCP CC.[74] At his first internal meeting at the Chinese Embassy in Pyongyang, Hao told his colleagues: I only have one task in North Korea, that is, friendship—to promote Sino-North Korean friendship and to safeguard Sino-North Korean unity. Don't shoot off your mouths. Don't say anything or do anything that will be harmful to Sino-North Korean unity. From now on, we will only report good news about North Korea, not bad news. You cannot report on the shortcomings and problems in North Korea.[75]

Although China treated North Korea with "absolute sincerity" and on many occasions North Korea deeply appreciated it, Kim Il-sung still maintained an "equidistant diplomacy" between China and the Soviet Union. Even though Kim was resentful of Khrushchev's foreign policy, the Soviet Union was economically much stronger than China. Thus, whenever Moscow extended an olive branch, Kim was always willing to accept it. On the occasion of Kim Il-sung's fiftieth birthday, the Soviet Union published a collection of Kim Il-sung's writings and speeches. An introductory essay about the collection appeared in *Kommunist*. Kim acted promptly to write a foreword for the collection, and *Rodong sinmun* published a front-page story about it.[76] On April 18, 1962, Pak Sŏng-ch'ŏl relayed Kim Il-sung's oral message to Ambassador Hao: "We hope that China and the Soviet Union will achieve unity. We will march forward along our own recognized road. We do not care what others have to say."[77]

China was unable to offer the amount of economic aid that North Korea requested,[78] and it appears that, with any small move on the part of the

Soviets, Kim Il-sung would waver. Therefore, to secure Kim's continuous support for China in the struggle against "revisionism," Mao had to make concessions on migration and to sacrifice territory.

Mao's Concessions on Migration and Territory

The migration of ethnic Koreans between Northeast China and North Korea was a complicated issue. It was worrisome for the PRC because the direction of the flow out of China toward an ethnic "homeland" had the potential of encouraging other ethnic minorities in China.[79] An examination of the history of Koreans in Northeast China demonstrates that the PRC attempted to achieve a workable policy toward those crossing the Korean border and to accommodate the DPRK's concerns about defining nationality, including the handling of cases of Sino–Korean marriages and exit procedures for ethnic Koreans, allowing Korean nationals to visit China, and dealing with cases of illegal border crossings.[80]

Because many Korean families lived on both sides of the border, China and North Korea were slack in terms of border administration. In the early 1950s, Chinese and Koreans could come and go between Northeast China and North Korea without passports or visas. Chinese citizens were only required to apply for travel documents from the relevant provincial or municipal public security organs in order to travel to North Korea.[81] In July 1953, China and the DPRK signed the "Regulations on Chinese and Korean Border Transit." Residents wishing to cross the border could use travel documents issued by the county or municipal public security bureaus. The Public Security Department of the Northeast People's Government stipulated that all citizens eighteen years old or older could apply for travel documents to go to North Korea to visit relatives and friends, to attend schools, to see doctors, or to attend weddings or funerals.

In March 1955, China and the DPRK reached another agreement whereby the two sides agreed to implement a new transit system, as of July 1, to strengthen entry and exit management.[82] With the exception of Korean residents and nationals in the border area and certain government workers, everyone would need a passport and a visa to cross the border. But travel permits were issued by provincial- and municipal-level organs (e.g., Heilongjiang, Jilin, Liaoning, Lüshun, and Dalian) and at many entry/exit points (including Andong, Changdian, Hekou, Ji'an, Kaishantun, Linjiang,

Nanping, Sanhecun, and Tumen).[83] The procedures were much simpler for North Korean citizens to apply for travel documents to visit relatives in China or to take up long-term residence.[84] Under such conditions, it was impossible to implement effective management of visa issues along the border. For example, by 1957, 4,896 of the 9,791 Korean residents in Changbai Korean Autonomous County had migrated to North Korea.[85]

Applying for travel documents to visit the DPRK for short periods was a different matter than applying for residence, though the former had some influence on the latter. The core issue was that North Korea was in need of laborers for economic reconstruction after the war, especially laborers with special skills. Chinese policy toward the outflow of Korean residents to a great extent was to satisfy the DPRK's demand for laborers.

After the cease-fire in Korea, the North Korean government immediately began its economic recovery and reconstruction programs. One of the greatest obstacles to reconstruction was the shortage of skilled laborers. To resolve this problem, in 1953 and 1954 Pyongyang began to mobilize officials to engage in physical work.[86] In 1957, as Pyongyang entered its First Five-Year Plan period, "the shortage of skilled labor proved to be an insuperable obstacle."[87] The DPRK government was thus very interested in recruiting skilled labor from among the Koreans residing in foreign countries.

There were large numbers of Koreans in the Soviet Union.[88] In April and May 1958, the DPRK proposed to the Soviet Union that those Koreans with dual citizenship who were then residing in North Korea could remain there permanently. It also requested that all Koreans working in the Soviet Far East return to the DPRK ahead of schedule. It expressed special interest in those Koreans residing in Sakhalin who lacked any citizenship. The Soviet government consented to Pyongyang's requests.[89] Pyongyang also actively mobilized those Koreans residing in Japan to return to North Korea. In August 1954, DPRK Foreign Minister Nam Il appealed to the Koreans in Japan to return to their country. Chosen Soren, the pro-DPRK General Association of Koreans in Japan, actively coordinated this endeavor. In 1957, the North Korean government began sending large sums of money, totaling some 120 million Japanese yen, to Chosen Soren to provide support for education. On September 8, 1958, the tenth anniversary of the founding of the DPRK, Kim Il-sung instructed that all returning overseas Koreans should be warmly received. In 1959, 2,942 Koreans returned from Japan, and by 1962 the number had reached 74,335.[90]

Pyongyang was very interested in the Korean residents in China as a potential pool of skilled labor. There were many more Korean residents in China than there were in the Soviet Union, and it was much easier for the Koreans in China to return to the DPRK than it was for the Koreans in Japan. To encourage Mao Zedong to take action, in May 1960 Kim Il-sung told Mao that 200,000 of the 600,000 Koreans living in Japan would return to the DPRK by the end of 1960.[91]

According to Chinese documents, in May 1954, soon after the Korean armistice, some Koreans with Chinese citizenship and some Korean nationals in Northeast China and Mongolia applied to return to the DPRK. The Chinese government immediately approved their requests.[92] In August 1955, the DPRK government took the unprecedented initiative to ask the Chinese government to approve the return of sixty-two Korean technical personnel. The Chinese government made an exception and allowed them to return to the DPRK.[93]

During the first year of the First Five-Year Plan, the DPRK began to mobilize Koreans in China to migrate to North Korea. By the end of 1957, more than fifty thousand Koreans in China had migrated to North Korea to participate in the economic reconstruction. But shortly thereafter, more than forty thousand of them returned to China due to the undesirable conditions in Korea.[94] During his visit to China in November 1958, Kim Il-sung asked if the Chinese government could transfer some Korean nationals residing in Northeast China to the DPRK. The Chinese government responded favorably and agreed to return forty thousand Korean nationals to North Korea before March 1959 so that they could participate in the spring plowing season. To enhance the DPRK's labor force, the Chinese Embassy in Pyongyang interviewed thirteen thousand Chinese nationals in the DPRK and asked them if they were interested in receiving North Korean citizenship. But the majority wished to retain their Chinese citizenship.[95]

With respect to marriages between Korean women and Chinese men, Chinese policy was much more favorable to the North Korean side. A Chinese Interior Ministry document dated October 1958 pointed out that, "Due to its shortage of labor, the DPRK government maintains tight control over Korean women who want to marry Chinese men. We should play a supporting role. . . . If a Korean woman wants to marry a Chinese man, we should make it difficult; we should dissuade Chinese men from marrying Korean women. When we cannot prevent such marriages, we should encourage the Chinese men to relocate to North Korea to start their families."[96]

In the spring of 1961, a large number of Koreans in Northeast China illegally crossed the border to North Korea. Allegedly, the North Korean government had contrived the incident. According to Ministry of Public Security statistics, between January 1961 and March 1962 more than 38,590 people attempted to illegally cross the Sino–North Korean border in Liaoning and Jilin provinces to reach the DPRK. Among them, 29,133 were successful. By May 1962, fifty-five thousand of the seventy-one thousand people who had attempted to illegally cross the border had made it.[97]

Why was the Chinese government unable to effectively curb this massive exodus? The deterioration in Sino–Soviet relations was the most important contributing factor. Divergences between the CCP and the CPSU in the late 1950s over both foreign policy—China's bombardment of Jinmen in 1958 and border clashes with India in 1959—and domestic policy—the Great Leap Forward and the People's Commune movement—seriously worsened the relationship between the two former Communist allies. In July 1960, Soviet leader Nikita Khrushchev made the fateful decision to recall all Soviet experts posted throughout China. Thus, the Sino–Soviet disagreement over ideology expanded to the state-to-state relationship. Both Sino–Soviet party-to-party and state-to-state relationships were on the verge of collapse. The Ita incident in the spring of 1962 seriously affected Chinese leaders' thinking about China's national security interests and accelerated Mao Zedong's determination to break with the Soviet Union.[98]

Between late 1958 and early 1960, China and North Korea signed a series of protocols and border trade agreements, including an agreement on joint use of the Shuifeng (Sup'ung) reservoir (for fish breeding) and an agreement on river shipping along their joint riparian boundary.[99] Under such circumstances, when the illegal crossings began to gain momentum, the Chinese side failed to adopt effective countermeasures and deferred to North Korea's position. As the problem became more serious, the Chinese government avoided the issue so as not to upset the North Korean government. On May 10, 1961, the Ministry of Public Security reported to the CCP CC and the State Council on the situation in Northeast China.[100] On May 24, the Ministry of Public Security and the Ministry of Foreign Affairs proposed that China should consult with North Korea to resolve the problem in accordance with the existing agreements regarding illegal border crossings. They proposed to instruct Ambassador Qiao Xiaoguang to raise the issue with the North Korean Foreign Ministry.[101]

We do not know whether the CCP CC and the State Council discussed this issue. But the Foreign Ministry's instructions to Ambassador Qiao ultimately were quite different from the May 24 proposal. They read, "The Foreign Ministry will respond in detail on the issue of ethnic Koreans illegally crossing the border to [North] Korea. But our overall principle is that we will not resort to diplomatic channels. We should try to reassure the Koreans in China by working with them. It is acceptable for [North] Korea to set up reception stations. Recently, Chinese-[North] Korean relations have been in very good shape. Do not overreact to ethnic Koreans illegally crossing the border [to North Korea]. So it is not necessary for you to go to Jilin on a fact-finding mission."[102]

In order to maintain a good relationship with Pyongyang and to counter the Soviet Union, Beijing tolerated Pyongyang's violation of the Sino–Korean agreement on the handling of illegal border crossings. Additionally, the Chinese government wanted to avoid an embarrassing situation during Kim Il-sung's forthcoming visit to the PRC in July 1961. In their conversation on July 11, Zhou Enlai broached with Kim the topic of the exodus of Koreans from Northeast China. Zhou said, "Many people in Yanbian have fled [to your country]. It is acceptable for able-bodied people to go to North Korea because they can work. But the results would be troublesome if elderly people were also to leave China. How many are young people?" When Kim responded that there had been more than ten thousand young people and ten thousand elderly, Zhou continued, "It is a combination of the young and the old. It is difficult to demarcate the boundary between our two countries. We adopted an open-door policy with you. We will give you as many people as you want." When Kim explained that it was difficult to persuade those people in Korea to return to China because the DPRK had already welcomed back the Koreans from Japan, Zhou told Kim that it was not necessary to send them back to China.[103] In view of Zhou's attitude, the Ministry of Foreign Affairs instructed the Chinese Embassy in the DPRK on how to handle the exodus issue: "Do not resort to diplomatic measures and do not take up the matter with the Korean side."[104]

The massive exodus of Koreans from Northeast China to the DPRK also created problems for North Korea. After arriving in the DPRK, many became disappointed with their working and living conditions. According to a December 1961 report from the Chinese Embassy in Pyongyang, more than 1,500 people either wanted to return to China or became unsettled internal migrants in the DPRK. Some resorted to smuggling, speculation, or profiteering, and others spread infectious diseases, thus causing much concern among the North Koreans.[105]

The Chinese government was soon confronted with the issue of those who had illegally fled to North Korea and then wanted to return to China. In 1961, 7,528 people who had fled to North Korea from Jilin province returned to China voluntarily, representing 58.5 percent of the total number of those who had fled from Jilin to North Korea.[106] However, the Chinese Embassy in Pyongyang had difficulties in dealing with those who applied to return to China. Embassy staff knew that the DPRK only "allows people to come, but does not allow them to leave."[107] In view of Premier Zhou's attitude, on July 11 the Ministry of Foreign Affairs instructed its embassy in Pyongyang, "With respect to those Koreans who crossed the border and now want to return [to China], the Embassy should not accept or hear their cases. They should ask the [North] Korean side for assistance. . . . With respect to the Han Chinese, if the [North] Korean side has helped them settle, we should not bother with them. If the [North] Korean side proposes to send some back, please ask the [North] Korean side to repatriate them in accordance with the mutually agreed regulations. If such people come to the Embassy, you may issue an entry permit."[108] For those who had already crossed the border and had returned to China, the CCP Jilin Provincial Committee ordered, "You should resolutely persuade them to return to [North] Korea. Otherwise, this might result in a massive exodus of North Korean citizens to China. It might create misunderstandings and even undermine the friendly relations between our two countries."[109] In handling this issue, the Chinese yielded to the interests of the North Koreans out of respect for its overall foreign policy agenda, that is, to keep Pyongyang closer to Beijing than to Moscow.

In receiving émigrés, North Korea was mainly interested in able-bodied people, especially specialists with technical skills. But the North Korean government was soon faced with a potentially massive exodus. In March 1962, Foreign Minister Pak Sŏng-ch'ŏl accused China of "not strictly observing the agreement on people-to-people exchanges," which had led to the large numbers of Koreans holding Chinese citizenship crossing the border. Pak further claimed, "The number of people who illegally cross the border is increasing day by day. Some have even died. This has had negative political effects and has disturbed social order." He hoped that the two governments would negotiate an agreement that would allow the Koreans to come and go.

After learning of Pak's complaints, Zhou Enlai offered oral instructions: "We should admit our mistakes and apologize to the Korean side."[110] The Ministry of Foreign Affairs and the Ministry of Public Security instructed Ambassador Hao Deqing to make an appointment with Pak to submit the following statement: "The migration of numerous ethnic Koreans in China to the DPRK has created difficulties and trouble for your side. Your side has taken action to find jobs for them. We are grateful for your help. There are many reasons for this situation. In addition to the usual historical factors, the direct cause is the difficulties in our country. We will need more time to resolve our problems. Please pardon us!"[111]

Thereafter, the Chinese government paid more attention to the ethnic Korean residents in China. In principle, it approved the requests of all Korean residents and nationals who applied to return to North Korea. It also established a joint office of personnel from the Public Security Bureau, the civil administration, customs, and the Nationality Affairs Commission to dissuade people from illegally crossing the border.[112] North Korea also adopted measures to strengthen border administration.[113] By the second half of 1962, the mass exodus of Korean residents in Northeast China had been contained.

CCP policies and actions with respect to migration to North Korea were motivated by two factors. First, by the early 1960s North Korea was one of China's few remaining international partners.[114] An August 1963 CCP CC document stated, "At present, as international revisionists are colluding with the imperialists and reactionaries in all countries to oppose the Chinese and the people of the world, the Korean Workers' Party stands closely by our side and is our faithful comrade in arms. China and the DPRK are on very good terms and support each other. We should be cautious in handling issues with [North] Korea. We must do a good job and we cannot afford to handle [relations with North Korea] unsatisfactorily."[115] Second, China already had a very large population. It was thus acceptable to allow some Koreans to leave the country. At one point, Mao told Kim Il-sung, "In Northeast China there are over one million Koreans who belong to both of us. If necessary, you may recruit soldiers from among them. If they want to return [to Korea], we will let them go. In any case, we have a very large population."[116]

Meanwhile, the PRC also accommodated the DPRK's wish to settle the border disputes.[117] We know little about the contacts between the two sides or the details of the actual negotiations. However, from the declassified documents in the archives of the Chinese Foreign Ministry and *The Chronology of Zhou Enlai*, we can sketch the 1962 process to demarcate a common Sino-North Korean border.

On February 18, 1962, North Korean Foreign Minister Pak Sŏng-ch'ŏl invited Chinese Ambassador Hao Deqing on a hunting trip. During a picnic, Pak asked Hao if it would be possible to resolve the Sino–Korean border problem through internal consultations. On February 28, the Chinese Foreign Ministry responded to a request from the Chinese Embassy in North Korea, stating that the Chinese government would agree to a resolution of the Sino–Korean border issue. On March 3, Hao again met with Pak and relayed the response of the Ministry of Foreign Affairs. He then inquired about a date and location for the negotiations. On March 26, Pak proposed to Hao that China and the DPRK hold negotiations on April 10, at the vice foreign ministerial level, in Andong and Sinŭiju. On March 30, Zhou Enlai called a meeting of responsible cadres to discuss the Sino–Korean and Sino–Mongolian border disputes. It was at this meeting that the Chinese plan was initially drawn up.

Between April 4 and April 8, officials from the North Korean Foreign Ministry and the Chinese Embassy in North Korea met to discuss the time, location, and the members of their respective delegations, and between April 10 and April 14, the Sino-North Korean border negotiations were held in Andong. The Chinese delegation was headed by Vice Foreign Minister Ji Pengfei and the Korean delegation was led by Vice Foreign Minister Yu Chang-sik. After five rounds of talks, each side proposed a plan for demarcating the border. On April 18, Hao Deqing visited Vice Foreign Minister Yu in Sinŭiju to exchange views on the border issue. On the same day, Hao also met with Pak Sŏng-ch'ŏl and proposed a postponement of the next round of border negotiations, to which Pak agreed.[118] It is likely that the Chinese delegation felt uncomfortable about the North Korean proposal.

During this period, the Second Asian Department of the Chinese Foreign Ministry asked the Foreign Affairs Office of Jiangsu province to locate historical materials on the Sino–Korean border. The Second Historical Archives of China in Nanjing held the official documents of the Beiyang government and the Nationalist government. But when the Nationalist government was overthrown, in 1949, Jiang Jieshi fled to Taiwan and took all the important documents with him. On April 19, the Foreign Affairs Office of Jiangsu province replied, "After contacting the Nanjing Historical Materials Arrangement Division and consulting all available sources, we could not find any materials on Tianchi [天池, Heaven Lake; Ch'ŏnji Lake in Korean] and Huangchaoping, which are located along the Sino–North Korean border. Hence, we were unable to locate any materials on the Sino–Korean border."[119] Judging from the documents that the Foreign Ministry asked the Foreign Affairs Office to attempt to locate, it is clear that North Korea's plan for the border demarcation involved ownership of Tianchi. The lack of documentation in the Chinese archives made it difficult for the Chinese delegation to come up with an effective plan to conduct the negotiations.

During his April 30 meeting with Han Ik-su, the North Korean ambassador to China, Deng Xiaoping, general secretary of the CCP CC, said, "Between fraternal parties, we should not conduct diplomacy. There should be internal consultations. . . . We should maintain comradely relations." When the discussions turned to the border issue, Deng said, "We hold identical views on this. The remaining issue is how to delimit the boundary. This is a matter of drawing a line for the boundary. It is not a big deal."[120] Deng's words are indicative of three important points about the Chinese position: first, China had assumed that it would not be a major problem and thus it was not fully prepared; second, China was taken by surprise about North Korea's plan to delimit the boundary (obviously a major issue); and third, because China and North Korea were fraternal countries, it should have been easy to resolve the border issue. This indicates that Chinese leaders were considering accepting North Korea's plan.

On June 3, Zhou Enlai met with officials from the CCP Northeast Bureau to review the Sino-North Korean border issue.[121] It seems that the CCP CC had already made a general policy decision regarding delimiting the boundary and it was then soliciting opinions from local officials. On June 28, Zhou met with Pak Kŭm-ch'ŏl, head of the delegation from the DPRK's Supreme People's Assembly, and Ambassador Han Ik-su. After the meeting, Zhou discussed the Sino–Korean border issue with Ambassador Han.[122] It is quite possible that Zhou explained China's plan to resolve the border issue. On September 15, Yu Chang-sik notified Hao Deqing that North Korea would consent to the Chinese plan and would welcome Vice Foreign Minister Ji Pengfei to Pyongyang for negotiations. Therefore, on

September 25 Ji flew to Pyongyang. On October 3, the two sides signed the minutes of the negotiations. On October 11, Zhou Enlai and Chen Yi secretly visited North Korea and held talks with Kim Il-sung, and on October 12, the Sino–Korean Border Treaty was signed in Pyongyang.[123] On November 7, the Supreme People's Assembly of the DPRK approved the Sino–Korean Border Treaty.

On November 24, Chen Yi chaired the 122nd plenary session of the State Council, which approved the treaty. It was then delivered to the National People's Congress for consideration. At the Congress meeting, Ji Pengfei stated, "The Sino–Korean border is over 1,300 kilometers long. It is obvious that the two countries both border on the Yalu and the Tumen rivers. But there has been contention concerning the Baitoushan [白头山; Paektusan in Korean] area at the origin of the two rivers. The Baitoushan boundary differs on Chinese and North Korean maps. In view of the national sentiments of each side toward Baitoushan and the actual situation, it is fitting to divide the boundary at Baitoushan. The smooth resolution of the border issue has enhanced the friendship and unity of our two countries."[124] On the same day, the seventieth meeting of the Standing Committee of the National People's Congress approved the Sino–Korean Border Treaty. On December 11, Ji Pengfei and the North Korean chargé d'affaires, Chŏng Pong-kyu, on behalf of their respective governments, exchanged the instruments of ratification in Beijing. On March 20, the Protocol on the Sino–Korean Border was signed in Beijing. Liu Shaoqi, Zhou Enlai, and Pak Sŏng-ch'ŏl attended the ceremony.[125]

What did North Korea ask for and what concessions did China make during these negotiations? The presently available documentation indicates that North Korea's territorial demands in 1962 focused on ownership of Tianchi at the top of Changbai Mountain (长白山; Paektu Mountain in Korean) and a redefinition of the source of the Tumen River. In the end, "the two sides agreed to divide the disputed Changbai Mountain through the crater lake, which formed the crux of the dispute."[126] The so-called crater lake was Tianchi. As Zhou Enlai later explained to U.S. President Richard Nixon, "We finally solved the question by dividing and sharing the lake."[127] The core of the treaty that was signed in October 1962 involved acceptance of Kim Il-sung's proposal and the ceding of a large part of Tianchi and Changbai Mountain to North Korea. Chen Xiaolu, son of Foreign Minister Chen Yi, reportedly overheard his father's staff discussing the Sino-North Korean border negotiations. Chen Xiaolu said, "At the very beginning of the negotiations, North Korea proposed extending the Sino–North Korean boundary to the Liao River. It had also requested that Yanbian be handed over to North Korea. Later, it requested that the highest peak on Changbai Mountain and Tianchi be given to North Korea. In short, the North Korean negotiating strategy was to harass us with unreasonable demands. Its purpose was to get the highest peak on Changbai Mountain and Tianchi."[128]

The North Korean leaders knew that they had made huge territorial gains by signing the border treaty with the Chinese.[129] According to the minutes of the talks held from September 26 to October 2, 1962, on the Sino–Korean border issue, the Chinese and North Korean delegations, headed by Ji Pengfei and Yu Chang-sik, respectively, negotiated and came to a basic agreement on resolving the Sino–Korean border issue, which was beneficial to the resolution of concrete technical and procedural issues.[130] Together with the Sino–Korean Border Treaty signed by Zhou Enlai and Kim Il-sung and the Protocol on the Sino–Korean Border, these documents delineated the Sino–North Korean boundary.

In accordance with the Sino–Korean Border Treaty, a joint Sino–Korean Boundary Commission (ZhongChao Bianjie Lianhe Weiyuanhui, 中朝边界联合委员会) was established. It met for the first time in Pyongyang in early January 1963.[131] From May 13 to November 15, 1963, the commission conducted a comprehensive survey of the Sino–Korean border, established boundary markers, and defined ownership of the islets and shoals, thus fixing the 1,334-kilometer-long Sino–Korean border, which included the Changbai Mountain region. North Korea acquired 54.5 percent of Tianchi, consisting of 98 square kilometers that had been held by China, and China retained only 45.5 percent.[132] With respect to the source of the Tumen River, between the Jiandao Treaty of 1909 and the Sino–Korean Border Treaty of 1962, China lost about 500 square kilometers (see figure 5.2). On the basis of the new border treaty, on May 5, 1964, China and North Korea signed the Mutual Cooperation Agreement for Joint Use and Management of the Sino–Korean Border Rivers.[133]

According to the official Chinese position, China decided to accept the Sino–North Korean boundary along Tianchi and Changbai Mountain in order to cater to North Korean national sentiment. But why did the North Koreans insist on occupying Tianchi and Changbai Mountain? It is true that the Koreans had long revered Paektu Mountain as the sacred birthplace of the Korean dynasties.[134] But Kim Il-sung had very practical

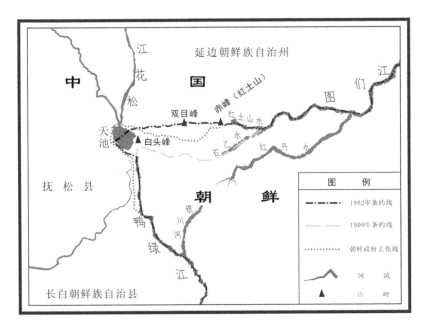

Figure 5.2 Map of the disputed Sino–North Korean border.

political considerations as well. First, the North Korean media had long claimed that Kim Il-sung had engaged in the anti-Japanese struggle in the thick forests of Changbai Mountain, making extraordinary contributions to Korea's liberation. If Changbai Mountain did not belong to North Korea, it would mean that Kim had not really led the anti-Japanese struggle of its people.

In fact, it was largely due to this consideration that North Korea raised the border issue. In February 1962, North Korea managed to try out on the Chinese Embassy the idea that Kim Il-sung had once been a guerrilla fighter in the area of Jinjiang Hot Spring (northwest of Tianchi) and that North Korea therefore wanted to build a monument there.[135] Second, Kim Il-sung might have also considered this issue from a longer-term perspective, with regard to the legitimacy of the succession of his son, Kim Jong-il. In his memoirs, Kim Il-sung claims that "Kim Jong-il was born in the early morning of February 16, 1942, in the thick forest of Paektusan. . . . [He] was a Korean boy born on the fiery battlefield as guns were roaring."[136] If Kim Jong-il had been born in a foreign country, it would have been embarrassing for him to become North Korea's top leader. Bringing

Tianchi and Changbai Mountain under North Korean jurisdiction would thus solve this problem.

As a matter of fact, however, Kim Jong-il was not born in the thick forest of Changbai Mountain. By October 1941, Kim Il-sung had already left Changbai Mountain for the Soviet Far East. With the exception of leading small guerrilla groups to Northeast China in 1941, he remained at a secret Soviet training camp until the Japanese surrender in September 1945. Therefore, Kim Jong-il was born in the Soviet Far East.[137] But, following the demarcation of the Sino–North Korean border, North Korea publicized with great fanfare the myth of Kim Il-sung's anti-Japanese guerrilla activities in Changbai Mountain and of Kim Jong-il's birthplace in the thick forests of Changbai Mountain.

On October 7, 1964, soon after the signing of the Protocol on the Sino–Korean Border, Mao spoke about the border issue with a visiting North Korean party and government delegation. He said that Korea had originally bordered China along the east of the Liao River but that the ancient Chinese emperors had driven the Korean people to the Yalu River and they had occupied Korean territory. When Pak Kŭm-ch'ŏl, deputy chairman of the DPRK's Supreme People's Assembly, told Mao that they were very satisfied with the current boundary, Mao stated, "That is why we plan to make our Northeast your great hinterland, which is much larger than the Liao River region." Pak replied, "We settled the border issue in 1962. Premier Zhou Enlai knows that we have satisfactorily resolved our differences over Paektu Mountain and Chongji. The prime minister [Kim Il-sung] is very pleased. Making use of Northeast China as our great hinterland and the boundary line are two very different matters."[138]

"Northeast China Is Your Great Hinterland"

Historically, both Korea and Vietnam were vassals and protectorates of China. The CCP attached great importance to its relations with Korea and Vietnam, its two most important partners in the surrounding region. In Mao's view, China was the center of the Asian Revolution and also the rear base for both North Korea and Vietnam.[139] North Korea and Vietnam, standing at the forefront of the anti-U.S. imperialist struggle, represented China's security barriers. It was thus natural for China to offer assistance to these two allies.[140] From a geopolitical perspective, North Korea had become even more important to China following the rise of the CCP in the socialist bloc in 1957, especially after Sino–Soviet relations began to deteriorate.

When Kim Il-sung visited China as North Korea's head of state, in late 1953, Mao told him, "In the struggle against the imperialist invasion of China, the Korean people helped us. Without the heroic struggle of the Korean people, China could not have been safe. . . . The Korean people are at the first line of defense, and we are at the second line of defense, i.e., the rear."[141] At the time, Mao was discussing the issue from the perspective of mutual assistance in the anti-imperialist struggle. In December 1958, Mao once again said that China's Northeast was Korea's rear base. He told Kim Il-sung, who was then visiting China, "At the beginning of the U.S. invasion of Korea, I said, Northeast China is your rear base—all yours. You can move your government offices, schools, and air force to wherever you want. Moreover, the whole of China is your rear base."[142] Mao was still talking about providing assistance to North Korea in the future anti-U.S. imperialist struggle. The Soviet Union and China each signed alliance treaties with North Korea in 1961; the common target of each was the Western bloc. Thereafter, however, in Mao's view North Korea's alliance with China began to experience subtle changes.

The year 1962 was critical in the development of Sino–Soviet relations. It was in this year that the CCP identified the Sino–Soviet dispute as a struggle between "the enemy and us." This created the ideological foundation for the breakdown in CCP–CPSU party relations. The Twenty-Second Congress of the CPSU in October 1961 had demonstrated the disagreements between the CCP and CPSU in terms of their basic viewpoints and programs. Thereafter, the CCP announced in inner-party circles that the CCP and the CPSU "differ over matters of principle," or the issue of who would prevail over whom, and that the CCP would never forsake its position.[143] The CCP then informed North Korea of its views of the international situation and its policy. In February 1962, when North Korean Ambassador Yi Yŏng-ho was about to leave his position, Liu Shaoqi, Deng Xiaoping, and officials from the Foreign Ministry and the CCP International Liaison Department took turns speaking with him. Their main messages were that Khrushchev was a revisionist to the core and was sinking ever more deeply, that differences in the International

Communist Movement were inevitable, that the Soviet Union would take major anti-China steps, and that China would unite with Korea to deal with such difficulties.[144]

It was under these circumstances that North Korea proposed that the Sino–Korean border issue be resolved. China signed the border treaty with North Korea basically on Pyongyang's terms, sacrificing territory to win over a political ally. After the signing of the treaty, Mao felt that the Chinese and the North Koreans belonged to the same family. From the Chinese perspective, China had provided massive economic aid to North Korea after the Korean War and had satisfied Pyongyang's territorial claims. Therefore, North Korea should feel deeply grateful and should have no second thoughts about China. At an April 26, 1963, meeting with a delegation from *Rodong sinmun*, Mao said, "The whole of the Northeast is your rear base. Please have more contacts with it!. . . You should become familiar with Liaoning, Jilin, and Heilongjiang provinces. Send more people there to research and investigate. . . . If something big were to occur, if a world war were to break out, you can make use of this area." Mao also urged North Korea to send military delegations to the Northeast. "It is better to send one delegation each year" so that North Korea would understand the army, navy, and air force there.[145] In late May 1963, Mao met with Kim Il-sung in Wuhan and said, "The whole of Northeast China is Korea's rear base. . . . Should a war break out in the future, the great rear base will be turned over to Comrade Kim Il-sung for a 'unified command.'"[146] Mao was serious. He not only considered Northeast China to be Korea's rear base but also believed that Kim should manage it. This was something new.

After the Ita incident in May 1962, the clashes on the Sino–Soviet border began to escalate. The CCP Central Military Commission held a conference on Sino–Soviet and Sino–Mongolian border defense, in September and October 1963. The conference reconfirmed the guiding principles of the CCP CC on border defense: "Neither advance forward nor retreat. Do not take an initiative to stir up trouble. Strike only after the other side attacks first." It also proposed that "we have to be militarily prepared to deal with a possible border conflict provoked by the revisionists."[147] Under such circumstances, Northeast China was not only the rear base for a future anti-U.S. imperialist war of invasion but also was becoming an outpost for possible military conflicts provoked by the revisionists.

In February 1964, Mao told Kim Il-sung that it was possible that the Soviet Union might engage in a war with China if it failed to subdue it by other means.[148] At the CCP CC work conference, held from May 15 to June 17, Mao shifted the goal of China's Third Five-Year Plan from resolving the issue of "food, clothing, and daily necessities" to war preparedness. He proposed the Third Front construction project and the establishment of military industries in every province.[149] When explaining the division of the Third Front area, Zhou Enlai opined, "The northwest and northeast provinces are the first line of defense against revisionism. . . . The Third Front defense is in Qinghai, southern Shaanxi, southern Gansu, and Panzhihua in Sichuan."[150] At a July 1964 CCP CC Politburo meeting, Mao said, "Do not pay attention only to the east and ignore the north; and do not pay attention only to imperialism and ignore revisionism. We must prepare for war on both fronts." This was the first time that Mao formally raised the issue of preparing for a potential defensive war against the Soviet Union.[151]

At the time, Mao repeatedly stated that he would turn Northeast China over to Kim's management. On the one hand, this showed that he was considering making Northeast China into a strategic buffer zone in the case of a future conflict with the Soviet Union. On the other hand, it demonstrated his trust in North Korea as an ally. At a September 5, 1964, meeting with a Chinese government economic delegation, Kim mentioned that Northeast China was North Korea's rear base. Chinese Ambassador Hao Deqing said, "In a sense, you are also the rear base of our Northeast. Our northern neighbor has become revisionist and we cannot rely on it. We need your help." Kim replied, "This is worrisome."[152]

For Kim, Mao's suggestion that he manage Northeast China was most welcome. In August 1959, the North Korean Consulate General in Changchun asked the Chinese for permission to attend the next meeting of the Heilongjiang Provincial People's Congress. In June 1963, while accompanying Ch'oe Yong-gŏn on a tour of the Northeast, Zhou Enlai said that Chairman Mao had already said that Northeast China was Korea's rear base, but Heilongjiang was the rear of the rear base and North Korea could contact it directly if anything needed to be dealt with. He said that the central government would request that the Northeast Bureau send cadres to North Korea to investigate and learn.[153] Kim Il-sung responded promptly. In July, he invited the leading people in the party, government, and military from the Northeast Bureau, the three provinces in the Northeast, and Andong city to secretly visit North Korea.[154] When receiving the first group of visiting Chinese officials from the Northeast, on October 8, Kim said that the Korean people would never forget Northeast China. He said that he had often dreamed about Northeast China and would secretly visit Northeast China with a team of ministers the following year.[155]

In September 1964, Kim Il-sung did indeed secretly visit Northeast China, and Deng Xiaoping traveled to Shenyang to accompany him. Kim told Deng that he had come "to meet with you [Deng] in order to carry out Chairman Mao's instructions. Northeast China is Korea's rear base and both sides should establish close contacts." Deng briefed Kim on the situation in the Northeast and told him, "This region is at your disposal. How to manage it? Premier, please tell them." Deng later added, "If there is anything you want to do here, ask Comrade Song Renqiong. In Northeast China, you can give orders." After Deng departed, Kim, accompanied by Song Renqiong, first secretary of the CCP Northeast Bureau, and Wu Xiuquan, vice director of the CCP CC International Liaison Department, traveled from Shenyang to Qiqihar in Northeast China.[156] From Kim's perspective, Northeast China had already fallen into his lap.

China's economic aid and concessions on migration and territory did win some political dividends from Pyongyang. According to a report by the Chinese Embassy, beginning in early 1962 North Korean propaganda reports had already adopted the Chinese position in terms of opposing the views of the Soviets.[157] At a KWP CC meeting on March 8, 1962, Kim vigorously criticized revisionism, using the same language that was used in CCP newspapers. Kim said, "Modern revisionism is the main danger to the International Communist Movement. . . . The revisionists negate the general principles of the socialist revolution—the leadership of the Marxist–Leninist party and the proletariat dictatorship. . . . The revisionists distort the basic principle of Marxism–Leninism—the theory of class struggle."[158]

According to an April 1962 report from the Hungarian Embassy in Pyongyang, college students "were warned against corresponding with foreign (fraternal) countries." Several local party organs "voluntarily" canceled their subscriptions to the Soviet newspaper *Pravda*.[159] During the visit of Yuri Andropov (head of the CPSU CC Department for Liaison with Communist and Workers' Parties in the Socialist Countries) to North Korea, in January 1963, Kim condemned him to his face, censuring Moscow for interfering in North Korea's internal affairs in 1956 and clearly indicating that the KWP would not allow any attack on the CCP.[160] In February 1963, Pak Sŏng-ch'ŏl told Mr. Guo, director of the PRC's

Liaison Office in Kaesong, "The Korean Workers' Party has consistently maintained that there is no socialist camp without China. Therefore, Premier Kim Il-sung has recently proposed a new slogan: "The socialist camp led by the Soviet Union and China."[161]

In May, the CCP invited Kim Il-sung to secretly visit China, seeking his opinions on its "Proposal Concerning the General Line of the International Communist Movement." Kim, together with eight Korean scholars, visited China to review the article with members of the CCP team drafting the "Nine Polemics." Mao was very pleased with the results.[162] When Ch'oe Yong-gŏn met Liu Shaoqi in China in June, he told Liu that he had long been considering that the center of the world revolution should shift to China: "China should play a more important role in promoting world revolution. The Korean Workers' Party now realizes that revisionism is the enemy, and it is important to distinguish the enemy from friends. Korea will always side with China."[163] In praising the KWP, the Chinese Embassy in Pyongyang stated, "Although it [the KWP] has avoided a direct confrontation with the Soviet Union at the front line, it has provided China with critical support in the international struggle."[164] In an internal document, International Liaison Department leaders pointed out that the KWP "now has very good relations with us. We can discuss anything with them. In particular, since the beginning of the antirevisionist struggle, they have agreed with us in both words and deeds. We always consult them when anything important occurs."[165]

By the time Liu Shaoqi visited Pyongyang in September 1963, Sino–North Korean relations had reached a high water mark. To demonstrate his support for the Chinese in the Sino–Soviet split, Kim made the following points to Liu:

> The KWP is not afraid of the split in the International Communist Movement. Since coming to power, Khrushchev has continuously pressured the KWP, interfering in our internal affairs and engaging in subversion. The KWP long ago split with Khrushchev in terms of ideology. China is a big party, and if you break with Khrushchev, the KWP will resolutely side with you. As for the polemics with the CPSU, the KWP is unwilling to continue to stand on the second line—we have assembled a team of scholars to write several articles and we will become directly involved in the struggle.[166]

Although they were in general agreement, Kim also allowed some room for leeway. For instance, even though Kim accepted Liu's suggestion that the KWP should participate in the writing of the polemics against revisionism, the KWP would not be mentioned publicly by name. Kim also rejected Liu's proposal for a Sino–North Korean joint declaration.[167]

As Soviet-North Korean relations deteriorated, North Korea's standing and role in Northeast China became ever more important and China paid increasing attention to solidarity and friendship with North Korea. In April 1964, Kim Il-sung wanted to pay a visit to the Chinese side of the construction site of the Yunfeng (Unbong) hydroelectric power station, but he was embarrassed to raise this issue with the Chinese. So he proposed inviting the head of the Chinese site to visit the Korean side to celebrate May Day. After being informed of Kim's true intentions, the Chinese government invited Kim to visit. The Chinese government told those at the Chinese site that they should be prepared to report openly to Kim about the construction work and not to keep any secrets.[168]

At an April 28 meeting with Pak Se-Ch'ang, the newly appointed North Korean ambassador to China, Liu Shaoqi said, "Relations between our two countries are very good. Relations between our two parties are very good as well. This friendly relationship will continue to develop. . . . If you need any assistance, we are willing to provide help."[169] On the same day, Zhou Enlai praised North Korea for cooperating with China during the mid-April Afro–Asian Solidarity Conference (the preparatory meeting for the Second Afro–Asian Conference) and at the Legal Workers' Conference. He told the North Korean ambassador, "We are in complete agreement about the antirevisionist struggle. The revisionists treat us as one and the same."[170]

Even though he was resentful of Soviet foreign policy and Soviet-North Korean relations were deteriorating, Kim Il-sung still attempted to maintain normal relations with the Soviet Union whenever possible. In any event, the Soviet Union was capable of offering North Korea much more economic and military aid than China was. In a conversation with Czechoslovak Ambassador Václav Moravec on December 21, 1962, Yi Chu-yŏn tried to defend his position by describing the situation in the DPRK. He placed two apples on a table, calling the one on the left China and the one on the right the Soviet Union. Then he put a third apple in the center and called it Korea. Thereafter, he took a knife and cut this apple in half and then posed the following question to Ambassador Moravec: "Should we do it this way—move one half over there and the other half over here? This is impossible. If you were in such a situation, just like us you would have no other choice. For a long time we tried to do everything possible to prevent the differences of opinion from becoming public. . . . We still want to maintain our friendship with both China and the Soviet Union. Our differences of opinion should not have an impact on this."[171]

After Khrushchev's fall, in October 1964, the new Soviet leadership under Leonid Brezhnev and Aleksei Kosygin began to alter Soviet foreign and domestic policies, and Soviet-North Korean relations gradually improved. Kim Il-sung was a practical politician as well as a shrewd diplomat. Despite China's economic and military aid and its concessions on migration and territory, China was only able to keep a grateful Kim at its side for three to four years (1961-1965). During those years, Kim was closer to Beijing than to Moscow. As East German diplomats observed in 1963, despite the rhetoric of closeness with China, good economic relations with Eastern Europe remained indispensable for North Korea to fulfill its ambition to achieve economic development. North Korea might have been closer to China ideologically, but, in practice, the DPRK would have no choice but to swing back to the Soviet position sooner or later.[172]

CHAPTER VI

The Lowest Ebb, 1966–1969

C hina's relations with North Korea, especially from 1966 to 1969, during the Cultural Revolution, have received relatively little scholarly attention. Earlier studies, such as those by political scientist Donald S. Zagoria, argue that North Korea's "relations with China began deteriorating in the mid-1960s once the Chinese Cultural Revolution got under way."[1] South Korean scholar Chin-Wee Chung contends that Pyongyang moved closer to Moscow during the 1965–1969 period mainly because Beijing "was incapable of providing military assistance adequate to North Korean needs," and in the event of a North Korean military confrontation with the United States, North Korea would need Soviet military support and nuclear protection.[2] German-American scholar Bernd Schaefer's excellent study documents "the challenges and opportunities Kim Il-sung faced as a result of China's Cultural Revolution." He notes that the effects of the Cultural Revolution on Pyongyang's foreign policy were actually "greater than previously realized."[3] Schaefer's study, mainly based on East German archives, essentially examines Pyongyang's foreign policy from the perspective of North Korea. Relying on Chinese and Eastern European sources in the Wilson Center Digital Archive, Chinese scholar Dong Ji argues that even though Sino–North Korean relations were at a low ebb during the first three years of the Cultural Revolution (1966–1969), both Beijing and Pyongyang showed restraint and prevented the relationship from further deteriorating. Although political relations were tense, economic and trade relations continued.[4] In an eighteen-page article on Sino–North Korean relations in the 1960s, Chinese scholar Cheng Xiaohe devotes only two pages to the 1966–1969 period, contending that, "As North Korean–Soviet relations warmed, the KWP [Korean Workers' Party] and the CCP [Chinese Communist Party] found themselves at odds on two key issues: how to judge [Leonid] Brezhnev and how to evaluate Soviet assistance to Vietnam."[5]

According to newly acquired Chinese and Russian sources, Eastern European Communist-era documents, and CIA analytical reports, China's relationship with North Korea had worsened substantially during the eighteen months prior to the May 1966 beginning of the Cultural Revolution. By that time China already believed that the KWP was carrying out a "revisionist" policy. This chapter examines China's relationship with North Korea from 1965 to 1969 primarily from the Chinese perspective. We contend that the main reason for the deterioration in Sino–North Korean relations was China's radical and uncompromising foreign and domestic policies. However, it is important to distinguish between the Red Guards' verbal attacks on North Korean leaders and the position of the Chinese government. A review of North Korea's relations with Beijing and Moscow from 1966 to 1969 reveals that Pyongyang did not have as much leverage over its two Communist allies as has generally been believed. Instead, Pyongyang was mainly reacting to policy changes in Beijing and Moscow, and it thereby adjusted its policies in order to better protect its own national security and interests.

Sino–North Korean Disputes

Previous studies have already found that the Soviet Union under the leadership of Leonid Brezhnev and Aleksei Kosygin began to modify its policy toward the radical Asian Communist parties, especially in North Vietnam and North Korea. This was an important contributing factor in the deterioration of Pyongyang's relations with Beijing. It has also been pointed out that China's policy during the Cultural Revolution was an additional key factor in the worsening of relations between China and North Korea. Bernd Schaefer argues that Nikita Khrushchev's "overthrow in 1964 therefore allegedly paved the way for a smoother relationship, but in actuality it was Mao Zedong's decision to launch the Cultural Revolution that was the decisive factor."[6]

We go a step further, to argue that Sino–North Korean relations were already extremely strained when the Cultural Revolution began in May 1966. As an August 1966 CIA analysis points out, "In the past 18 months the Chinese have suffered their most serious setbacks in the Far East. The ruling parties of North Korea and North Vietnam have edged away from Peking, and the Communist Party in Japan can no longer be counted on for support. The Communist Party in Indonesia—which had been supporting Peking—was shattered in the wake of the abortive coup last fall. China's relations with Cuba, Peking's only diplomatic toehold in the Western Hemisphere, have also sunk to an all-time low, and Peking is no longer able to work through pro-Castro activities in Latin America."[7]

In terms of economic policy, according to reports from the Chinese Embassy in North Korea, in July 1964 North Korea began implementing a "cooperative brigade material incentive system" and distributing the means of production to certain cooperative brigades in Kangwŏn-do. At the start of each year, the North Korean government established production quotas for the cooperative brigades, and at the end of each year those brigades that had overfilled their production quotas were rewarded. This was similar to the policy of fixing production quotas for each household, which was implemented in China in 1962 but shortly thereafter rejected by Mao Zedong.

The Chinese Embassy in North Korea was fixated on this policy. A Chinese report criticized the practice on five counts. First, the huge disparities in distribution would contribute to the divide between the rich and the poor. Second, when the means of production were distributed to smaller units, it would be difficult for the cooperative farms to allocate the means of production and manpower. This would negatively affect collective economic development. Third, this could also lead to a greater burden on the cooperative brigades because of heavier production demands from upper levels. Fourth, if the cooperative brigades could not fulfill their quotas because of natural disasters, they could blame both God and man and hold grudges against the collectives and brigades. And finally, this practice could weaken peasant collectivism and encourage capitalism.[8] In May, the Hungarian ambassador to North Korea, József Kovács, reported that, due to its poor economic performance, the North Korean government was taking measures "to increase agricultural production by considering material interests to a certain extent. Cooperative brigades are given a certain amount of land for collective cultivation and brigade members can distribute their products among one another."[9]

North Korea's relations with both its two Communist allies also began to experience major changes during the eighteen months prior to the summer of 1966. After Khrushchev's removal, the Communist Party of the Soviet Union (CPSU) leadership took steps to improve relations with the North Koreans, "who had gone considerably further than the North Vietnamese in their outspoken support of the Chinese position and in waging open polemics with Moscow." Pyongyang was also interested in improving relations with Moscow. Kim Il, vice chairman of the KWP Central Committee (CC), led a delegation to Moscow in November 1964 to attend the celebration on the anniversary of the CPSU's October Revolution. During this period, the KWP insisted that the Soviets stick fast to two principles: "a fundamental revision of Soviet policies toward the United States to expedite a world-wide 'anti-imperialist struggle,' and an end to all Soviet attempts to dictate the North Korean party or to interfere in its internal affairs."[10] When, shortly after Khrushchev's fall, Kim Il-sung met Mao Zedong, in November 1964, Kim told Mao that "Brezhnev is tactless and very inexperienced." This implied that China and North Korea should not have undue expectations about the new Soviet leaders.[11]

But North Korea soon began to cool its relations with Beijing. A December 3, 1964, *Rodong sinmun* (Workers' Newspaper) editorial openly criticized Chinese dogmatism. It stated that "we cannot talk about the victory of the cause of all peoples for peace, national independence, and social progress apart from the struggle against imperialism," and the article demanded that the socialist bloc and all revolutionary forces "put pressure on and deal a blow to the imperialists from all directions."[12] At the time, Moscow was calling for a strengthening of joint anti-imperialist actions ("unity of action") by the socialist bloc against U.S. imperialism in Vietnam, but the Chinese were adamantly opposed to the Soviet Union.[13] The *Rodong sinmun* editorial was a veiled attack on the Chinese position and a statement of support for the Soviet Union.

Soviet Premier Aleksei Kosygin's visit to North Korea in February 1965 was seen as a turning point in Soviet–North Korean relations. Kosygin and Kim Il-sung discussed the resumption of Soviet economic and military aid to Pyongyang. Kim also promised not to criticize the March 1965 twenty-six-party Moscow Conference (although in fact only nineteen parties actually attended), at which the North Koreans, like the North Vietnamese, were not in attendance.[14] Political scientist Chin W. Chung has pointed out, "The tone of Kosygin's speeches in Pyongyang and Moscow clearly indicated Moscow's willingness to pay a price to bring a member of the Chinese camp back into the Soviet fold."[15] In December 1965, Kim Il-sung told Kim Pyŏng-chik, North Korean ambassador to the Soviet Union, that Kim "requests that Brezhnev receive him" and that he was very interested in Soviet economic aid.[16]

By early 1966, it was clear that Kim Il-sung was moving much closer to Moscow than to Beijing. He was obsessed with improving national defense, and the post-Khrushchev Soviet leaders were willing to provide military equipment. Following Kosygin's 1965 visit to North Korea, Moscow signed two new defense agreements with Pyongyang, enhanced aid for a series of advanced industrial projects, and greatly expanded trade. On June 20, 1966, the Soviet Union and North Korea also signed economic and technical cooperation agreements that stipulated that the Soviet Union would provide loans, experts, and technical aid to establish a series of mineral, energy, and petrochemical projects between 1966 and 1972.[17] This marked the resumption of Soviet aid to North Korea that had been suspended since December 1962.[18]

In March 1967, North Korea signed a military cooperation agreement with the Soviet Union.[19] By the time of the *Pueblo* incident of January 23, 1968 (when the Democratic People's Republic of Korea [DPRK] captured a U.S. reconnaissance ship), "the North Korean armed forces had been completely reequipped with late-model Soviet military hardware, including submarines, T-54 and T-55 tanks, Komar missile boats, radar, ground-to-air missiles, and MiG-21 jet fighters." The Soviet Union "more than doubled the number of ground-to-air missile sites in North Korea, from fourteen to thirty-five, representing a total of 210 launchers."[20]

When China began to apply pressure on Fidel Castro, thus adding tensions to Sino–Cuban relations, Kim Il-sung showed his support for Cuba by personally attending a reception at the Cuban Embassy, on January 3, 1966. This marked the beginning of a moral alliance with Castro based on their common anti-Mao grievances. Castro was delighted to have such an ally—an independent-minded leader of a small Communist country who resisted pressure from the big Communist powers. In March 1966, Castro effusively praised Kim, stating "Kim Il-sung is one of the most distinguished, brilliant, and heroic socialist leaders in the world today."[21]

Beijing attempted to pressure the KWP not to send a delegation to attend the Twenty-Third Congress of the CPSU in March 1966, but Pyongyang paid no heed. At the time, Soviet Foreign Minister Andrei Gromyko met with DPRK Foreign Minister Pak Sŏng-ch'ŏl and told Pak that the Soviet Union fully supported the position of the DPRK with regard to Korean unification and the withdrawal of American forces from South Korea. The Soviet Union deemed DPRK government policy to be correct and to serve the interests of the entire socialist camp.[22]

Pyongyang's relations with Moscow continued to warm. In May 1966, Pyongyang sent a directive to Chosen Soren, a pro–North Korean organization of Koreans in Japan, charging Beijing with sabotaging bloc unity. The directive also blamed the Chinese for openly disparaging Soviet aid to Vietnam and for calling Cuba a revisionist nation. Pyongyang issued direct attacks on the CCP through private channels after the Japanese Communist Party and the Cubans clashed with the Chinese. This directive is the best indication that Pyongyang was moving closer to Moscow after Khrushchev's fall.[23] In late May, Brezhnev secretly met with Kim Il-sung in Vladivostok, promising to increase Soviet military and economic aid to North Korea. During their meeting, Kim Il-sung "characterized the Cultural Revolution as 'massive idiocy.'"[24]

China and North Korea also differed on how best to assist the Vietnamese Communists in the war against the United States. Both American intelligence and Soviet diplomats reported that Beijing pressured Pyongyang "to unleash military operations against the Americans on the Korean Peninsula," but North Korea resisted China's request.[25] It is likely that Kim Il-sung "skillfully took advantage of Beijing's belligerent statements to depict China as the prime aggressor, and thus conceal his own growing militancy from the USSR."[26] In the view of the Soviets, the North Koreans "disassociated themselves from the Chinese standpoint that stressed the necessity of launching a guerrilla war in South Korea."[27] Instead, in September 1966, North Korea agreed to provide pilots to fight on behalf of the North Vietnamese Air Force. Between 1967 and 1969, a total of eighty-seven North Korean Air Force personnel went to Vietnam.[28]

Pyongyang's differences with Beijing were exacerbated as a result of the Cultural Revolution. On July 20, 1966, seven weeks after the Brezhnev–Kim secret meeting in Vladivostok, the North Korean party issued another internal directive to Chosen Soren. It began by explaining both the virtues and faults of the current Soviet leadership, but its attacks on the Chinese leadership were much more serious. The CCP was said to be "treading a very dangerous path today." It had turned to "extreme leftist adventurism" and was "attempting to impose [its] . . . line of thinking on Communist parties of other countries." It censured the CCP's attitude toward the Soviet Union and China's obstructionist position against "unity of action" in Vietnam. The DPRK also held Mao personally responsible for the ongoing purge of intellectuals in China, calling this yet another manifestation of Mao's "extreme leftism," and it expressed worry about the harmful effects that the Chinese Cultural Revolution might have on the attitudes of intellectuals toward Communists in other countries.[29]

A subsequent editorial in *Rodong sinmun*, on August 12, 1966, covering much the same material as the July directive, asserted Pyongyang's independence from both the CPSU and the CCP. At a conference of KWP delegates held on October 5, 1966, Kim Il-sung officially confirmed this position. He declared that the KWP would not indiscriminately follow the ideological line or policy of any other party. He warned that "no one should make exaggerated or distorted appraisals of any fraternal country or party, or place any such party" in the same category as the enemy. This represented an indirect attack on the CCP.[30] According to a report by the German Democratic Republic (GDR) Embassy in Pyongyang, "DPRK officials would crack jokes about events across the border, and even about Chairman Mao himself. Mao had become senile, Koreans remarked to Amb. Vigoa, and perhaps the only remedy for him was Korean ginseng root." Pyongyang "portrayed the Cultural Revolution as incomprehensible and the Red Guards as 'just kids who know nothing about politics.'"[31]

From the second half of 1966 to the end of 1968, North Korean newspapers and magazines published a series of editorials that criticized leftist opportunism, dogmatism, and chauvinism.[32] These were actually indirect attacks on China. As Romanian diplomat N. Popa reported in May 1967, "Although well aware of how North Korea exploits its relations with China, [China] adopted an indifferent, immovable and expectative attitude, a position which implied no consequences or replies to the various actions undertaken by the North Koreans with a view to aggravating their relations with China. Therefore, the Chinese did not publish any materials on DPRK–PRC relations, they did not respond to the declarations made at press conferences or in newspapers, which should be noted as an exception to the rule."[33]

In April 1968, Kim Il-sung told a visiting Socialist Unity Party of Germany Politburo member, "Currently there are big differences of opinion with the Chinese, but they still say they will fight together with us against U.S. imperialism if that proves necessary. They say our deep differences are of a tactical and not a strategic nature. They slander us as revisionists but we always stay calm. When the Red Guards insult us, the Chinese tell us that the party and government are not responsible. Only if e.g. *People's Daily* [Renmin Ribao] attacks us would they be responsible."[34]

According to Chinese statistics, from 1967 to 1969 Chinese press coverage of North Korea dropped to only seventeen items, a mere fraction of the reporting in previous years.[35] As Romanian diplomat N. Popa reported, "Sino–Korean relations have been marked since the fall of 1964 by a certain deterioration, which has been constantly aggravating, especially politically, culturally and in the consular area, without affecting economic–commercial relations and the level of diplomatic representation."[36] The level of diplomatic representation of the two countries during most of this period was that of chargés d'affaires. Chinese ambassador Jiao Reyu left Pyongyang for China on October 26, 1966, and did not return to his post. China did not send its new ambassador, Li Yunchuan, to North Korea until March 1970, a month before Zhou Enlai's visit to North Korea in April 1970. Although there was only a Chinese chargé d'affaires present in Pyongyang in 1967, North Korea sent Hyŏn Chunkŭk as ambassador to China on June 20, 1967. On the consular front, individual traffic and border commerce were halted, as were repatriations and family visits. Chinese-language schools in the DPRK were closed down for an unlimited duration.[37]

Chinese Perceptions of the North Korean Leadership

As noted, from 1965 to 1969 Chinese relations with North Korea cooled. There were no exchanges of high-level delegations. But although political relations were tense, normal diplomatic and economic relations were maintained. Internal communications provided by Chinese sources reveal that some Chinese leaders regarded the KWP as revisionist. Because of the nationwide turmoil in China, several Red Guard publications openly attacked the North Korean leadership, especially Kim Il-sung. But these did not represent the views and attitudes of the central leadership, especially Mao Zedong and Premier Zhou Enlai. Mao and Zhou never publicly said anything negative about Kim Il-sung.

At the National Day reception at the North Korean Embassy in Beijing on September 9, 1966, Foreign Minister Chen Yi implicitly criticized Pyongyang, saying, "In order to fight against imperialism, one has to fight against modern revisionism. All real revolutionaries must make a clear distinction about the modern revisionists, resolutely disclose the scabs on their true faces, and never take so-called 'joint actions' with them."[38] But North Korea simply ignored China's warning. *Guoji gongyun cankao ziliao*, an internal publication of the Xinhua News Agency, pointed out in March 1967, "In diplomacy, North Korea has moved closer to the Soviet Union."[39]

On November 17, 1966, Tao Zhu, who had recently been promoted to the Standing Committee of the CCP CC Politburo and ranked fourth among Chinese leaders, told delegates from the Mao Zedong Thought Red Guard Shenyang headquarters that Northeast China was very important because it represented the front line of China's national defense. Tao said, "Your [region] is encircled on three sides by Soviet revisionists, Mongolian revisionists, and Korean revisionists. . . . Your region is very important."[40]

Apparently this was the first time that a high-level Chinese leader openly accused North Korea of revisionism. In October 1967, in a talk on the international situation, Yao Wenyuan, a leading radical who was then the second secretary of the Shanghai Municipal CCP Committee and later would become a member of the so-called Gang of Four, said:

There are only three Marxist–Leninist parties and three socialist countries in today's world—China, Albania, and Vietnam. . . . North Korea is reckless in its anti-China activities, accusing us of great-power chauvinism, sectarianism, and left-adventurism . . . epithets hurled on us by the Soviet revisionists . . . of rejecting unity of action on the Vietnam issue with the Soviet Union. . . . At the Fifth Congress of the KWP, Kim Il-sung delivered an anti-China report. . . . There is no Mao Zedong Thought in North Korea, but the masses and leftist KWP members worship Chairman Mao and love Chairman Mao. Kim Il-sung belongs to a privileged stratum and is a degenerate element. . . . The domestic economic situation in North Korea is very poor and the so-called Ch'ŏllima movement was simply an exaggeration. Ordinary people earn very little, whereas people of the privileged strata enjoy high salaries. . . . We have not exposed them in our newspapers. . . . It is all right for you to know the real situation in North Korea, but please do not disseminate this information.[41]

Yao Wenyuan was not the only one to speak out openly about North Korean revisionism. On October 19, 1967, in a speech on the international situation to cadres and staff of the central government, Feng Biao, director of the international news section of *Renmin ribao*, told the audience, "Day by day [North] Korea is opposed to Mao Zedong Thought and to China. [North] Korea advocates its road of neutrality, opposition to imperialism but not to revisionism, and it always sits on its own bench. This is impossible. It can be perceived that [North] Korea has serious problems in the political arena as well as in the economic arena."[42]

The view that the North Koreans had become revisionists was widely shared among Chinese leaders as well as among ordinary citizens. Even Foreign Ministry officials accepted this opinion. On May 20, 1975, long after the Sino–North Korean rapprochement, Foreign Minister Qiao Guanhua was invited to speak to provincial leaders on international issues and Chinese foreign policy. When he began to talk about the Korean War and Kim Il-sung, he noticed that his audience started to whisper among themselves. He said:

You are calling him an "old revisionist." When Kim Il-sung was visiting Beijing [in April 1975], some among those who came out to welcome him were in low spirits. The Premier [Zhou] said we should learn from the North Koreans. How can we learn from them if they are revisionists? The North Korean comrades face a difficult situation and we should take that into consideration. . . . North Korea was first closer to us, but it later became estranged from us and grew closer to the Soviet revisionists. Soon revisionism began to run rampant in North Korea. The North Koreans later got the worst of Soviet revisionism and were afraid of the revival of militarism in Japan. He [Kim Il-sung] soon sent Ch'oe Yong-gŏn to China. Kim

[Il-sung] ordered that the monuments and memorial halls for the slain Chinese People's Volunteers be rebuilt.[43]

In a conversation with a visiting GDR party and state delegation in April 1968, DPRK foreign minister Pak Sŏng-ch'ŏl said, "During the last three years, we have had almost no party-to-party contacts with China. They accuse us of revisionism and no longer call us comrades. Nonetheless, we still want to maintain solidarity with them."[44]

The Soviet invasion of Czechoslovakia in August 1968 aroused strong worldwide condemnation and concern among the socialist countries. To stabilize the situation, the CPSU decided to host a World Communist and Workers' Parties Conference in Moscow to promote "the unity of all Communist and workers' parties." When the Soviet ambassador relayed an invitation from the CPSU CC to the KWP, Kim Il-sung was noncommittal, declaring that such a conference would result in a further rupture in the International Communist Movement. Although pressured by Moscow, the KWP did not send any delegates to the conference.[45]

Evidently, Kim Il-sung wanted to leave some leeway in his relations with China. After the Sino–Soviet border clashes on Zhenbao Island, in March 1969, Brezhnev wrote to Kim Il-sung to request that North Korea publish a Soviet statement for the purpose of "influencing the Chinese so that they would not complicate the situation." Kim turned down the Soviet request on the grounds that Pyongyang had no influence over China.[46] Years later, Kim Il-sung told Erich Honecker, "Relations with China were poor during the 'Cultural Revolution' . . . China agitated against the 'Korean revisionists' over loudspeakers that were set up along the entire Sino–Korean border." However, due to fears of the United States in the South, Pyongyang was eager to improve relations with China after the end of the radical phase of the Cultural Revolution, in 1969.[47]

Red Guard Attacks on Kim Il-sung

The Red Guards attacked everyone except Mao Zedong and his presumptive successor, Lin Biao, prior to Lin's downfall in September 1971. The attacks by the Red Guards on Kim Il-sung were not particularly serious, but the central government had no control over them. First, in mid-January 1967, two Red Guard posters claimed that Kim Il-sung had been deposed and Deputy Premier Kim Kwang-hyŏp had been arrested. On February 19, large-character posters signed by "Chinese soldiers who were participants in the Korean War" were put up in the center of Beijing, accusing Kim Il-sung of betraying Marxism–Leninism, of following revisionist policies, and of being "Khrushchev's disciple."[48] Zhou Enlai tried to mollify Pyongyang and dissociate Beijing from the posters by telling a meeting of Zhejiang Red Guards that the rumor of a coup had been fabricated in South Korea and that Kim Il-sung was still premier.[49]

North Korean reactions to the Red Guard assertions were modest and measured. Pyongyang did not attack the CCP publicly. On January 26, 1967, the Korean Central News Agency issued a statement denying that a coup had taken place and warning Beijing against any reiteration of such "false propaganda." The statement indicated Korean sensitivity to any charges of disunity, insisting that party and government leaders, as well as the people and the Korean People's Army, were "firmly united in one ideology" under the party headed by Kim Il-sung. Because the Chinese Embassy in Pyongyang refused to remove materials about the Red Guard movement from the bulletin board in front of the embassy building, the North Korean government set up a blockade on the road leading to the embassy, to prevent North Korean pedestrians from seeing the materials.[50] When "news agencies and official press organs in Bulgaria, USSR, Czechoslovakia, GDR, and Poland" reported on the Red Guard attacks against Kim Il-sung, the DPRK Ministry of Foreign Affairs summoned the chiefs of the respective diplomatic missions and "handed [them] a formal complaint for having published calumnious writings about the North Korean party and state leadership in their respective newspapers." The Ministry of Foreign Affairs required that "from then on news agencies in their respective countries [should] not release, using Chinese or any other sources, calumnious reports on the DPRK and its leadership." A Romanian diplomat quipped that "the North Koreans took the easy way out, chiding the aforementioned countries instead of confronting the PRC."[51] This clearly indicated that Pyongyang was doing all that it could not to provoke Beijing.

For a while, the Chinese Embassy in Pyongyang waged a silent battle against North Korea. A poster erected on the roof of the embassy stated, "Those Fighting Against Imperialism Must Also Fight Against Revisionism!" In response, the North Koreans hung a poster on the opposite side of the street that read, "Firmly Uphold the Unity of the Socialist Camp!"[52]

Red Guard accusations continued until the spring of 1968. In February 1968, a Guangdong Red Guard bulletin claimed, "Kim Il-sung is an out-and-out counterrevolutionary revisionist of the Korean revisionist clique as well as a millionaire, an aristocrat, and a leading bourgeois element in Korea. His house commands a full view of the Moranbong, the Taedong River, and the Pot'ong River. . . . The estate covers an area of several tens of thousands square meters and is surrounded on all sides by high walls. All sides of the estate are dotted with sentry posts. One has to pass through five or six doors before one arrives at the courtyard. This is really reminiscent of the great palaces of past emperors."[53]

Like many ordinary Chinese, ethnic Koreans in China were persecuted and suspected of spying for North Korea. Many lost their jobs, were taken into custody, or were "struggled against" (criticized or physically abused at a public meeting), locked up, and interrogated. The area of Yanbian in particular was hard hit. From August 1967 to October 1970, more than ten thousand "North Korea revisionist spies" were arrested in Yanbian.[54] In October 1967, East German diplomats reported that the "bodies of Korean casualties were displayed on a freight train traveling from the Chinese border town of Sinŭiju into the DPRK, along with graffiti that read: 'Look, this will be also [sic] your fate, you tiny revisionists!'"[55]

No Chinese sources have surfaced revealing that Mao Zedong and Zhou Enlai ever had any plans to spread the Cultural Revolution to North Korea or Vietnam. Meanwhile, Albania was the only country that openly supported the Cultural Revolution.[56] In fact, beginning in September 1967, Zhou Enlai took great care to improve Chinese relations with North Korea. To do so, he even took advantage of a visiting foreign head of state, President Moktar Ould Daddah of Mauritania, who was visiting China in October 1967. Daddah, who was also scheduled to visit North Korea, Cambodia, and Egypt, was received by Mao Zedong. In his negotiations with the Mauritanian guests, Zhou emphasized that China wanted to resolve international issues in accordance with the five principles of peaceful coexistence.

On the way to the airport to see off Daddah, on October 24, Zhou asked Daddah to convey a three-point message to Kim Il-sung, to Prince Sihanouk of Cambodia, and to President Nasser of Egypt. He said, "China has always taught overseas Chinese to abide by the laws of the country in which they live. However, China does not have control over their activities. There have been shortcomings in the work of the Chinese embassies. We are not trying to hide this, but we are making efforts to improve it. The imperialists defile China, but China's policy toward [North] Korea, Cambodia, and Egypt has never changed. China has always supported their struggles against the imperialists."[57]

Three days later, after visiting North Korea, Daddah stopped over in Beijing on his way to Cambodia. He brought Zhou Enlai a four-point message from Kim Il-sung that stated that Korea's policy toward China had not and would never change in the future; that Kim had a very profound friendship with Chairman Mao Zedong and Premier Zhou Enlai, and he cherished the friendship they had built up in their common struggle; that although the leaders disagreed with each other on some issues, there were no serious problems in their relations, and these could be resolved through face-to-face discussions; and that Kim trusted that if Korea were attacked, China would come to its aid, as it had done many times in the past.[58] Obviously, Kim Il-sung knew his limits and was attempting to reassure the Chinese leaders of his position.

The Continuation of Normal Diplomatic and Economic Relations

After the Sino–Soviet differences were openly revealed in the early 1960s, Chinese leaders began to link China's economic aid with opposition to the Soviet Union. When DPRK foreign minister Pak Sŏng-ch'ŏl was in Beijing in March 1964, PRC President Liu Shaoqi and Premier Zhou Enlai held long briefings with him about "the situation concerning the struggle against revisionism." Both Liu and Zhou urged Pyongyang to stand firm and not to fear any anticipated economic pressures from Moscow. They pledged that China would do its best to support the DPRK.[59] One month later, Zhou informed Pak Se-Ch'ang, the DPRK's newly appointed ambassador to Beijing, that the PRC was prepared to sign another agreement with North Korea on technical aid.[60] In return, on September 5, Kim Il-sung assured Fang Yi, chairman of the PRC's State Commission on Foreign Economic Liaisons, that the DPRK would stand together with "Chinese comrades" in pursuit of an "independent national economy" as well as in opposition to Soviet "revisionism."[61]

Meanwhile, Beijing accommodated Pyongyang's requests for economic aid, in December 1965, by providing a loan of $3 million to help purchase "war preparation" material. The Chinese also agreed to assist North Korea by exporting North Korean rice to Western Europe through Hong Kong. China's "generosity" was highly appreciated by the DPRK leadership.[62] Vice Premier Kim Il expressed heartfelt thanks to the Chinese, stating, "We can only rely on China—no one else. . . . In the International Communist Movement, for the purpose of countering modern revisionism and defending the purity of Marxism–Leninism, we should unite to fight our common enemy."[63]

During his June 1966 trip to Albania, Zhou Enlai told Albanian leaders that North Korea ranked second only to Vietnam in terms of priority for Chinese foreign aid.[64] But PRC economic aid to North Korea came to a halt in the summer of 1966, during the Cultural Revolution.[65] After the KWP Congress of October 1966, all Sino-North Korean cultural cooperation programs were terminated, but Sino-North Korean bilateral trade continued.[66] Annual trade supply agreements and agreements on science and technology cooperation were signed, but they had less substance.[67] A CIA report on North Korea's foreign trade indicates that, in 1966, Communist countries accounted for 87 percent of North Korea's total trade of about $445 million, with the USSR and China together representing 75 percent of the total ($290.4 million). This share had remained relatively constant since 1964. North Korea's most important imports from China were coke, minerals, cotton, and sugar. According to the CIA analysis, "Imports had consistently exceeded exports, until in 1966, when North Korea achieved an export surplus with both the Free World and the Communist Countries."[68]

According to Chinese government sources, China exported more and bought less from North Korea. North Korea used a Chinese loan to make up the difference. After completion of the second Sino-North Korean long-term trade agreement (from 1963 to 1967), China and North Korea did not sign another trade agreement and the volume of trade decreased dramatically. The total volume of trade between China and North Korea reached more than $200 million in 1966 (Chinese exports were $114 million and Chinese imports were $88 million), $176 million in 1967, but only $110 million in 1968, a decrease of 37.5 percent from the previous year, and only $92 million in 1969.[69]

An East German document reported that a nineteen-member Chinese delegation visited North Korea to negotiate a trade agreement on January 29, 1968. But DPRK Deputy Prime Minister Yi Chu-yŏn told a Soviet official in December 1967 that "there were no prospects at all for a trade agreement between the DPRK and the PRC for the year of 1968."[70] Beijing was obviously unhappy about Pyongyang's overall attitude toward the Cultural Revolution. Nonetheless, trade relations with North Korea continued.

On March 18, 1967, China's Ministry of Foreign Trade and the First Ministry of Light Industry issued a circular regarding the export of granulated sugar to North Korea. It stated that, in 1967, China would provide North Korea with 40,000 tons of granulated sugar from Jilin, Heilongjiang, and Shanxi provinces. The circular stressed that "exporting to North Korea is currently an antirevisionist political task." The ministries declared, "Please step up coordination among relevant work units. Motivate revolutionary workers and staff to work hard on this assignment. Concentrate on ideological work as well as on processing, allocating, and transporting arrangements. Ensure that exports to North Korea are carried out on time with good quality and quantity."[71] According to a June 15, 1967, report by a Romanian diplomat:

A Chinese team of specialists working on military and civilian telecommunications and a team working on electronics are in North Korea. A Chinese team of specialists working on oil exploration just returned from North Korea. Chinese specialists are currently building the tower of the new television station. . . . Recently, the Chinese government finished its equipment deliveries to North Korea and from now on it will offer technical assistance to the DPRK for assembling and organizing production at a new factory for transmission-reception portable military radio stations. . . . China continues to give North Korea military assistance, in other words, nonrefundable aid, in the form of gasoline and fuel for jet planes.[72]

We now know that, from 1968 to 1973, China had to suspend construction of the subway in Beijing in order to assist Pyongyang to build its own subway (designed by the Soviets). All the engineers, workers, construction materials, and vehicles came from China. This represented a huge drain on the Chinese economy.[73]

Why did North Korea play down its economic contacts with China during these years? In a conversation with Romanian Ambassador N. Popa, Chinese chargé d'affaires Wang Peng argued that "North Korean leaders try to justify the lack of a wide variety of foodstuffs and consumer goods in front of the North Korean population" and the "North Korean authorities are trying to obtain material advantages from other European socialist countries, especially from the USSR."[74] It is understandable that North Korea would try to procure more from its two giant neighbors and would attempt to maintain neutrality in the Sino–Soviet dispute. Political scientist Byung Chul Koh has argued that North Korea's overall posture in the Sino–Soviet dispute during the 1965-1968 period was "one of neutrality— not neutrality pure and simple but with a slight slant in favor of Moscow."[75] We argue that during this period North Korea was actually closer to Moscow than it was to Beijing but that Pyongyang made great efforts not to openly offend Beijing. In March 1968, an East German diplomat reported that there were "no publications arguing directly against the CCP line, Mao Zedong as a person, or other members of the leading group in the PRC."[76]

China's Urgent Invitation

In the second half of the 1960s, North Korea launched a series of attacks on the United States and South Korea, including numerous incidents in the demilitarized zone along the 38th parallel, from May 1967 to January 1968; a sneak attack on the Blue House—South Korea's presidential palace—on January 21, 1968; the *Pueblo* incident on January 23, 1968; and the shooting down of a U.S. EC-121 spy plane in April 1969.[77] Tensions between Washington and Pyongyang were very high.

The Chinese response to the *Pueblo* incident was slow in coming. On January 28, 1968, five days after the incident, the Chinese government issued a statement: "The Chinese government and people firmly support the Korean government and people's righteous stance against the reckless provocation by the U.S. imperialists."[78] According to reports by East German diplomats, after the Blue House attack and the *Pueblo* incident, China sent engineering troops to repair North Korean weapons and equipment. A nineteen-member Chinese delegation visited Pyongyang to negotiate a trade agreement on January 29.[79]

In mid-February, Zhou Enlai sent a personal message to Kim Il-sung, in which he "proposed to jointly normalize Sino–Korean relations and to leave past quarrels behind . . . [and] mentioned the traditional friendship between the Chinese and the Korean people and reassured Kim Il-sung of the candor with which the Chinese people would be ready at any given point in time to give its full support to the Korean people."[80] After a conversation with Chinese Chargé d'Affaires Wang Peng on March 16, Romanian diplomat A. Lazar reported, "Contrary to the harsh language used previously by Chinese diplomats toward the DPRK party and state leadership and about DPRK internal and foreign policy, it was noticeable that Wang Peng completely changed his approach, having become an active supporter of the forceful line promoted by the DPRK."[81]

Historians have debated about why North Korea became so belligerent in the late 1960s.[82] Perhaps Kim Il-sung intentionally created these crises in order to draw together his two Communists allies in a common cause against the United States and South Korea. But Mao was in no hurry to improve relations with Pyongyang as he was fully preoccupied with the Cultural Revolution and China's domestic problems. Furthermore, the Chinese leadership was still angry about Kim's close relationship with the Soviet "revisionists." In October 1968, the North Korean Embassy extended an invitation to Beijing to send a delegation to the celebration on the twentieth anniversary of the establishment of the DPRK, on the condition that the Chinese delegation would not be allowed "to verbally attack other socialist countries while in North Korea." China turned down the invitation.[83] "Beijing justified this snub by noting the participation of Soviet 'revisionists' in the festivities."[84]

According to East German documents, "DPRK officials spread rumors that China intended to make use of North Korean defectors who had fled after the failed 1956 coup attempt against Kim Il-sung."[85] This, indeed, was indicative of the North Korean leader's fears. According to the Russian archives, North Korea dismissed several cadres who had fought in China during the War of Resistance against Japan but who also remained loyal to Kim Il-sung. These included Kim Ch'ang-man, a member of the Political Council of the KWP, and Ha Ang-ch'ŏn, an alternate member of the Political Council.[86] At a KWP plenum in November 1968, numerous senior military officers were purged, including Minister of People's Defense Kim Ch'ang-pong, Deputy Minister of People's Defense O Paek-ryong, and Army Chief of Staff Ch'oe Kwang, all of whom were accused of being "pro-China."[87]

But China remained very restrained. During the early period of the Cultural Revolution, when tensions in Sino–North Korean relations were escalating, the living conditions of North Korean cadres who had defected to China improved, and they were resettled in major cities such as Beijing, Shanghai, Qingdao, Taiyuan, and Xi'an.[88] But the Chinese rejected Sŏ Hwi's request to "organize forces to enter North Korea to launch a struggle." The CCP International Liaison Department instructed, "Do not allow them to establish organizational connections. Scatter them in different localities. Organize them to study and conduct research on North Korea."[89] Obviously, Chinese leaders had no intention of making use of them for the purpose of opposing Kim Il-sung. Nevertheless, the Chinese might have felt uncomfortable about treating these people too harshly and thus provided them with better accommodations.

It has been widely rumored that there were minor border skirmishes between China and North Korea when Chinese and Soviet troops clashed on Zhenbao Island in March 1969. Citing East German documents, Bernd Schaefer argues that there were indeed some minor border incidents between the PRC and DPRK in 1969.[90] A Bulgarian diplomat in Pyongyang reported, "The border incidents became more frequent. A more serious incident, later confirmed by Kim Il-sung, occurred on March 15, 1969. Eighty unarmed Chinese crossed the border and entered a Korean village. They plundered livestock before retreating."[91] A Soviet document confirms the same episode. On March 17, 1969, Kim Il-sung told Soviet Ambassador N. G. Sudarikov that, on March 15, "around fifty Chinese crossed the border along the Tumen River and entered a Korean village, which is about 200 meters from the river." When a contingent of North Korean frontier troops arrived, they escaped, "taking away several bulls and handcarts."[92]

Years later, Kim Il-sung would tell the same story to Eastern European leaders, in slightly different versions. For instance, in October 1973 he told Todor Zhivkov, first secretary of the Bulgarian Communist Party, about "armed Chinese soldiers and officers" penetrating into North Korea. He said:

> In this village we had soldiers and armed villagers (along the border our people carry arms), about fifty people; and the Chinese penetrated into our country with 100 armed soldiers and officers. I was out in the country at the time (on Saturdays and Sundays I usually go out in the country to read) and they told me about this infiltration by the Chinese soldiers. I gave instructions to our people to let

them in and not to shoot at them straight away. But if they tried to advance farther into our territory and carry out actions, our people were to block their way and capture at least five of them alive. The Chinese soldiers, however, penetrated into our territory and then withdrew without undertaking any action. There were also similar, but less significant, incidents in other places along the border.[93]

In May 1984, Kim also spoke about this with East German leader Erich Honecker. He said, "While I was recuperating in the country, I received a call from our minister of state security that Chinese troops were crossing the Tumen [River] onto our territory. I gave the order not to shoot, but to let them come ahead so that we could take them on our territory, if necessary. We sent a group of soldiers there. Then the Chinese withdrew."[94]

It is quite possible that the memorandum of this conversation, prepared by Todor Zhivkov himself after the meeting and filtered through interpreters, is not accurate. The stenographic record of the May 1984 conversation between Erich Honecker and Kim Il-sung is more reliable. According to that record, Kim did mention the Chinese troops but he did not use the word "armed." Indeed, the so-called border skirmishes revealed North Korea's hypersensitivity and overreaction.[95] According to reminiscences and interviews with educated youth who had been sent to work in Yanbian, military conflicts never occurred along the Sino–North Korean border. They recalled that educated youth from Shanghai all wore yellow cotton-padded clothing and caps provided by the Shanghai Municipal Revolutionary Committee. It is likely that the North Koreans mistakenly thought they were Chinese troops. North Korea thus cut down trees along the border and built underground bunkers in order to prevent Chinese troops from engaging in sneak attacks.[96]

After the Soviet Union and China became involved in military conflicts in the wake of the Zhenbao incident in March 1969, Mao Zedong no longer actively promoted revolution in the same way that he had during the early years of the Cultural Revolution, and he no longer had an incentive to criticize socialist states, especially North Korea, for being revisionist or insufficiently revolutionary. The Ninth Congress of the CCP, in April 1969, brought the radical phase of the Cultural Revolution to an end. Mao and Zhou were again in effective control of Chinese foreign policy making, and they attempted to rectify some of the more radical policies of the previous years. To demonstrate China's goodwill, Mao held friendly talks with emissaries from forty countries during the International Workers' Day holiday on May 1, 1969. This demonstrated China's intention to develop friendly relations with other countries. On numerous occasions, Chinese leaders, especially Premier Zhou, took the initiative to admit the mistakes of China's previous ultra-leftist policy. Mao conveniently explained away his own responsibility by stating that some Chinese had been chauvinists and ultra-leftists.[97]

Beginning in early June 1969, Chinese ambassadors who had been recalled at the beginning of the Cultural Revolution gradually began to return to their posts.[98] Chinese diplomacy was returning to normalcy. The stabilization of Chinese politics was also favorable to an improvement in Sino–North Korean relations.

After the downing of a U.S. spy plane in April 1969, Assistant to the President for National Security Affairs Henry Kissinger told President Richard Nixon that "the Chinese have not endorsed the North Korean position during the recent tension."[99] The August 8, 1969, "Response to National Security Study Memorandum 14" states, "Although North Viet-Nam and North Korea pursue largely independent policies, sometimes in conflict with those of the PRC, Peking has a major national security interest in their continued existence and would almost certainly intervene militarily if the Communist regime of either country were seriously threatened."[100]

Meanwhile, there were signs of strains in Soviet–North Korean relations. Several days after the *Pueblo* incident, at the January 27, 1968, UN Security Council session, P. D. Morozov, Soviet representative to the UN, publicly defended North Korea.[101] In private, however, the Soviet Union did not support Korea's seizure of the *Pueblo* or its shooting down of the American EC-121 reconnaissance plane in April 1969. Donald Zagoria notes, "After each incident the Soviets dispatched high-level Politburo members to Pyongyang and publicly warned the North Korean ruler that the defense of the socialist camp had to be 'collective,' i.e., that unilateral attacks on the United States would not be sanctioned."[102]

In principle, China was more supportive of Kim's military adventurism. Naturally, Pyongyang wanted to improve relations with Beijing. Therefore, North Korea gradually abandoned its closer relations with the Soviet Union and made efforts to improve relations with China. On May 12, 1969, when Nikolai Podgorny, chairman of the Presidium of the Supreme Soviet of the Soviet Union, visited North Korea for a week, he was unable to prevent Pyongyang from moving closer to China.[103] The KWP did not attend the World Communist and Workers' Parties Conference in Moscow in June 1969. One of the items on the agenda of the conference was to establish an anti-China "Asian collective security" system.[104] Chin-Wee Chung has pointed out that another factor behind the improved Sino-North Korean relationship was their "shared hostility toward Japan" and fear of a revival of Japanese militarism.[105]

After attending the funeral of Vietnamese leader Ho Chi Minh on September 10, 1969, Ch'oe Yong-gŏn, chairman of the Presidium of the Supreme People's Assembly of the DPRK, visited Beijing. Zhou Enlai met with Ch'oe on two occasions and thanked him for transmitting Kim Il-sung's wish to improve bilateral relations. Ch'oe told Zhou that North Korea did not support the Soviet proposal to establish an "Asian collective security" system that would be targeted against China.[106] To improve Sino-North Korean relations, the North Korean side stipulated two conditions: first, the Chinese should not interfere "in the internal affairs of the DPRK, including the dismantling of the speakers along the border"; and second, the Chinese should not interfere "in DPRK relations with the Soviet Union. The PRC accepted both."[107] To hide the improvement in Sino-North Korean relations from the Soviet Union, on September 19 Kim Il-sung told N. M. Shubnikov, a high-ranking diplomat at the Soviet Embassy in North Korea, that China and North Korea could not agree on much and had major differences. He said that the meeting between Ch'oe and Zhou had achieved nothing.[108]

Sino-North Korean relations continued to improve on the eve of the twentieth anniversary of the founding of the PRC, in October 1969. Even though Beijing had decided in principle that no foreign delegations would be invited to attend the anniversary celebrations, China issued an invitation to Pyongyang at 3:20 P.M. on September 30. Although Kim Il-sung was not in Pyongyang at the time, he tacitly understood the significance of China's invitation, and he immediately called a meeting to discuss the issue.[109] At 6:25 P.M., Pyongyang replied that Ch'oe Yong-gŏn would lead a high-level North Korean government and party delegation to attend China's National Day celebration. The North Korean delegation arrived in Beijing at 11:30 that evening. The next day, Mao met with Ch'oe at the gate tower of Tiananmen (the Gate of Heavenly Peace) and told him, "Now the United States has a much closer relationship with Japan, and it also has pursued a closer relationship with South Korea and Taiwan. . . . They

Figure 6.1 Mao Zedong and Ch'oe Yong-gŏn at the gate tower of Tiananmen, Beijing, October 1, 1969.

intend to attack you. But their target is not only you; their main target is China. Therefore, our two countries must become closer. . . . Relations between our two countries are very special, and our aims are identical, so we should improve our relations."[110]

Ch'oe proposed that Mao invite Kim Il-sung to visit China to discuss issues affecting the two countries. Mao promised to send Premier Zhou Enlai to North Korea and that, thereafter, he would also invite Kim Il-sung to China.[111] Mao's conversation with Ch'oe established a solid foundation for a Sino–North Korean reconciliation.

The deterioration in Sino–North Korean relations from 1965 to 1969 was mainly due to the radicalization of China's domestic and foreign policies. Chinese leaders were disappointed with North Korea after Brezhnev and Kosygin assumed power and increased aid to North Korea. Meanwhile, Kim Il-sung attempted to keep an equal distance between Beijing and Moscow, and Pyongyang was unwilling to closely follow Beijing in the International Communist Movement or to support China's anti-Soviet position. But for historical reasons, including their common hostility toward the United States, relations between Beijing and Pyongyang were restrained. Even during the chaotic years, from 1966 to 1969, each attempted to maintain a semblance of normal diplomatic and economic contacts and to prevent any further worsening in their relations.

As soon as the high tide of the Cultural Revolution had subsided and the domestic political situation in China had stabilized, Pyongyang was eager to restore relations with Beijing. After the military clashes with the Soviet Union on Zhenbao Island, in March 1969, the Soviet Union became China's foremost enemy, and Mao began to consider improving relations with the United States. But for many years Mao had presented himself as the leader of the world revolution, and he was thus unwilling to completely abandon his class position and to move toward a more nationalist stance that placed priority on national interests. To salvage his shaky revolution-ary credentials, Mao considered the interests of its smaller allies, such as North Korea, Vietnam, and Albania. Therefore, before the process of rap-prochement with the United States could proceed in full swing, China first had to mend fences with North Korea. It was only in this way that Mao could justify his new policy toward the United States as a tactical move.

CHAPTER VII

China's Last Ally, 1970–1976

The Sino–American rapprochement in the early 1970s, which Henry Kissinger considered a "diplomatic revolution," is a watershed event in world history. Its impact should be examined on at least two levels. First, at the level of the process, the rapprochement not only was an issue between the United States and China but also involved the triangular relationship among the United States, China, and the Soviet Union as well as the interests of the allies of both China and the United States. Second, in terms of outcome, the rapprochement affected many other countries, which thereafter had to adjust their respective policies toward both China and the United States.

Previous studies on alliance relationships after the Sino–American rapprochement have focused on its effects on Taiwan, Vietnam, the Soviet Union, and Japan.[1] However, its effects on Korea have received scant attention in scholarly studies.[2] For instance, Chris Tudda's 2012 book on the Sino–American rapprochement, which is based primarily on U.S. documents, does not touch on the Korean issue.[3] Gregg Brazinsky's chapter traces the evolution of China's Korean policy from 1968 to 2000, providing useful but brief treatment of the period from 1970 to 1975.[4]

After the outbreak of the Korean War, the Korean Peninsula became a strategic front line in the Cold War confrontation. Both China and the United States were heavily involved in the contest between North and South Korea. Before the Sino–American rapprochement, China and North

Korea remained hostile to both the United States and South Korea. Any changes in Sino–American relations naturally forced them to modify their respective policies toward their allies. But neither China nor the United States was willing to once again become involved in a war on behalf of the Koreans. Hence, both North and South Korea also began to modify policies toward each other. Two issues remained high on their agendas: sovereignty (in particular, representation at the UN) and security (in particular, the issue of the U.S. troops stationed in South Korea).

This chapter traces China's policies toward North Korea from 1970 to 1976. It examines Chinese views with respect to the Korean issue during the Sino–American rapprochement negotiations as well as Chinese policy toward North Korea in the subsequent deliberations at the UN. It attempts to address the question of how and why China could maintain friendly relations with Pyongyang while at the same time seeking détente with the United States. It is worthwhile to compare the developing Sino–Vietnamese relations with Sino–North Korean relations during this period. Although Premier Zhou Enlai ranked Indochina as the most urgent issue for the relaxation of tensions in the Far East, and in his numerous talks with U.S. officials he urged the United States to withdraw its troops from Vietnam, North Vietnam turned to the Soviet Union for help and China's relations with Vietnam deteriorated dramatically.[5]

It is understandable that, when he was first told about Henry Kissinger's secret visit to Beijing in July 1971, Kim Il-sung was surprised. But China still managed to maintain friendly relations with Pyongyang. How could this be? During this process, what issues did the two countries agree upon and on what issues did they disagree? What was China's foreign policy priority—to defend Pyongyang or to pursue détente with Washington? This chapter also discusses China's economic and military aid to North Korea during the first half of the 1970s and Kim Il-sung's attempt to be the next apostle in the line of world revolutionary leaders during the waning years of Mao Zedong's life.

The Korean Issue in the Sino–American Rapprochement Talks

When, in March 1969, two bloody conflicts between Chinese and Soviet border garrison forces erupted on Zhenbao Island (Damansky Island in

Russian), located on the Ussuri River, China's security situation worsened dramatically. The conflict soon spread to other areas as tensions increased along the entire length of the border. These incidents immediately brought China and the Soviet Union to the brink of a major military confrontation. According to Henry Kissinger, Soviet leaders even considered conducting a preemptive nuclear strike against their former Communist ally.[6] It is not surprising that Beijing's leaders felt compelled to make major changes in China's foreign policy and security strategies.

After the Ninth Party Congress, in April 1969, Mao Zedong authorized Zhou Enlai to make arrangements for four senior marshals—Chen Yi, Ye Jianying, Xu Xiangqian, and Nie Rongzhen—to continue their joint study on the international situation.[7] In mid-May, Zhou Enlai, following Mao's instructions, asked the four marshals to "pay attention to" international affairs. He urged them to meet two to three times each month to discuss important issues on international security and to provide the party Central Committee (CC) with their opinions.[8]

The marshals' study group concluded that it was unlikely that the Soviet Union would wage a large-scale war against China. Nevertheless, it emphasized the need for Beijing to be prepared for a worst-case scenario. In this context, Chen Yi and Ye Jianying contended that, in order for China to be prepared for a major confrontation with the Soviet Union, it should play "the American card." In a written September 17 report entitled "Our Views About the Current Situation," the marshals pointed out that although Moscow was intending to "wage war against China" and had actually deployed forces, the Soviet leadership was unable "to reach a final decision" because of political considerations. The marshals proposed that, in addition to waging "a tit-for-tat struggle against both the United States and the Soviet Union," China should use "negotiation as a means to struggle." Perhaps, the report noted, the Sino–American ambassadorial talks should be resumed "when the timing is proper."[9]

The report by the four marshals' study group provided Mao and Zhou with a strategic assessment that emphasized the benefits of improving Sino–American relations. Both strategically and psychologically, the war scare had created the necessary conditions for the CCP leadership to reconsider the long-standing People's Republic of China (PRC) policy of confrontation with the United States. The perception of an extremely grave threat to China's national security posed by the Soviet Union

Figure 7.1 Zhou Enlai is warmly welcomed by Kim Il-sung during Zhou's visit to the Democratic People's Republic of Korea, April 1970.

convinced Mao to end the existing conceptual restrictions so as to improve relations with the United States.[10]

China's relations with North Korea began to improve after Ch'oe Yong-gŏn's trip to Beijing in September and October 1969. In April 1970, after Zhou Enlai visited North Korea, Sino-North Korean relations quickly recovered from the chill of the Cultural Revolution period. Zhou's primary mission was to lure Pyongyang away from Moscow.[11] In October 1970, Kim Il-sung secretly visited China and Mao met Kim at the state guest house (something Mao had never done for any Western visitor), whereupon Mao made a self-criticism of China's radical policy and in fact revoked China's criticism of Kim during the previous years.[12] Thereafter, China resumed its aid to North Korea, which had been suspended during the Cultural Revolution.

But Sino–North Korean relations were not simply restored to their pre–Cultural Revolution status. China also had to acknowledge Pyongyang's autonomy and independence in foreign affairs. One week after Kim's visit, on October 17, Beijing and Pyongyang signed the Agreement on Chinese

Economic and Technical Aid to North Korea and the Long-Term Trade Agreement.[13] Thus, China actually mended fences with North Korea before the process of rapprochement with the United States entered into full swing.

It took about two years for Washington and Beijing to establish a mechanism for high-level talks. The process began with mutual probing and signaling in 1969 and negotiations via the Warsaw channel in early 1970. With the collapse of the Warsaw channel in the spring of 1970, Beijing and Washington communicated with each other via a secret Pakistani channel. Thereafter, the famous "Ping-Pong diplomacy" took place, in April 1971. After receiving Richard Nixon's message indicating his intention to visit China, Zhou Enlai chaired a May 26 Politburo meeting to establish China's "basic principles" for its new relations with the United States, which also included a demand that the United States withdraw from Korea. In late May 1971, after twenty-two years of confrontation, the Chinese government, via the Pakistani channel, extended an invitation to President Nixon to visit China. Henry Kissinger, assistant to the president for national security affairs, secretly visited Beijing in July of 1971 to discuss the presidential visit with Chinese leaders.[14]

Kissinger's visit to China to prepare the agenda for the forthcoming visit represented the first face-to-face meeting between senior leaders from the PRC and the United States. During Kissinger's forty-eight hours in Beijing, he participated in six meetings, totaling seventeen hours, with Zhou Enlai and other Chinese officials. The Kissinger–Zhou talks focused on the anticipated Mao–Nixon summit, Taiwan, Indochina, U.S.–Japan relations, and U.S. relations with the Korean Peninsula. The two sides also haggled over the wording in the announcement of Nixon's visit to China.[15]

The Korean issue was discussed at some length during the first meeting between Zhou and Kissinger. On the afternoon of July 9, Zhou urged that the United States withdraw from Korea, and Kissinger indicated that it would not be a problem. Zhou said, "Your troops in South Korea should withdraw. We withdrew our people voluntarily from Korea back in 1958."[16] At their meeting on July 10, Kissinger explained that the Korean situation would very much depend on general relations in the area. If the war in Indochina ended, U.S.–PRC relations developed, and Republic of Korea (ROK) troops in Vietnam withdrew, then it was conceivable that most U.S. troops in Korea would also be withdrawn before the end of President Nixon's second term. Kissinger said, "Frankly, I don't think that the

Korean problem need detain us very long. I am certain that a political evolution is occurring in which this will take care of itself. Our military presence in South Korea is not a permanent feature of our foreign policy." Kissinger told Zhou that Nixon would talk with him regarding the precise timetable for a U.S. withdrawal from South Korea.[17]

It seems that Kissinger's declaration went beyond the formulation in National Security Decision Memorandum 48, issued on March 20, 1970. The memorandum stated that "the President has decided to reduce the U.S. military presence in Korea by 20,000 personnel by the end of FY 71." It also pointed out, "Further withdrawals of substantial numbers of U.S. personnel beyond the 20,000 personnel decided upon are not now planned, though they may be considered when substantial ROK forces return from Vietnam or compensating improvements in ROK forces are well underway."[18] Thus, Kissinger's declaration, without many policy implications, was mainly for the purpose of creating a congenial atmosphere for the Sino–American talks. Later in their conversation, when Zhou expressed concerns that, following the U.S. withdrawal from the Korean Peninsula, Japanese forces might move in, Kissinger said, "It is absolutely against President Nixon's policy to project Japan's military power outside its home islands into areas for possible offensive uses." When Zhou noted that there was only an armistice agreement between the two Koreas and that North Korea felt threatened by the presence of U.S. forces in the South, Kissinger said, "We oppose military aggression by South Korea against North Korea. . . . We believe that it would help maintain Asian peace if you could use your influence with North Korea to not use force against the U.S. and against South Korea." Zhou raised no objections.[19] It seems that both Washington and Beijing were interested in maintaining stability on the Korean Peninsula.

But the Sino–American reconciliation had troubling implications for China's erstwhile Communist allies outside of the Soviet bloc, who had relied on China to stand up to the "American imperialists." Thus, Zhou Enlai had a tough job of selling North Vietnam, North Korea, and Albania on China's new policy toward Washington. Soon after Kissinger departed Beijing, Zhou visited Hanoi, on July 13 and 14, and Pyongyang, on July 15, to explain to Vietnamese and North Korean leaders China's new policy toward the United States. Although he stated that China would never barter away its principles and would continue to assist the Vietnamese in their struggle against the United States, he failed to convince them.

In fact, China's diplomatic priority was to improve relations with the United States by welcoming Kissinger and Nixon to China.

The North Vietnamese were so angry that they tilted more obviously toward the Soviet Union.[20] The North Vietnamese Embassy in China formally requested that the Chinese government not arrange for North Vietnamese interns in China to watch newsreels about Nixon's visit to China.[21] Albania, which had vigorously supported China's policy during the Cultural Revolution, felt betrayed by China's reconciliation with the United States. The Party of Labour of Albania CC formally wrote to the CCP CC, resolutely opposing Sino–American collusion and censuring the Chinese policy of "opportunism."[22] In his memoirs, Albanian leader Enver Hoxha states that this development "fell like a bombshell on us Albanians, on the Vietnamese, the Koreans, not to mention the others."[23]

In his deliberations with Kim Il-sung, Zhou described China's new strategy as the formation of a united front with the American people against the U.S. imperialists. It seems that Zhou was successful in convincing Kim. At first, Kim was somewhat surprised, or even shocked, but he did not view China's improved relations with the United States as a betrayal.[24] Zhou tried to persuade Kim that the prospects of a Sino–American rapprochement would drive the United States off the Korean Peninsula. Zhou told Kim that this was identical to China's efforts to bring about Taiwan's return to China. As Zhou firmly stated that China would never abandon its principles, Kim seemed to be persuaded to accept the Chinese position and came to voice support for China's changed policy toward the United States.[25] As a CIA study notes, "North Korea apparently believes that, by welcoming these events, it will further many of its own objectives."[26]

In the wake of the Sino–American reconciliation and the changing international situation, Pyongyang began to adjust its policy. Early on June 10, during a meeting with Romanian leader Nicolae Ceaușescu in Pyongyang, Kim Il-sung elaborated on North Korea's complex strategy. In addition to achieving Korean unification, North Korea hoped to elevate its stature by taking advantage of China's entry into the UN. Kim stated that he regarded "peaceful means" as the only feasible option to achieve Korean unification. He insisted that all other solutions "could trigger a global-scale war." He also noted that neither China nor the Soviet Union wanted "to get involved in such a confrontation." Thus, from North Korea's perspective, unification might be achieved if revolutionary activities were to grow in the South and the U.S. Army were to withdraw. Kim stated, "Should Park Chung Hee be overthrown, we will be able to discuss the unification of our country with anyone who desires this."[27]

On July 30, Vice Premier Kim Il visited China to introduce North Korea's eight-point program for the peaceful unification of Korea, which had been promulgated by the Supreme People's Assembly of the Democratic People's Republic of Korea (DPRK) in April. He also asked the Chinese to transmit the program to the United States. The eight-point program, which focused on the withdrawal of foreign troops and the dissolution of the United Nations Commission for the Unification and Rehabilitation of Korea (UNCURK), made no reference to inter-Korean relations or unification issues.[28]

On August 6, during a visit by Prince Norodom Sihanouk, Cambodian leader-in-exile, Kim Il-sung publicly praised China's reconciliation with the United States. He announced that Nixon's visit to China "will not be the march of a victor but a journey of the defeated. . . . This is a great victory for the Chinese people and a victory for the revolutionary people of the world." He intended to use this formulation to mitigate the impact of the Sino–American rapprochement on the North Korean people. He then announced that he would meet all political parties, "including the [ruling] Democratic Republican Party, and all social organizations and individual personages in South Korea" to improve North–South relations and to work toward unification.[29] This was the first time that Kim had accepted the South Korean ruling party as a legitimate negotiating partner. But, on the same day, Kim also pointed out in *Rodong sinmun* (Workers' Newspaper), the official newspaper of the Korean Workers' Party (KWP), that Koreans should not be cheated by the imperialist détente strategy and should make concerted efforts to strike against the U.S. imperialists.[30] Nonetheless, the ensuing North–South dialogue was initiated due to the impact of the Sino–American rapprochement.

To alleviate North Korea's fears about a Sino–American deal on the Korean issue, China enhanced military cooperation with Pyongyang. On August 5, in an interview with James Reston of the *New York Times*, Zhou Enlai said that China had supported North Korea's position on the *Pueblo* incident and the EC-121 crisis. He pointed out, "To solve the Korean question, a way must be found to bring about a rapprochement between the two sides and to move toward a peaceful unification of Korea." Zhou suggested that a peace treaty to replace the armistice should be in order.[31]

From August 18 to September 7, a high-level North Korean delegation visited China and the PRC promised to provide Pyongyang with free military equipment.[32] Not only did China want to clarify to the United States its position regarding North Korea, it also sought to reassure Pyongyang that the Sino–American rapprochement would not endanger the security and interests of the DPRK. As Kissinger later explained to Nixon, "The Chinese are no doubt well prepared to pay this kind of a price to shift Kim Il-sung into a less belligerent stance on the peninsula."[33]

During his public trip to China in October 1971, Kissinger held ten meetings with Zhou Enlai.[34] This time their discussions on Korea lasted longer than their discussions in July. Due to a request from North Korea, Zhou ranked Korea as number three on the agenda (immediately behind Vietnam and Taiwan in terms of importance), giving it a higher priority than he had in July. In addition to the U.S. withdrawal from Korea, Zhou spoke about allowing North Korea to participate unconditionally in the UN debates. Apparently, Zhou had already anticipated the PRC's role in the UN as a champion on behalf of North Korea. Zhou stressed that the UN should treat South and North Korea equally. He emphasized that the PRC, as a big country, could afford to wait on issues of direct concern, such as Taiwan, whereas the more urgent matters were those concerning China's smaller friends, such as Indochina and Korea, which did not have such a broad perspective.[35]

Zhou then handed over to Kissinger the eight-point program of the North Korean government. The document consisted of a series of generally abusive demands, including that Washington should withdraw U.S. forces and military support for Korea, provide North Korea with equal status, prevent Japanese influence, disband the UNCURK, leave the Korean question to be decided by the Koreans themselves, and allow North Korea to unconditionally participate in the UN debates. Kissinger sharply retorted that the Nixon administration was dedicated to improving relations and easing tensions in East Asia, but he rejected the translation of this goal into a series of unilateral demands. The United States was prepared to move in certain directions, but it could not accept a paper that listed all the things that the United States "must" do and that referred to its South Korean ally as a "puppet." The PRC had never done this, and the United States respected it for standing by its friends. But it was important that North Korea (and North Vietnam) show some of the same spirit as its large ally.

Kissinger then clarified U.S. objectives on the peninsula. The United States was prepared to discuss the possibility of a more permanent legal basis for the existing situation, but it was not interested in a legal situation that allowed for a reopening of hostilities. Kissinger stated that the United States was already reviewing the UNCURK issue and that it recognized North Korea as a fact of life. Zhou stressed that the PRC was interested in equal legal status for both Koreas and that unification should be left to the future.[36]

In later exchanges, Kissinger said that it was U.S. policy not to allow Japanese military forces to enter South Korea, but only to the extent that the United States was able to control this. As tensions in the Far East diminished, the number of U.S. forces would continue to decline and could be expected to be small. In any event, the United States would not allow South Korean military attacks while U.S. forces remained there. As an end to a complicated process, but not as an immediate objective, the United States could envisage North Korea as a lawful entity in the UN and elsewhere. There was merit in giving North Korea fair representation in discussions about the peninsula. As for final reunification, the United States had not studied this problem, but it believed that it should be accomplished peacefully. At the end of their discussions, Zhou seemed to have accepted the U.S. position that the Korean issue would take time but that, in the interim, opinions could be exchanged. Zhou was more interested in dissolution of the UNCURK than in a U.S. withdrawal. Kissinger believed that China was not particularly interested in Korean unification.[37]

In the draft communiqué for the President's visit, both China and the United States agreed to disagree. Instead of superficially and vaguely emphasizing common and shared points, each side would state its own position on specific issues (including Korea). This would allow each side to retain its credibility while at the same time putting together a mutually acceptable joint statement. In Kissinger's words, "The very novelty of the approach might resolve our perplexities."[38] Therefore, the Chinese supported North Korea's eight-point program and called for abolition of the UNCURK. The United States honored its commitments to South Korea and endorsed reduced tensions and increased communications on the peninsula. This indicates that China had placated North Korea but was in no hurry to facilitate U.S. military withdrawal for Korean unification.

After his secret trip to Beijing from November 1 to November 3, 1971, Kim Il-sung became even more convinced that a North–South dialogue under the auspices of the North could achieve unification.[39] He now saw this as a contingent but useful strategy. On November 15, in his address to the Twenty-Sixth Plenary Session of the UN General Assembly (UNGA), Qiao Guanhua, vice foreign minister and head of the Chinese delegation, declared that the Chinese government and people resolutely supported the DPRK's eight-point program for unification, its just demands for repealing unlawful UN resolutions on Korea, and dissolution of the UNCURK.[40] Kim thus felt reassured about China's support for North Korea while it was negotiating with the Americans. On December 2, in a speech to party cadre education instructors, Kim Il-sung said, "The annals of the world revolutionary struggle know no instance in which Communists relinquished their anti-imperialist stand or gave up the revolution simply because they concluded a treaty or held a dialogue with the imperialists. The Soviet Union continued the revolutionary struggle without giving up its anti-imperialist stand, even though it had signed a nonaggression treaty with fascist Germany. In no circumstance will the Chinese Communist Party, which has fought for a long time against domestic reactionaries and imperialist aggressors, abandon the revolution or act against the interests of the socialist countries just because of Nixon's visit."[41]

In early January 1972, Alexander Haig, deputy assistant to the president for national security affairs, led an advance team to Beijing. Its mission was to make technical arrangements for Nixon's forthcoming visit. Zhou Enlai told Haig that the "situation in Vietnam is different from that which pertained in Korea. In Korea, he was heavily involved and agreement could be reached with U.S."[42] Zhou's statement is indicative of the tensions in China's relationship with North Vietnam. North Vietnam had made a futile attempt to persuade the Chinese to call off President Nixon's trip to China. In contrast, Kim Il-sung did not object to Sino–American engagement. Kim apparently hoped that it would facilitate a U.S. troop withdrawal and achieve Korean unification. In an interview with the Japanese newspaper *Yomiuri Shimbun* on January 10, Kim proposed that once a peace agreement was signed and U.S. troops had withdrawn, North and South Korea should carry out a large-scale disarmament.[43] Many in the U.S. government were concerned about the timing of such a peace agreement, that is, whether it should be signed before or after the U.S. troop withdrawal.

On January 26, 1972, a North Korean Foreign Ministry delegation headed by Vice Premier Pak Sŏng-ch'ŏl flew to Beijing to prepare with their Chinese colleagues discussion of issues related to the Korean Peninsula during President Nixon's trip to China. Several members of the delegation remained in Beijing while Nixon was there in the later part of February. Some sources claim that Kim Il-sung also secretly visited Beijing, which Pyongyang denied but Moscow confirmed.[44] Nevertheless, when the U.S. President was in China, from February 21 to February 28, 1972, there were no direct talks between the U.S. delegation and the North Korean delegation. China kept the North Koreans away from the Nixon delegation.[45]

While in Beijing, Nixon and Zhou Enlai exchanged views on a broad range of international issues. They touched briefly on the Korean issue, but only to confirm what Zhou had previously discussed with Kissinger. Zhou said, "As for the question of Korea, we know of course your ideas, and of course you also know our ideas. First, the official policy of the president is that he is prepared to finally withdraw troops from Korea in the future, and also to prevent the entry of Japanese forces into South Korea because this would not be beneficial to the cause of peace in the Far East. How does one promote contacts between North and South Korea? How does one promote peaceful reunification? That question will take a long time." Nixon replied, "The Koreans, both the North and the South, are emotionally impulsive people." He called for the United States and the PRC to restrain the two Koreas from initiating conflicts that could lead to a large war among the Great Powers.[46]

The Shanghai Communiqué, which was released at the end of the presidential visit on February 27, states, "The United States will maintain its close ties with and support for the Republic of Korea . . . [and] will support efforts of the Republic of Korea to seek a relaxation of tension and increased communication on the Korean Peninsula." The PRC "firmly supports the eight-point program for the peaceful unification of Korea" and stood for the abolition of the "UN Commission for the Unification and Rehabilitation of Korea."[47] At this point, China might have come to the conclusion that the withdrawal of U.S. forces from the Korean Peninsula in the near future was not vital to the PRC and would be impossible to achieve.

On March 3, Zhou met with leading officials from the CCP CC and the State Council to explain the Shanghai Communiqué. Zhou said, "We have constantly supported North Korea's eight-point program." Regarding the UNCURK, he said, "It is equal to aggression against [North] Korea and China if this commission is not abolished." He reported that the United States had agreed to abolish the UNCURK at the twenty-seventh or twenty-eighth meeting of the UNGA.[48]

A *Rodong sinmun* editorial on March 4 stated that "it is a good thing" for China to achieve a rapprochement with the United States because it would be conducive to relaxing the international situation. Regarding China's statement on the Korean issue, it referred to "the support of the fraternal Chinese people for our people in order to force the U.S. imperialists to withdraw from South Korea, and to achieve the just course of national unification under the premise of self-determination and peace." The editorial reiterated the position of the North Korean government, condemning U.S. silence in the Shanghai Communiqué on the issue of the withdrawal of U.S. troops and dissolution of the UNCURK.[49] It should be noted that, during this period, *Renmin ribao* reprinted many articles from Korean newspapers and periodicals, but it did not reprint this article. This indicates that the Chinese leaders might have realized that the North Koreans were unhappy that the Shanghai Communiqué failed to mention the withdrawal of U.S. troops from South Korea.

On March 7, 1972, Zhou Enlai visited Pyongyang to brief Kim Il-sung on the Sino–American negotiations during Nixon's visit. Zhou mentioned, in particular, Nixon's tacit agreement that "Japanese forces will not be allowed to enter. Nor will the United States allow Japanese forces to enter South Korea." Although the Shanghai Communiqué stated that "neither is prepared to negotiate on behalf of any third party," China had reminded the United States that "China and North Korea represent one side at the Korean Military Armistice Commission." According to a Chinese report, Kim was very pleased.[50] Pyongyang then issued a lengthy statement praising the Shanghai Communiqué.

According to Erich Merten, chargé d'affaires in the East German Embassy in Pyongyang, Kim was very satisfied with the results of Nixon's visit to China, in particular with China's support in the Shanghai Communiqué of North Korea's position. The DPRK press reprinted the Shanghai Communiqué almost verbatim.[51]

Meanwhile, China paid more attention to cultivating its delicate relationship with North Korea. On the occasions of Kim's sixtieth birthday, on April 15, 1972, and the fortieth anniversary of the Korean People's Army, on April 25, Mao and Zhou sent congratulatory messages, and China dispatched large delegations for the occasions.[52]

On the one hand, North Korea attempted to use China's influence to achieve Korean unification;[53] on the other hand, Pyongyang's subsequent peace offensive was an indication of its dissatisfaction with China's position of not pressing harder for U.S. withdrawal. In March 1973, a Soviet diplomat reported, "The Chinese are not interested in Korean unification. . . . The Chinese were said not to have insisted enough on the withdrawal of U.S. troops from South Korea."[54]

In sum, in terms of the interests and sovereignty of South Korea, the United States was unwilling to discuss North Korea in depth during the rapprochement talks. But China did not want to alienate Pyongyang and thus drive it back to Moscow. Therefore, it had to convince Kim Il-sung that a Sino–American reconciliation would actually help Pyongyang achieve unification under his leadership.[55] It made numerous attempts to include the Korean issue in Sino–American talks and to present itself as a defender of North Korean interests.

The Korean Issue at the United Nations

After the end of the Korean War, the United Nations General Assembly met annually (except in 1960 and 1964) and debated three resolutions related to the Korean issue: acceptance of the UNCURK report, dissolution of the UNCURK, and withdrawal of UN and all other foreign forces. The United States and the ROK held that Korean reunification should take place through peninsula-wide elections supervised by the UNCURK. The PRC criticized this as a unilateral instrument of U.S. policy. In 1971, the United States and South Korea asked the UN to put off any discussions on the Korean issue, insisting on waiting for the results of the inter-Korean talks. The UN thus suspended discussion of the Korean issue in 1971.[56]

Because both the Soviet Union and China had a mutual defense treaty with North Korea (signed in July 1961) and the United States had a mutual defense treaty with South Korea (signed in 1953), the Sino–American rapprochement affected the structure of the confrontation on the Korean Peninsula (that is, China and North Korea, plus the Soviet Union, versus the United States and South Korea, plus Japan). After Nixon's trip to China in early 1972, both China and the United States made great efforts to avoid a direct confrontation over the Korean issue in the international arena. Pyongyang modified its international strategy by strengthening its international united front via the UN and the Non-Aligned Movement. In terms of North–South relations, Pyongyang launched a peace offensive toward the South Korean government in 1971 and initiated a North–South dialogue in order to force a U.S. troop withdrawal, to prevent Japanese intrusion into South Korea, and to win international recognition.[57] By following in China's footsteps, Pyongyang would gain expanded international recognition and eventual acceptance into the United Nations.

Pyongyang hoped to be invited to the Twenty-Seventh Session of the UNGA, in 1972, and to end the UN mission on the Korean Peninsula. But Seoul was against inviting Pyongyang and requested that a UN discussion on the Korean issue be postponed until after 1972, on the grounds that it might interfere with the inter-Korean dialogue. After six years of absence, China returned to the Korean Military Armistice Commission, at Panmunjom, in July 1971. China superficially called for a U.S. troop withdrawal in order to win over the hearts and minds of North Korea. But from a short-term perspective, China did not have a great strategic interest in a complete U.S. troop withdrawal. It was more worried about the Soviet Union than it was about the United States. According to the U.S. National Security Estimate of May 1972, Sino–North Korean cooperation in foreign policy rested on the basis of shared hostility toward "revisionism" and latent fears of Japanese expansionism. Thus, China supported the motion by Algeria and twelve other UN members to put the North Korean proposal on the agenda of the Twenty-Seventh Session of the UNGA so as "to create a favorable atmosphere for the autonomous and peaceful unification of Korea."[58]

Meanwhile, Washington attempted to postpone a UN debate on the Korean issue. On June 9, 1972, in a memo to Kissinger, National Security Council staff member Richard Solomon suggested, "While Chinese Foreign Ministry officials have expressed the view that debate on the Korean issue is unavoidable at the coming 27th UNGA, we might seek a coordinated position with Peking (and Moscow) to avoid an acrimonious public debate which would likely polarize positions just at a time when, in the light of the growing yet fragile contacts between Seoul and Pyongyang, deferment of a GA [General Assembly] debate would be of greatest interest to the major parties concerned."[59]

When Kissinger visited Beijing on June 22, 1972, he discussed the Korean issue with Zhou Enlai. Despite Kissinger's suggestion that China and the United States work together to avoid public debate on the issue at the UN, Zhou made it clear that China would put the Korean issue and the abolition of the UNCURK on the UN agenda in the fall of 1972.[60]

Zhou's position seemed to indicate that he had come to realize that it was not feasible to insist on an immediate U.S. troop withdrawal from South Korea. But in order to pacify Pyongyang, it was necessary that he work to include the issue of the UNCURK on the UNGA agenda in 1972.

The UNCURK had been established by a UNGA resolution in October 1950 for the purpose of creating a unified, independent, and democratic Korean government and "to exercise such responsibilities in connection with relief and rehabilitation in Korea." For Pyongyang, the existence of the UNCURK implied that the UN would ultimately manage Korean unification and thus Pyongyang opposed it. North Korea had always argued that unification must be the result of bilateral efforts by the two Koreas, outside of the UN. But South Korea considered the UNCURK to be the key to its peaceful reunification policy and an important link in the chain of UN sponsorship of the legitimacy of the ROK as "the only legal government in Korea." By the early 1970s, however, Washington no longer viewed the UNCURK as strategically important. Korean rehabilitation had been accomplished and there was no role for the UNCURK to play in Korean unification.[61] As Charles Armstrong and John Kotch note, "A key motivating factor in Washington's 'new thinking' on Korea was the growing presence and influence of Pyongyang in the international arena, in particular in the Third World movement at the UN, as well as the increased risk of being out-manoeuvred in the General Assembly's annual debate on Korea with the entry of the People's Republic of China in October 1971."[62]

Kissinger's report to Nixon about his June 1972 China trip stated that "Chou's (Zhou's) views have evolved on Korea as well. Although he maintained the principle of U.S. withdrawal, he indicated that we should keep our troops there for some time in order to keep out Japanese forces. The Chinese only demonstrated a diplomatic gesture of supporting North Korea in order to win over North Korea."[63] Nonetheless, the Chinese became the chief diplomatic champions for North Korea at the UN, at the expense of Moscow's competing claim.[64] Beijing demonstrated to Pyongyang that its flexible policy toward Washington would win benefits for North Korea that the Soviets simply could not deliver.

In November 1971, high-level delegates from Pyongyang and Seoul began to meet secretly for political talks—the so-called inter-Korean dialogue. The two sides issued a joint statement on July 4, 1972, that sought to achieve Korean unification under the umbrella of no foreign intervention and through peaceful means.[65] Pyongyang and Seoul had secretly agreed to exclude the Korean issue from the UN deliberations. Although the statement claimed that North and South Koreans were of one nation and one people, pursuing national unification without regard for ideologies or political systems, the role of the statement was at best minimal. South Korea was unwilling to give up its unique legal status at the UN (although it was not a full UN member) or to agree to any further withdrawal of U.S. troops. North Korea valued the legality and security protection the statement conferred on the North.[66]

In 1972, China and the United States reached a tacit agreement on the Korean issue at the UN. On July 19, Huang Hua, China's permanent representative to the UN, wrote to UN Secretary-General Kurt J. Waldheim, expressing China's support for the draft resolution by Algeria and twelve other countries to include the Korean problem on the agenda of the Twenty-Seventh Session of the UNGA. He also informed Waldheim that China was a cosponsor of the draft resolution.[67] In his conversation with Huang Hua on July 26, Kissinger said that the United States preferred to avoid a Korean debate in the General Assembly in 1972. The United States believed it would not be helpful to have a direct confrontation between China and the United States over the issue. Kissinger told Huang Hua that "if we avoided a debate in the UN this time we would use our influence to bring about a dismantling of the UNCURK" before the 1973 UNGA.[68] Huang's response was evasive. As Charles Armstrong and John Kotch point out, "With a large Third World coalition backed by the PRC demanding the dissolution of both UNCURK and the U.S.-led UN Command, Washington could no longer rely on the UN for carte blanche on its Korean policy, as had been the case since the beginning of the Cold War."[69]

However, the Chinese felt it would be difficult to persuade the North Koreans to accept the U.S. position. On July 31, 1972, the North Korean government issued a statement that demanded that the Twenty-Seventh Session of the UNGA include the draft resolution of Algeria and the twelve other countries to put the Korean question on the agenda.[70] In his meeting with Henry Kissinger on August 4, Huang Hua made yet another effort to persuade Kissinger to change his position, demanding that the United States reconsider its idea of postponing discussion of the Korean question to the 1973 UNGA. But Kissinger reiterated the U.S. position he had outlined to Huang on July 26, stating, "We do not want to be maneuvered into a position of being forced to do something that we might be prepared to do voluntarily and that one of our allies objects to very strenuously when it comes in this particular fashion."[71] What later transpired indicates that China had already agreed to postpone the discussion but wanted it put on the record, for the benefit of the North Koreans, that China had tried its best to persuade the United States to reconsider the issue.

During Kim Il-sung's secret visit to Beijing on August 22 to August 25, differences over this issue emerged between the Chinese and North Koreans. In his meeting with Kim Il-sung, Zhou Enlai avoided discussion of concrete issues, only repeating that it was in the interests of the people that China was involved in high-level diplomacy with the United States. But, he reiterated, China "observes principles while dealing with the Americans." Zhou also assured Kim, "We made it clear to the Americans that if you continue to stay in South Korea and provoke [the North], we have responsibility to [the North] and will participate if war were to erupt."[72] In a conversation on August 24 between N. M. Shubnikov, a high-ranking Soviet diplomat in Pyongyang, and Kim Tong-kyu, a member of the Political Committee of the KWP CC, Shubnikov said that the Soviet Union would support the DPRK's position if the DPRK rejected the U.S. proposal and insisted on the inclusion of the Korean issue on the agenda of the 1972 UN General Assembly.[73] On September 19, Huang Hua notified Kissinger that the Chinese side had accepted the U.S. position to postpone discussion of the Korean issue until after the U.S. elections in November.[74] Hence, due to U.S., UK, and Japanese insistence, the UNGA adopted (by a vote of 70 to 34, with 21 abstentions) another one-year moratorium on discussion of the Korean question.[75] Pyongyang viewed China's changing position as unsupportive. Although it eventually came to accept China's position, it saw China's action as a betrayal.[76]

Pyongyang realized that "a visible move to begin trade with the U.S. and/or initiate official or informal government to government contacts with the U.S. would have a favorable impact on North Korea's drive to increase its international prestige and influence, to establish diplomatic or trade relations with a larger number of third world countries and to gain membership in international organizations." Such a move would create doubts in Seoul about U.S. intentions and would also increase domestic and international pressures on Seoul to negotiate with the North, but it would weaken the ROK's negotiating position.[77]

North Korea made numerous failed efforts to establish direct contacts with the United States. On February 9, 1973, North Korean Foreign

Minister Hŏ Tam visited China and requested that China probe the United States regarding North Korea–U.S. contacts. On February 11, Zhou told Hŏ Tam that China would transmit Korea's request to Kissinger. North Korea hoped to establish contacts with the United States via China to help bring about a U.S. withdrawal. Zhou indicated that he would raise with Kissinger the following points: the Korean issue could only be resolved via the North–South dialogue, all foreign troops should be withdrawn from the Korean Peninsula, and the UNCURK should be abolished. He would also indirectly ask about direct North Korean contacts with the United States.[78] This reveals that the Chinese were not very enthusiastic about direct DPRK–U.S. contacts.

During his February 15 to February 19 visit, Kissinger indicated that the UNCURK would be abolished in the second half of the year. The United States would gradually withdraw from South Korea, and he would think about direct U.S.–North Korean contacts.[79] On February 20, Zhou informed Hŏ Tam about his conversation with Kissinger. Although as a general rule China still insisted that U.S. troops be withdrawn from South Korea, Beijing (unlike Pyongyang) did not demand immediate action by Washington. China was more concerned about UN legitimacy with regard to the Korean issue than about immediate U.S. withdrawal.

On August 27, 1973, Ri Jae-phil, deputy chief of mission at the DPRK Embassy in Beijing, called on Alfred Jenkins, deputy head of the U.S. Liaison Office, to discuss the issue of North Korea's membership in the World Health Organization and the sending of a permanent observer mission to the UN. This represented the first direct contact between U.S. and DPRK diplomats. David Bruce, head of the Liaison Office, believed that Pyongyang "could look upon Peking as a convenient—and safe—place to deal directly with the United States when or if such a course is determined."[80] On September 26, Kissinger informed Huang Hua about this contact and asked China to make contact with South Korea. However, Huang rejected Kissinger's proposal on the grounds that this would violate China's principle of "one Korea" and "one China."[81]

Meanwhile, the inter-Korean dialogue came to a halt in August 1973. Soon after the first meeting of the cochairmen of the South–North Coordinating Committee, in October 1972, North Korea began to demand a peace treaty with South Korea and a reduction of foreign troops. But South Korea was only interested in economic and social interactions between the two Koreas, not in military and political issues. In its June 23, 1973, declaration, South Korea recognized North Korea as an independent state and proposed that North and South Korea join the UN together.

In the words of Yi Hu-rak, director of the South Korean Central Intelligence Agency, South Korea's purpose in participating in the inter-Korean dialogue was to achieve peaceful coexistence between the two Koreas on the basis of keeping U.S. troops in the South. He expected this would lead to two Koreas in the UN.[82] On June 23, North Korea announced its "five-point plan for national unification," criticizing South Korea and opposing South and North Korea joining the UN together, on the grounds that it would lead to a permanent division on the Korean Peninsula. In August, North Korea terminated the inter-Korean dialogue, using the excuse that the South Korean Central Intelligence Agency had kidnapped opposition leader Kim Dae-jung.[83]

In 1973, China and the United States continued to cooperate on the Korean issue at the UN. Although China was a strong defender of North Korea's interests, Beijing nonetheless followed trends in the Sino–American détente, avoiding assistance to North Korea if doing so would seriously worsen its relations with the United States. On September 26, Secretary of State Henry Kissinger told Huang Hua, "We have agreed to the dissolution of UNCURK. If we could shelve the issue of the United Nations Command for one year at least. The problem now is that the armistice depends on the existence of the UN Command. That will give us an opportunity to look and work with you on this and to develop alternative legal arrangements." When Huang Hua suggested that South Korean President Park Chung Hee abandon his proposal to have both Koreas admitted to the United Nations together, Kissinger refused to make a commitment.[84]

Before the UNGA meeting, in November 1973, Kim Il-sung secretly traveled to Shenyang, China, to hold discussions with Zhou Enlai regarding Chinese and North Korean strategies at the Twenty-Eighth Session of the UNGA. Several months earlier, Vice Foreign Minister Qiao Guanhua had met with Kim Il-sung in Pyongyang to discuss the Korean issue at the UN. In early September, First Vice Foreign Minister Ri Jong-mok, head of the North Korean delegation to the UN, stopped over in Beijing en route to New York to coordinate with Qiao Guanhua. The Chinese delegation also collaborated closely with the North Korean delegation during the UN meetings.

After meeting with Kim in Shenyang, Zhou Enlai called an emergency meeting in Beijing to discuss China's strategy with regard to the Korean issue at the UNGA. Zhang Tingyan, then a desk officer for Korean affairs at the Foreign Ministry and later China's ambassador to South Korea (1992–1998), who was at the time a member of the Chinese delegation attending the UN meetings, was recalled to Beijing to report on the situation at the UN. The Chinese delegation was instructed to adopt a flexible strategy on the Korean issue at the UNGA.[85] Zhou was able to dissuade Pyongyang from insisting on a tough resolution that called for the immediate elimination of both the UNCURK and the United Nations Command (UNC), which was unacceptable to both Washington and Seoul. Zhang Tingyan's recollections reveal the intensity of the consultations and the collaboration between China and North Korea. It supports the thesis on how and why China could replace the Soviet Union as North Korea's champion at the UN.

At the 1973 UNGA meetings, China helped remove the twelve-year-old "Stevenson" formula, which discouraged North Korean participation in UN debates on the Korean issue, and then invited both North and South Korea to participate in the UN debates without a right to vote. In the context of Beijing's new détente policy toward the United States and Japan, Huang Hua fully cooperated with the U.S. permanent representative to the UN, John Scali, to extract a compromise from the two rival draft resolutions and to adopt a consensus statement on the Korean question at the UNGA, on November 18, 1973. He also convinced the North Koreans to accept the consensus statement.[86] The statement noted that "a joint communiqué was issued by the North and the South of Korea on July 4, 1972" and it expressed the hope that "the South and the North of Korea will be urged to continue their dialogue and widen their many-sided exchanges and cooperation in the above spirit so as to expedite the independent peaceful reunification of the country." It also immediately dissolved the UNCURK.[87]

The issue of the UN Command was more complicated and more important than the dissolution of the UNCURK, because the UNC was the mechanism for maintaining the cease-fire, had the authority to command troops in Korea, and legitimized the U.S. military presence.[88] The UNC was established in July 1950 by a UN resolution that requested that the United States assume command of all UN forces. It provided "the umbrella for U.S. operational control of ROK armed forces and the basis for a secret arrangement with Japan for the use of U.S. bases in Japan" for the defense of Korea.[89] The PRC had always objected to the presence of U.S. troops in Korea. In March 1973, Marshall Green, assistant secretary of state for East Asian affairs, pointed out in a State Department study that the UNC could prevent the South from attacking the North by maintaining the cease-fire agreement and acting as a psychological deterrent on the North.[90] Thus, the State Department came to view the UNCURK as a tactical issue but the UNC as a more important strategic issue. National Security Decision Memorandum 251 of March 1974 stipulated that the UNC could be dissolved only after the power of the UNC was transferred to the ROK–U.S. Combined Forces Command.[91]

On March 25, 1974, North Korea proposed signing a unilateral peace treaty with the United States. It stated that South Korea, under U.S. military control, was not even a signatory to the Korean Armistice Agreement, and it accused South Korea of refusing to sign a peace treaty during the inter-Korean dialogue.[92] It demanded that foreign troops be withdrawn from South Korea "at the earliest possible date." This was a reversal of its previous position that U.S. troops were to be withdrawn from Korea after the conclusion of a peace agreement. It seems that Pyongyang's new position was influenced by the January 1973 Paris Peace Accords, which ended direct U.S. military involvement in Vietnam.[93]

In order to force the Americans to agree to direct talks, North Korea created numerous crises along the Northern Limit Line (the sea line dividing the North from the South).[94] Pyongyang also made several attempts to establish direct contact with Washington via Egypt, Romania, and even the American banker David Rockefeller (a personal friend of Kissinger). On April 30, during Kissinger's visit to Egypt, Egyptian President Anwar Sadat told Kissinger that Pyongyang had asked him to help establish direct contact with the United States. Earlier, Kim Il-sung had also written to the U.S. Congress, but he never received a reply. Kissinger told Sadat that Kim had to make contact with the U.S. executive branch. The United States could "agree to initiate a dialogue with North Korea . . . but it should be secret and conducted through President Sadat."[95]

On August 26, 1974, Vasile Pungan, councilor to Romanian President Nicolae Ceaușescu, visited Kissinger at the State Department. He told Kissinger that North Korea desired "to establish contact with the United States" and had asked Romania to facilitate such contact. Kissinger replied, "I understand he wants a meeting with us. The question is: do we want a meeting? To be brutal, what will we get out of a meeting?" Kissinger further stated, "It is one thing to arrange a meeting with Mao. It is another thing to do something for Kim Il-sung, though his own estimation of his relative importance is not low." Although Kissinger did not dismiss the possibility of contact with North Korea, he showed very little interest.[96] Kissinger's statement demonstrated that North Korea was not sufficiently important, from a geostrategic perspective, for the U.S. government to compromise its ideals simply for the sake of meetings. Two other factors may also have contributed to this response. First, North Korea had verbally and abusively attacked Nixon (something the Chinese had never done); and second, the United States was concerned about the South Korean reaction.[97]

On April 12, 1974, in a memo to Kissinger on the topic of the PRC and termination of the UN command in Korea, Richard Solomon wrote, "Last summer, in preparing our position on the Korean issue for the fall session of the UN General Assembly, you indicated to PRC officials that we would be willing to reconsider the future of the UN Command if UNCURK were dissolved in a non-contentious manner." The memo further pointed out, "Peking will respond in generally favorable terms to our alternate arrangement for abolition of the UNC if it can be presented to Pyongyang as a transitional arrangement which would hold out some possibility for the eventual realization of North Korea's maximum goal of a complete U.S. withdrawal from Korea."[98]

On June 13, the United States relayed to the Chinese the content of National Security Study Memorandum 251 regarding dissolution of the UNC.[99] On July 31, China rejected the U.S. proposal, accusing the United States of attempting to continue to station its troops in Korea and of making the division of Korea permanent. This was most likely because North Korea had rejected the proposal. North Korea organized a lobbying effort, demanding that all foreign troops be withdrawn from Korea. Pressed by North Korea, on September 19 Huang Hua publicly called for the United States to withdraw its troops from Korea.[100]

On October 2, 1974, during the UNGA meetings, Qiao Guanhua and Kissinger discussed the UNC issue at a dinner party in honor of Qiao. During the day, Qiao had attacked détente, had criticized both superpowers, and had demanded the withdrawal of foreign forces from South Korea. But in their private conversation later that evening, Qiao enjoyed a good rapport with Kissinger. Qiao told Kissinger, "You understand that we maintain good relations with the Democratic People's Republic of Korea.

On this issue, we have to respect their views." Kissinger replied, "Our problem is that we cannot accept abolition of the United Nations Command if there is no legal basis on both sides for the continuation of the Armistice." Qiao told Kissinger that the details on the Korean question were of no great significance. He reminded his host, "As you know from your discussions with Chairman Mao, this is not a major issue if you look at it in terms of the overall world situation." Qiao also noted that China had delivered the revised U.S. proposal to North Korea but had not received any response.[101]

Partly due to deteriorating political developments in the United States (the Watergate scandal, which forced President Nixon to resign) and in China (the political setback of Premier Zhou Enlai, champion of good Sino–American relations) in 1974, China and the United States were unable to reach a compromise over the UNC. Kissinger observed that Nixon's resignation "was incomprehensible to the Chinese leaders" and "led to a collapse of congressional support for an active foreign policy in the subsequent congressional elections in November 1974." He noted that Foreign Minister Qiao Guanhua "turned confrontational" in their negotiations.[102] During his seventh visit to China, in November 1974, Kissinger intentionally avoided discussion of the Korean issue. In his report to President Gerald Ford, Kissinger claimed that the United States had achieved an advantage in the UN with respect to the Korean issue and had more supporters than China and North Korea.[103]

In view of their precarious position at the UN, in June 1975 the United States and South Korea proposed terminating the UNC by January 1, 1976, provided that China and North Korea would agree to continue the armistice agreement. According to Kissinger's talking points, the United States sent a letter to the UN Security Council on June 27, 1975, to announce U.S. willingness to dissolve the UNC on January 1, 1976, if the governments of the PRC and North Korea agreed to uphold the armistice by accepting the United States and the Republic of Korea as the "successors in command."[104] In a speech at the UN on September 22, 1975, Kissinger said it was important to pay attention to the efficacy of the armistice treaty. It was necessary for all involved parties to negotiate in order to achieve a transformation of the armistice arrangement. On September 26, in his speech at the UN, Qiao Guanhua publicly rebutted Kissinger's position, stating that the U.S. proposal was designed to prolong the stationing of U.S. troops in South Korea. The signatories to a peace treaty should be the United States and the DPRK. But Qiao later privately told Kissinger that this was only the view of the DPRK.[105]

On November 18, 1975, the UNGA adopted two contradictory resolutions—a pro-Seoul resolution (by a vote of 59 to 51, with 29 abstentions) and a pro-Pyongyang resolution (by a vote of 54 to 43, with 42 abstentions). The pro-Pyongyang resolution, introduced by China and Algeria and supported by forty-one other nations, called for an unconditional dissolution of the UNC and the withdrawal of all foreign troops stationed in South Korea under the flag of the UN, and asked that "the real parties to the armistice agreement" (meaning the United States, the PRC, and North Korea, but not South Korea) replace it with a peace agreement. The pro-ROK resolution called upon all parties concerned to negotiate a replacement to the armistice agreement.

The adoption of two contradictory resolutions by the UN rendered it impossible for either of the resolutions to be implemented.[106] The Korean issue would be frozen at the 1976 UNGA meeting as a consequence of the August 1976 ax murder incident.[107] The Korean issue gradually evolved into an international issue dominated by two related parties but also several other major powers, that is, China, the United States, the Soviet Union, and Japan. In 1978, a binational headquarters, the Republic of Korea–United States Combined Forces Command, was created, and South Korean military units with frontline missions were transferred from the UN Command to the Combined Forces Command operational control. As of today, the United States still has not withdrawn all of its troops from Korea.

According to a June 1975 analysis by the State Department, China was more concerned about blocking the expansion of Soviet influence in Korea and Indochina than in seeking to establish traditional hegemony in the area. It was primarily a result of China's decision to compete with Moscow for the goodwill of Kim Il-sung that the Chinese became burdened with the task of keeping Kim's emotional revolutionary and militaristic policies from escalating into a war on the peninsula. The U.S. analysis points out, "The Chinese prefer long-term stability on the peninsula—that is, a de facto situation of 'two Koreas.'"[108] Kim Il-sung did not agree with this idea. China thus increased economic and military support for Kim, apparently as part of the price for maintaining a clear advantage over the USSR in Pyongyang. A National Security Council memo of June 1976 noted that

Sino–Soviet rivalry "has helped deter Peking from playing any useful role in brokering compromise solutions to the Korean issue in the United Nations." Although it sought to discourage offensive military action by North Korea, China had "become the major supplier of military equipment to Pyongyang."[109]

China Becomes a Major Donor of Aid to North Korea

In the process of the Sino–American rapprochement, China and North Korea had a mutual need to sustain a friendly relationship. Beijing needed Pyongyang's political support, while Pyongyang attempted to take advantage of the Sino–American reconciliation to force U.S. troop withdrawal and to achieve Korean unification. As Bernd Schaefer notes, "Receiving North Korean support for its rapprochement with the United States was a major diplomatic achievement for the PRC. . . . For the time being, the fallout of Kissinger's trip to Beijing established the DPRK as Maoist China's closest international ally."[110]

But by 1973 Mao Zedong was no longer interested in fomenting revolution in the world in general or supporting Pyongyang's unification by force in particular. For instance, in 1972 a total of 445 people in eighteen

Figure 7.2 Kim Il-sung, accompanied by Deng Xiaoping, standing and waving as his motorcade passes through Tiananmen Square, April 18, 1975.

groups of "antigovernment" rebels from various parts of the world secretly went to China for military training. The number dropped to 232 people in eight groups in 1973, and by 1975 China had almost completely suspended this project.[111] Mao was extremely disappointed with the failure of his global revolution and its limited regional achievements. Following pronouncement of his theory of "three worlds" in 1973, he increasingly shifted his focus from supporting unsuccessful revolutionary movements to supporting anti-Soviet governments of various types. By 1974, he declared, "We may not mention that the current world tide is revolution."[112] This explains why the PRC declined to support Kim Il-sung's proposal to attack the South in April 1975.

Against the background of the Vietnam War coming to an end with a Communist victory, Kim made a public visit to Beijing with renewed energy. In his first public appearance in Beijing, on April 18, Kim declared Asia to be on a "high tide of revolution." If war were to break out in Korea, he said, "we will only lose the Military Demarcation Line but we will gain

Figure 7.3 Mao Zedong's last meeting with Kim Il-sung, at Zhongnanhai, Beijing, April 18, 1975.

the country's reunification." It would be "up to the U.S. whether or not there will be war in Korea." He also declared that "as members of the same nation," Koreans in the North would not stand by "with folded arms" if "revolution breaks out in the South"; the DPRK would "energetically support the South Korean people."[113]

However, there was a limit to China's support for North Korea. George H. W. Bush, then head of the U.S. Liaison Office in Beijing, recorded in his diary of April 24, 1975, "Kim Il-sung's talking militantly about Korea, China apparently downplaying this."[114] After Kim delivered his radical speech, Beijing's leaders demonstrated little interest in his ideas. When Kim was to meet Mao, the chairman pleaded illness in order to avoid confronting him and asked that Kim discuss political issues with Executive Vice Premier Deng Xiaoping. Deng told Kim that Beijing would not be in a position to commit its resources to Kim's revolutionary war plans.[115] Consequently, in Kim's farewell speech, he lowered his tone considerably. Accordingly, the final PRC–DPRK communiqué of April 1975 defined the "correct path to solve the problem of Korean reunification" by quoting Kim's 1972 three principles (that reunification should be peaceful, without foreign interference, and foster national unity despite different systems) and the "peaceful" DPRK Five-Point Program of 1973.[116] The PRC was obviously eager to prevent the Korean question from affecting its relations with the United States and Japan and to avoid becoming involved in a military conflict on the Korean Peninsula. Kim thus departed China without achieving his primary goal of receiving Beijing's approval for a military assault on the South.

Kim Il-sung wanted to visit the Soviet Union and Czechoslovakia in the second half of May, but the date he proposed did not suit Soviet and Czech leaders. Soviet-North Korean relations were decidedly cold at the time. Although China did not support a North Korean attack on the South, it also did not want to alienate its ally. Thus, it had to provide North Korea with more economic and military aid. In October 1970, China and North Korea signed a third long-term trade agreement, covering the period from 1971 to 1976. From 1970 to 1971, bilateral trade increased 45 percent. The volume of trade reached $395 million in 1976, which was 3.4 times more than that in 1970. China also provided aid to construct 101 plants, including antiaircraft radar plants and torpedo boat radar plants.[117] During this period, North Korean military delegations frequently visited China to request training, technical information, equipment, and aid.[118] By 1973,

Beijing had replaced Moscow as the leading supplier of weaponry to Pyong-yang.[119] China was clearly North Korea's primary donor of aid.

Kim Aspires to Lead the World Revolution

North Korea's pursuit of economic and political ties in the Third World began in the 1960s, "but it was in the 1970s that North Korea presented itself enthusiastically as a model for Third World development. . . . and Kim Il-sung tried with some success to present himself as a leader of the nonaligned Third World."[120] Propaganda material dated October 10, 1969, entitled "Great Leader, Kim Il-sung," which was translated into Russian and sent to Moscow from the Soviet Embassy in the DPRK, stated, "Kim Il-sung is not only the great leader of the DPRK, but also the one who can lead the world."[121] Without support from China and the Soviet Union for unification by force, Kim began to promote North Korea's cause internationally through active involvement in the Non-Aligned Movement. From Beijing, Kim Il-sung traveled to Algeria, Mauritania, Romania, and Bulgaria, finally arriving in Belgrade on June 6, 1975, where he met with President Josip B. Tito of Yugoslavia, cofounder of the movement.[122]

North Korea's diplomatic offensive in the Third World, in particular in the Non-Aligned Movement, reached a high point in 1975, when Pyong-yang was accepted to participate in the August foreign ministers' confer-ence of nonaligned nations held in Lima, Peru. In contrast, South Korea's request to participate was rejected, thus giving Pyongyang's diplomatic prospects a significant boost. This was an important development for North Korea, because many of the nonaligned countries strongly sup-ported North Korea in the UN in the 1970s. It also represented a victory for North Korea in its competition with the South.[123]

As China's revolutionary vigor gradually waned after rapprochement with the United States, Kim Il-sung aspired to replace Mao as the leader of the world revolution. In January 1972, when speaking with Japanese journalists, Kim Il-sung said, "The *Juche* idea is embodied, first of all, in the lines of political independence, economic self-sufficiency and national self-defence." He further stated, "The *Juche* idea is based on Marx's prin-ciple 'Workers of all countries, unite!' and is in full accord with proletar-ian internationalism."[124] In March, the Standing Committee of the Supreme

People's Assembly promulgated a government decree to issue a "Kim Il-sung medal"—the highest prize in the DPRK. The decree stated, "The great leader Comrade Kim Il-sung correctly and creatively resolved theoretical and practical issues in building the socialist system; [he] triumphantly opens the way to a complete victory of socialism and communism."[125]

Pyongyang also made a huge effort to globalize *Juche* and Kim Il-sung–ism. In October 1969, North Korea openly declared that Kim Il-sung "has turned the practice of Marxism–Leninism into a living weapon and has made all efforts to bring about the victory of the world revolution."[126] In May 1972, Kim Tong-kyu, a member of the Political Committee of the KWP CC, published an article in *Rodong sinmun* claiming that Kim Il-sung "has resolved the theoretical, strategic, and tactical issues in the International Communist Movement and world revolution." It further boasted that Kim Il-sung's theory "is Marxism–Leninism of our times, and it is the great battle banner of the working class and oppressed people. . . . Many revolutionaries and progressive people regard him as a wise and outstanding leader of our times."[127]

In February 1974, Kim Il-sung summed up his *Juche* idea as "Kim Il-sung-ism," thereby establishing his absolute authority.[128] A 1974 article in issue number 4 of *Kŭlloja*, a KWP journal, claimed, "The *Juche* idea has indeed showed revolutionary theory clearly to the people of the world, and it is an invincible revolutionary banner to encourage them to struggle and achieve success."[129] In November 1974, Kim Il-sung told Australian journalists, "This is the era of *Chajusong* [Independence] when people of the world want to live independently." Kim expected that the developing countries would follow North Korea's path of development. He advised, "I think, therefore, that if the developing countries are to adopt the *Juche* idea, they must under all circumstances apply it creatively, in keeping with their actual conditions."[130]

With North Korea's financial support, the first *Juche* idea study group was established in Mali in 1969. Many more would be established in Asia and Africa, with the number reaching 120 in more than fifty countries by 1971. By the end of 1970s, there were more than eight hundred *Juche* idea study groups throughout the world.[131] As Charles Armstrong writes, "Numerous International Seminars on the *Juche* Idea were held in various locations around the world, fully underwritten by the DPRK, and whose purpose seemed to be at least as much for internal North Korean propaganda as advancing 'science' abroad."[132]

Beginning in the early 1970s, North Korea increased its contacts with Third World countries. Additionally, the UNCURK was abolished in 1973, and in the same year the DPRK joined the World Health Organization. By June 1974, North Korea had established full diplomatic relations with more than seventy countries. In 1976, the number reached ninety-three, and North Korea was accepted as a member of numerous international organizations.[133] Soviet and Eastern European diplomats in North Korea noted that although the DPRK tried to remain in step with China's foreign policy orientation, at least in appearance, it "is not willing to openly follow the PRC in its anti-Soviet course." By the mid-1970s, Mao's intention was to unite with all Third World countries to oppose both American imperialism and Soviet hegemonism. But Kim still believed that "Enemy Number One of all progressive people is American imperialism."[134] Aspiring to be the leader of the world revolution, Kim Il-sung declared, at a March 4, 1974, mass rally in Pyongyang to welcome Houari Boumedienne, president of the Council of Revolution of the Algerian People's Democratic Republic, "We are convinced that if the people of all countries, small or poor, in Asia, Africa, Latin America and the rest of the world, in solid unity, strike hard at and bring pressure to bear upon imperialism everywhere, giving it no breathing space, they can defeat it and achieve the final victory of the revolution."[135]

By December 1955, Kim Il-sung had already come to appreciate the connection between internationalism and the Korean Revolution. He asserted that internationalism played a fundamental role in the Korean Revolution and could not be ignored. He further explained, "It would be wrong to advocate patriotism alone and neglect internationalist solidarity. For the victory of the Korean Revolution and for the great cause of the international working class, we should strengthen solidarity with the Soviet people, our liberator and helper, and with the peoples of all the socialist countries. This is our sacred internationalist duty."[136] Following the example of the Chinese, North Korea provided training and aid to many anti-government forces. For example, the North Koreans provided ideological and military training to fifty-three members of Mexico's Revolutionary Action Movement in 1969 and 1970.[137]

According to documents from the South Korean Foreign Ministry, North Korea's Ministry of National Defense established a Center for the Training and Political Instruction of Foreign Guerrillas, in 1966. During the next ten years, the center trained more than five thousand guerrillas from nine Central American countries, fifteen Middle Eastern and African countries, and six Asian countries. To export revolution abroad, North Korea used both legal and illegal methods. Pyongyang dispatched abroad many cultural, sports, and trade delegations, and distributed many copies of Kim Il-sung's writings throughout the world, in order to expand North Korea's influence. Through bribery, Pyongyang also supported the establishment of pro-North Korea "friendship associations." By training guerrilla fighters, distributing guerrilla-tactics handbooks, smuggling weapons via diplomatic pouches, and dispatching military advisers, Pyongyang helped establish revolutionary bases in several countries. After the 1973 Arab–Israeli War, North Korea publicly carried out its foreign policy of exporting revolution, for example by dispatching military advisers to Mozambique and Laos, participating in the Angolan Civil War, providing weapons and military personnel to the Jamaican Workers' Liberation League, offering technical aid to guerrilla fighters in Chile, becoming involved in antigovernment activities in Costa Rica, and training guerrilla fighters for the Communist Party of Thailand.[138]

On May 4, 1976, a *Rodong sinmun* editorial declared, "The *Juche* idea is the real banner of national liberation, class emancipation, and emancipation of mankind." In 1984, Kim Il-sung told East German leader Erich Honecker, "We have agricultural specialists in nearly all African countries," and "Ethiopia has obviously achieved the highest level of consolidation of any Marxist party" in Africa.[139] By the late 1970s, North Korea had sent more than 1,500 military advisers to Africa and had provided nearly $300 million in economic aid to twenty-one African countries. North Korea's standing in the Third World, especially in Africa, was rising, and was even surpassing China in certain respects. Some African countries seemed to be truly grateful to Pyongyang for its help. In October 1980, Robert Mugabe, prime minister of Zimbabwe, visited North Korea. Making a point of thanking Pyongyang for providing support during Zimbabwe's struggle for independence, he stated, "No one is better than President Kim Il-sung as a friend, brother, and ally."[140] In contrast, at that time China did not have a close relationship with Zimbabwe—Mugabe made only "a brief stop" in Beijing on his way home.[141]

In the view of many people, the center of world revolution moved from Beijing to Pyongyang after Mao Zedong's death, on September 9, 1976.

This also represented the end of an era in Sino-North Korean relations. North Korea held the most extravagant memorial events for any leader since the 1953 death of Stalin.[142] Kim Il-sung was truly saddened. Although between Mao and Kim there existed both gratitude and resentment, Kim was well aware that he would have lost power during the Korean War had Mao refused to dispatch the Chinese People's Volunteer Army to Korea. Additionally, North Korea would not have achieved the status and prestige it enjoyed in 1976 without the massive Chinese aid it had received over the years. Kim Il-sung might also have felt that the time had finally arrived for him to lead the world revolution.

During the period from 1970 to 1976, the PRC's overall foreign policy direction was to achieve rapprochement and maintain détente with the United States. But China also attempted to retain its revolutionary credentials and to consider the interests of its smaller allies, such as North Korea, Vietnam, and Albania. This was an impossible task. Vietnam and Albania openly opposed the Sino–American rapprochement, and as a consequence their relations with China deteriorated. Thus, North Korea became even more important to China. Beijing agreed to relay to the United States Pyongyang's demands with regard to the Korean Peninsula, and Chinese leaders maintained close contacts with the North Koreans. Zhou Enlai flew to Pyongyang to brief Kim Il-sung after Kissinger's secret visit and after Nixon's trip to China. Immediately following Kissinger's second trip to Beijing, Kim also made a secret visit to Beijing to learn about the U.S. position. But, in its talks with the Chinese, Washington did not feel a similar need to consult with Seoul regarding its policy toward the Korean Peninsula. Prior to Nixon's trip to China, South Korean President Park Chung Hee requested a meeting with the U.S. president, but his request was denied. Only after the U.S. Embassy in Seoul had made numerous attempts did Kissinger finally agree to visit South Korea, in November 1973. But he stopped there for only several hours.[143]

At UN meetings, Qiao Guanhua and Huang Hua strongly and publicly criticized the United States, demanding the withdrawal of foreign forces from South Korea and vociferously defending the DPRK position. But privately the Chinese seemed to accept the U.S. position that resolution of the Korean issue would take time. Gradually, China saw the presence of the U.S. forces on the Korean Peninsula as a stabilizing factor.

There are at least two main reasons why China was able to maintain friendly relations with North Korea, despite Pyongyang's obvious dissatisfaction with China's new policy orientation. First, the Soviet Union was not interested in unifying Korea by force, as proposed by Pyongyang, and it did not support such a move. Hence, maintaining good relations with Beijing was in Pyongyang's best interest. North Korea adjusted its policy accordingly and attempted to use the Sino–American détente to force the United States to withdraw from Korea and thereby to unify Korea on Pyongyang's terms. Second, China increased its economic and military aid to North Korea and became Pyongyang's largest donor. North Korea was China's last ally during Mao's later years.

By 1974, Pyongyang had become suspicious that, during Nixon's 1972 trip to China, Beijing had not sufficiently pressured Washington to force the withdrawal of the U.S. troops from the South. Beijing and Pyongyang started to diverge in pursuing their diplomatic and strategic goals, particularly with regard to the United States. Pyongyang therefore started to act alone, without prior consultation with Beijing, on major issues affecting the Korean Peninsula, such as dissolution of the UNC, a peace agreement between North Korea and the United States, and the withdrawal of U.S. troops from South Korea. Pyongyang made numerous futile attempts to begin direct negotiations with the United States. China also explicitly stated that it would not support North Korea's attempt to unify the Korean Peninsula by force. China's primary foreign policy goal during this period was to maintain détente with Washington in order to form a united front to counter the Soviet threat and to prevent a resumption of war on the Korean Peninsula. Thus, China's policy toward North Korea was based more on national security and geopolitical considerations than on ideological factors.

In his 2011 book, political scientist Thomas Christensen argues that disagreements between Moscow and Beijing during the Cold War often caused the two to try to outdo each other in supporting revolutions—such as, for instance, the Vietnamese revolution—and, from the perspective of America's policy makers, this rendered the Communist alliance "worse than a monolith."[144] During the period from 1970 to 1975, the tensions in Sino-North Korean relations were due to China's lack of sufficient support for DPRK aggression, rather than, as earlier, because it was hounding Pyongyang for not being sufficiently revolutionary. But with an improvement in Sino–North Korean relations, China could play a restraining role in North Korea.

The present study echoes Christensen's thesis. When Pyongyang's relations with Beijing were tense during the second half of the 1960s, North Korea acted more recklessly and with more hostility toward South Korea and the United States. We suggest that the relatively good relationship between Beijing and Pyongyang from 1970 to 1976 actually also benefited the United States. Washington was able to improve relations with Beijing while at the same time indirectly improving its security vis-à-vis Pyongyang. During this period, North Korea was far less aggressive and less confrontational toward South Korea and the United States. Thus, alienating the DPRK from the PRC did not seem to be in the interests of the United States.

Epilogue

China and North Korea in the Era of Deng Xiaoping

D uring the period from 1949 to 1972, China and North Korea were socialist countries, members of the International Communist Movement, and "fraternal countries" that maintained "brotherly relations." The United States was their shared common enemy. After Nixon's trip to China in February 1972 and the Sino–American rapprochement, Sino–U.S. relations underwent a fundamental change. The United States was no longer China's primary enemy. Rather, it was becoming a potential ally in China's conflict with the Soviet Union. This represented a major strike on the strategic foundation of the Sino-North Korean "special relationship." The inevitable consequence of Sino-North Korean disagreements over foreign and defense strategies weakened the geopolitical factors in their relationship. In Mao Zedong's later years, North Korea's role as China's security gateway and strategic buffer no longer existed. North Korea no longer served as China's "strategic shield" and China no longer was North Korea's "great hinterland."

China's post-1978 policy of "reform and opening" to the outside world shattered the economic foundation of the Sino–North Korean "special relationship." The strategy of Deng Xiaoping (who gradually emerged as China's paramount leader after Mao's death) to achieve economic development and modernization stood in stark contrast to Mao Zedong's reliance on ideological appeals to advance the Great Leap Forward. Deng charted a course that resulted in China's rapid economic development, successful reform, and opening to the capitalist international economy, while at the same time the country remained in the grip of one-party rule.[1] The core of the reform and opening was to allow for the existence of market mechanisms in foreign economic activities. In economic relations, it was necessary to abide by the principle of exchange of equal value. But this contradicted China's former policy toward North Korea whereby it only cared about political gain rather than economic considerations.

In foreign policy, Deng Xiaoping was determined to improve China's relations with the outside world so that the capitalist countries would be receptive to working with China. He thus sought to create a favorable international environment for China's economic development. Although he shared Mao's vision of national equality and restoration of China's lost glory, Deng's views and approaches after the late 1970s were very different from those of Mao. Mao regarded the outside world as hostile and he deemed a forthcoming world war to be inevitable. As a result, Mao's foreign and defense policies focused on safeguarding China's security. In contrast, Deng had a far better grasp of the intricacies of world affairs and was much more willing to tolerate a foreign presence in China. During his lifetime, Mao made only two trips to foreign countries, whereas Deng traveled to many foreign countries and clearly enjoyed speaking with the foreign press. Additionally, while Mao was distrustful of the West, Deng hoped that Western allies would treat China with its due dignity and help contribute to its building of a strong country. In June 1985, Deng argued that a world war was unlikely in the near future and he stressed that it would be possible to sustain world peace. In 1989, he similarly declared that the "international situation is relaxing and world war can be averted."[2] Rather than respond to external threats, Deng's foreign and defense policy focused on the development of China's national strength.[3]

The Democratic People's Republic of Korea (DPRK) was quite concerned about China's post-1978 policy of reform and opening to the outside world. After initial hesitation, Beijing decided in the early 1980s to endorse Kim Il-sung's succession plan—to install his son Kim Jong-il as his successor—even as the Soviet Union evinced serious reservations.[4] During this period, China's relations with the Soviet Union gradually improved. But Kim Il-sung continued to play a balancing game of diplomacy between Beijing and Moscow, receiving aid from both allies. However, by the late 1980s Pyongyang felt under siege when both Beijing and

Moscow gradually improved relations with South Korea. Beijing and Moscow were obviously impressed with South Korea's economic success.[5]

Toward the end of 1985, Deng's policy toward North Korea began to change. On December 13, 1985, Deng invited Hu Yaobang, general secretary of the Chinese Communist Party (CCP), and Yang Shangkun, vice chairman of the Central Military Commission, to discuss Chinese policy toward North Korea. Deng said, "We should draw lessons from our dealings with North Korea. We should not give the North Koreans the wrong impression that whatever they ask for we will give them." Deng resolutely rejected Pyongyang's recent request that North Korean MiG-21 pilots who had completed training in China would remain in China for another five years and then return to North Korea with Chinese aircraft. Deng said, "Of course, the North Koreans are unhappy. Let it be. We should prevent them from dragging us into trouble. We have made huge efforts to aid Vietnam, Albania, and North Korea. Now Vietnam and Albania have fallen out with us. We should be prepared for the third one [North Korea] to fall out with us, though we should try our best to prevent that from happening."[6]

In the wake of the Tiananmen Square incident and the fall of the Communist regimes in Eastern Europe, in 1989, and in the Soviet Union, in 1991, Beijing and Pyongyang became fellow sufferers who could commiserate with each other. In return for North Korea's firm support of internationally isolated China after the Tiananmen Square incident, Beijing agreed to provide 150 million renminbi in economic and military aid to Pyongyang during the 1991–1995 period.[7]

In the late 1970s, when Deng Xiaoping first initiated his reform and opening policy, Sino–South Korean relations were cool. On September 7, 1978, South Korean newspapers cited Japanese media reports on Deng Xiaoping's interview with a Japanese press delegation. According to these reports, Deng had said, "The Soviet Union is attempting to expand its influence in South Korea, but China is not interested in establishing contacts with South Korea."[8] During his visit to the United States in January 1979, Deng told U.S. President Jimmy Carter that China "cannot have direct contacts with South Korea because if we were to do that we would lose the possibility of working with other parties. These are very sensitive problems."[9]

Meanwhile, as an important measure to bring about a reconciliation on the Korean Peninsula, China actively promoted U.S.–North Korean contacts and North–South Korean dialogues. In January 1979, when meeting with a U.S. Senate delegation, Deng relayed Kim Il-sung's request for the resumption of North–South dialogues and the establishment of direct U.S.–North Korean talks.[10] On April 23, Deng told Kim Il-sung that if North Korea were to increase its commercial activities and bilateral personnel exchanges with the United States and Japan, this would be beneficial to North–South dialogues.[11] On August 28, 1979, Deng Xiaoping told visiting U.S. Vice President Walter Mondale, "Our present suggestion is that the U.S. considers getting in touch directly with the DPRK and leave aside the tripartite talks. Such contact can be held at many different levels and in the course of such contact maybe some modalities acceptable to both sides can be arranged."[12] On September 27, Han Nianlong, deputy foreign minister and head of the Chinese delegation, told the UN General Assembly that China supported U.S.–North Korean contacts, that a peace treaty should replace the armistice treaty, and that China would support North–South dialogues for the realization of Korean unification.[13] Such circumstances created a condition for a relaxation of Sino–South Korean relations.

But economic factors would soon play an important role in China's relations with South Korea. As Chin-Wee Chung writes, "China cannot ignore the fact that the ROK [Republic of Korea] is an emerging power in East Asia. The ROK, in cooperation with the United States and Japan, could make a significant contribution to Chinese economic modernization by providing technology at a low cost and by cooperating in the expansion of Chinese trade."[14] In early spring 1979, several internal Chinese magazines and journals began to publish articles and reference materials on South Korea's economic development.[15] Some South Korean sources claim that indirect trade between China and South Korea began in 1976.[16] According to Samuel Kim, Chinese–South Korean trade totaled $19 million in 1979, but by 1980 it had reached $188 million—a tenfold increase. In the same year, Chinese–North Korean trade totaled $677 million. By 1984, the amount of Chinese–North Korean and Chinese–South Korean trade was about the same ($498 million and $443 million, respectively). But by 1985, the amount of Chinese–North Korean trade had decreased to $488 million, whereas the amount of Chinese–South Korean trade had increased to $1.161 billion. Thereafter, in the early 1990s, there were structural changes in China's trade with both North and South Korea. In 1990, the amount of Chinese–South Korean trade totaled $3.821 billion, whereas the amount of Chinese–North Korean trade was only $483 million. In 1992, the amount of Chinese–South Korean trade increased to $6.375 billion, whereas the amount of Chinese–North Korean trade was only $696 million.[17]

In July 1982, the Chinese Foreign Ministry drafted a document entitled "Request for Instructions Regarding Adjusting our Attitude Toward South Korea in International Multilateral Activities." It proposed that "China should allow South Korea to attend activities of multilateral international organizations of which South Korea is a member and that China is entrusted to host. Likewise, the Chinese should also travel to South Korea for similar international gatherings."[18] China's central government leaders soon approved this request. On July 20, 1983, Li Xiannian, president of the People's Republic of China (PRC), chaired a meeting of the Foreign Affairs Leadership Small Group of the CCP Central Committee (*Zhongyang waishi lingdao xiaozu*, 中央外事领导小组), which discussed how to adjust China's policy toward South Korea and how to pacify North Korea.[19]

On August 24, the Chinese government formally submitted a bid to host the 1990 Eleventh Asian Games. Chinese Foreign Minister Wu Xueqian announced that China would invite all member states of the Olympic Council of Asia, including South Korea, to participate in the Asian Games if the Chinese bid were to be successful. This represented an important step toward improving relations with South Korea.[20] Thereafter, Deng Xiaoping issued numerous instructions on changing Chinese policy toward South Korea. He emphasized the strategic importance of improving relations with South Korea, arguing that it would be beneficial to promoting China's policy of reform and opening, restraining Japan and isolating Taiwan, and relaxing tensions on the Korean Peninsula. In particular, Deng stated, the development of economic relations between China and South Korea "can benefit us and also benefit South Korea." In May 1984, Deng Xiaoping made a point of entrusting Hu Yaobang, who was scheduled to visit North Korea, with explaining to Kim Il-sung that an improvement in Sino–South Korean relations would also be beneficial to North Korea.[21] On September 4, the Foreign Affairs Leadership Small Group of the CCP Central Committee announced, "South Korea has been making gestures to us; in particular, the South Koreans hope to establish direct trade with us. We insist on our current policy, but we should adopt a more active attitude toward indirect trade."[22]

The first official contacts between the People's Republic of China and the Republic of Korea occurred in May 1983, when Shen Tu, administrator of the Civil Aviation Administration of China, traveled to South Korea to negotiate the return of Flight 296, a hijacked Chinese airliner. After the negotiations, the passengers and flight crew were safely returned to China. This incident thus presented a fresh opportunity for direct contacts and dialogues between the two countries.[23] Subsequently, the two countries established the "Hong Kong channel," whereby the director of the Hong Kong office of the Xinhua News Agency and the consul general of the Republic of Korea in Hong Kong represented the two governments in handling emergency issues, such as the Chinese navy torpedo boat incident, when sailors attempt to cross over into South Korea and Chinese pilots attempted to defect to Taiwan. Both sides were happy with this arrangement.[24]

Person-to-person contacts between the PRC and the ROK mainly took place in connection with trade and sports. As noted, Sino–South Korean trade began in the late 1970s. But at the time it involved only a small number of businessmen and enterprises and thus had very little societal impact. But sports exchanges attracted wide public attention in both countries. After the success of the "Ping-Pong diplomacy" between China and the United States in 1971, sports exchanges had become a main avenue for Chinese foreign exchanges. They played a similarly important role in opening up relations with South Korea. In February 1984, a South Korean tennis team visited China to compete in a Davis Cup qualifying match held in Kunming. This was the first time that South Korean athletes had set foot in the PRC. In April, a Chinese team traveled to Seoul to participate in the Eighth Asian Youth Basketball Championship.[25] Thereafter, sports exchanges between the PRC and the ROK became routine occurrences.

In May 1986, China notified South Korea, via the Hong Kong channel, that China would participate in the 1986 Asian Games and that it regarded this as good opportunity to improve Chinese relations with South Korea.[26] On August 17, *Renmin ribao* (People's Daily) revealed that China would field a contingent of 515 athletes and officials for the games, the fourth-largest representation, after the ROK with 673, Japan with 575, and India with

540.[27] Pyongyang was clearly unhappy about this. On August 20, *Rodong sinmun* (Workers' Newspaper) published an article stating that the Asian Games "should not become a political plaything of splittists."[28] However, Beijing simply ignored Pyongyang's complaints. The 1986 Asian Games in Seoul greatly enhanced Sino–South Korean relations. The South Korean public "felt very good" about the Chinese delegation. The Chinese also felt that South Korea had "demonstrated a friendly attitude toward cooperation." Through official channels, the Chinese stated its wish "to increase collaborative relations with South Korea in every field, while also preparing for the 1990 Asian Games."[29]

After Roh Tae-woo became president of the ROK, in February 1988, he launched his *Nordpolitik* (Northern diplomacy). He was willing to engage in trade and formal diplomatic relations with Communist countries, and he requested that North Korea expand economic and cultural exchanges with the South and invited the leaders of the two Koreas to hold a summit meeting.[30] He attempted to use the improving relations with China as his political capital. He promised ROK citizens that he would break the deadlock in relations with China, stipulating a national policy of "China first, and the Soviet Union second."[31] In March, China decided to elevate Sino–South Korean indirect trade to nongovernmental direct trade, beginning in Shandong province.[32] Deng Xiaoping attached to an internal document the following instructions: "The time is ripe for us to develop economic and cultural relations with South Korea. We should move a bit faster and wider."[33] In spite of protests and pressure from Pyongyang, China actively participated in the 1988 Summer Olympics in Seoul, further promoting the development of Sino–South Korean relations.[34]

The establishment of Sino–South Korean economic and trade offices in the respective countries was a prelude to the establishment of political and diplomatic relations. In September 1988, South Korea proposed that China establish a nongovernmental trade office in South Korea.[35] On November 5, Beijing informed visiting North Korean Foreign Minister Kim Young-nan, "Due to the continuous expansion of trade relations between China and South Korea, it has become inevitable that China and South Korea exchange trade offices."[36] In January 1989, the China Council for the Promotion of International Trade formally proposed to the Korea Trade Promotion Corporation, a semigovernmental organization under the Ministry of Trade and Industry (in South Korea), that negotiations should begin on the exchange of trade offices.[37]

On April 23, prior to the visit of CCP General Secretary Zhao Ziyang to North Korea, Deng Xiaoping asked Zhao to deliver the following message to Kim Il-sung: "In consideration of the DPRK's position, China has lost a great opportunity to develop economic relations with South Korea. China is now far behind the Soviet Union and Eastern Europe in this regard. This situation should not continue. China is considering developing economic relations with South Korea, but it will continue to support the DPRK politically."[38] However, the tragic events in Tiananmen Square in early June 1989 disrupted Sino–South Korean negotiations and contacts. When Kim Il-sung, who supported Beijing in the wake of the June 4 incident and the subsequent international sanctions, asked Jiang Zemin, the new CCP general secretary, not to establish a trade office in South Korea as this would further isolate North Korea, Jiang responded that the issue could be delayed.[39] But China, which was confronting Western economic sanctions, soon welcomed courting from enthusiastic South Korean entrepreneurs.

When Jiang Zemin visited North Korea in March 1990, he told North Korean leaders, "Your opposition to our establishment of a trade office in South Korea is understandable, but it is inevitable." On April 25, Vice Premier Tian Jiyun, who was also chairman of the Small Steering Group on Coordinating the Economy and Trade with South Korea, secretly met in Beijing with Lee Sun-seok, president of the Sunkyung Group, one of the largest conglomerates in South Korea. This was the first time that a senior Chinese government official had met with a South Korean dignitary. Tian Jiyun told Lee Sun-seok, "With the further development of relations between our two countries, the exchange of trade offices will be imperative." Such proposed trade offices "as a matter of fact will be semi-official" and should "enjoy status equivalent to that of a consulate."[40] When Kim Il-sung visited China, in September, Jiang Zemin again said, "Sino–South Korean trade relations are developing very rapidly and it is inevitable that nongovernmental trade offices will be established." Kim Il-sung thus had no choice but to accept this reality.[41]

On October 20, the China Chamber of International Commerce signed an agreement with the Korea Trade Promotion Agency on the exchange of trade offices between the two countries.[42] Externally, the trade offices were nongovernmental, but internally they enjoyed official status. Eleven of the twenty members of the South Korean staff in the trade office in Beijing were officials from the South Korean Ministry of Foreign Affairs.

They had the authority to carry out consular duties and they enjoyed full diplomatic immunity. The exchange of trade offices established a foundation for the development of Sino–South Korean political relations.[43]

Beginning in the early 1980s, China started to pay attention to improving relations with South Korea. But, in consideration of North Korea's interests, China refrained from developing political and formal diplomatic relations. After the exchange of trade offices, China adopted a more active posture to promote the establishment of full diplomatic relations. In May and June 1991, China persuaded (or even forced) North Korea into accepting the proposition that North and South Korea should join the UN as two separate states. China also attempted to facilitate North–South Korean dialogues and U.S.–North Korean talks.[44]

On September 17, 1991, together with the ROK, North Korea was admitted to the UN. The admission of both South Korea and North Korea to the United Nations was important to China because once and for all it disentangled "the 'two Korea' issue from the 'one China' principle."[45] With the further relaxation of relations between North and South Korea, as well as between North Korea and the United States, political conditions were ripe for the establishment of full diplomatic relations between China and South Korea. Therefore, in early 1992 China initiated the process of normalizing relations with South Korea.[46]

During the conference of the UN Economic and Social Commission for Asia and the Pacific, held in Beijing in April 1992, Qian Qichen and Lee Sang-ok, foreign ministers of China and South Korea, respectively, met to discuss China's proposal for negotiations on diplomatic normalization between the two countries. After two rounds of negotiations in Beijing, on May 13 and June 2 and 3, diplomats from the two countries met in Seoul, on June 21 and 22, to draft the communiqué for normalizing diplomatic relations.[47] Contrary to China's usual practice of consulting North Korea on anything related to North Korean interests, Beijing informed Pyongyang only *after* China had already made this decision. When the Soviet Union normalized diplomatic relations with South Korea, in September 1990, North Korea protested angrily. *Rodong sinmun* accused the Soviets of "selling the dignity and honor of the great socialist country and selling the interests and trust of an ally."[48]

To comfort Kim Il-sung, Chinese leaders promised Kim on two occasions, in September 1990 and October 1991, that China would not establish full diplomatic relations with South Korea.[49] Nonetheless, on Kim Il-sung's eightieth birthday, in April 1992, Beijing informed Pyongyang that China was considering normalizing relations with South Korea. When Kim Il-sung asked if China could postpone such normalization of diplomatic relations with South Korea for another year, China was noncommittal.[50] On July 15, when Foreign Minister Qian Qichen went to Pyongyang to inform Kim Il-sung of China's decision to establish full diplomatic relations with South Korea, Kim coldly replied, "The DPRK will adhere to socialism and will overcome any difficulties on its own."[51]

Finally, in August 1992 China and South Korea established full diplomatic relations, which ended nearly half a century of hostilities between the two countries. Because the United States had no intention of invading China and therefore South Korea was not a bridgehead for attacking China, North Korea was no longer China's shield and strategic buffer. The geostrategic importance of the Korean Peninsula to China thus underwent fundamental changes. Indeed, on October 5, 1991, prior to the normalization of relations between China and South Korea, Deng Xiaoping told Kim Il-sung, who was then visiting Beijing, "China and the DPRK have a special relationship. But it is not reflected in appearance. We have close fraternal ties, but we are not allies."[52] On October 8, Jiang Zemin told Ishida Koshiro, visiting secretary-general of the Komei party of Japan, that "China and North Korea are not allies."[53]

The normalization of diplomatic relations between China and South Korea cut the last cord in the "brotherly" political foundation of Sino-North Korean relations. The strategic, economic, and political foundations of the Sino–North Korean "special relationship" collapsed completely, and relations between China and North Korea cooled considerably. Although Beijing and Pyongyang attempted to project a semblance of political unity, they were strange bedfellows.[54] Since then, North Korea no longer pays much attention to China's interests and attitudes in international politics. Instead, it attempts to make utmost use of the contradictions among global and regional powers to ensure regime survival and security.[55] The DPRK's most blatant action has been the creation of the "nuclear crisis." During Kim Jong-il's tenure, North Korea did not consider Chinese interests with regard to the nuclear weapons issue. It continuously undermined the six-party talks and flagrantly conducted two nuclear tests.[56] Nevertheless, it remained highly dependent on China economically and it managed to acquire from China much-needed aid to ensure survival of the regime.

What do we learn from a study of the evolution of Sino-North Korean relations from 1949 to 1976? We can summarize the following three main features of the relationship.

First, from the perspective of cultural traditions, after World War II, Sino-North Korean relations underwent a process of transformation from suzerain–vassal relations to modern state-to-state relations. The transformation represented a struggle between China's concept of suzerain–vassal state relations and North Korea's *Juche* idea and resistance to "flunkeyism." Both China and North Korea were under the control of powerful dictators who formulated their respective foreign policies. As soon as the PRC was established, in 1949, Mao Zedong sought to restore China's dominant position along its borders. Familiar with the Chinese classics, he had memorized the ruling techniques of the emperors of the Heavenly Kingdom.

Thus, with respect to issues related to North Korea, Mao relied on the traditional tributary system. But during this period, the tributary system was promoted in the name of revolution. Mao's lifetime ambition was to make China the center of the Asian Revolution, or even the world revolution, that is, to establish China as a revolutionary "celestial empire." In its attempts to achieve this goal, China paid a heavy price. If North Korea submitted to and remained in step with China's political line and recognized Mao's leadership, China was willing to suffer losses of territory, population, and economic interests. This, indeed, was a salient feature of the ancient suzerain–vassal state relationship.

As the leader of a small state, Kim Il-sung's ideas were completely opposite those of Mao. Ancient Korean leaders had advocated flunkeyism, relying on the suzerain–vassal relationship with China to defend Korea's national security and political status in East Asia. In modern times, because of China's declining status in international affairs, Korea suffered the great humiliation of its colonization by Japan. After the Second World War, North Korea saw the light of independence, but it had to accept protection by the Soviet Union during the early period of the Cold War.

Throughout his lifetime, Kim Il-sung, who had come of age politically during the War of Resistance against Japan, pursued independence and Korean reunification. After the death of Stalin and the end of the Korean War in 1953, Kim lost no time in proposing his *Juche* idea and opposing flunkeyism. He believed that this was the only way that Korea could achieve true independence and he could establish his personal dictatorship. With respect to diplomatic relations, the evolution in Sino-North Korean relations was indicative of the transformation from traditional suzerain–vassal relations to modern state-to-state relations. Although international political realities and ideological conflicts required Sino-North Korean unity, they also entailed different diplomatic agendas. Such contradictory agendas constituted a fundamental source of the instability in the Sino-North Korean alliance.

Second, from the geopolitical perspective, relations between China, a major power, and North Korea, a small and weak power, were asymmetric and unequal during the Cold War period. The relationship was a case of the not uncommon phenomenon of the "tail wagging the dog." In an alliance, the smaller and weaker country usually submits to the larger and more powerful country. But from the early 1950s to Mao Zedong's death in 1976, North Korea generally held the upper hand in the relations between the two countries. When there were tensions and conflicts, China ultimately had to make concessions to satisfy North Korean needs.

Why was this the case? Aside from Kim Il-sung's indomitable will and his diplomatic skill in winning advantages for his side, it was largely due to the international background of the Cold War and to geopolitical factors. North Korea, which was at the nexus of Chinese, American, and Soviet security interests in Northeast Asia, was vitally important strategically. During the confrontation between the two blocs, from 1950 to 1959, both China and the Soviet Union had to consider the interests and demands of North Korea, the gateway to socialism in the Far East. During the period of Sino–Soviet competition for a leading role in the socialist bloc, from 1960 to 1965, each side flattered and extended favors to North Korea in order to win its support.

After China was excluded from the socialist bloc, in 1966, North Korea was one of its few remaining allies, thereby holding even more political capital to squeeze concessions from China. In their bilateral relations, China, the "elder brother," valued "leadership"—that is, the ability to exercise control over major issues of principle, such as relations with the Soviet Union—whereas North Korea, the "younger brother," cared more about "interests." In order to win Kim Il-sung's political support, Mao had no choice but to ignore North Korea's vacillation and opportunistic policies. This allowed Kim Il-sung to gain the upper hand in its relations with China.

Mao could tolerate North Korea's growing demands for material aid but not its political betrayal. Most of the time, North Korea was able to receive a large amount of material aid from China even though the relationship was only lukewarm. During the Sino–Soviet confrontation, North Korea "sat on the fence." The contradictions in Sino-North Korean relations were not exposed to the general public in either of the two countries, nor were they disclosed to their enemies. Otherwise, the alliance would have been rendered illegitimate and would no longer have served its deterrence purposes. This is the reality of the Sino-North Korean alliance during the Cold War.

Third, from the perspective of codes of conduct and political norms, the Sino-North Korean alliance was indicative of the structural problems in relations among the socialist states. China and North Korea were both socialist nations under the leadership of Communist parties. Similar to Sino–Soviet relations, China's diplomatic interactions with North Korea during the Cold War represented a typical case of the immature modern state-to-state relations among the socialist bloc countries. But Sino-North Korean relations did not reject the influence of party-to-party relations within the International Communist Movement. To a great extent, state relations followed the political principles of party-to-party relations.

In modern state-to-state relations, the core common principle is the acceptance of sovereignty and equality among nations. But there were inherent structural drawbacks in the socialist alliance. First, according to Communist political theory, the concepts of state and sovereignty do not exist. The Communists had long claimed that "The proletarian has no motherland" and "Workers of the world, unite!" Even after assuming power, the Communist parties still accepted internationalism as a paramount principle. Second, there is no concept of equality in Communist ideology. The constitutions of the Communist parties stipulated the organizational principle that the junior party is always subordinate to its superior and the entire party obeys the Central Committee.

This leader–subordinate relationship in party-to-party relations was transplanted to state-to-state relations. It was commonly accepted that the "leader of this big Communist family" could interfere at will in the internal affairs of "other members of the socialist family." The "younger brother" could be capricious and act shamelessly, whereas the "elder brother" had to endure humiliation in order to carry out its important mission. This situation existed in both Sino–Soviet relations and Sino-North

Korean relations. But China's role was transformed from that of the "younger brother" in Sino–Soviet relations to that of the "elder brother" in Sino-North Korean relations. Although the leaders of the Communist countries gradually came to understand that every country should be accorded equal rights and that national interests should be the core guiding principle in state-to-state relations, no party could reject proletarian internationalism or the importance of unity in the International Communist Movement, lest they risk forsaking the principles of Marxism–Leninism and negate the legitimacy of Communist political power. Such contradictions thus contributed to the continuing tensions in Sino-North Korean relations.

Notes

Introduction: Refuting a Historical Myth

1. The official name of North Korea is the Democratic People's Republic of Korea, or DPRK. It was established in September 1948.
2. A careful review of *Renmin ribao* [People's Daily] over the past sixty years reveals that the newspaper never published anything negative about North Korea. During the period of deteriorating relations between the two countries, official Chinese newspapers reported very little about North Korea. North Korean newspapers adopted a similar practice, though they did occasionally attack China by innuendo. For instance, in the early years of the Cultural Revolution, *Rodong sinmun* [Workers' Newspaper] published a statement censuring the Red Guards' rumor mongering about North Korea's internal affairs. Nevertheless, we have noticed that China's relations with North Korea have worsened precipitously since 2013. On May 3, 2017, the Korean Central News Agency published an editorial entitled "Buyao zai zuo luankan Chao Zhong guanxi zhizhu de weixian de yanxing" [Stop the Words and Deals That Undermine the Foundation of Sino–North Korean Relations]. For the first time, Pyongyang publicly made unwarranted charges against Beijing because China's official media had published numerous articles censuring North Korea's nuclear weapons program. On May 4, Beijing fired back. *Renmin ribao*'s overseas edition editorial board released an article, via its official WeChat account, entitled "Chaozhongshe, Ni piping Zhongguo de yanlun hen wuli" [Korean Central News Agency: Your Criticism of China Is Very Unreasonable]. The article concludes, "The Sino–DPRK relationship is no longer 'traditional' friendship. The bilateral relations should be redefined in the spirit of the new era." On May 5, the article was reprinted on a popular Chinese-language Web site (see http://news.ifeng.com/a/20170505/51047069_0.shtml).

3. This is at least the case in terms of Chinese publications. See, for example, Jilin-sheng Shekeyuan [Jilin Province Academy of Social Sciences], ed., *ZhongChao guanxi tongshi* [A General History of Sino–Korean Relations], 4 vols. (Chang-chun: Jilin renmin chubanshe, 1996).

   Between 2001 and 2002, the major Chinese journal on the Korean Peninsula, *Dongbeiya luntan* [Forum on Northeast Asia], published eighty-one articles on topics related to the Korean Peninsula, but none of these articles deal with Sino–North Korean relations. Between 2003 and 2005, *Dongbeiya luntan* published 158 articles on the Korean Peninsula, but only five are on the topic of Sino–North Korean relations. The arguments in these articles are very similar to those in *Renmin ribao*. See Piao Jianyi and Ma Junwei, eds., *Zhongguo dui Chaoxian bandao de yanjiu* [Chinese Studies on the Korean Peninsula] (Beijing: Minzu chubanshe, 2006). A search of the keywords "China and Korea" in a popular Chinese academic electronic database (www.cnki.net) generates around eight hundred journal articles written during the period from 1990 to 2017. In general, articles on the history of Sino–North Korean relations focus on the period prior to the founding of the People's Republic of China (PRC) in 1949 or to the history of the "War to Resist American Aggression and Aid Korea." Fewer than ten studies cover the period from the Korean armistice in 1953 to the end of the Cold War in 1991, and those articles primarily extol the Sino–North Korean friendship. Thus, the sensitivity of the topic for Chinese scholars is clearly manifest.

4. Yang Zhaoquan, "Jianguo 60 nian lai woguo de Chaoxian-Hanguo shi he Zhong-Chao Zhong-Han guanxi yanjiu zongshu" [Survey of Studies on the History of North and South Korea, and the History of Sino-North Korean and Sino-South Korean Relations], *Chaoxian-Hanguo lishi yanjiu* [Historical Studies on North and South Korea] 12 (2012): 470.

5. In the PRC, the history of the Sino–North Korean friendship is typically traced back to the Korean War period (1950–1953), when the Chinese sent troops to save Kim Il-sung's regime. However, in North Korea, the history begins during the colonial period, when Koreans fought with the Chinese against the Japanese in Manchuria and when Korean and Chinese armies joined forces to fight Chiang Kai-shek's Guomindang during the Chinese Civil War (1946–1949). For a thoughtful analysis, see Heonik Kwon, "The Korean War and Sino–North Korean Friendship," *Asia Pacific Journal* 11, no. 4 (August 8, 2013): 1–19.

6. See, for example, Mike Myung-Kun Yiu, "The Factors of North Korean Neutral Behavior in the Sino–Soviet Conflict," *International Behavioral Scientist* 4, no. 1 (March 1972): 1-10; Seung-kwon Synn, "Kim Il-sung Between Moscow and Peking," *Korean Journal of International Studies* 5, no. 2-3 (Spring-Summer 1974): 7-16; Deok Kim, "Sino–Soviet Dispute and North Korea," *Korea Observer* 10, no. 1 (Spring 1979): 3-30.

7. V. A. Shin, *Kitai i koreiskie gosudarstva vo vtoroi polovine XX stoletiia* [China and North Korea in the Second Half of the Twentieth Century] (Moscow: ID-vo MGU, 1998), 6-7, 11-12.

8. See, for example, Hazel Smith, *North Korea: Markets and Military Rule* (Cambridge: Cambridge University Press, 2015); Andrew Scobell, *China and North*

Korea: From Comrades-in-Arms to Allies at Arm's Length (Carlisle Barracks, PA: Strategic Studies Institute, U.S. Army War College, March 2004); Jae Ho Chung, *Between Ally and Partner: Korea–China Relations and the United States* (New York: Columbia University Press, 2007); Scott Snyder, *China's Rise and the Two Koreas: Politics, Economics, Security* (Boulder, CO: Lynne Rienner, 2009).

9. Charles K. Armstrong, "Trends in the Study of North Korea," *Journal of Asian Studies* 70, no. 2 (May 2011): 357–371.

10. Yi Chong-sŏk, *Pukhan-Chungguk kwan'gye, 1945–2000* [The Sino-North Korean Relationship, 1945–2000] (Seoul: Chungsim, 2000).

11. Charles K. Armstrong, *Tyranny of the Weak: North Korea and the World, 1950–1992* (Ithaca, NY: Cornell University Press, 2013).

12. These documents are no longer open to the public, thus rendering this research even more important. In early 2013, when asked about access to those formerly declassified files in the Chinese Ministry of Foreign Affairs archives, ministry spokesperson Hong Lei declared that the facility was "in the process of upgrading its computer system for technical reasons." However, there have been reports that the new restrictions were put in place after a Japanese journalist obtained a 1950 Chinese document that describes the disputed Senkaku/Diaoyu Islands as part of Japan, thereby contradicting the current position of the Chinese government. See "Curtailed Access to China's Diplomatic Archives Fuels Senkaku Conjecture," *Japan Times*, February 1, 2013.

13. The most important is Zhonggong Zhongyang Duiwai Lianluobu [International Liaison Department of the Chinese Communist Party Central Committee], ed., *Mao Zedong yu waibin tanhua jilu huibian* [A Collection of Records of Mao Zedong's Conversations with Foreign Guests], various vols. (Beijing: unpublished internal edition, 1977), in the authors' personal collection. Because this collection remains classified and is available to only a small number of Chinese Communist Party historians, we are unable to reveal more information about this collection. Nonetheless, throughout the present volume many memoranda (as well as memoranda of conversations, and minutes) regarding Mao Zedong's conversations with visiting foreign delegations or foreign leaders are cited.

14. See Sergey S. Radchenko, "The Soviet Union and the North Korean Seizure of the USS *Pueblo*: Evidence from the Russian Archives," *Cold War International History Project Working Paper* 47 (April 2005); James F. Person, introduction to "New Evidence on North Korea in 1956," *Cold War International History Project Bulletin* 16 (Fall 2007-Winter 2008): 447–454; James F. Person, ed., "Limits of the 'Lips and Teeth' Alliance: New Evidence on Sino–DPRK Relations 1955–1984," *North Korea International Documentation Project Reader* 2 (March 2009). Also see the Wilson Center's online Cold War International History Project digital archive, at http://digitalarchive.wilsoncenter.org/theme/cold-war-history.

15. These documents are available at the online Central Intelligence Agency library (http://www.foia.cia.gov/historical-collections), from the U.S. Department of State (http://www.state.gov/s/inr), and in two important databases— the Declassified Documents Reference System and the Digital National Security Archive.

16. For recently published U.S. diplomatic documents, see U.S. Department of State, Office of the Historian, *Foreign Relations of the United States, 1969–1976, Richard M. Nixon/Gerald R. Ford*, vol. 17, *China, 1969–1972* (Washington, DC: Government Printing Office, 2006); and vol. 18, *China, 1973–1976*; and U.S. Department of State, Office of the Historian, *Foreign Relations of the United States, 1969–1976*, vol. E-13, *Documents on China, 1969–1972* (Washington, DC: Government Printing Office, 2006), http://history.state.gov/historicaldocuments/frus1969-76ve13/comp1.

17. Interview with Kim Kang in Taiyuan, China, February 16–February 17, 2010, and with Kim Ch'ung-sik in Taiyuan, China, February 2010 and February 2011.

18. The No. 88 Independent Infantry Brigade is also known as the Anti-Japanese United Army Training Brigade, which was organized by the Soviet Far Eastern Command in July 1942, in the area east of Khabarovsk.

19. "Flunkyism" is a term denoting the Confucian ideal of a small state serving a big power in order to survive, referring especially to the 1392–1895 period of Korean history, when the Korean Yi dynasty paid tribute to China's Ming and Qing dynasties.

20. Steven R. David, "Explaining Third World Alignment," *World Politics* 43, no. 2 (January 1991): 233-256; Michael N. Barnett and Jack S. Levy, "Domestic Sources of Alliances and Alignments: The Case of Egypt, 1962-73," *International Organization* 45, no. 3 (Summer 1991): 369-395; Eric A. Miller and Arkady Toritsyn, "Bringing the Leader Back In: Internal Threats and Alignment Theory in the Commonwealth of Independent States," *Security Studies* 14, no. 2 (April-June 2005): 325-363.

21. John M. Owen, "When Do Ideologies Produce Alliances? The Holy Roman Empire, 1517-55," *International Studies Quarterly* 49, no. 1 (March 2005): 73-99; Mark L. Haas, *The Ideological Origins of Great Power Politics, 1789–1989* (Ithaca, NY: Cornell University Press, 2005), 16-17, 29, 51, 88-90, 95, 98-102, 107, 148-158, 214-216, 222; Stephen M. Walt, *The Origins of Alliances* (Ithaca, NY: Cornell University Press, 1987), 33-35.

22. The reasons for the formation of alliances are not mutually exclusive. For example, when states form alliances for the purpose of ideological support and promotion, they are also likely combining capabilities to balance shared ideological threats.

23. Glenn H. Snyder, *Alliance Politics* (Ithaca, NY: Cornell University Press, 1997), 4; Walt, *Origins of Alliances*, 18-19; Kenneth N. Waltz, *Theory of International Politics* (New York: McGraw-Hill, 1979), 126-127; John J. Mearsheimer, *The Tragedy of Great Power Politics* (New York: Norton, 2001), 156. On the differences between defensive and offensive alliances, see Randall L. Schweller, "Bandwagoning for Profit: Bringing the Revisionist State Back In," *International Security* 19, no. 1 (Summer 1994): 72-107.

24. See, for example, Thomas J. Christensen and Jack Snyder, "Chain Gangs and Passed Bucks: Predicting Alliance Patterns in Multipolarity," *International Organization* 44, no. 2 (Spring 1990): 137-168; Evan N. Resnick, "Strange

Bedfellows: U.S. Bargaining Behavior with Allies of Convenience," *International Security* 35, no. 3 (Winter 2010/2011): 144-184.

25. See Giorgi Gvalia, David Siroky, Bidzina Lebanidze, and Zurab Iashvili, "Thinking Outside the Bloc: Explaining the Foreign Policies of Small States," *Security Studies* 22, no. 1 (January-March 2013): 98-131.

26. In addition to recent systematic works on major bilateral relations, such as Sino–American relations, Sino–Soviet relations, and Sino–Japanese relations, there also are works focusing on China's foreign relations and foreign policy. Many of these appear in the form of journal articles, essay collections, and PhD dissertations. Two monographs are particularly noteworthy: Niu Jun, *Lengzhan yu xin Zhongguo waijiao de yuanqi, 1949-1955* [The Cold War and the Genesis of New China's Diplomacy, 1949-1955] (Beijing: Shehui kexue wenxian chubanshe, 2012); and Li Qianyu, *Cong Wanlong dao A'erjier: Zhongguo yu liuci YaFei huiyi (1955-1965)* [From Bandung to Algiers: China and the Six Afro-Asian Conferences (1955-1965)] (Beijing: Shijie zhishi chubanshe, 2016).

1. Victory and Expansion of the Revolution in China and North Korea, 1945-1950

1. Niu Jun, *Lengzhan yu xin Zhongguo waijiao de yuanqi (1945–1955)* [The Cold War and the Genesis of New China's Diplomacy (1945–1955)] (Beijing: Shehui kexue wenxian chubanshe, 2012), chap. 3, part 1.

2. See Pu Xuanling, *Dongbei KangRi yiyongjun* [The Anti-Japanese Volunteer Army in the Northeast] (Beijing: Zhongguo youyi chubanshe, 1998). See also A. N. Pochtarev, "Iz istorii Sovetsko-Koreiskikh otnoshenii v 1920–1950e dofy" [The History of Soviet–Korean Relations, 1920–1950], *Novaia i noveishaia istoria* [Modern and Contemporary History] 5 (1999): 135–160.

3. During what is also called the Manchurian incident, Japanese military personnel detonated a small quantity of dynamite close to a railway line owned by Japan's South Manchuria Railway, near Mukden (now Shenyang), on September 18, 1931. Japan used this as a pretext for its subsequent invasion of northeastern China, known as Manchuria.

4. For a recent study on the relationship between Chinese and Korean Communists from 1919 to 1936, based on newly available sources, see Shen Zhihua, "Tongming xianglian: Chaoxian gongchandang rongru Zhonggong de lishi guocheng (1919–1936)" [Sharing a Similar Fate: The Historical Process of the Merger of the Korean Communists with the Chinese Communist Party (1919–1936)], *Shehui kexue zhanxian* [Social Science Front] 2 (2015): 68–85. For an English version of the article, see Shen Zhihua, "Sharing a Similar Fate: The Historical Process of the Korean Communists' Merger with the Chinese Communist Party (1919–1936)," *Journal of Modern Chinese History* 11, no. 1 (2017): 1–28.

5. Shi Yuanhua, ed., *Zhongguo gongchandang yuanzhu Chaoxian duli yundong jishi, 1921–1945* [A History of the Chinese Communist Party's Assistance to the Korean Independence Movement, 1921-1945] (Beijing: Zhongguo shehui

kexue chubanshe, 2000), 269–273, 299; Liu Jinzhi, ed., *ZhongChao ZhongHan guanxi wenjian ziliao huibian, 1919–1949* [Collection of Documents on China's Policies toward North and South Korea, 1919–1949] (Beijing: Zhongguo shehui kexue chubanshe, 2000), 727, 801. See also Kim Donggil, "Prelude to War? The Repatriation of Koreans from the Chinese PLA, 1949–50," *Cold War History* 12, no. 2 (May 2012): 229.

6. Archive of the President of the Russian Federation (APRF), f. 3, op. 65, d. 840, l. 16, in Pochtarev, "Iz istorii sovetsko-koreiskikh otnoshenii," 140.

7. Central Archive of the Ministry of Defense, Russian Federation (TsAMORF), f. 1896, op. 1, d. 1, l. 1; d. 4, l. 29, in Pochtarev, "Iz istorii sovetsko-koreiskikh otnoshenii," 140–143. For an article-length study of the No. 88 Independent Infantry Brigade, based on newly available documentation, see Zhihua Shen, "On the Eighty-Eighth Brigade and the Sino–Soviet–Korean Triangular Relationship: A Glimpse at the International Antifascist United Front During the War of Resistance Against Japan," *Journal of Modern Chinese History* 9, no. 1 (2015): 3-25.

8. For details, see Andrei Lankov, *From Stalin to Kim Il-sung: The Formation of North Korea, 1945–1960* (London: C. Hurst, 2002), 1–48; In Deok Gang, ed., *A Complete Book of North Korea* (Seoul: Research Center of the Far East Issue, 1974), 1:254–255; Dae-Sook Suh, *Kim Il-sung: The North Korean Leader* (New York: Columbia University Press, 1988), 95–101; Zhihua Shen, *Mao, Stalin and the Korean War: Trilateral Communist Relations in the 1950s*, trans. Neil Silver (London: Routledge, 2012), 38-43.

9. Zhongyang Dang'anguan [China Central Archives], *Zhonggong zhongyang wenjian xuanji* [Selection of Documents of the Central Committee of the Chinese Communist Party] (Beijing: Zhonggong zhongyang dangxiao chubanshe, 1991), 15:223.

10. Shi Yuanhua, *Zhongguo gongchandang yuanzhu Chaoxian duli yundong jishi*, 389–390.

11. Zhonggong Zhongyang Wenxian Yanjiushi [Chinese Communist Party Central Committee Party Literature Research Office], ed., *Chen Yun wenji* [Collected Writings by Chen Yun] (Beijing: Zhongyang wenxian chubanshe, 2005), 1:447–452.

12. Shi Yuanhua, *Zhongguo gongchandang yuanzhu Chaoxian duli yundong jishi*, 394; Li Xiangshu, "Guanyu Wu Ting de kangRi geming huodong yanjiu" [A Study of Mu Chong's Anti-Japanese Revolutionary Activities], master's thesis, Institute of Modern History, Chinese Academy of Social Sciences, 2006, 56; Jin Jingyi, "Guanyu Zhongguo jundui zhong Chaoxianzu guanbing fanhui Chaoxian de lishi kaocha" [A Historical Investigation into the Return to Korea of Ethnic Korean Officers and Soldiers from the Chinese Army], *Shixue jikan* [Collected Papers on Historical Studies] 3 (May 2007): 56. Also see Kim, "Prelude to War?" 230.

13. Yanbian Chaoxianzu Zizhizhou Dang'anguan [Archives of Yanbian Korean Autonomous Prefecture], ed., *Yanbian diwei Yanbian zhuanshu zhongyao wenjian huibian* [A Compilation of Important Documents of the Yanbian Prefectural Party

Committee and the Prefectural Commissioner's Office] 1 (unpublished, December 1986), cited in Xu Longnan, "Yanbianji Chaoxian renminjun tuiwu junren caifanglu" [Record of Interviews with Ex-servicemen of the Korean People's Army in Yanbian], in *Lengzhan guojishi yanjiu* [Cold War International History Studies], ed. Li Danhui (Beijing: Shijie zhishi chubanshe, 2008), 7:265-287. For more details on the ethnic Korean troops, see Zhongguo Chaoxianzu Lishi Zuji Bianji Weiyuanhui [Editorial Committee on the History of Koreans in China], *Sheng li* [Victory] (Beijing: Minzu chubanshe, 1992), 57–83.

14. In the Chinese Communist Party (CCP)–controlled *Jiefang ribao* [Liberation Daily], *JinChaJi ribao* [JinChaJi Daily], and *Renmin ribao* [People's Daily], between 1946 and 1948 the Laodong dang (Korean Workers' Party) was referred to as the "Laogong dang," *Jin Richeng* (Kim Il-sung) was translated as "Gai Misheng" or "Jin Yisun," *Jin Kefeng* (Kim Tu-bong) was translated as "Jin Tuoben" or "Jin Doufeng," and *Pak Hŏn-yŏng* was translated as "Bai Hengning." These mistranslations indicate that CCP leaders were unfamiliar with the situation in Korea. For details, see Liu Jinzhi, *ZhongChao ZhongHan guanxi wenjian ziliao huibian, 1919–1949*, 1217, 1249, 1403–1575.

15. Wu Dianyao and Song Lin, *Zhu Lizhi zhuan* [A Biography of Zhu Lizhi] (Beijing: Zhonggong dangshi chubanshe, 2007), 468-470.

16. "Report, Zhu Lizhi to Li Fuchun and the Northeast Bureau, June 27, 1947" and "Political Report, Zhu Lizhi to the Northeast Bureau," in *Jinian Zhu Lizhi wenji* [Collection of Papers in Memory of Zhu Lizhi], ed. Zhonggong Henanshengwei Dangshi Yanjiushi [Party History Office of the Henan Provincial Chinese Communist Party Committee] (Beijing: Zhonggong dangshi chubanshe, 2007), 239–241, 242–244.

17. Wu Dianyao and Song Lin, *Zhu Lizhi zhuan*, 461; Ding Xuesong et al., "Huiyi dongbei jiefang zhanzheng qijian dongbeiju zhu Chaoxian banshichu" [Recollections of the Northeast Bureau Office in North Korea During the Chinese Civil War in the Northeast], *Zhonggong dangshi ziliao* [Materials on the History of the Chinese Communist Party] 17 (1986): 197–200, 202–204.

18. In Jae-Jung Suh, ed., *Origins of North Korea's* Juche: *Colonialism, War, and Development* (Lanham, MD: Lexington Books, 2013), 57.

19. Based on U.S. intelligence, Bruce Cumings writes, "Kim Il-sung sensed the immense strategic blessing of a Chinese Communist victory . . . and therefore in early 1947 he began dispatching tens of thousands of Koreans to fight with Mao and to swell the existing Korean units to division size, a 'volunteer' army that prefigured the Chinese 'volunteers' that returned the favor in the fall of 1950." Cumings, *Korea's Place in the Sun: A Modern History*, updated ed. (New York: W. W. Norton, 2005), 238–239. This is a distilled version of an argument he makes in Cumings, *The Origins of the Korean War*, vol. 2, *The Roaring of the Cataract, 1947–1950* (Princeton, NJ: Princeton University Press, 1990), 350–376. In light of Chinese and Russian archival sources, Kim Donggil refutes this argument, concluding, "Chinese documents verify that ethnic Korean units in the PLA [People's Liberation Army] were indigenous in Northeast China and that the North Korean regime never dispatched soldiers to Manchuria to

assist Communist China during the Chinese Civil War." Kim, "Prelude to War?" 238.

20. Zhonggong Henanshengwei Dangshi Yanjiushi, *Jinian Zhu Lizhi wenji*, 239–241; Ding Xuesong and Yang Dehua, *Diyiwei nü dashi: Ding Xuesong huiyilu* [The First Female Ambassador: Memoirs of Ding Xuesong] (Nanjing: Jiangsu renmin chubanshe, 2000).

21. Zhonggong Henanshengwei Dangshi Yanjiushi, *Jinian Zhu Lizhi wenji*, 241; Jin Jingyi, "Guanyu Zhongguo jundui zhong Chaoxianzu guanbing fanhui Chaoxian de lishi kaocha," 58; Xu Longnan, "Yanbianji Chaoxian renminjun tuiwu junren caifanglu," 266-287.

22. *Collected Works of Kim Il-sung* (Pyongyang: Korean Workers' Party Press, 1993), 8:284–389.

23. Zhonghua Renmin Gongheguo Waijiaobu and Zhonggong Zhongyang Wenxian Yanjiushi [People's Republic of China Ministry of Foreign Affairs and Chinese Communist Party Central Committee Party Literature Research Office], eds., *Mao Zedong waijiao wenxuan* [Selected Diplomatic Papers of Mao Zedong] (Beijing: Zhongyang wenxian chubanshe and Shijie zhishi chubanshe, 1994), 66, 94.

24. "Revolutionary internationalism" refers to the perception that all Communist revolutions are part of a single global class struggle rather than separate, localized events. Both Mao Zedong and Kim Il-sung believed that the Chinese Communist revolution and the Korean Communist revolution were part of the same revolution, and thus the two countries should always provide each other with aid for their common endeavors.

25. Anastas I. Mikoyan expressed his support for a CCP-led Asian Communist Bureau during a secret trip to Xibaipo in February 1949. See APRF, f. 39, op. 1, d. 39, ll. 47–53, in *Russko-kitaiskie otnoshenie v XX veke, Dokumenty i materialy*, Tom V, *Sovetsko–kitaiskie otnoshenie, 1946–fevral'1950*, Kniga 2: *1949—fevral'1950 gg.* [Russian–Chinese Relations in the Twentieth Century: Documents and Materials, vol. 5: Soviet–Chinese Relations, February 1946-1950, no. 2: 1949-February 1950], ed. Andrei M. Ledovskii, R. A. Mirovshchkaia, and V. S. Miasnikov (Moscow: PIM, 2005), 62–66. The Burmese, Malaysian, and Indo-Chinese Communist parties also wrote to the CCP Central Committee to suggest the establishment of an intelligence bureau that would include all Asian Communist parties. But Mao Zedong thought that the time was not yet ripe, due to the ongoing Chinese Civil War. See Shen Zhihua, ed., *Chaoxian zhanzheng: Eguo dang'anguan de jiemi wenjian* [The Korean War: Declassified Documents from the Russian Archives] (Taipei: Zhongyang yanjiuyuan, Jindaishi yanjiusuo, 2003), 188-189. During Liu Shaoqi's trip to the Soviet Union in July 1949, Stalin again suggested that an East Asian Communist alliance be established. See Sergei N. Goncharov, John W. Lewis, and Xue Litai, *Uncertain Partners: Stalin, Mao and the Korean War* (Stanford, CA: Stanford University Press, 1993), 71–73, 232–233. See also, based on Shi Zhe's oral account, Shi Zhe, *Zai lishi juren shenbian: Shi Zhe huiyilu* [By the Side of the Great Man: Reminiscences of Shi Zhe], ed. Li Haiwen, 2nd rev. ed. (Beijing: Zhongyang wenxian chubanshe, 1995), 413–414.

26. The Soviet Communist Party was called the All-Union Communist Party (Bolsheviks) from 1925 to 1952. It was renamed the Communist Party of the Soviet Union (CPSU) in 1952. For convenience, we use CPSU throughout.

27. Telegram, Terebin to Kuznetsov, July 28, 1948, APRF, f. 3 9, op. 1, d. 31, l. 41, in Ledovskii, Mirovitskaia, and Miasnikov, *Russko-kitaiskie otnosheniia v XX veke*, 451-452.

28. Zhihua Shen and Yafeng Xia, *Mao and the Sino–Soviet Partnership, 1945–1959: A New History* (Lanham, MD: Lexington Books, 2015), 19-20.

29. For a study on Soviet policy toward China from 1947 to 1948, see Shen and Xia, *Mao and the Sino–Soviet Partnership*, 11-20.

30. Memorandum of conversation between Anastas Mikoyan and Mao Zedong, February 3, 1949, APRF, f. 39, op. 1, d. 39, ll. 47-53.

31. Telegram, Shtykov to Vishinsky, May 15, 1949, APRF, f. 3, op. 65, d. 9, ll. 51-55. For Stalin's meeting with Kim Il-sung, Moscow, March 5, 1949, see Christian Ostermann et al., eds., *Stalin and the Cold War, 1945–1953: A Cold War International History Project Document Reader*, prepared for the conference on Stalin and the Cold War, 1945-1953, Yale University, September 23-26, 1999, 434-439. This document does not mention the Cominform. It is not known whether it was brought up in other secret conversations.

32. Telegram, Kovalev from Stalin, May 18, 1949, APRF, f. 45, op. 1, d. 331, ll. 59-61.

33. In 1948-1949, Stalin expelled Yugoslavia from the International Association of Socialist States because its leader, Josip B. Tito, wanted to remain independent. On several occasions, Mao Zedong mentioned that Stalin distrusted him, and Stalin indeed had concerns about Mao's loyalty. In December 1948, Ivan Kovalev was recalled to Moscow by Stalin. In their conversation, Stalin directly referred to the CCP's position with respect to the "Yugoslav incident" and demanded to know on which side the Chinese stood. Ivan Kovalev, "The Stalin–Mao Dialogue," *Far Eastern Affairs* (Moscow) 1 (1992): 100-113; and 2 (1992): 94-111.

34. Telegram, Stalin to Kovalev, May 26, 1949, APRF, 45, op. 1, d. 331, ll. 73-75.

35. Telegram, Liu Shaoqi to the General Office of the CCP Central Committee, July 27, in Zhonggong Zhongyang Wenxian Yanjiushi and Zhongyang Dang'anguan [Chinese Communist Party Central Committee Party Literature Research Office and Central Archives], eds., *Jianguo yilai Liu Shaoqi wengao* (*JYLSW*) [Liu Shaoqi's Manuscripts Since the Founding of the State] (Beijing: Zhonggong zhongyang wenxian chubanshe, 2005), 1:40-41; Jin Chongji, ed., *Liu Shaoqi zhuan* [A Biography of Liu Shaoqi] (Beijing: Zhonggong zhongyang wenxian chubanshe, 1998), 651-652; Shi Zhe, *Zai lishi juren shenbian*, 412-415; Kovalev, "The Stalin–Mao Dialogue," 2: 98–100. Kovalev may have made a mistake in recalling that the Cominform issue was initiated by Liu Shaoqi.

36. Yan Mingfu, "1957 nian xingshi yu Fuluxiluofu fangHua" [The Situation in 1957 and Voroshilov's Visit to China], *Bainian chao* [Hundred-Year Tide] 2 (2009): 13-17.

37. Acheng [Shan Ruhong], *Wo jianfu de shiming-Magong zhongyang zhengzhiju weiyuan Acheng huiyilu* [My Mission: Memoirs of Malayan Communist Party Central Committee Member Acheng] (Kuala Lumpur: Ershiyi shiji chubanshe, 2007), 4:11–37.

38. *Renmin ribao*, October 9, 1949.

39. *Renmin ribao*, November 17, 1949, and November 22, 1949.

40. See also Liu Ningyi, *Lishi huiyi* [Historical Recollections] (Beijing: Renmin ribao chubanshe, 1996), 140-144, 374-376. The Asian Liaison Bureau of the World Federation of Trade Unions officially began operations in early 1952. Its main tasks included collecting information about the Asian and Australasian nations, strengthening ties between the labor movements in the Asian and Australian nations and the World Federation of Trade Unions, and providing practical assistance to the working classes in Asia and Australia. In March 1958, the seventeenth meeting of the Executive Committee of the World Federation of Trade Unions abolished the Asian Liaison Bureau. See *JYLSW*, 2:138-139.

41. *JYLSW*, 2:176 177.

42. *JYLSW*, 3:27.

43. Liu Chongwen et al, eds., *Liu Shaoqi nianpu, 1898–1969* [A Chronology of Liu Shaoqi, 1898-1969] (Beijing: Zhongyang wenxian chubanshe, 1996), 2:245.

44. For a comprehensive introduction to this theory, see Mineo Nakajima, "The Sino–Soviet Confrontation: Its Roots in the International Background of the Korean War," *Australian Journal of Chinese Affairs* 1 (January 1979): 28–29; Kim Donggil, "'Sanguo tongmoulun' fenxi: Chaoxian zhanzheng qiyuan zai sikao" [An Analysis of the "Theory of Conspiracy Among the Three States": Reconsidering the Origins of the Korean War], *Dangdai Zhongguoshi yanjiu* [Contemporary China History Studies] 3, no. 2 (2006): 112-113.

45. Shen Zhihua, *Chaoxian zhanzheng*, 170, 172–173.

46. Shen Zhihua, *Chaoxian zhanzheng*, 187–88; APRF, f. 45, op. 1, d. 331, ll. 59–61. See also Archive of Foreign Policy of the Russian Federation (AVPRF), f. 059a, op. 5a, 11, d. 3, ll. 46–53.

47. Zhongguo Renmin Jiefangjun Dongbei Junqu Silingbu [Military Command of the Northeast Military Region of the People's Liberation Army], ed., *Dongbei sannian jiefang zhanzheng junshi ziliao* [Military Materials on the Three-Year War of Liberation in the Northeast] (unpublished, October 1949), 76–77; Shen Zhihua, *Chaoxian zhanzheng*, 205–208, 215. Also see Kim Donggil, "Zhongguo renmin jiefangjun zhong de Chaoxian shi hui Chaoxian wenti" [Some New Insights on the Return of the Ethnic Korean Divisions in the PLA to North Korea], *Lishi yanjiu* [History Research] 6 (2006): 103–114; Jin Jingyi, "Guanyu Zhongguo jundui zhong Chaoxianzu guanbing fanhui Chaoxian de lishi kaocha," 52–61; and Xu Longnan, "Yanbianji Chaoxian renminjun tuiwu junren caifanglu," 266-287.

48. APRF, f. 45, op. 1, d. 334, ll. 8–9, *Novaia i noveishaia istoriia* 5 (2005): 89–90.

49. APRF, f. 45, op. 1, d. 334, ll. 8–9, *Novaia i noveishaia istoriia* 5 (2005): 281.

50. *JYLSW*, 1:319–320.

51. See Nie Rongzhen, *Nie Rongzhen huiyilu* [Memoirs of Nie Rongzhen], 2nd ed. (Beijing: Jiefangjun chubanshe, 1983), 744.

52. *JYLSW*, 1:320. For the Russian version, see APRF, f. 45, op. 1, d. 334, l. 22, *Novaia i noveishaia istoriia* 5 (2005): 90.

53. Park Myong Rim, "The Outbreak and Origins of the Korean War" [in Korean], PhD diss., Korea University, Seoul, August 1994; Xu Longnan, "Yanbianji Chaoxian renminjun tuiwu junren caifanglu," 273, 277, 281.

54. Zhongguo Renmin Jiefangjun Zhongnanqu Disi Yezhanjun Zhengzhibu [Political Department of the Fourth Field Army of the Central–South Military Region of the People's Liberation Army], ed., *Chaoxian shi Zhongguo qinmi de lingbang gonghuannan de zhanyou* [North Korea Is China's Close Neighbor and Comrade-in-Arms in Sharing Hardship] (unpublished, October 1950), 20–24.

55. Zhongguo Renmin Jiefangjun Zongcanmoubu [People's Liberation Army General Staff], *Zhongguo renmin jiefangjun junshi gongzuo dashiji, 1949.10–1987.12* [A Record of Major Events in PLA Military Affairs, October 1949–December 1987] (unpublished, December 1988), 1:4; Xu Longnan, "Yanbianji Chaoxian renminjun tuiwu junren caifanglu," 280-281.

56. Telegram, Liu Shaoqi to the Central Committee of the Chinese Communist Party, July 27, 1949, authors' personal collection; Shi Zhe, *Zai lishi juren shenbian*, 412; Kovalev, "The Stalin–Mao Dialogue," 2: 98–100. Hereafter, all documents cited without specific sourcing are part of the authors' personal collection.

57. Shen Zhihua, *Chaoxian zhanzheng*, 230, 238–254.

58. Shen Zhihua, *Chaoxian zhanzheng*, 255–260.

59. Shen Zhihua's interview with Andrei M. Ledovskii, Moscow, July 31, 1996. Ledovskii was Soviet consul general in Shenyang during the 1950s and one of the few scholars who had easy access to the Archives of the President of the Russian Federation.

60. APRF, f. 45, op. 1, d. 332, ll. 47–48, *Novaia i noveishaia istoriia* 5 (2005): 92–93. According to Shepilovkii, the "yet" had been added by Stalin. This indicates that Stalin understood that, in principle, Mao did not oppose reunification by military means but was concerned about the timing.

61. Shen Zhihua, *Chaoxian zhanzheng*, 276.

62. Vladislov Zubok and Constantine Pleshakov, *Inside the Kremlin's Cold War: From Stalin to Khrushchev* (Cambridge, MA: Harvard University Press, 1996), 65-66; Evgueni Bajanov, "Assessing the Politics of the Korean War, 1949–51," *Cold War International History Project Bulletin* 6-7 (Winter 1995–1996): 87.

63. Yang Kuisong, "Sidalin weishenme zhichi Chaoxian zhanzheng? Du Shen Zhihua zhu 'Mao Zedong, Sidalin yu Chaoxian zhanzheng'" [Why Did Stalin Support the Korean War? On Reading Shen Zhihua's "Mao Zedong, Sidalin yu Chaoxian zhanzheng"], *Ershiyi shiji* [Twenty-First Century] 81 (February 2004): 130–144. The English translation is cited in Shen, *Mao, Stalin and the Korean War*, 10.

64. For a detailed description of why Stalin changed his policy toward the Korean Peninsula in January 1951 and decided to support Kim Il-sung's attack on South Korea, see Shen, *Mao, Stalin and the Korean War*, p. 118.

65. Telegram, Shtykov to Vyshinsky, January 19, 1950, in AVPRF, f. 059a, op. 5a, d. 3, p. 11, ll. 87-91.

66. For details, see Shen Zhihua, *Mao Zedong, Sidalin yu Chaoxian zhanzheng* [Mao Zedong, Stalin, and the Korean War], 3rd ed. (Guangzhou: Guangdong renmin chubanshe, 2013), 129–158.

67. Kathryn Weathersby, introduction to "New Russian Documents on the Korean War," *Cold War International History Project Bulletin*, 6–7 (Winter 1995–1996): 39 (translated from APRF, ll. 151–154, f. and op. not given; and AVPRF, f. 059a, op. 5a, d. 3, 11, ll. 100–103).

68. AVPRF, f. 059a, op. 5a, 11, d. 3, ll. 100–103. "Filippov" was a pseudonym for Stalin.

69. APRF, f. 45, op. 1, d. 331, l. 55.

70. Russian State Archive of Sociopolitical History, f. 558, op. 11, d 334. ll. 56, 57, *Novaia i noveishaia istoriia*, no. 5 (2005): 94–95.

71. AVPRF, ed., "Khronologiia osnovnykh sobytii kanuna i nachal'nogo perioda koreiskoi voiny, ianvar' 1949–oktiabr' 1950 gg." [A Chronology of the Basic Events on the Eve of and During the First Period of the Korean War, January 1949–October 1950], manuscript, 30–31. See also Goncharov, Lewis, and Xue, *Uncertain Partners*, 145.

72. A former high-ranking North Korean military officer recalled that, before the outbreak of the Korean War, all Soviet military aid was shipped to North Korea by sea, not by the Chinese railroad. The purpose was to prevent China from learning about North Korea's mobilization for the forthcoming war. Cited in Goncharov, Lewis, and Xue, *Uncertain Partners*, 153, 163.

73. See Li Haiwen, "Zhonggong zhongyang jiujing heshi jueding zhiyuanjun chuguo zuozhan?" [When Did the Chinese Communist Party Central Committee Make the Decision to Dispatch the Chinese People's Volunteers to Fight Abroad?], *Dang de wenxian* [Party Literature] 5 (1993): 85.

74. Important studies on this issue include Chen Jian, *China's Road to the Korean War: The Making of the Sino–American Confrontation* (New York: Columbia University Press, 1994); A. V. Torkunov, *Zagadochnaia voina: Koreiskii konflikt 1950–1953 godov* [The Mysterious War: The Korean Conflict of 1950–1953] (Moscow: Rosspen, 2000); and Shen Zhihua, *Mao Zedong, Sidalin yu Chaoxian zhanzheng.*

75. Zhonggong Zhongyang Wenxian Yanjiushi [Chinese Communist Party Central Committee Party Literature Research Office], ed., *Zhou Enlai nianpu, 1949–1976* [A Chronology of Zhou Enlai, 1949-1976] (Beijing: Zhonggong zhongyang wenxian chubanshe, 1997), 1:54; AVPRF, "Khronologiia osnovnykh sobytii kanuna," 38; Archives of the Ministry of the Foreign Affairs of China 118-00080-03, 67–68; Zhonggong Zhongyang Wenxian Yanjiushi and Zhongyang Dang'anguan [Chinese Communist Party Central Committee Party Literature Research Office and Central Archives], ed., *Jianguo yilai Zhou Enlai wengao* [Zhou Enlai's Manuscripts Since the Founding of the State] (Beijing: Zhongyang wenxian chubanshe, 2008), 3:31–32, 60.

76. AVPRF, "Khronologiia osnovnykh sobytii kanuna," 35–37. Establishment of the Northeast Defense Army was announced on July 7. See Zhonggong Zhongyang Wenxian Yanjiushi, *Zhou Enlai nianpu*, 2:52–53. The fact that Zhou informed the Soviets of the establishment of the Northeast Defense Army five days before the formal announcement is indicative of Zhou's eagerness.

77. Memorandum of conversation between Roshchin and Zou Dapeng on July 4, 1950. Quoted in O. A. Westad, "The Sino–Soviet Alliance and the United States: Wars, Policies, and Perceptions, 1950–1961," paper presented at an international conference on the Cold War in Asia, Hong Kong, January 1996.

78. At this point, the CCP had ceased its campaign to liberate Taiwan. Su Yu, commander in chief of the Taiwan campaign, was reappointed commander of the Northeast Defense Army. See Zhonggong Zhongyang Wenxian Yanjiushi, *Zhou Enlai nianpu*, 2:52–53.

79. APRF, f. 45, op. 1, d. 331, l. 79.

80. APRF, f. 45, op. 1, d. 331, l. 82.

81. Zhonggong Zhongyang Wenxian Yanjiushi, *Zhou Enlai nianpu*, 1:51. Chai Chengwen served as the direct contact between the Chinese government and Kim Il-sung during the Korean War.

82. TsAMORF, f. 5, op. 918795, d. 122, ll. 303–305.

83. TsAMORF, f. 5, op. 918795, d. 122, ll. 352–355.

84. Author's interview with Chai Chengwen, September 12, 2000. Wang Dagang, former Chinese deputy military attaché in Pyongyang, recalls the same situation; they could only learn about the war from local ethnic Chinese or ethnic Korean cadres in China. See David Tsui, "Did the DPRK and the PRC Sign a Mutual Security Pact?," paper presented at an international conference on the Cold War in Asia, Hong Kong, January 1996.

85. Regarding the aborted visit, at a military meeting on August 26, 1950, Zhou Enlai explained that China canceled it on its own accord. See Zhonggong Zhongyang Wenxian Yanjiushi and Zhongguo Renmin Jiefangjun Junshi Kexueyuan [Chinese Communist Party Central Committee Party Literature Research Office and Academy of Military Science of the People's Liberation Army], eds., *Zhou Enlai junshi wenxuan* [Selected Military Writings by Zhou Enlai] (Beijing: Renmin chubanshe, 1997), 4:45–46. But he later told the Soviet ambassador that the North Korean government had canceled it. See AVPRF, "Khronologiia osnovnykh sobytii kanuna," 52–54. Witnesses have confirmed the latter explanation. See Goncharov, Lewis, and Xue, *Uncertain Partners*, 163.

86. Gao Gang's speech at the Shenyang military conference, August 13, 1950. Quoted in Junshi Kexueyuan Junshi Lishi Yanjiubu [History Research Department of the Academy of Military Science], ed., *KangMei yuanChao zhanzhengshi* [A History of the War to Resist America and to Aid Korea] (Beijing: Junshi kexue chubanshe, 2000), 1:91–92.

87. AVPRF, "Khronologiia osnovnykh sobytii kanuna," 45, 47.

88. AVPRF, "Khronologiia osnovnykh sobytii kanuna," 48–49; Chen, *China's Road to the Korean War*, 273. Yi Sang-jo also recalled this. See Yoshiko Sakurai, "Chuci pilu Chaoxian zhanzheng zhenxiang" [The First Publication on the Truth of the Korean War], *Bungei shunju* [Spring and Autumn of Literature and Art] 68, no. 5 (April 1990): 171–172.

89. Zhonggong Zhongyang Wenxian Yanjiushi and Zhongyang Dang'anguan, *Jianguo yilai Zhou Enlai wengao*, 3:247–251.

90. TsAMORF, f. 5, op. 918795, d. 1227, ll. 666–669.

91. Weathersby, introduction to "New Russian Documents on the Korean War," 45 (translated from APRF, f. 45, op. 1, d. 347, ll. 5–6, 10–11 [original copy]; and AVPRF, f. 059a, op. 5a, d. 4, 11, ll. 155–156).

92. Weathersby, introduction to "New Russian Documents on the Korean War," 45 (translated from APRF, f. 45, op. 1, d. 347, ll. 12–13; and AVPRF, f. 059a, op. 5a, d. 4, 11, ll. 159–160).

93. Interview with Chai Chengwen, September 12, 2000. Yi Sang-jo also recalled that Kim Il-sung refused to retreat. See Yoshiko Sakurai, "Chuci pilu Chaoxian zhanzheng zhenxiang," 171–172.

94. APRF, f. 45, op. 1, d. 331, ll. 123–126, quoted in Torkunov, *Zagadochnaia voina*, 106–108.

95. Shen Zhihua, *Chaoxian zhanzheng*, 542–545.

96. Zhonggong Zhongyang Wenxian Yanjiushi and Zhongyang Dang'anguan, *Jianguo yilai Zhou Enlai wengao*, 3:311–312.

97. APRF, f. 45, op. 1, d. 331, ll. 133–135, quoted in Torkunov, *Zagadochnaia voina*, 109–111.

98. APRF, f. 45, op. 1, d. 331, l. 131, quoted in Torkunov, *Zagadochnaia voina*, 109.

99. TsAMORF, f. 5, op. 918795, d. 125, ll. 86–88.

100. TsAMORF, f. 5, op. 918795, d. 125, ll. 89–91.

101. APRF, f. 45, op. 1, d. 347, ll. 41–45, 46–49.

102. APRF, f. 45, op. 1, d. 334, ll. 97–98.

103. For a detailed account of the decision-making process and Mao Zedong's calculations regarding Chinese entry into the Korean War, see Shen Zhihua, *Mao Zedong, Sidalin yu Chaoxian zhanzheng*, 251–330. For the most recent study, see Shen Zhihua, "Sidalin, Mao Zedong yu Chaoxian zhanzheng zai yi" [Reconsidering Stalin, Mao Zedong, and the Korean War], *Shixue jikan* [Collected Papers of History Studies] 1 (2007): 51–65.

11. Sharp Contradictions Among the Leadership, 1950–1953

1. Telegram, Mao Zedong to Kim Il-sung, October 8, 1950; telegram, Peng Dehuai to Mao Zedong, October 10, 1950; interview with Chai Chengwen, September 12, 2000.

2. Archive of the President of the Russian Federation (APRF), f. 45, op. 1, d. 334, ll. 97–98. It is worth noting that this telegram was intended only for Beijing, and Kim Il-sung was unaware of it.

3. Telegram, Peng Dehuai to Mao Zedong, October 25, 1950; interview with Chai Chengwen, September 12, 2000.

4. Kathryn Weathersby, introduction to "New Findings on the Korean War," *Cold War International History Project Bulletin* 3 (Fall 1993): 16. By October 30, 1950, nine Korean People's Army (KPA) infantry divisions and special units, a total of 117,000 men, had withdrawn to Northeast China for regrouping. See APRF, f. 45, op. 1, d. 347, ll. 81–83. Yi Sang-jo has recalled that 350,000 to 360,000 KPA soldiers received training in China. See Yoshiko Sakurai, "The First Publication

on the Truth of the Korean War: Former Senior Official (Yi Sang-jo) Exposes the Fabricated 'Kim Il-sung Myth' " [in Japanese], *Bungei shunju* [Spring and Autumn of Literature and Art] 68, no. 5 (April 1990): 173.

5. Interview with Chai Chengwen, September 12, 2000; Wang Yan, ed., *Peng Dehuai nianpu* [A Chronology of Peng Dehuai] (Beijing: Renmin chubanshe, 1998), 445.

6. Telegram, Peng Dehuai to Mao Zedong, October 25, 1950, and November 2, 1950.

7. Junshi Kexueyuan Junshi Lishi Yanjiubu [History Research Department of the Academy of Military Science], ed., *KangMei yuanChao zhanzhengshi* [A History of the War to Resist America and to Aid Korea] (Beijing: Junshi kexue chubanshe, 2000), 2:167.

8. Interview with Chai Chengwen, September 12, 2000; Junshi Kexueyuan Junshi Lishi Yanjiubu, *KangMei yuanChao zhanzhengshi*, 2:167; telegram, Peng Dehuai to Mao Zedong, November 11, 1950; Wang Yan, *Peng Dehuai nianpu*, 449.

9. Telegram, Peng Dehuai to Mao Zedong, November 8 and 18, 1950.

10. Zhonggong Zhongyang Wenxian Yanjiushi and Zhongyang Dang'anguan [Chinese Communist Party Central Committee Party Literature Research Office and Central Archives], eds., *Jianguo yilai Zhou Enlai wengao* [Zhou Enlai's Manuscripts Since the Founding of the State] (Beijing: Zhongyang wenxian chubanshe, 2008), 3:473, 491.

11. Zhonggong Zhongyang Wenxian Yanjiushi and Zhongyang Dang'anguan, *Jianguo yilai Zhou Enlai wengao*, 3:475–476.

12. Junshi Kexueyuan Junshi Lishi Yanjiubu, *KangMei yuanChao zhanzhengshi*, 2:167–168; Zhou Enlai Junshi Huodong Jishi Bianxiezu [Editorial Committee of the Record of Zhou Enlai's Military Activities], ed., *Zhou Enlai junshi huodong jishi, 1918–1975* [A Record of Zhou Enlai's Military Activities, 1918–1975] (Beijing: Zhongyang wenxian chubanshe, 2000), 2:162–163.

13. Interview with Chai Chengwen, September 12, 2000; Junshi Kexueyuan Junshi Lishi Yanjiubu, *KangMei yuanChao zhanzhengshi*, 2:167; telegram, Peng Dehuai to Mao Zedong, November 11, 1950.

14. Telegram, Razuvayev to Stalin, December 1,1950, Central Archive of the Ministry of Defense, Russian Federation (TsAMORF), f. 5, op. 918795, d. 124, ll. 499–501, in V. N. Vartanov, *Voiia v Koree 1950–1953 gg.: Dokumenty i materialy* [Korean War Documents, 1950–1953] (Moscow: unpublished, 1997), 293–295.

15. Zhonggong Zhongyang Wenxian Yanjiushi and Zhongguo Renmin Jiefangjun Junshi Kexueyuan [Chinese Communist Party Central Committee Party Literature Research Office and Academy of Military Science of the People's Liberation Army], eds., *Zhou Enlai junshi wenxuan* [Selected Military Writings by Zhou Enlai] (Beijing: Renmin chubanshe, 1997), 4:100; Zhou Enlai Junshi Huodong Jishi Bianxiezu, *Zhou Enlai junshi huodong jishi, 1918–1975*, 2:164.

16. Razuvayev to Shtemenko, November 22, 1950, TsAMORF, f. 5, op. 918795, d. 124, ll. 308–310, in Vartanov, *Voiia v Koree 1950–1953 gg.*, 282. On July 4, 1950, Kim Il-sung became top commander of the KPA; throughout the war, he did not resign from this position, and he continued to issue directives to the KPA.

17. Zhou Enlai Junshi Huodong Jishi Bianxiezu, *Zhou Enlai junshi huodong jishi, 1918–1975*, 2:168–169; Zhonggong Zhongyang Wenxian Yanjiushi and Zhongguo Renmin Jiefangjun Junshi Kexueyuan, *Zhou Enlai junshi wenxuan*, 4:122–123; Zhonggong Zhongyang Wenxian Yanjiushi and Zhongyang Dang'anguan, *Jianguo yilai Zhou Enlai wengao*, 3:611–612.

18. Interview with Chai Chengwen, September 12, 2000; telegram, Mao Zedong to Peng Dehuai, December 6, 1950; telegram, Peng Dehuai to Mao Zedong, December 2, 1950; Wang Yan, *Peng Dehuai nianpu*, 453.

19. Telegram, Peng Dehuai to the 9th Regiment, December 13, 16, and 19, 1950; Wang Yan, *Peng Dehuai nianpu*, 465.

20. Telegram, Mao Zedong to Chinese People's Volunteer Army (CPVA) headquarters, December 8, 1950.

21. Zhou Enlai Junshi Huodong Jishi Bianxiezu, *Zhou Enlai junshi huodong jishi, 1918–1975*, 2:169–171.

22. For an article on the entry of the Soviet Air Force into the Korean War, see Zhihua Shen, "China and the Dispatch of the Soviet Air Force: The Formation of the Chinese–Soviet–Korean Alliance in the Early Stage of the Korean War," *Journal of Strategic Studies* 33, no. 2 (April 2010): 211-230.

23. Zhonggong Zhongyang Wenxian Yanjiushi and Zhongyang Dang'anguan, *Jianguo yilai Zhou Enlai wengao*, 3:427.

24. APRF, f. 45, op. 1, d. 335, ll. 71–72.

25. Zhou Enlai Junshi Huodong Jishi Bianxiezu, *Zhou Enlai junshi huodong jishi, 1918–1975*, 2:178–179; Shen Zhihua, *Mao Zedong, Sidalin yu Chaoxian zhanzheng* [Mao Zedong, Stalin, and the Korean War], 3rd ed. (Guangzhou: Guangdong renmin chubanshe, 2013), 333–341.

26. Shen Zhihua, ed., *Chaoxian zhanzheng: Eguo dang'anguan de jiemi wenjian* [The Korean War: Declassified Documents from the Russian Archives] (Taipei: Zhongyang yanjiuyuan, Jindai yanjiusuo, 2003), 748. On July 6, 1952, Kim Il-sung sent a letter to CPVA headquarters to inform them of the decision of the Politburo of the Korean Workers' Party (KWP) to appoint Kim Ung as deputy minister of national defense, Ch'oe Yong-gŏn as deputy commander of the Joint Command, and Kim Kwang-hyŏp as commander of the Front Command of the KPA. See Junshi Kexueyuan Junshi Lishi Yanjiubu, *KangMei yuanChao zhanzhengshi*, 3:269.

27. Junshi Kexueyuan Junshi Lishi Yanjiubu, *KangMei yuanChao zhanzhengshi*, 3:269, 394.

28. "Yi Sang-jo to the KWP Central Committee," October 12, 1956, Russian State Archive of Contemporary History (RGANI), f. 5, op. 28, d. 410, ll. 233-295.

29. Telegram, Peng Dehuai to Mao Zedong, December 19, 1950; Wang Yan, *Peng Dehuai nianpu*, 456.

30. Zhonggong Zhongyang Wenxian Yanjiushi and Zhongyang Dang'anguan, *Jianguo yilai Zhou Enlai wengao*, 3:625–626.

31. See Shen Zhihua, "KangMei yuanChao zhanzheng juece zhong de Sulian yinsu" [The Soviet Factor in the War to Resist the U.S. and to Aid Korea], *Dangdai Zhongguoshi yanjiu* [Contemporary China History Studies] 1 (2000): 28–39.

32. *Mao Zedong junshi wenji* [Collection of Mao Zedong's Military Writings] (Beijing: Junshi kexue chubanshe and Zhongyang wenxian chubanshe, 1993), 6:245–246, 249–250.

33. Peng Dehuai Zhuanji Bianxiezu [Editorial Committee for the Peng Dehuai Biography], ed., *Peng Dehuai junshi wenxuan* [Selected Military Writings by Peng Dehuai] (Beijing: Zhongyang wenxian chubanshe, 1988), 383; telegram, Peng Dehuai to Kim II Sung, January 3, 1951; Wang Yan, *Peng Dehuai nianpu*, 464.

34. APRF, f. 3, op. 1, d. 336, ll. 81–82.

35. The Party Committee of CPVA headquarters reported that the Chinese troops were short of manpower and supplies, physically weakened, and were unable to continue to fight until transportation and supplies were replenished and they had had some time to rest and regroup. Telegram, Party Committee of CPVA headquarters to the Chinese Communist Party Central Committee, January 8, 1951. See also Yang Feng'an and Wang Tiancheng, *Jiayu Chaoxian zhanzheng de ren* [The Man Who Controlled the Korean War] (Beijing: Zhonggong zhongyang dangxiao chubanshe, 1993), 222.

36. Peng Dehuai, *Peng Dehuai zishu* [An Account in Peng Dehuai's Own Words], unpublished internal reference, 350.

37. Telegram, Razuvayev to Vasilevskii, December 13, 1950, TsAMORF, f. 5, op. 918795, d. 124, ll. 667-68, in Vartanov, *Voiia v Koree 1950–1953 gg.*, 300.

38. Telegram, Razuvayev to Vyshinskii, December 30, 1950, TsAMORF, f. 5, op. 918795, d. 124, ll. 750-52, in Vartanov, *Voiia v Koree 1950–1953 gg.*, 303–305.

39. Wang Yan, *Peng Dehuai nianpu*, 463.

40. *Neibu cankao* [Internal Reference] 21 (February 21, 1951): 21-61. *Neibu cankao* began publication in 1949 and ended in 1964. Containing intelligence on domestic events and translations of foreign news reports, it served as a confidential news bulletin for top Chinese Communist Party leaders. Found in overseas libraries, it is now a part of the historical record, providing unique insights into what information China's central leaders received on a daily basis. The authors secured access to this material at the Universities Service Centre, Chinese University of Hong Kong.

41. Interview with Chai Chengwen, September 12, 2000; telegram, Peng Dehuai to Mao Zedong, January 1, 1951; telegram, Chai Chengwen to Peng Dehuai, January 8, 1951; Wang Yan, *Peng Dehuai nianpu*, 465–466.

42. Wang Yazhi, "KangMei yuanChao zhanzheng zhong de Peng Dehuai, Nie Rongzhen" [Peng Dehuai and Nie Rongzhen During the War to Resist America and to Aid Korea], *Junshi shilin* [Journal of Military History] 1 (1994): 11.

43. Wang Yan, *Peng Dehuai nianpu*, 465.

44. Interview with Chai Chengwen, September 12, 2000; memorandum of conversation, Peng Dehuai and Kim Il-sung, January 10-11, 1951.

45. Interview with Chai Chengwen, September 12, 2000; Wang Yan, *Peng Dehuai nianpu*, 466.

46. Interview with Chai Chengwen, September 12, 2000.

47. Interview with Chai Chengwen, September 12, 2000; Wang Yan, *Peng Dehuai nianpu*, 466.

48. Wang Yan, *Peng Dehuai nianpu*, 461; Hong Xuezhi, *KangMei yuanChao zhanzheng huiyi* [Recollections of the War to Resist America and to Aid Korea] (Beijing: Jiefangjun wenyi chubanshe, 1990), 111–112; Lei Yingfu, "KangMei yuanChao zhanzheng jige zhongda juece de huiyi (xuwan)" [Recollections About Several Important Policy Decisions During the War to Resist America and to Aid Korea (Part 3)], *Dangde wenxian* [Party Literature] 5 (1994): 41.

49. Kathryn Weathersby, introduction to "New Russian Documents on the Korean War," *Cold War International History Project Bulletin*, nos. 6–7 (Winter 1995–96): 55–56 (translated from APRF, f. 45, op. 1, d. 337, ll. 1–3).

50. APRF, f. 45, op. 1, d. 337, ll. 37–40.

51. Telegram, Razuvayev to Moscow, April 1951, in Shen Zhihua, *Chaoxian zhanzheng*, 1022–1026.

52. RGANI, f. 5, op. 28, d. 314, ll. 48.

53. For an article-length study on this issue, see Zhihua Shen and Yafeng Xia, "Mao Zedong's Erroneous Decision During the Korean War: China's Rejection of the UN Cease-Fire Resolution in Early 1951," *Asian Perspective* 35, no. 2 (April–June 2011): 187–209.

54. V. N. Razuvayev's investigation report to Soviet Deputy Foreign Minister Valerian Zorin, May 1, 1951. See Shen Zhihua, ed., *Guanyu Chaoxian zhanzheng de Eguo dang'an yuanwen fuyinjian* [Copies of Original Documents on the Korean War in the Russian Archives] (Shanghai: Center for Cold War International History Studies, East China Normal University, 2004), 9:1178–1195. Unpublished.

55. The damage rate of CPVA cargo trucks had reached 84.6 percent by 1951. *KangMei yuanChao zhanzheng houqin jingyan zongjie: Zhuanye qinwu* [Summary of the Logistics Experience in the War to Resist America and to Aid Korea: Professional Logistics Affairs] (Beijing: Jindun chubanshe, 1987), 2:140.

56. Zhang Mingyuan, "Fengxue zhanqin: Yi kangMei yuanChao zhanzheng de houqin baozhang" [War Logistics During Windy and Snowy Days: Recollections of Logistics Support During the Korean War], *Dangdai Zhongguo shi yanjiu* [Contemporary China History Studies] 6 (2000): 34; *KangMei yuanChao zhanzheng houqin jingyan zongjie: Zhuanye qinwu*, 2:6.

57. Wang Yan, *Peng Dehuai nianpu*, 449; Zhang Mingyuan, "Fengxue zhanqin," 29.

58. Interview with Chai Chengwen, September 12, 2000; telegram, Peng Dehuai to Mao Zedong, December 7, 1950.

59. Zhonggong Zhongyang Wenxian Yanjiushi and Zhongyang Dang'anguan, *Jianguo yilai Zhou Enlai wengao*, 3:618; *KangMei yuanChao zhanzheng houqin jingyan zongjie: Zhuanye qinwu*, 2:6.

60. *KangMei yuanChao zhanzheng houqin jingyan zongjie: Jiben jingyan* [Summary of the Logistics Experience in the War to Resist America and to Aid Korea: Basic Experience] (Beijing: Jindun chubanshe, 1987), 41–42; Zhang Mingyuan, "Fengxue zhanqin," 34.

61. *KangMei yuanChao zhanzheng houqin jingyan zongjie: Ziliao xuanbian (Tielu yunshu lei)* [Summary of the Logistics Experience in the War to Resist America and to

Aid Korea: Collection of Materials (Railways and Transportation)] (Beijing: Jiefangjun chubanshe, 1988), 2:273, 282, 285.

62. Zhang Mingyuan, *Wo de huiyi* [My Recollections] (Beijing: Zhonggong dang-shi chubanshe, 2004), 370.

63. *KangMei yuanChao zhanzheng houqin jingyan zongjie: Ziliao xuanbian (Tielu yunshu lei)*, 2:283–284; Zhang Mingyuan, "Fengxue zhanqin," 34.

64. *KangMei yuanChao zhanzheng houqin jingyan zongjie: Zhuanye qinwu*, 2:3–4, 6.

65. Interview with Chai Chengwen, September 12, 2000.

66. Telegram, Ye Lin, Zhang Mingyuan, and Peng Min to Gao Gang, February 19, 1951.

67. Telegram, Ye Lin, Zhang Mingyuan, and Peng Min to Gao Gang, March 15, 1951; telegram, Peng Dehuai to Gao Gang and Zhou Enlai, March 22, 1951.

68. Telegram, Zhou Enlai to Peng Dehuai and Gao Gang, March 25, 1951.

69. Zhang Mingyuan, "Fengxue zhanqin," 34.

70. Shen Zhihua, *Chaoxian zhanzheng*, 724–725.

71. Telegram, Zhou Enlai to Peng Dehuai and Gao Gang, March 25, 1951.

72. Zhou Enlai Junshi Huodong Jishi Bianxiezu, *Zhou Enlai junshi huodong jishi, 1918–1975*, 2:204.

73. *KangMei yuanChao zhanzheng houqin jingyan zongjie: Zhuanye qinwu*, 2:6–7; *KangMei yuanChao zhanzheng houqin jingyan zongjie: Jiben jingyan*, 66–67.

74. Peng Dehuai, *Peng Dehuai zishu*, 352.

75. Dean Acheson, *Present at the Creation: My Years in the State Department* (New York: W. W. Norton, 1987), 652.

76. Nie Rongzhen, *Nie Rongzhen huiyilu* [Memoirs of Nie Rongzhen], 2nd ed. (Beijing: Jiefangjun chubanshe, 1983), 591; David Rees, *Korea: The Limited War* (New York: St. Martin's, 1964), 225–256.

77. Telegram, Kim Il-sung to Peng Dehuai, May 30, 1951; telegram, Mao Zedong to Peng Dehuai, June 11, 1951; Chai Chengwen and Zhao Yongtian, *Banmendian tanpan* [The Panmunjom Negotiations] (Beijing: Jiefangjun chubanshe, 1989), 125; Qi Dexue, *Chaoxian zhanzheng juece neimu* [Inside Stories Behind the Decision Making During the Korean War] (Shenyang: Liaoning daxue chubanshe, 1991), 177.

78. APRF, f. 45, op. 1, d. 339, ll. 23, 28–29, 31–32.

79. Shen Zhihua, *Chaoxian zhanzheng*, 1022–1026.

80. Yafeng Xia, *Negotiating with the Enemy: U.S.–China Talks During the Cold War, 1949–1972* (Bloomington: Indiana University Press, 2006), 60–62.

81. As revealed in a letter to Stalin, before November 14, 1951, Mao still believed that an agreement on the POW issue could easily be achieved. See APRF, f. 45, op. 1, d. 342, ll. 16–19.

82. Razuvaev's work report for the first season of 1952, in AVPRF, f. 0102, op. 8, d. 35, 10, ll. 157–158, cited in A. Volokhova, "Dokumenty, arkhivy: Peregovopy o peremirii v Koree (1951–1953 gg.) (po materialam Arkhiva vneshnei politiki Rossii)" [Documents, Archives: Truce Negotiations in North Korea (1951-1953) (based on Material from the Russian Archive on Foreign Policy)], *Problemy Dal'nego Vostoka* [Problems of the Far East] 2 (2000): 104.

83. Mao Zedong to Filippov [Stalin], February 8, 1952, in APRF, f. 45, op. 1, d. 342, ll. 81–83.

84. Razuvayev's work report for the first season of 1952, in AVPRF, f. 0102, op. 8, p. 35, d. 10, ll. 157–158, cited in Volokhova, "Dokumenty, arkhivy," 104.

85. Razuvayev's work report for the second season of 1952, in AVPRF, f. 0102, op. 8, p. 36, d. 11, l. 19, cited in Volokhova, "Dokumenty, arkhivy," 104.

86. Zhonggong Zhongyang Wenxian Yanjiushi and Zhongguo Renmin Jiefangjun Junshi Kexueyuan, *Zhou Enlai junshi wenxuan*, 4:289–290; for the full text, see Weathersby, introduction to "New Russian Documents," 78.

87. Zhou Enlai Junshi Huodong Jishi Bianxiezu, *Zhou Enlai junshi huodong jishi, 1918–1975*, 2:280.

88. Razuvayev to Vasilevskii, July 17, 1952, in APRF, f. 45, op. 1, d. 343, ll. 72–75, 65–68.

89. After the Korean armistice went into effect, Kim Il-sung consulted with Mao in Beijing on how to deal with the detained POWs. Mao's advice was that it was already too late to hand them over to the other side and that doing so would provide the Americans with evidence to accuse the Chinese–North Korean side of violating the armistice agreement. Kim agreed, and he later told the Soviets that measures would be taken to scatter the prisoners of war in the northern parts of the country so as to prevent them from escaping or establishing contacts with the Commission of Neutral States that was supervising the armistice. AVPRF, f. 0102, op. 9, p. 46, d. 14, l. 2; p. 50, d. 67, ll. 59–60. cited in Volokhova, "Dokumenty, arkhivy," 106, 108.

90. Xu Yan, *Diyici jiaoliang: KangMei yuanChao zhanzheng de lishi huigu* [First Encounter: Recollections and Reflections on the War to Resist America and to Aid Korea] (Beijing: Zhongguo guangbo dianshi chubanshe, 1990), 285.

91. Ciphered telegram, Mao to Filippov [Stalin], July 18, 1952, *Cold War International History Project Bulletin* 6-7 (Winter 1995–1996): 78.

92. Zhonggong Zhongyang Wenxian Yanjiushi [Chinese Communist Party Central Committee Party Literature Research Office], ed., *Zhou Enlai nianpu, 1949–1976* [A Chronology of Zhou Enlai, 1949-1976] (Beijing: Zhonggong zhongyang wenxian chubanshe, 1997), 1:250.

93. Telegram from Filippov [Stalin] to Mao Zedong, July 16, 1952; for the full text, see Weathersby, introduction to "New Russian Documents," 77–78.

94. Minutes of Stalin–Zhou Enlai conversations, August 20 and September 19, 1952, in APRF, f. 45, op. 1, d. 329, ll. 54–72, 91–101. For two different views, see Haruki Wada, "Stalin and the Japanese Communist Party, 1945–1953: In the Light of New Russian Archival Documents," paper presented at an international conference on the Cold War in Asia, Hong Kong, January 1996; and Vojtech Mastny, *The Cold War and Soviet Insecurity: The Stalin Years* (New York: Oxford University Press, 1996), 147–148.

95. Hong Xuezhi's report on Stalin's remarks at the banquet, November 18, 1952.

96. Shen Zhihua, *Chaoxian zhanzheng*, 1214-1221.

97. Zhou Enlai's statement in support of the Soviet proposal, November 28, 1952, Chinese Foreign Ministry Archives 113-00118-01, 35.

98. For details, see Shen Zhihua, "1953 nian Chaoxian tingzhan: ZhongSu lingdao-ren de zhengzhi kaolü" [The Korean Armistice in 1953: The Political Consid-erations of the Chinese and Soviet Leaders], *Shijie shi* [World History] 2 (2001): 2-18.

99. Ciphered telegram, resolution, USSR Council of Ministers, with draft letters from the Soviet government to Mao Zedong and Kim Il-sung, and the directive to the Soviet delegation at the United Nations, March 19, 1953, in *Cold War International History Project Bulletin* 6-7 (Winter 1995-1996): 80; Pang Xianzhi and Jin Chongji, eds., *Mao Zedong zhuan 1949–1976* [A Biography of Mao Zedong] (Beijing: Zhongyang wenxian chubanshe, 2003), 1:180.

100. Peng Dehuai, *Peng Dehuai zishu*, 352.

101. Jae-Jung Suh, ed., *Origins of North Korea's Juche: Colonialism, War, and Develop-ment* (Lanham, MD: Lexington Books, 2013), 57.

102. It is worth noting that scholars use factional identifications only for narrative convenience. According to the Soviet ambassador to North Korea, S. P. Suzda-lev, the KWP consisted of members from the "Soviet faction," the "China fac-tion," and the "domestic faction" (from both the South and the North). See Suzdalev diary, January 21, 1954, in AVPRF, SD44886. Apart from the Southern faction, these cannot be identified as "factions" from the perspective of organi-zational activities. James F. Person points out that it is important not to overstate the group identities of the Soviet and Yan'an "factions," which are largely post hoc labels affixed by Kim Il-sung to tarnish his enemies. Person, " 'We Need Help from Outside': The North Korean Opposition Movement of 1956," *Cold War International History Project Working Paper* 52 (August 2006).

III. Chinese Economic Aid and Kim's *Juche* Idea, 1953–1956

1. We use the term "faction" only for convenience. We believe that members of the so-called Moscow and Yan'an factions did not engage in organizational activ-ities against Kim Il-sung or others. Many of those involved in the August 1956 incident were not members of the so-called Yan'an faction.

2. *Juche*, commonly translated as "self-reliance," is best understood as being the master of one's own fate. See Jae-Jung Suh, ed., *Origins of North Korea's Juche: Colonialism, War, and Development* (Lanham, MD: Lexington Books, 2013).

3. Dae-Sook Suh, *Kim Il-sung: The North Korean Leader* (New York: Columbia University Press, 1988), 301.

4. Throughout the early Ming dynasty, due to China's strength on land and sea, China became the suzerain of many tributary or vassal states. These included Korea, the Ryukyu Islands, Annam (Vietnam), Burma, Siam (Thailand), and a host of other states in Southeast and Central Asia—from Bengal to the Philip-pines to Samarkand. These states did not enjoy sovereignty and they were regarded as vassals of the suzerain. Rulers or envoys of the vassal states offered tribute or gifts to the suzerain and in return they received the Chinese emperor's

seal of recognition and return gifts, which, in general, were much in excess of the tributes. Historically, Korea was a very important "outer vassal" of the Chinese empire. Korea paid tribute to China three times every year during the Ming dynasty and four times every year during the Qing dynasty.

5. Chen Jian, "Reorienting the Cold War: The Implications of China's Early Cold War Experience, Taking Korea as a Central Test Case," in Tsuyoshi Hasegawa, ed., *The Cold War in East Asia, 1945–1991* (Stanford, CA: Stanford University Press, 2011), 88.

6. Zhonggong Zhongyang Wenxian Yanjiushi and Zhongguo Renmin Jiefangjun Junshi Kexueyuan [Chinese Communist Party Central Committee Party Literature Research Office and Academy of Military Science of the People's Liberation Army], eds., *Jianguo yilai Mao Zedong junshi wengao* (*JYMJW*) [Mao Zedong's Military Writings Since the Founding of the State] (Beijing: Zhongyang wenxian chubanshe, 2010), 1:235-236.

7. *Postwar Reconstruction and Development of the National Economy of the DPRK* (Pyongyang: Foreign Languages Publishing House, 1957), 8.

8. Natalia Bazhanova, *Kiroe sŏn Puk Han kyŏngje* [The North Korean Economy at a Crossroads], trans. Yang Chunyong (Seoul: Hanguk kyŏngjie sinmunsa, 1992), 8.

9. Soviet Embassy to the Democratic People's Republic of Korea (DPRK), Diary report, July 7, 1954, Archive of Foreign Policy of the Russian Federation (AVPRF), f. 0102, op. 10, p. 53, d. 8.

10. *Postwar Reconstruction and Development of the National Economy of the DPRK*, 8. According to an April 1955 Soviet document, the war damage inflicted on North Korea was calculated at 430 billion won (14 billion rubles, or $3.5 billion). See N. Fedorenko and B. Ponomarev to the Communist Party of the Soviet Union Central Committee, "Information About the Situation in the DPRK," April 1955, North Korea International Documentation Project Archives.

11. Charles K. Armstrong, " 'Fraternal Socialism': The International Reconstruction of Korea, 1953-62," *Cold War History* 5, no. 2 (May 2005): 162.

12. Nineteen divisions departed in 1954–1955 and the remainder stayed until 1958.

13. Kim Il-sung to Soviet Ambassador Suzdalev, "General Report on Basic Reconstruction of Important Enterprises Relating to Heavy Industry," July 31, 1953, AVPRF, f. 0102, op. 9, p. 44, d. 8. Cited in Armstrong, "Fraternal Socialism," 163.

14. Shen Zhihua, ed., *Chaoxian zhanzheng: Eguo dang'anguan de jiemi wenjian* [The Korean War: Declassified Documents from the Russian Archives] (Taipei: Zhongyang yanjiuyuan, Jindaishi yanjiusuo, 2003), 1326.

15. Kim Il-sung, *All for the Postwar Rehabilitation and Development of the National Economy* (Pyongyang: Foreign Languages Publishing House, 1961); Robert Scalapino and Chong-sik Lee, *Communism in Korea* (Berkeley: University of California Press, 1972), 1:528; Zhonggong Zhongyang Duiwai Lianluobu [International Liaison Department of the Chinese Communist Party Central Committee], ed., *Jin Richeng wenji, 1945–1967* [Collection of Kim Il-sung's Works, 1945–1967] (unpublished, 1982), 51–52.

16. Armstrong, "Fraternal Socialism," 163–164.

17. "Foreign Assistance to the DPRK, 1953–60," in Natalia Bazhanova, *Kiroe sŏn Puk Han kyŏngje* [North Korean Economy at the Crossroads], trans. Yang Chu-yong (Seoul: Hanguk kyŏngje sinmunsa, 1992), 22, cited in Armstrong, "Fraternal Socialism," 165.

18. AVPRF, f. 3, op. 65, p. 779, d. 2, ll. 11–12.

19. Russian State Archive of Contemporary History (RGANI), f. 5, op. 28, d. 412, ll. 170–172; Bernd Schaefer, "Weathering the Sino–Soviet Conflict: The GDR and North Korea, 1949-1989," *Cold War International History Project Bulletin* 14-15 (Winter 2003-Spring 2004): 25–71; Armstrong, "Fraternal Socialism," 168–169, 174–175.

20. Zhonggong Zhongyang Wenxian Yanjiushi [Chinese Communist Party Central Committee Party Literature Research Office], ed., *Zhou Enlai nianpu, 1949–1976* [A Chronology of Zhou Enlai, 1949-1976] (Beijing: Zhonggong zhongyang wenxian chubanshe, 1997), 1:334–335.

21. The respective exchange rates in the 1950s were four rubles to one U.S. dollar and two Chinese yuan to one U.S. dollar.

22. Fedorenko's investigative report, December 31, 1953, AVPRF, f. 0102, op. 7, d. 47, ll. 115–120; *Renmin ribao* [People's Daily], November 24, 1953, 1. On the Sino–Korean agreement on North Korean trainees in China and Chinese experts sent to North Korea, see Shanghai Municipal Archives, A 38-2-352, 50–52; Shen Jueren, ed., *Dangdai Zhongguo duiwai maoyi* [Contemporary China's Foreign Trade] (Beijing: Dangdai Zhongguo chubanshe, 1992), 1:300.

23. Armstrong, "Fraternal Socialism," 164. See also Deok Kim, "Sino–Soviet Dispute and North Korea," *Korea Observer* 10, no. 1 (Spring 1979): 12.

24. Zhonggong Zhongyang Wenxian Yanjiushi, *Zhou Enlai nianpu, 1949–1976*, 1:335.

25. RGANI, f. 5, op. 28, d. 314, ll. 45–48. Other sources indicate that fraternal aid constituted 35 percent of North Korea's 1954 budget.

26. *Renmin ribao*, March 31, 1954; June 25, 1954; May 9, 1954; May 28, 1954; June 6, 1954; October 25, 1957; October 31, 1958.

27. *Renmin ribao*, March 23, 1954.

28. Hyeon Uk Nam, *China and Soviet Assistance to North Korea and the Status of Trade, 1946–1978* [in Korean] (Seoul: Korea Institute of National Unification, February 1979), 10. Unpublished.

29. Li Fuchun's report on Sino–North Korean trade negotiations, September 30, 1957, State Planning Commission Archives. The Eastern European archives provide very different numbers on Sino–North Korean trade. See Avram Agov, "North Korea in the Socialist World: Integration and Divergence, 1945-1970," PhD diss., University of British Columbia, 2010, 206–207.

30. Shanghai Municipal Archives, A 38-2-352, 1–4; Shi Lin, ed., *Dangdai Zhongguo de duiwai jingji hezuo* [Contemporary China's Economic Cooperation with Foreign Countries] (Beijing: Zhongguo shehui kexue chubanshe, 1989), 26; *Renmin ribao*, August 25, 1956.

31. Agov, "North Korea in the Socialist World," 256–257.

32. *Renmin ribao*, February 3, 1956; March 26, 1956.

33. RGANI, f. 5, op. 28, d. 412, ll. 164–167, 174–176; Center for the Preservation of Contemporary Documentation (TsKhSD), f. 5, op. 28, d. 314, ll. 200–207; National Archives of Hungary XIX-J-1-j Korea, 7. doboz, 5/f, 006054/1955, *Cold War International History Project Bulletin*, 14–15 (Winter 2003–Spring 2004): 107–108; Scalapino and Lee, *Communism in Korea*, 1:535.

34. RGANI, f. 5, op. 28, d. 314, ll. 197-199; TsKhSD, f. 5, op. 28, d. 314, ll. 200-207.

35. Sera Shin, "Politicheskaya bor'ba v rukovodstve KNDR v 1953–1956 gg.: Prichiny i dinamika" [Political Struggle Within the DPRK Leadership in 1953–1956: Reasons and Dynamics], *Problemy dal'nego Vostoka* [Problems of the Far East] 3 (2009): 129; Balázs Szalontai, " 'You Have No Political Line of Your Own': Kim Il-sung and the Soviets, 1953–1964," *Cold War International History Project Bulletin* 14-15 (Winter 2003-Spring 2004): 90; interview with Kim Ch'ung-sik, former head of the Organization Department of the Pyongyang Municipal Committee of the Korean Workers' Party (KWP), February 17, 2010.

36. Zhonggong Zhongyang Duiwai Lianluobu, *Jin Richeng wenji, 1945–1967*, 116–131.

37. Nobuo Shimotomai, "Kim Il-sung's Balancing Act Between Moscow and Beijing, 1956-1972," in Hasegawa, *The Cold War in East Asia, 1945–1991*, 126.

38. AVPRF f. 0102, op. 13, p. 53, d. 5, ll. 131-145; Schaefer, "Weathering the Sino–Soviet Conflict," 28. It is worth noting that at the Sixth Plenum of the Supreme People's Assembly of the DPRK in December 1953, "Kim Il-sung analyzed in detail the agreement signed between the Government of the DPRK and the Governments of the Soviet Union, the People's Republic of China, Poland, Czechoslovakia, the German Democratic Republic, Romania, Bulgaria and Hungary, stressing what great assistance these countries promised to give to Korea in rebuilding its national economy destroyed by American invaders." Embassy of the Polish Republic in Korea, report no. 8, for the period of December 1 to December 31, 1953, North Korea International Documentation Project Archives. We argue that this speech was made about one month after Kim's trip to the Soviet Union and that his main point was to stress his diplomatic success rather than to praise his generous allies.

39. Shen Zhihua, ed., *Sidalin yu Tietuo: Su Nan chongtu de qiyuan jiqi jieguo* [Stalin and Tito: The Origins and Outcome of the Soviet–Yugoslav Conflict] (Guilin: Guangxi shifan daxue chubanshe, 2002); T. V. Volokitina et al., *Moskva I Vostochnaia Evropa: Stanovlenie politicheskikh rezhimov sovetskogo tipa: 1949–1953: Ocherki istorii* [War in Korea 1950-1953: Documents and Materials] (Moscow: Rosspen, 2002); Liu Shaoqi, "Lun guoji zhuyi yu minzu zhuyi" [On Internationalism and Nationalism], *Dongbei ribao* [Northeast Daily], November 8, 1948.

40. Edvard Kardelj, *Kade'er huiyilu, 1944–1957* [Memoirs of Kardelj, 1944–1957], trans. Li Daijun et al. (Beijing: Xinhua chubanshe, 1981), 160–162; Wu Xiuquan, *Huiyi yu huainian* [Recollections and Remembrances] (Beijing: Zhonggong zhongyang dangxiao chubanshe, 1991), 297.

41. RGANI, f. 5, op. 28, d. 410, ll. 73–85, 171–194.

42. RGANI, f. 5, op. 28, d. 412, ll. 86–117, 253-276, 316–333.

43. Hungarian Legation Document, 12. doboz, 25/j, 005594/1956, cited in Szalontai, "You Have No Political Line of Your Own," 91.

44. RGANI, f. 5, op. 28, d. 411, ll. 143–159.

45. RGANI, f. 5, op. 28, d. 410, ll. 309–314, 315–333, 334–359.

46. For details, see Zhihua Shen and Yafeng Xia, "Hidden Currents During the Honeymoon: Mao Zedong, Khrushchev and the 1957 Moscow Conference," *Journal of Cold War Studies* 11, no. 4 (Fall 2009): 74–117.

47. TsKhSD, f. 5, op. 28, d. 314, ll. 12–15, 33–63, 212–214, 271–279; d. 410, ll. 22–25.

48. TsKhSD, f. 5, op. 28, d. 314, ll. 33–63. See also TsKhSD, f. 5, op. 28, d. 412, ll. 126–127.

49. Chinese Ambassador Ni Zhiliang left his post in Pyongyang in March 1952. China did not have an ambassador in Pyongyang until Pan Zili was appointed in January 1955. Additionally, the Soviet record regarding the War Museum has proven to be reliable to this day. Shen Zhihua visited it in 2006 and Xia Yafeng visited it in June 2014.

50. Its predecessor, the North Korean Workers' Party, was established in 1946. It merged with the South Korean Workers' Party to form the Korean Workers' Party in 1949.

51. There is still no consensus on how Hŏ Ka-i died. Many believe that he was assassinated by an agent working on behalf of Kim Il-sung. See Andrei Lankov, *Crisis in North Korea: The Failure of De-Stalinization, 1956* (Honolulu: University of Hawai'i Press, 2004), 17; Kim Hak-chun, *Chaoxian wushiqinian shi* [Fifty-Seven Years of North Korean History], trans. Zhang Ying, in Translated Series on China's Northeast Border (unpublished internal reference, 2005), 213; Yi Chong-sŏk, *Pukhan-Chungguk kwan'gye, 1945–2000* [The Sino-North Korean Relationship, 1945-2000] (Seoul: Chungsim, 2000), 200.

52. Suh, *Kim Il-sung*, 130–134; and Zhonggong Zhongyang Duiwai Lianluobu [International Liaison Department of the Chinese Communist Party Central Committee], ed., *Chaoxian laodongdang lijie zhongyang quanhui gaikuang* [Basic Facts on the Central Committees of the Congresses of the Korean Workers' Party] (unpublished, 1981), 12–14.

53. Suh, *Kim Il-sung*, 135–136.

54. See Gang In Deok, ed., *A Complete Book of North Korea* (Seoul: Research Center of the Far East, 1974), 1:260–261; Suh, *Kim Il-sung*, 107–122; Committee on Korean Central Yearbook, ed., *General Book of North Korea (1945–1968)* (Seoul: Institute Communist Circle Issue, 1968), 175–176; and Kim Nam-sik and Sim Chi-yŏn, *Pak Hŏn-yŏng nosŏn pip'an* [The Criticism of Pak Hŏn-yŏng's Line] (Seoul: Segye, 1986). The work by these Korean scholars is confirmed in the Russian documents. See TsKhSD, f. 5, op. 28, d. 314, ll. 33–63. According to the KWP resolution "On Further Strengthening the Struggles Against Reactionary Ideologies in the Literary and Art Sectors," Pak Ch'ang-ok was removed from the KWP Political Committee of the Central Committee and Pak Yŏng-bin was removed from the KWP Political Committee and the Central Committee. TsKhSD, f. 5, op. 28, d. 410, ll. 57–67.

55. Suh, *Kim Il-sung*, 125–126.

56. *Pravda*, 15 February 1956, p. 7; 18 February 1956, p. 5; 20 February 1956, p. 3; Meeting Records of the CPSU Presidium, 30 January 1956, RGANI, f. 3, op. 8, d. 389, I. 43–510b.

57. See Zhihua Shen and Yafeng Xia, *Mao and the Sino-Soviet Partnership, 1945–1959: A New History* (Lanham, MD: Lexington Books, 2015), pp. 134–135.

58. James F. Person, "New Evidence on the 1956 September Plenum of the Korean Workers' Party," paper presented at the International Workshop on "The Cold War and the Two Koreas," Woodrow Wilson International Center for Scholars, April 19, 2016, p. 3.

59. Person, "New Evidence on the 1956 September Plenum of the Korean Workers' Party," p. 3.

60. TsKhSD, f. 5, op. 28, d. 411, ll. 164–168.

61. TsKhSD, f. 5, op. 28, d. 410, ll. 137–139.

62. TsKhSD, f. 5, op. 28, d. 486, ll. 1–17; Suh, *Kim Il-sung*, 128–130; TsKhSD, f. 5, op. 28, d. 412, ll. 220–222, 207–211.

63. TsKhSD, f. 5, op. 28, d. 410, ll. 163–170.

64. TsKhSD, f. 5, op. 28, d. 412, ll. 202–203.

65. TsKhSD, f. 5, op. 28, d. 412, ll. 227–229; d. 410, ll. 174–177.

66. TsKhSD, f. 5, op. 28, d. 410, ll. 222–223.

67. TsKhSD, f. 5, op. 28, d. 314, ll. 33–63.

68. TsKhSD, f. 5, op. 28, d. 410, ll. 57–67.

69. TsKhSD, f. 5, op. 28, d. 410, ll. 163–170.

70. TsKhSD, f. 5, op. 28, d. 314, ll. 271–279; d. 412, ll. 222–224. Pak Ch'ang-ok and Pak Yŏng-bin visited the Soviet Embassy in Pyongyang to reflect upon the situation. See TsKhSD, f. 5, op. 28, d. 410, ll. 120–121, 57–67; d. 412, ll. 220–122, 225.

71. TsKhSD, f. 5, op. 28, d. 412, ll. 190–196.

72. TsKhSD, f. 5, op. 28, d. 412, ll. 238–241.

73. TsKhSD, f. 5, op. 28, d. 410, ll. 210–214.

74. This is a problematic assertion, given Ch'oe Yong-gŏn's loyalty to Kim Il-sung and his position at the August plenum. This report that they successfully won Ch'oe Yong-gŏn and Kim Tu-bong over to their side was more a reflection of the opposition's desire to enlist Ch'oe than an actual switching of sides.

75. Interview, Kim Ch'ung-sik, February 17, 2010.

76. Memorandum of conversation, Mao Zedong and Anastas Mikoyan, September 19, 1956. When Shen Zhihua asked Kim Ch'ung-sik whether the Yan'an faction cadres had requested help from the Chinese Embassy in Pyongyang, he replied that they had not, because they did not want to make any trouble for China. Interview with Kim Ch'ung-sik, February 17, 2010.

77. TsKhSD, f. 5, op. 28, d. 410, ll. 335–337.

78. Mu Chŏng returned to China after he was removed from his post and escaped trial. See Suh, *Kim Il-sung*, 107–109. According to Soviet intelligence, the Chinese military was not happy with how Kim Il-sung had treated Pak Il-u. TsKhSD, f. 5, op. 28, d. 314, ll. 212–214. During Kim Il-sung's trip to Beijing in

November 1953, Mao requested that Kim not execute Pak Hŏn-yŏng. Moscow offered the same advice via its military advisers. But Kim ignored this advice. Later, when the Soviet ambassador asked Kim about it, Kim was offended and even argued with the ambassador. See memorandum of conversation, Mao and Mikoyan, September 18, 1956, TsKhSD, f. 5, op. 28, d. 412, ll. 214–216.

79. Several years later, Kim Il-sung blamed Soviet Ambassador Ivanov for supporting the opposition. See minutes of Mao Zedong and Kim Il-sung conversation, July 13, 1961; minutes of conversation between the Party of Labor of Albania Delegation and Kim Il-sung, September 25, 1961, Arkivi Qendor Shtetëror [Albanian Central State Archive], MPP Korse, D 4, V, 1961.

80. Memorandum of conversation between DPRK Foreign Minister Nam Il and Soviet Chargé d'Affaires A. Petrov, July 24, 1956, RGANI, f. 5, op. 28, d. 410, ll. 301–303, in *Cold War International History Project Bulletin* 16 (Fall 2007–Winter 2008): 480–481. Later, the opposition blamed Ch'oe Yong-gŏn for "betraying" them. However, Ch'oe Yong-gŏn had long been a Kim Il-sung loyalist. It was at Kim's insistence that Ch'oe was promoted to vice chairman of the KWP in 1955, and when Kim was in Eastern Europe and the Soviet Union in June–July 1956, Ch'oe was left in charge in North Korea. It is very unlikely that Ch'oe would have joined the opposition. It is more likely that members of the opposition had hoped to use Ch'oe's name to attract more supporters and later blamed Ch'oe for their failure.

81. Petrov diary, July 20–August 3, 1956, RGANI, f. 5, op. 28, d. 410, ll. 309–314; Petrov diary, August 2, 1956, RGANI, f. 5, op. 28, d. 410, l. 313; Ivanov diary, August 6, 1956, RGANI, f. 5, op. 28, d. 410, ll. 335–337.

82. Ivanov diary, August 7, 1956, RGANI, f. 5, op. 28, d. 410, ll. 335–341.

83. TsKhSD, f. 5, op. 28, d. 410, ll. 335–359, 317–321.

84. Yun Kong-hŭm's remarks at the KWP Congress, August 30, 1956, State Archive of the Russian Federation (GARF), f. 5446, op. 98, d. 721, ll. 182–202; "Letter from Sŏ Hwi, Yun Kong-hŭm, Yi P'il-gyu, and Kim Kang to the Chinese Communist Party Central Committee," September 5, 1956, GARF, f. 5446, op. 98, d. 721, ll. 176–177.

85. "Letter from Sŏ Hwi, Yun Kong-hŭm, Yi P'il-gyu, and Kim Kang to the Chinese Communist Party Central Committee," September 5, 1956, GARF, f. 5446, op. 98, d. 721, ll. 170–190; memorandum of conversation, Mikoyan's conversation with the KWP delegation, September 16, 1956, GARF, f. 5446, op. 98, d. 728, ll. 48–57. Interview with Kim Kang, February 16, 2010, Taiyuan, China.

86. KWP Central Committee (CC) resolution, August 31, 1956, GARF, f. 5446, op. 98, d. 721, ll. 14–25; and *Rodong sinmun* [Workers' Newspaper], September 6, 1956.

87. Lankov, *Crisis in North Korea*, 111.

88. GARF, f. 5446, op. 98, d. 721, l. 153.

89. Memorandum of conversation, Mao Zedong and Kim Il-sung, May 21, 1960.

90. Memorandum of conversation, Mao Zedong's meeting with the CPSU CC delegation, September 18, 1956.

91. Petrov diary, August 3, 1956, RGANI, f. 5, op. 28, d. 410, ll. 313–314.

92. Interview with Kim Ch'ung-sik, February 17, 2010.

93. Ivanov diary, August 17, 1956, RGANI, f. 5, op. 28, d. 410, ll. 346–347.

94. Interview with Kim Kang, February 16, 2010.

95. The Chinese sent a delegation led by Marshal Nie Rongzhen, who was a Chinese Communist Party (CCP) CC member but not a Politburo member, to attend the KWP's Third Congress.

96. Person, "New Evidence on the 1956 September Plenum of the Korean Workers' Party," 2–3.

97. Ivanov diary, September 6, 1956, RGANI, f. 5, op. 28, d. 410, ll. 326–332.

98. Ivanov diary. The relevant documents are from TsKhSD, f. 5, op. 28, d. 410, ll. 319–321, 322–325, 327–332; d. 412, ll. 302–303.

99. Interview with Kim Kang, February 16, 2010.

100. Ivanov diary, TsKhSD, f. 5, op. 28, d. 410, ll. 319–321, 322–325, 327–332; d. 412, ll. 322–325.

101. Letter, Sŏ Hwi et al. to the Chinese Communist Party Central Committee, September 5, 1956, GARF, f. 5446, op. 98, d. 721, ll. 161–181. It is most likely that the document was first written in Chinese and then translated into Russian (a total of twenty pages of typewritten Russian text). Based on later developments, we are confident that this document was handed over to the CPSU by the CCP. This indicates that the CCP and the CPSU still remained in close consultation on major issues at the time.

102. Ivanov diary, TsKhSD, f. 5, op. 28, d. 410, ll. 319–321, 322–325, 327–332; d. 412, ll. 224–228. Even the minister of posts and telecommunications, who was in the Soviet Union for medical treatment, feared facing arrest if he returned home. See memorandum of conversation, Mao and Mikoyan, September 18, 1956.

103. "CPSU Presidium Resolution," September 6, 1956, RGANI, f. 3, op. 14, d. 56, l. 3; "Minutes, CPSU Presidium Meeting," September 6, 1956, RGANI, f. 3, op. 12, d. 1005, l. 30; A. A. Fursenko et al., eds., *Prezidium TsK KPSS 1954–1964*, tom 1 [Communist Party of the Soviet Union Central Committee Presidium, 1954–1964, vol. 1], *Chernovye protokol'nye zapisi zasedanii stenogrammy* [Draft Protocols of Meetings, Stenographic Records, and Decrees] (Moscow: Rosspen, 2003), 166–167.

104. Minutes, Ponomarev's conversation with Yi Sang-jo, RGANI, f. 5, op. 28, d. 410, ll. 228–232.

105. For details, see Zhihua Shen and Yafeng Xia, *Mao and the Sino–Soviet Partnership, 1945-1959: A New History* (Lanham, MD: Lexington Books, 2015), 148.

106. For details, see Shen Zhihua, "Sugong ershida fei Sidalinhua jiqi dui ZhongSu guanxi de yingxiang" [The Twentieth Congress of the CPSU, De-Stalinization, and Its Effects on Sino–Soviet Relations], in Li Danhui, ed., *Guoji lengzhanshi yanjiu* [Cold War International History Studies] (Shanghai: Huadong shifan daxue chubanshe, 2004), 1:28–69. For the CPSU CC resolution, see RGANI, f. 3, op. 14, d. 39, ll. 1, 30–34; K. Aimermakher et al., *Doklad N. S. Khushcheva o kul'te lichnosti Stalina naXXs'ezde KPSS dokumenty* [Khrushchev's Report on Stalin's Personality Cult in the Documents of the Twentieth Congress of the CPSU] (Moscow: Rosspen, 2002), 352–368.

107. TsKhSD, f. 5, op. 28, d. 410, ll. 228–232.

108. TsKhSD, f. 5, op. 28, d. 412, ll. 302–303.

109. Suh, *Kim Il-sung*, 131–133.

110. "Instructions to the CPSU Delegation at the Eighth Congress of the CCP Concerning the Situation in the KWP," RGANI, f. 3, op. 12, d. 109, ll. 4-12.

111. "Conversation with the KWP Delegation at the Eighth Congress of the CCP," September 17, 1956, GARF, f. 5446, op. 98c, d. 718, ll. 48–57.

112. Report from A. I. Mikoyan to the CPSU CC, September 17, 1956, GARF, f. 5446, op. 98c, d. 718, l. 47, cited in Person, "New Evidence on the 1956 September Plenum of the Korean Workers' Party," p. 9.

113. Report from A. I. Mikoyan to the CPSU CC, September 17, 1956, GARF, f. 5446, op. 98c, d. 718, l. 47, cited in Person, "New Evidence on the 1956 September Plenum of the Korean Workers' Party," p. 8.

114. Report from A. I. Mikoyan to the CPSU CC, September 17, 1956, GARF, f. 5446, op. 98c, d. 718, l. 47, cited in Person, "New Evidence on the 1956 September Plenum of the Korean Workers' Party," p. 8.

115. Minutes, Mikoyan's conversation with the Korean delegation, September 17, 1956, GARF, f. 5446, op. 98c, d. 718, ll. 48–57.

116. Record of a Conversation between A. I. Mikoyan and the Chinese Leadership, September 18, 1956, GARF, f. 5446, op. 98c, d. 718, l. 35–38; Memcon, Mao's Conversation with Mikoyan, September 18, 1956. (This is the Chinese version of the Memcon, in authors' personal collection.)

117. Person, "New Evidence on the 1956 September Plenum of the Korean Workers' Party," p. 10.

118. Person, "New Evidence on the 1956 September Plenum of the Korean Workers' Party," p. 10. See also Memcon, Mao's Conversation with Mikoyan, September 18, 1956.

119. Memcon, Mao's Conversation with Mikoyan, September 18, 1956, cited in Person, "New Evidence on the 1956 September Plenum of the Korean Workers' Party," p. 10.

120. Record of a Conversation between A. I. Mikoyan and the Chinese Leadership, September 18, 1956, GARF, f. 5446, op. 98c, d. 718, l. 35–38, cited in Person, "New Evidence on the 1956 September Plenum of the Korean Workers' Party," p. 10.

121. Memcon, Mao's Conversation with Mikoyan, September 18, 1956.

122. Mikoyan's Report to the CPSU CC, September 19, 1956, GARF, f. 5446, op. 98c, d. 718, l. 35–46; Memcon, Mao's Conversation with Mikoyan, September 18, 1956.

123. See Person, "New Evidence on the 1956 September Plenum of the Korean Workers' Party," p. 10.

124. Memcon, Mao's Conversation with Mikoyan, September 18, 1956. See also Person, "New Evidence on the 1956 September Plenum of the Korean Workers' Party," pp. 11–12.

125. Memcon, Mao's Conversation with Mikoyan, September 18, 1956, cited in Person, "New Evidence on the 1956 September Plenum of the Korean Workers' Party," pp. 11–12.

126. Record of a Conversation between A. I. Mikoyan and the Chinese Leadership, September 18, 1956, GARF, f. 5446, op. 98c, d. 718, l. 35–38.

127. See Person, "New Evidence on the 1956 September Plenum of the Korean Workers' Party," p. 10.

128. Memcon, Mao's Conversation with Mikoyan, September 18, 1956.

129. Based on Russian transcript of the conversion between Mao and Mikoyan on September 18, James Person writes, Mao "half-jokingly quipped 'the KWP leadership does not listen to the CCP advise 100%, and it does not listen to you 30%.'" See Person, "New Evidence on the 1956 September Plenum of the Korean Workers' Party," p. 12. As what Mao said was originally in Chinese and then was translated into Russian, we believe that our rendition here is accurate. See Memcon, Mao's Conversation with Mikoyan, September 18, 1956.

130. Minutes, Mao Zedong's conversation with the Korean delegation, September 18, 1956.

131. Lankov, *Crisis in North Korea*, 138.

132. Zhihua Shen, "Jin Richeng zuoshang quanli dingfeng: Yingdui Zhong Su gongtong ganyu" (Kim Il-sung Moves to the Pinnacle of Power: Coping with the Joint Sino-Soviet Intervention), *Ershiyi shiji* (Twenty-first Century), no. 154 (April 2016), p. 84. See also Person, "New Evidence on the 1956 September Plenum of the Korean Workers' Party," p. 11.

133. Lankov, *Crisis in North Korea*, 140. See also James F. Person, "North Korea in 1956: Reconsidering the August Plenum and the Sino-Soviet Joint Intervention," *Cold War History* (September 25, 2018), pp. 17–18. Available at https://doi.org/10.1080/14682745.2018.1509849.

134. Person, "North Korea in 1956," p. 13.

135. Minutes of the Korean Workers' Party Standing Committee Meeting, September 20, 1956, GARF, f. 5446, op. 98c, d.718, ll. 17–34.

136. Minutes of the Korean Workers' Party Standing Committee Meeting, September 20, 1956, GARF, f. 5446, op. 98c, d.718, ll. 17–34, cited in Person, "New Evidence on the 1956 September Plenum of the Korean Workers' Party," p. 13.

137. On September 20, 1956, the KWP CC Standing Committee "tentatively scheduled" the plenum for September 22. Then, the KWP CC plenum was postponed to 23 September 1956 at the meeting on 22 September. See Person, "North Korea in 1956," p. 16.

138. Report by A. I. Mikoyan to the CPSU CC, September 21, 1956, GARF, f. 5446, op. 98c, d.718, ll. 12–16, cited in Person, "New Evidence on the 1956 September Plenum of the Korean Workers' Party," p. 14.

139. Mikoyan's Report to the CPSU CC, September 23, 1956, GARF, f. 5446, op. 98c, d. 718, l. 3–6. See also Person, "North Korea in 1956," pp. 16-17.

140. Mikoyan's Report to the CPSU CC, September 23, 1956, GARF, f. 5446, op. 98c, d. 718, l. 3–6.

141. Minutes, KWP Central Committee plenum, September 23, 1956, GARF, f. 5446, op. 98c, d. 721, ll. 31–43.

142. Minutes, Mao Zedong's Conversation with the Soviet Delegation, September 23, 1956 (This is the Chinese version of the Memcon, in authors' personal collection), cited in Person, "North Korea in 1956," p. 17.

143. Minutes, Mao Zedong's Conversation with the Soviet Delegation, September 23, 1956, cited in Person, "North Korea in 1956," p. 17.

144. Shen, "Jin Richeng zuoshang quanli dingfeng: Yingdui Zhong Su gongtong ganyu," p. 89; Zhihua Shen, "Alliance of 'Tooth and Lips' or Marriage of Convenience? The Origins and Development of the Sino–North Korean Alliance, 1946–1958," trans. Min Song, U.S.–Korea Institute at SAIS Working Paper 08–09 (December 2008), p. 20; and Person, "North Korea in 1956," pp. 17–18.

145. Person, "North Korea in 1956," p. 19.

146. See Memcon, Mao and Mikoyan, September 23, 1956; TsKhSD, f. 5, op. 28, d. 486, ll. 1–17, 26, 28–33; d.412, ll. 344–347; d.411, ll. 295–296.

147. North Korea was not opposed to the UN as an international body. As early as 1956, with the support of the North Korean government, the Soviet Union had proposed that the DPRK be permitted to join the UN, together with the Republic of Korea. But the United States rejected this proposal. See Barry K. Gills, *Korea Versus Korea: A Case of Contested Legitimacy* (London: Routledge, 1996), 73.

148. Ivanov diary, November 28, 1956, RGANI, f. 5, op. 28, d. 411, ll. 301–302; "Work Report of 1956, the Soviet Embassy in China," April 18, 1957, RGANI, f. 5, op. 28, p. 103, d., 409, ll. 139–163.

149. Mao Zedong's conversation with Pavel Yudin, November 30, 1956.

150. Chinese Foreign Ministry Archives 109-00743-10, 52–54.

151. RGANI, f. 5, op. 28, d. 410, ll. 315–333; RGANI, f. 5, op. 28, d. 486, ll. 1–17.

152. RGANI, f. 5, op. 28, 103, d. 409, ll. 139–163.

153. RGANI, f. 5, op. 28, d. 411, ll. 287–288.

154. RGANI, f. 5, op. 28, d. 411, ll. 287–313.

155. Chinese Foreign Ministry Archives 106-01129-01, 21.

156. Person, "New Evidence on the 1956 September Plenum of the Korean Workers' Party," p. 10.

IV. Mao's Policy of Mollification, 1957–1960

1. For a detailed study of China's role in the Polish and Hungarian crises, see Zhihua Shen and Yafeng Xia, *Mao and the Sino–Soviet Partnership, 1945–1959: A New History* (Lanham, MD: Lexington Books, 2015), chap. 6.

2. Russian State Archive of Contemporary History (RGANI), f. 5, op. 28, d. 412, ll. 364-365; RGANI, f. 5, op. 28, d. 411, ll. 297–300.

3. Center for the Preservation of Contemporary Documentation (TsKhSD), f. 5, op. 28, d. 412, ll. 364–365.

4. RGANI, f. 5, op. 30, d. 228, ll. 15–36.

5. Archive of the President of the Russian Federation (AVPRF), f. 0102, op. 13, d. 5, ll. 1-2.

6. TsKhSD, f.5, op. 28, d. 412, ll. 292–294, 297–300.

7. AVPRF, f. 0102, op. 13, d. 5, ll. 1-15.

8. AVPRF, f. 0102, op. 13, d. 5, ll. 44-113.

9. Shen and Xia, *Mao and the Sino–Soviet Partnership*, chaps. 5, 6, and 8.

10. Victor Cha writes, "Internal splits within the Chinese leadership after the war were fortuitous for Kim Il-sung as well. Peng Dehuai, who was commander in chief of Chinese forces during the Korean War, wanted to oust Kim for his mistakes. Peng would have probably been successful had he not fallen out with Mao. Peng's criticism of Mao's Great Leap Forward eventually led to his demise, thereby allowing Kim to stay in place." Cha, *The Impossible State: North Korea, Past and Future* (New York: Ecco, 2012), 76. Cha does not provide his sources for this claim, and the historical record indicates that this is incorrect. Mao had a change of heart about North Korea in early 1957, and by late 1958 China had already withdrawn all Chinese People's Volunteer Army (CPVA) forces from North Korea. Peng's criticism of the Great Leap Forward occurred in August 1959, and in the fall he was purged by Mao. By 1959, Sino-North Korean relations had already improved and stabilized.

11. AVPRF, f. 0102, op. 13, d. 5, ll. 146-164.

12. RGANI, f. 3, op. 12, d. 1007, ll. 64-65.

13. AVPRF, f. 0102, op. 13, d. 5, ll. 275-300.

14. Chinese Foreign Ministry Archives (CFMA) 117-00665-03, 10-11, 14-15, 20-24.

15. Li Fuchun's report on the Sino–North Korean trade negotiations, September 30, 1957; Li Fuchun's report on the Sino–North Korean trade negotiations, October 4, 1957, State Planning Commission Archives; AVPRF, f. 0102, op. 13, d. 5, ll. 260-264, 274-280, 255-256.

16. Shen Jueren, ed., *Dangdai Zhongguo duiwai maoyi* [Contemporary China's Foreign Trade] (Beijing: Dangdai Zhongguo chubanshe, 1992), 1:301, 2:371.

17. *Renmin ribao* [People's Daily], October 25, October 26, October 30, and November 9, 1957.

18. Arkhiv Rossiiskoi Academii Nauk [Russian Academy of Sciences Archives], f. 1636, op. 199, d. 1-6; AVPRF, f. 0102, op. 13, d. 5, ll. 322–324.

19. Junshi Kexueyuan Junshi Lishi Yanjiubu [History Research Department of the Academy of Military Science], ed., *KangMei yuanChao zhanzhengshi* [A History of the War to Resist America and to Aid Korea] (Beijing: Junshi kexue chubanshe, 2000), 3:519.

20. *Renmin ribao*, September 9, 1954, and March 26, 1955; Zhonggong Zhongyang Wenxian Yanjiushi [Chinese Communist Party Central Committee Party Literature Research Office], ed., *Zhou Enlai nianpu, 1949–1976* [A Chronology of Zhou Enlai, 1949-1976] (Beijing: Zhonggong zhongyang wenxian chubanshe, 1997), 1:562.

21. Telegram, Mao Zedong to Kim Il-sung and CPVA headquarters, November 24, 1954; Zhou Enlai and Peng Dehuai to the Chinese People's Volunteer Army delegation in Kaesŏng, CPVA headquarters, and CPVA Logistics Department, December 6, 1954, cited in Junshi Kexueyuan Junshi Lishi Yanjiubu, *KangMei yuanChao zhanzhengshi*, 3:474.

22. Annual Work Report (1956), Soviet embassy in China, April 18, 1956, RGANI, f. 5, op. 28, 103, d. 409, ll. 139–143.

23. Minutes of Mao Zedong's conversation with the Communist Party of the Soviet Union Central Committee delegation, September 18, 1956; minutes of Mao's conversation with Yudin, November 30, 1956.

24. For details, see Zhihua Shen and Yafeng Xia, "New Evidence for China's Role in the Hungarian Crisis of October 1956: A Note," *International History Review* 31, no. 3 (September 2009): 558-575.

25. Telephone interview with Sergey Radchenko, September 2015.

26. RGANI, f. 5, op. 28, p. 103, d. 409, ll. 139–143; Dmitri Shepilov to the Communist Party of the Soviet Union Central Committee, January 4, 1957; Shen Zhihua and Li Danhui, eds., *ZhongSu guanxi: Eguo dang'an yuanwen fuyinjian huibian* [Sino–Soviet Relations: Collection of Copies of Original Documents in the Russian Archives] (Shanghai: Center for Cold War International History Studies, East China Normal University, 2004), 11:2810–2813. Unpublished.

27. Shen Zhihua, ed., *Eluosi jiemi dang'an xuanbian: ZhongSu guanxi, 1945–1991* [Selected Collection of Declassified Russian Archives: Sino–Soviet Relations, 1945-1991] (Shanghai: Dongfang chubanshe, 2015), 7:129-131.

28. Minutes of the conversation between Khrushchev and Mao Zedong, October 2, 1959, in *Novaia i noveishaia istoriia* [Modern and Contemporary History] 2 (2001): 94-106.

29. According to a Soviet Embassy report, some Chinese Communist Party (CCP) officials had become conceited and arrogant because China was successful in its socialist construction, thereby enhancing its international prestige. Their opinion was that Chinese officials had revealed their great power chauvinism when dealing with North Korean, Vietnamese, and Mongolian comrades. RGANI, f. 5, op. 28, p. 103, d. 409, ll. 111-112.

30. Zhonggong Zhongyang Wenxian Yanjiushi, *Zhou Enlai nianpu, 1949–1976*, 2:5-6. This document gives the impression that, in his January 1957 conversation with Zhou Enlai, Khrushchev agreed to China's proposal for a unilateral withdrawal from Korea. This was not the case. It was Mao Zedong who, in November 1957, first proposed China's unilateral withdrawal from Korea.

31. For the predicament of the Soviet Union after its suppression of the Hungarian Revolution, see Shen and Xia, "New Evidence for China's Role in the Hungarian Crisis of October 1956"; Zhihua Shen and Yafeng Xia, " 'Whirlwind' of China: Zhou Enlai's Shuttle Diplomacy in 1957 and Its Effect," *Cold War History* 10, no. 4 (November 2010): 513-535.

32. See Shen Zhihua, *Zhonghua renmin gongheguoshi. Di 3 juan. Sikao yu xuanze: Cong zhishifenzi huiyi dao fan youpai yundong, 1956–1957* [History of the People's Republic of China, vol. 3, Pondering and Choosing: From the Conference on Intellectuals to the Anti-Rightist Campaign, 1956-1957] (Hong Kong: Chinese University Press, 2008), chaps. 6, 7, and 8.

33. Minutes of Mao Zedong's conversation with Yi Yŏng-ho, June 21, 1957. Also *Renmin ribao*, June 22, 1957.

34. *Renmin ribao*, August 15, 1957.

35. AVPRF, f. 0102, op. 13, d. 51, ll. 215-222.

36. "Several Issues in the CPVA's Relations with the North Korean Party, Government, Army, and People Since the Armistice," *Neibu cankao* [Internal Reference] 2073 (December 8, 1956): 158-163; "Problems in the CPVA's Relations with the Korean People," *Neibu cankao* 2111 (January 22, 1957): 427-429.

37. Pang Xianzhi and Feng Hui, eds., *Mao Zedong nianpu, 1949–1976* [A Chronology of Mao Zedong, 1949-1976] (Beijing: Zhongyang wenxian chubanshe, 2013), 3:241; *Yang Shangkun riji* [Yang Shangkun's Diary] (Beijing: Zhongyang wenxian, chubanshe, 2001), 1:289.

38. Minutes of the conversation between Zhou Enlai and Soviet Ambassador Yudin, January 8, 1958, CFMA 109-00828-01, 4-7; Chinese Embassy in the Soviet Union to the Foreign Ministry, January 16, 1958, CFMA 109-01813-01, 1-2; memorandum of conversation between Mao and Yudin, February 28 1958; AVPRF, f. 0100, op. 51, p. 432, d. 6, ll. 86-96.

39. Russian Academy of Sciences Archives, f. 1636, op. 1, d. 199, ll. 1-6. Victor Cha contends that Mao and Kim Il-sung argued at the 1957 Moscow Conference. Mao refused to hand over those Yan'an faction cadres who had fled to China after the 1956 August incident, and Kim complained about the presence of Chinese troops in North Korea. Cha writes, "Without a hint of hesitation, an equally perturbed Mao brusquely assured Kim that all troops would be withdrawn, and within one year, they were." Cha, *The Impossible State*, 322. We now know that this is incorrect.

40. Andrei Lankov, *Crisis in North Korea: The Failure of De-Stalinization, 1956* (Honolulu: University of Hawai'i Press, 2004), 161-62; AVPRF, f. 0102, op. 13, d. 5, ll. 322-324.

41. Hebei Provincial Archives 855-4-1307, 64-65; *Guoji shishi tongbao* [International Affairs Bulletin] 3 (March 10, 1958); *Renmin ribao*, February 7, 1958.

42. Division of Research and Analysis for the Far East, "Intelligence Report: Implications of Communist Chinese Withdrawal from North Korea," March 17, 1958, MF2510409-0073, available from the University of Hong Kong main library.

43. Kim Yong-hyeon, "Studies on the Nationalization of North Korea's Military: Focusing on the Years from 1950 to 1960" [in Korean], PhD diss., Graduate School of Dongkuk University, 2001, 81-82; Park Yeong-sil, "The Chinese People's Volunteers Army's Aid to and Withdrawal from North Korea After the Armistice" [in Korean], *Chŏngsin munhwa yŏn'gu* [Korean Studies Quarterly] 29, no. 4 (2006): 265–291; Kim Yong-hyeon, "A Study of the Role of the Chinese People's Volunteer Army After the Korean War" [in Korean], *Pukhan Yŏn'gu Hakhoe* [North Korean Studies Review] 10, no. 2 (2006): 148–162; Park Jung-cheol, "A Study of Sino-North Korean Relations Regarding the Withdrawal of the Chinese People's Volunteer Army" [in Korean], *Kunsasa yŏn'gu ch'ongsŏ* [Military History Studies Series] 5 (March 2008): 212; Yi Sang-suk, "The Causes and Impact of the Withdrawal of the Chinese People's Volunteer Army from North Korea in 1958" [in Korean], *Pukhan Yŏn'gu Hakhoe* [North Korean Studies Review] 13, no. 1 (2009): 104.

44. Junshi Kexueyuan Junshi Lishi Yanjiubu, *KangMei yuanChao zhanzhengshi*, 3:520.

45. V. A. Shin, *Kitai i koreiskie gosudarstva vo vtoroi polovine KhKh stoletiia* [China and North Korea in the Late Twentieth Century] (Moscow: ID-vo MGU, 1998), 25.

46. Jin Chongji, ed., *Zhou Enlai zhuan* [A Biography of Zhou Enlai] (Beijing: Zhongyang wenxian chubanshe, 1998), 1371-1372; Zhonggong Zhongyang Wenxian Yanjiushi and Zhongguo Renmin Jiefangjun Junshi Kexueyuan [Chinese Communist Party Central Committee Party Literature Research Office and Academy of Military Science of the People's Liberation Army], eds., *Jianguo yilai Mao Zedong junshi wengao* [Mao Zedong's Military Writings Since the Founding of the State] (Beijing: Zhongyang wenxian chubanshe, 2010), 2:371.

47. Memorandum of conversation, Zhou Enlai and P. Yudin, January 8, 1958, CFMA 109-00828-01, 4–7; Yan Mingfu and Zhu Ruizhen, "Mao Zedong dierci fang Su he 1957 nian Mosike huiyi (yi)" [Mao Zedong's Second Trip to the Soviet Union and the 1957 Moscow Conference (Part 1)], *Zhonggong dangshi ziliao* [Materials on the History of the Chinese Communist Party] 4 (2005): 30.

48. Chinese Embassy in Moscow to Chinese Ministry of Foreign Affairs, January 16, 1958, CFMA 109-01813-01, 1–2.

49. *Renmin ribao*, February 6, February 7, and February 22, 1958.

50. Jin Chongji, *Zhou Enlai zhuan*, 2:370; *Renmin ribao*, February 21 and October 18, 1958; TsKhSD, f. 5, op. 49, d. 135, ll. 1–75.

51. *Renmin ribao*, October 5, October 21, October 25, October 26, and October 27, 1958; minutes of Mao Zedong's conversation with the North Korean government delegation, November 25, 1958.

52. Interviews with Hong Sun-Kwan, October 2005; Kim Kang, February 2010; and Kim Ch'ung-sik, November 23, 2010.

53. The number seventeen is from Kim Ch'ung-sik; according to Kim Kang, there were only sixteen. However, according to Mao Zedong's conversation with Yudin, there were fifteen Yan'an faction cadres in China by November 30, 1956. The names of several others, such as Yi Kyu-ch'ŏl, Pak Hyŏn, Kim Chŏng-nyong, and Kim Chi-hong, also appear in Chinese documents.

54. For details, see Zhihua Shen and Yafeng Xia, "Hidden Currents During the Honeymoon: Mao Zedong, Khrushchev and the 1957 Moscow Conference," *Journal of Cold War Studies* 11, no. 4 (Fall 2009): 74–117.

55. Letter, Kim Ch'ung-sik to Wu De, March 4, 1957, Jilin Provincial Archives 1-13/1-1957.41, 174.

56. Minutes of the conversation between Fu Zhensheng and Kim Ch'ung-sik, March 16, 1957, Jilin Provincial Archives 1-13/1-1957.41, 169.

57. Foreign Affairs Office, Jilin Province asks for instructions from Jilin Provincial CCP Committee, April 28, 1957, Jilin Provincial Archives 1-13/1-1957.41, 182.

58. Letter, Kim Chun-kŭn and Yi Hŭi-sang to the CCP Central Committee, June 28, 1957; letter, Jilin Province to CCP International Liaison Department (ILD); and letter in reply, CCP ILD to Jilin province, July 1 and July 9, 1957, Jilin Provincial Archives 1-13/1-1957.41, 183–184.

59. Memorandum of conversation, Zhou Enlai and Liaoning provincial cadres, February 21, 1958, Jilin Provincial Archives 1-14/1-1958.94, 106–118.

60. Opinion of the United Front Department of the CCP Sichuan Provincial Committee regarding the resettlement of Korean cadres, February 15, 1958;

CCP Sichuan Provincial Committee to the CCP ILD, February 16, 1958, Sichuan Provincial Archives, Jianchuan 1-7-617, 5, 6-7.

61. CCP ILD to CCP Sichuan Provincial Committee United Front Department, April 23, 1958, Sichuan Provincial Archives, Jianchuan 1-7-617, 9-10.

62. ILD circular regarding the handling of the Korean Workers' Party runaway cadres, September 8, 1958, Sichuan Provincial Archives, Jianchuan 1-7-617, 19-20.

63. Work arrangements and behavior of the four runaway North Korean cadres in China, December 7, 1958, Sichuan Provincial Archives, Jianchuan 1-7617, 21-23.

64. Minutes of Mao Zedong's conversation with Kim Il-sung, July 13, 1961.

65. Minutes of Mao Zedong's conversation with Pak Kŭm-ch'ŏl, June 21, 1962.

66. Wu Xiuquan to Wang Jiaxiang and the Central Committee, asking for instructions and submitting reports regarding the handling of North Korean antiparty factionalists, April 24, 1962, Sichuan Provincial Archives, Jianchuan 1-7-813, 8-9; ILD to CCP Sichuan and Shanxi provincial committees, May 17, 1962, Sichuan Provincial Archives, Jianchuan 1-7-813, 7.

67. ILD opinions on how to handle those North Korean antiparty elements who illegally fled to our country (summary of conference discussion), June 13, 1962, Sichuan Provincial Archives, Jianchuan 1-7-813, 17-20.

68. CCP Sichuan Provincial Committee United Front Department, *Qingkuang jianbao* [Briefing on the Situation] 11 (April 25, 1962), Sichuan Provincial Archives, Jianchuan 1-7-813, 10-13; ILD to the CCP Sichuan Provincial Committee, opinion regarding how to handle Yun Kong-hŭm, September 26, 1962, Sichuan Provincial Archives, Jianchuan 1-7-813, 4. Their cases were not redressed until 1981. See Sichuan Provincial Archives, Jianchuan 1-7-617, 1-10; Jianchuan 1-7-813, 7-20; Shanxi Provincial Archives C54-2009-66-3; C54-1011-39-8; C59-1-83-14.

69. This is a claim Bernd Schaefer made in his article. See Bernd Schaefer, "Weathering the Sino–Soviet Conflict: The GDR and North Korea, 1949-1989," *Cold War International History Project Bulletin* 14-15 (Winter 2003-Spring 2004): 27.

70. Minutes of Chen Yi's conversation with Han Ik-su, April 20, 1962, CFMA 106-01380-02, 49-52; minutes of Liu Shaoqi's conversation with Han Ik-su, April 21, 1962, CFMA 106-01380-05, 53-60.

71. *Renmin ribao*, March 9, 1958.

72. A. A. Fursenko et al., eds., *Prezidium TsK KPSS 1954–1964*, tom 1 [Communist Party of the Soviet Union Central Committee Presidium, 1954–1964, vol. 1], *Chernovye protokol'nye zapisi zasedanii stenogrammy* [Draft Protocols of Meetings, Stenographic Records, and Decrees] (Moscow: Rosspen, 2003), 960–961; Committee on Korean Central Yearbook, *General Book of North Korea (1945–1968)* (Seoul: Institute Communist Circle Issue, 1968), 178–179; Gang In Deok, ed., *Pukhan chŏnsŏ* [A Complete Book of North Korea] (Seoul: Research Center of the Far East Issue, 1974), 1:262–263.

73. Internal speeches of the North Korean leaders, January 1958, CFMA 204-00612-01, 28–39.

74. Lin Yunhui, *Zhonghua renmin gongheguoshi. Di 4 juan. Wutuobang yundong: Cong dayuejin dao dajihuang, 1958–1961* [The History of the People's Republic of China,

vol. 4, The Utopian Movement: From the Great Leap Forward to the Great Famine, 1958-1961] (Hong Kong: Chinese University Press, 2008), chaps. 1–3.

75. According to Jae-Jung Suh, Kim Il-sung "turned to internal resources, material and human, as the main locomotive of economic development, launching in December 1956 the mass mobilization campaigns to promote rapid economic development, the Ch'ŏllima Movement." See Jae-Jung Suh, ed., *Origins of North Korea's* Juche: *Colonialism, War, and Development* (Lanham, MD: Lexington Books, 2013), 10. Although the Ch'ŏllima Movement resembled the Great Leap Forward in both rhetoric and practice, the outcomes were quite different. Whereas the Great Leap Forward was short-lived and its results were immediately disastrous, "the outcome of the North Korean economic campaigns of the late 1950s was more ambiguous, and for decades Ch'ŏllima remained the enduring symbol of North Korea's 'human wave' approach to economic development," Charles K. Armstrong observes. "Between 1972 and 1992, Ch'ŏllima was even enshrined in the North Korean constitution as the 'general line of socialist construction in the DPRK.' " Armstrong, *Tyranny of the Weak: North Korea and the World, 1950–1992* (Ithaca, NY: Cornell University Press, 2013), 103, 111.

76. Robert Scalapino and Chong-Sik Lee, *Communism in Korea* (Berkeley: University of California Press, 1972), 1:540.

77. *Rodong sinmun* [Workers' Newspaper], June 13, 1958.

78. *Waishi gongzuo tongbao* [Bulletin on Foreign Affairs Work] 4 (October 11, 1958): 3-5.

79. *Rodong sinmun*, January 27, 1959; *Geguo gongchandang gaikuang* [General Situation of the Communist Parties of the World] 9 (1959): 11-12.

80. Minutes of Mao Zedong's conversation with the North Korean government delegation, November 25, 1958.

81. CFMA 106-01129-04, 44-63; 204-00315-03, 42-51; 204-00315-04, 53-55; 106-01131-01, 2-17; *Renmin ribao*, October 11, 1958; December 9, 1958; May 20, 1959; *Neibu cankao* [Internal Reference] 2719 (March 3, 1959): 19-20.

82. Kim Il-sung, "On Communist Education," speech at a short course for the agitators of the city and prefecture party committees of the country, November 20, 1958, in Kim Il-sung, *Selected Works* (Pyongyang: Foreign Languages Publishing House, 1971), 1:406-408. Also see Scalapino and Lee, *Communism in Korea*, 1:541.

83. Zhonggong Zhongyang Wenxian Yanjiushi [Party Documents Research Office of the Chinese Communist Party Central Committee], ed., *Jianguo yilai Mao Zedong wengao* (*JYMWG*) [Mao Zedong's Manuscripts Since the Founding of the State] (Beijing: Zhongyang wenxian chubanshe, 1993), 8:41-43.

84. AVPRF, f. 0102, op. 14, d. 6, ll. 30–60; CFMA 203-00111-04, 84-86.

85. CFMA 204-00614-02, 36-38.

86. Reference materials for the Sino–North Korean negotiations on supplying equipment and constructing power plants, August 5, 1958, CFMA 204-00315-04, 57-67, 69-71; AVPRF, f. 0102, op. 14, d. 3; *Renmin ribao*, September 28, 1958.

87. See Nam Hyŏn-uk, *Chungsoŭi taebugwŏnjo mit muyŏkhyŏnhwang, 1946–1978* [China and Soviet Assistance to North Korea and the Status of Trade,

1946–1978] (Seoul: Korea Institute of National Unification, February 1979), 11. Unpublished.

88. Shanghai Municipal Archives, B 163-2-666, 1-9.
89. Shanghai Municipal Archives, B 134-1-11, 1-4.
90. CFMA 204-00064-01, 1-8; CFMA 204-00064-02, 9-25.
91. *Renmin ribao*, November 23, 1958.
92. Minutes of Mao Zedong's conversations with the North Korean government delegation, November 25 and December 6, 1958.
93. AVPRF, f. 0102, op. 14, d. 6, ll. 1–25.
94. On Kim Il-sung's purges in 1958, see Zhihua Shen, "Alliance of 'Tooth and Lips' or Marriage of Convenience? The Origins and Development of the Sino-North Korean Alliance, 1946-1958," trans. Min Song, *U.S.–Korea Institute at SAIS Working Paper* 08-09 (December 2008).
95. Balázs Szalontai, *Kim Il-sung in the Khrushchev Era: Soviet–DPRK Relations and the Roots of North Korean Despotism, 1953–1964* (Stanford, CA: Stanford University Press, 2006), 120. Also see Lankov, *Crisis in North Korea*, 165-169.
96. Scalapino and Lee, *Communism in Korea*, 1:522-525. Also see Dae-Sook Suh, *Kim Il-sung: The North Korean Leader* (New York: Columbia University Press, 1988), 154; Adrian Buzo, *The Guerilla Dynasty: Politics and Leadership in North Korea* (London: I. B. Tauris, 1999), 58. In March 1958, the First Conference of Korean Workers' Party Representatives reinforced the decisions of the August 1956 plenum and eliminated Kim's major Soviet- and China-aligned rivals.
97. AVPRF, f. 0102, op. 14, 6; AVPRF, f. 0102, op. 14, 3.
98. *Renmin ribao*, February 1, 1959.
99. AVPRF, f. 0102, op. 14, d. 6, ll. 26-64; *Pravda*, January 30, 1959.
100. AVPRF, f. 0102, op. 14, d. 6, ll. 26-64; *Magyar Országos Levéltár* [Hungarian National Archives, Budapest], XIX-J-1-j Korea, 11. doboz, 24/b, 001660/1960, *Cold War International History Project Bulletin* 14-15 (Winter 2003-Spring 2004): 112-114.
101. *Renmin ribao*, March 19, 1959.
102. *Renmin ribao*, January 17, 1959; March 26, 1959, 4; May 9, 1959, 4.
103. Kim Il-sung, *Jin Richeng zhuzuo ji* [Works of Kim Il-sung] (Pingrang: Waiwen chubanshe, 1983), 12:489, 491-493; Balázs Szalontai and Sergey Radchenko, "North Korea's Efforts to Acquire Nuclear Technology and Nuclear Weapons: Evidence from Russian and Hungarian Archives," *Cold War International History Project Working Paper* 53 (August 2006): 4; *Renmin ribao*, February 22, 1959.
104. "Mao Zedong zai bada erci huiyishang di erci jianghua" [Mao Zedong's Second Speech at the Second Plenum of the Eighth Party Congress], May 17, 1958, Jilin Provincial Archives 1/1–14/59, 6-9.
105. Zhonggong Zhongyang Wenxian Yanjiushi [Chinese Communist Party Central Committee Party Literature Research Office], ed., *Jianguo yilai zhongyao wenxian xuanbian* [Selected Important Documents Since the Founding of the State] (Beijing: Zhongyang wenxian chubanshe, 1995), 11:450.
106. Jilin Provincial Archives 1/1-14/71, 6-11. Translation from Roderick Mac-Farquhar, Timothy Cheek, and Eugene Wu, eds., *The Secret Speeches of Chairman*

Mao: From the Hundred Flowers to the Great Leap Forward (Cambridge, MA: Council on East Asian Studies, Harvard University, 1989), 443-444.

107. Jilin Provincial Archives 1/1-14/72, 1-6; *JYMWG*, 7:553-554; translation from MacFarquhar, Cheek, and Wu, *Secret Speeches of Chairman Mao*, 516.

108. CFMA 106-01131-01, 2-17.

109. *Geguo gongchandang dongxiang* [Trends in the Communist Parties of the World] 91 (January 13, 1959). It is worth noting that these radical expressions were deleted from a later published collection of Kim Il-sung writings. See Kim Il-sung, *Jin Richeng zhuzuo ji*, 12:489-511.

110. CFMA 106-01129-04, 62-63.

111. *Geguo gongchandang dongxiang* 82 (December 25, 1958).

112. Minutes of Mao Zedong's conversation with the North Korean government delegation, December 6, 1958.

113. *Geguo gongchandang dongxiang* 13 (1959). This was also deleted from a later published collection of Kim Il-sung's writings. See Kim Il-sung, *Jin Richeng zhuzuo ji*, 13:9.

114. *JYMWG*, 7:554.

115. Jilin Provincial Archives 1/1-14/72, 1-6.

116. *JYMWG*, 7:570.

117. Hebei Provincial Archives 855-4-1268, 130-135.

118. *Waishi dongtai* [Trends in Foreign Affairs] 53 (1959): 14-15; *Waishi dongtai* 82 (1959): 13-15; CFMA 106-01132-04, 1-5.

119. Cited from Balázs Szalontai, " 'You Have No Political Line of Your Own': Kim Il-sung and the Soviets, 1953–1964," *Cold War International History Project Bulletin* 14-15 (Winter 2003-Spring 2004): 93.

120. *Geguo gongchandang jiankuang* 29 (1959): 4-5.

121. Hebei Provincial Archives D 822-312-511, 14-31.

122. *Waishi dongtai* 48 (1959): 8-18; *Renmin ribao*, September 14, 1959; November 27, 1959.

123. *Sulian he qita xiongdidang guojia baokan cailiao* [Periodical Materials from the Soviet Union and Other Fraternal Parties] 28 (August 27, 1959); and 29, 30 (August 28, 1959); *Rodong sinmun*, August 28, 1959.

124. *Waishi dongtai* 90 (1959): 2-3.

125. Shanxi Provincial Archives C54-1011-39, 76. During Kim Il-sung's secret visit to China in May 1960, Mao reprimanded Peng Dehuai in front of Kim Il-sung. According to their conversation, Peng Dehuai was responsible for all the tensions in Sino-North Korean relations from the period of the Korean War to the August incident of 1956. See minutes of Mao Zedong's conversation with Kim Il-sung, May 21, 1960.

v. North Korea's Balancing Act, 1961-1965

1. Zhihua Shen and Yafeng Xia, *Mao and the Sino–Soviet Partnership, 1945–1959: A New History* (Lanham, MD: Lexington, 2015), chaps. 9 and 10; Danhui Li and Yafeng Xia, "Competing for Leadership: Split or Détente in the Sino–Soviet Bloc, 1969-1961," *International History Review* 30, no. 3 (September 2008): 545-574.

2. Russian State Archive of Contemporary History (RGANI), f. 5, op. 30, d. 337, ll. 70-92; Balázs Szalontai, " 'You Have No Political Line of Your Own': Kim Il-sung and the Soviets, 1953–1964," *Cold War International History Project Bulletin* 14-15 (Winter 2003-Spring 2004): 93-95; Archive of Foreign Policy of the Russian Federation (AVPRF), f. 0102, op. 16, d. 6, ll. 28-61.

3. Robert Scalapino and Chong-Sik Lee, *Communism in Korea* (Berkeley: University of California Press, 1972), 1:543.

4. AVPRF, f. 0102, op. 14, d. 6, ll. 78-116.

5. *Renmin ribao* [People's Daily], August 31, 1959.

6. AVPRF, f. 0102, op. 14, d. 6, ll. 117-144, 154-185; AVPRF, f. 0102, op. 16, d. 6, ll. 28-61, 72-122.

7. AVPRF, f. 0102, op. 16, d. 6, ll. 184-187; RGANI, f. 5, op. 30, d. 337, ll. 70-92.

8. AVPRF, f. 0102, op. 14, d. 6, ll. 186-216; Szalontai, "You Have No Political Line of Your Own," 94.

9. Minutes of Mao Zedong's conversation with Kim Il-sung, May 21, 1960; Shen Zhihua, ed., *ZhongSu guanxi shigang, 1917–1991* [History of Sino–Soviet Relations, 1917-1991] (Beijing: Xinhua chubanshe, 2007), 261-262.

10. Minutes of Mao Zedong's conversation with Kim Il-sung, May 21, 1960.

11. AVPRF, f. 0102, op. 16, d. 85, ll. 5–19.

12. AVPRF, f. 0102, op. 16, d. 7, ll. 1-15. See also "GDR [German Democratic Republic] Ambassador to Pyongyang K. Schneidewind to SED [Socialist Unity Party of Germany] Central Committee, August 30, 1960," North Korea International Documentation Project Archives.

13. AVPRF, f. 0102, op. 16, d. 7, ll. 31-35, 36-37.

14. A. M. Puzanov's diary entries from June 29 to August 8, 1960, AVPRF, f. 0102, op. 16, d. 7, ll. 16–42.

15. AVPRF, f. 0102, op. 16, d. 7, ll. 16–42, 72–101.

16. Chinese Foreign Ministry Archives (CFMA) 109-02090-01, 3-7, 1318.

17. "Report, Embassy of Hungary in North Korea to the Hungarian Foreign Ministry, 2 July 1960," Magyar Országos Levéltár [Hungarian National Archives, Budapest] XIX-J-1-j Korea, 8. doboz, 5/f, 0029/RT/1960, *Cold War International History Project Bulletin* 14-15 (Winter 2003-Spring 2004): 116.

18. CFMA 204-00492-06, 61-62.

19. CFMA 109-02090-02, 35.

20. *Renmin ribao*, October 14, 1960.

21. Zhonggong Zhongyang Wenxian Yanjiushi [Chinese Communist Party Central Committee Party Literature Research Office], ed., *Zhou Enlai nianpu, 1949–1976* [A Chronology of Zhou Enlai, 1949-1976] (Beijing: Zhonggong zhongyang wenxian chubanshe, 1997), 2:355-356.

22. "Intelligence Report no. 8370, October 28, 1960," in National Institute of Korean History, ed., *Office of Intelligence Research (OIR) Report on the Korean Problems* (Seoul: NIKH, 2003), 5: 455-56, cited in Dongjun Lee, "The Politics of Lips and Teeth: Reexamining the 1961 Sino-North Korean Alliance Treaty from the Chinese Perspective," *Korean Journal of Security Affairs* 16, no. 2 (December 2011): 93.

23. *Renmin ribao*, October 14, 1960.

24. *Renmin ribao*, October 19, 1960; Shanghai Municipal Archives, B 163-2-1033, 2-8.

25. Lin Yunhui, *Zhonghua renmin gongheguoshi. Di 4 juan. Wutuobang yundong: Cong dayuejin dao dajihuang, 1958–1961* [The History of the People's Republic of China, vol. 4, The Utopian Movement: From the Great Leap Forward to the Great Famine, 1958-1961] (Hong Kong: Chinese University Press, 2008), chap. 8; Shen Jueren, ed., *Dangdai Zhongguo duiwai maoyi* [Contemporary China's Foreign Trade] (Beijing: Dangdai Zhongguo chubanshe, 1992), 1:301.

26. Central Intelligence Agency, Office of Current Intelligence, *Sino–Soviet Competition in North Korea*, ESAU 15-61 (April 5, 1961). https://www.cia.gov/library /readingroom/docs/esau-14.pdf.

27. Zhonggong Zhongyang Wenxian Yanjiushi [Chinese Communist Party Central Committee Party Literature Research Office], ed., *Jianguo yilai Mao Zedong wengao* [Mao Zedong's Manuscripts Since the Founding of the State] (Beijing: Zhongyang wenxian chubanshe, 1987–1998), 8:41-43.

28. Zhonggong Zhongyang Wenxian Yanjiushi, *Zhou Enlai nianpu*, 2:371.

29. Telegram, State Foreign Culture Commission and Foreign Ministry to Chinese Embassy in North Korea, November 17, 1960, CFMA 116-00498-07, 51.

30. *Renmin ribao*, January 25 1960; telegram, Qiao Xiaoguang to Foreign Ministry, March 8, 1960; Chinese Embassy in North Korea to Foreign Ministry, March 21, 1961, CFMA 106-00577-04, 60-61, 62-63.

31. Yan Mingfu, "Huiyi liangci Mosike huiyi he Hu Qiaomu" [Recollections on the Two Moscow Conferences and Hu Qiaomu], *Dangdai Zhongguoshi yanjiu* [Contemporary China History Studies] 3 (1997): 14–19; *Yang Shangkun riji* [Yang Shangkun's Diary] (Beijing: Zhongyang wenxian chubanshe, 2001), 1:562, 573-576, 598-599, 616-617; Li and Xia, "Competing for Leadership," 570-572.

32. Report of the Chinese Embassy in North Korea, December 28, 1960, CFMA 106-00579-03, 124-135; January 17, 1961, CFMA 109-03052-06, 8-21.

33. Telegram, Qiao Xiaoguang to Foreign Ministry, April 14, 1961; telegram, Foreign Ministry to Ambassador Qiao, April 16, 1961; Qiao Xiaoguang to Foreign Ministry: North Korean government statement, April 17, 1961, CFMA 106-01361-03, 41-42, 48-49, 51-53.

34. CFMA 109-02090-02, 36-37.

35. Nobuo Shimotomai, "Kim Il-sung's Balancing Act between Moscow and Beijing, 1956-1972," in Tsuyoshi Hasegawa, ed., *The Cold War in East Asia, 1945–1991* (Stanford, CA: Stanford University Press, 2011), 133.

36. Shimotomai, "Kim Il-sung's Balancing Act," 133-34; AVPRF, f. 0102, op. 16, d. 7 ll. 151-171.

37. The Chinese Embassy in Pyongyang reported that, prior to October 1960, North Korea had avoided taking a position in the Sino–Soviet dispute. Thereafter, however, it adopted a much clearer pro-Chinese position. CFMA 109-03052-06, 8-21.

38. CFMA 109-02090-02, 40-41; *Renmin ribao*, December 28, 1960.

39. Shijie Zhishi Chubanshe [World Knowledge Publisher], ed., *Guoji tiaoyue ji, 1945–1947* [Collection of International Treaties, 1945-1947] (Beijing: Shijie zhishi chubanshe, 1959), 212, 439-441; Shijie Zhishi Chubanshe, ed., *Guoji tiaoyue ji,*

1948–1949 [Collection of International Treaties, 1948-1949] (Beijing: Shijie zhi-shi chubanshe, 1959), 35-38, 52-53, 86-89, 167-168.

40. AVPRF, f. 07, op. 23a, p. 18, d. 235, ll. 1-4.

41. V. P. Tkachenko, *Koreiskii poluostrov i interesy Rossii* [The Korean Peninsula and Russian Interests] (Moscow: Izd. firma "Vostochnaia literatura," 2000), 17.

42. Russian State Archive of Socio-Political History, f. 558, op. 11, d. 334, ll. 56, 57; A. M. Ledovskii, "Stalin, Mao Tszedun i koreiskaii voina, 1950-1953 godov" [Stalin, Mao Zedong, and the Korean War, 1950-1953], *Novaia i noveishaia istoriia* [Modern and Contemporary History] 5 (2005): 94-95.

43. "Jianxun" [News in Brief], *Waishi dongtai* [Trends in Foreign Affairs] 97 (1959): 15.

44. Zhonggong Zhongyang Wenxian Yanjiushi, *Jianguo yilai Mao Zedong wengao*, 9:88.

45. Cables and dispatches between the Foreign Ministry in Beijing and its ambassadors in the Democratic People's Republic of Korea (DPRK) and Vietnam on the issue of signing the Treaty of Friendship and Cooperation with Mongolia, March 11–June 3, 1960, CFMA 106-01359-03.

46. Memorandum of conversation between Vice Foreign Minister Luo and North Korean Ambassador Yi Yŏng-ho, May 31, 1960, CFMA 106-01359-01.

47. Tkachenko, *Koreiskii poluostrov i interesy Rossii*, 19-20.

48. Letter, Chinese Embassy in North Korea to the Foreign Ministry and International Liaison Department, June 10, 1961, CFMA 106-00580-01, 2-5; *Renmin ribao*, June 8, 1961. Earlier, on September 14, 1960, Kim Il-sung told the Soviet ambassador that he expected to sign a treaty of friendship, cooperation, and mutual assistance with the Soviet Union during Khrushchev's visit to Korea. He noted that the Korean side "has no objection to the draft treaty." See Puzanov's diary entries from September 12 to September 30, 1960, AVPRF, f. 0102, op. 16, d. 7, ll. 102–129.

49. Tkachenko, *Koreiskii poluostrov i interesy Rossii*, 16-18, cited in Lee, "The Politics of Lips and Teeth," 94.

50. Cable, Qiao Xiaoguang to the Foreign Ministry, June 28, 1961; report, Foreign Ministry to the State Council, July 8, 1961, CFMA 114-00206-01, 1-2, 16-21.

51. Cable, Chinese Embassy in North Korea to the Foreign Ministry, June 29, 1961, CFMA 114-00206, 3-5; July 4, 1961, CFMA 204-00765-03, 27-28.

52. Foreign Ministry to the State Council, July 8, 1961, CFMA 114-00206-01, 16-21.

53. Foreign Ministry propaganda notice on the North Korean government and party delegation's visit to China, July 8, 1961, CFMA 201-00761-05, 54-57. The contents of the Soviet–Korean and Sino–Korean treaties can be found in *Renmin ribao*, July 8, 1961, and July 12, 1961, respectively.

54. Chinese draft and finalized text of the Sino–Korean joint communiqué and explanations, July 14, 1961, CFMA 204-01456-01, 1-8, 13-18.

55. Shimotomai, "Kim Il-sung's Balancing Act," 134-135.

56. Zhonggong Zhongyang Wenxian Yanjiushi, *Zhou Enlai nianpu*, 2:423-424; *Renmin ribao*, July 13, 1961.

57. Lee, "The Politics of Lips and Teeth," 86. Jin Baizhu makes a similar observation, arguing that the Sino–North Korean alliance treaty was an important component of China's 1961 foreign strategy, which sought to delimit boundary lines, stabilize relations with China's neighbors, and assemble supporters in the socialist bloc in terms of the Sino–Soviet confrontation. China took the initiative to propose the signing of the alliance treaty with North Korea. See Jin Baizhu, "Examining the Motives for the Formation of the Sino–Korean Alliance: On the Process of the Formation of the Sino–Korean Alliance" [in Japanese], *Zhongguo yanjiu yuebao* [Chinese Studies Monthly] 64, no. 5 (May 2010): 1-14.

58. Chinese Embassy in North Korea, North Korea's formulations on several major domestic and international issues, CFMA 106-01129-01, 28-37.

59. Chinese Embassy in North Korea to Foreign Ministry, August 3, 1961, CFMA 106-00579-12, 19-21.

60. Chinese Embassy in North Korea to Xinhua News Agency, August 3, 1961, CFMA 106-00578-03, 19-21.

61. Christian F. Ostermann and James F. Person, eds., *The Rise and Fall of Détente on the Korean Peninsula, 1970–1974* (Washington, DC: Woodrow Wilson International Center for Scholars, 2011), 26-35.

62. RGANI f. 5, op. 30, d. 337, ll. 70-72; Shi Lin, ed., *Dangdai Zhongguo de duiwai jingji hezuo* [Contemporary China's Economic Cooperation with Foreign Countries] (Beijing: Zhongguo shehui kexue chubanshe, 1989), 32, 630-632.

63. Nam Hyŏn-Uk, *Chungsoŭi taebugwŏnjo mit muyŏkhyŏnhwang* [Chinese and Soviet Assistance to North Korea and the Status of Trade, 1946–1978] (Seoul: Korea Institute of National Unification, February 1979), 5. Unpublished.

64. CFMA 204-00612-02, 53-97.

65. Chinese Embassy in North Korea to the International Liaison Department and the Foreign Ministry, November 28, 1961, CFMA 109-03023-04, 134-135.

66. CFMA 109-03222-07, 146; Szalontai, "You Have No Political Line of Your Own," 97.

67. Bernd Schaefer, "Weathering the Sino–Soviet Conflict: The GDR and North Korea, 1949-1989," *Cold War International History Project Bulletin* 14-15 (Winter 2003-Spring 2004): 29.

68. Chinese Embassy in North Korea to the Foreign Ministry, January 9, 1962; Trade Counselor's Office, Chinese Embassy, to the Ministry of Foreign Trade, February 1, 1962, CFMA 109-03222-07, 133-136.

69. Minutes of Zhou Enlai's conversation with DPRK vice premier Yi Chu-yŏn, December 13, 1961, CFMA 106-01381-06.

70. Hebei Provincial Archives 907-5-178, 31-33.

71. Minutes of the conversation between Kim Il and Ye Jizhuang, January 7, 1962, CFMA 106-01381-04, 32-35.

72. Minutes, Mao Zedong's meeting with Kim Il-sung, July 13, 1961. At the time, Mao was neither old nor confused. He may have merely been attempting to satisfy Kim Il-sung. Also, neither Mao nor Zhou Enlai believed that Qiao Xiaoguang had made serious mistakes in North Korea. Thus, he was not demoted or punished. On July 22, only a few days after he was recalled from Pyongyang, Qiao

was appointed executive secretary of the Chinese Communist Party (CCP) Committee of the Guangxi Autonomous Region. See Zhonggong Zhongyang Zuzhibu [Chinese Communist Party Central Committee Central Organization Department], ed., *Zhongguo gongchandang zuzhishi ziliao, 1921–1997* [Materials on the Organizational History of the Chinese Communist Party, 1921-1997] (Beijing: Zhonggong dangshi chubanshe, 2000), 5:651.

73. The North Koreans reported that Qiao Xiaoguang was "unfit" for the job. See AVPRF, f. 0102, op. 13, d. 5, ll. 52-55, 147-151.

74. CFMA 106-00577-06, 67-68.

75. Interview with He Zhangming, November 29, 2013, Beijing. He was at that time a counselor at the Chinese Embassy in Pyongyang.

76. CFMA 109-03222-07, 145.

77. CFMA 106-00645-01, 97-98.

78. Szalontai, "You Have No Political Line of Your Own," 96.

79. Telegram from the ministries of Foreign Affairs and Public Security to the Chinese Embassy in North Korea on the illegal border crossings of ethnic Koreans, May 1961, CFMA 118-01026, 82-83.

80. For a comprehensive study of China's policies toward Korean cross-border migration from 1950 to 1962, see Zhihua Shen and Yafeng Xia, "Chinese-North Korean Relations and China's Policy Toward Korean Cross-Border Migration, 1950-1962," *Journal of Cold War Studies* 16, no. 4 (Fall 2014): 1-26.

81. State Council instructions on travel rules between China and North Korea, March 27, 1955, Dalian Municipal Archives 2-2-794, 26.

82. Han Zheshi, ed., *Changbai Chaoxian zizhixian zhi* [Gazetteer of Changbai Korean Autonomous County] (Beijing: Zhonghua shuju, 1993), 302; An Longzhen, *Yanbian Chaoxianzu zizhizhou zhouzhi* [Gazetteer of Yanbian Korean Autonomous Prefecture] (Beijing: Zhonghua shuju, 1996), 545.

83. State Council instructions on the transit system between China and North Korea, March 27, 1955, Dalian Municipal Archives 2-2-794, 25-27.

84. Cable, Chinese Embassy in North Korea to the Foreign Ministry's Consular Department, February 16, 1959, CFMA 118-00806-03, 69-70; Foreign Ministry's Consular Department to the Chinese Embassy in North Korea, November 14, 1960, CFMA 118-01159-20, 27.

85. Han Zheshi, *Changbai Chaoxian zizhixian zhi*, 46, 302-303.

86. "Hungarian Embassy to the DPRK," May 16, 1955, Hungarian Legation Document, 5, doboz, 5/c, 006050/1955, cited in Szalontai, "You Have No Political Line of Your Own," 96. Also see Balázs Szalontai, *Kim Il-sung in the Khrushchev Era: Soviet–DPRK Relations and the Roots of North Korean Despotism, 1953–1964* (Stanford, CA: Stanford University Press, 2006), 121-124.

87. Szalontai, "You Have No Political Line of Your Own," 93. According to the DPRK State Planning Commission, 1.078 million workers and staff had registered in 1958. But in order to accomplish its 1959 plan, 1.517 million workers were needed. Cited in Soviet Ambassador A. M. Puzanov's diary entries from November 6 to December 7, 1959, in AVPRF, f. 0102, op. 14, d. 6, ll. 258–292.

88. The number of Koreans in the Russian Far East reached forty-four thousand in 1915. See Wang Xiaoju, *Eguo dongbu yimin kaifa wenti yanjiu* [Studies on Immigration and Development in Russia's Far East] (Beijing: Zhongguo shehui kexue chubanshe, 2003), 138. There were about 182,300 Koreans living in Russian Siberia in 1939. See Che Zhejiu, "Zhongguo Chaoxianzu de xingcheng jiqi bianhua" [The Formation and Changes in China's Korean Situation], *Yanbian daxue xuebao* [Journal of Yanbian University] 3 (1998): 137-138.

89. A. M. Puzanov's diary entries from April 9 to April 28, 1958, in AVPRF, f. 0102, op. 14, d. 6; minutes of the conversation between M. C. Kapitsa and counselor of the North Korean Embassy in the Soviet Union, June 17, 1958, AVPRF, f. 0102, op. 14, d. 5.

90. Zheng Xinzhe, *Zai Ri Chaoxianren lishi jiqi xianzhuang yanjiu* [Studies on the History and Current Situation of Koreans in Japan] (Beijing: Zhongguo fangzheng chubanshe, 2007), 132-135. Effective propaganda on the part of the DPRK brought many overseas Koreans back to North Korea. But by 1963, when returnees discovered the actual situation in North Korea, the number of returnees dropped dramatically. Tessa Morris-Suzuki reveals the tragic tale of ninety thousand Koreans who returned to North Korea from Japan. Tessa Morris-Suzuki, *Exodus to North Korea: Shadows from Japan's Cold War* (Lanham, MD: Rowman & Littlefield, 2007).

91. Minutes of Mao's conversation with Kim Il-sung, May 21, 1960.

92. Request for instructions and approval, Yan Baohang to Xi Zhongxun, May 12, 1954, CFMA 118-00027-03, 4-5.

93. On assisting sixty-two Korean technical personnel to return to Korea, August 5 to August 13, 1955, CFMA 118-00301-01, 1-20. In accordance with the regulations at the time, it was much more difficult for foreign nationals with technical skills to migrate to other countries.

94. On the illegal migration of Koreans in China and Chinese nationals (meeting records), December 5, 1957, CFMA 118-01026-01, 13-20.

95. A. M. Puzanov's diary entries from January 21 to March 14, 1959, AVPRF, f. 0102, op. 14, d. 6, 11. 26–64.

96. Interior Ministry's internal views on the issue of Chinese men marrying Korean women, October 8, 1958, Hubei Provincial Archives SZ67-01-0540-003.

97. Request for instructions from the Foreign Ministry and the Ministry of Public Security regarding Korean residents illegally crossing the border, March 23, 1962, CFMA 118-011025-02, 1-3.

98. In the early 1960s, thousands of local ethnic minorities in Ili, Xinjiang, fled to the Soviet Union. By late May 1962, the total number reached 61,361, most of whom had been recruited by the Association of Soviet Nationals. This exodus is known as the Tacheng incident in the Ili region (or the "Ita incident"). For an authoritative study, see Li Danhui, "Dui 1962 nian Xinjiang I Ta shijian qiyin de lishi kaocha: Laizi Zhongguo Xinjiang de dang'an cailiao" [A Historical Investigation of the 1962 Ili and Tacheng Incidents in Xinjiang: Archival Materials from Xinjiang], in Li Danhui, ed., *Beijing yu Mosike: Cong lianmeng zouxiang duikang* [Beijing and Moscow:

From Alliance to Confrontation] (Guilin: Guangxi shifan daxue chubanshe, 2002), 480–509. For details on Mao Zedong's determination to break with the Soviet Union, see Danhui Li and Yafeng Xia, *Mao and the Sino–Soviet Split, 1959–1973: A New History* (Lanham, MD: Lexington, 2018), chaps. 1 and 2.

99. Zhonghua Renmin Gongheguo Waijiaobu Tiaoyue Falüsi [Treaty and Law Department of the PRC Ministry of Foreign Affairs], ed., *Zhonghua renmin gong-heguo bianjie shiwu tiaoyue ji: Zhong Chao juan* [Collection on Border Affairs of the People's Republic of China: Volume on China and Korea] (Beijing: Shijie zhishi chubanshe, 2004), 169-186, 195-257.

100. Report by the Party Committee of the Ministry of Public Security on Koreans in China illegally crossing to [North] Korea, May 10, 1961, CFMA 118-01026-03, 69-70.

101. Report of the Ministry of Foreign Affairs and the Ministry of Public Security on Koreans in China illegally crossing to [North] Korea, May 24, 1961, CFMA 118-01026-05, 131-132.

102. Written instructions, Ministry of Foreign Affairs to Qiao Xiaoguang, June 6, 1961, CFMA 118-01026-06, 104.

103. Minutes of Zhou Enlai's conversation with Kim Il-sung, July 11, 1961, CFMA 204-0145-01, 1-12.

104. Report, Chinese Embassy in North Korea to the Foreign Ministry's Consular Department, July 24, 1961, CFMA 118-01026-07, 112-115.

105. Report, Chinese Embassy in North Korea to the Foreign Ministry's Consular Department and the Ministry of Public Security, December 2, 1961, CFMA 118-01026-07, 125-128.

106. Request for instructions from the Foreign Ministry and the Ministry of Public Security on the issue of illegal border crossings of Koreans, March 23, 1962, CFMA 118-01025-02, 1-3.

107. Report, Chinese Embassy in North Korea to the Foreign Ministry's Consular Department, July 24, 1961, CFMA 118-01026-07, 112-115.

108. Letter, Second Asian Department to Consular Department, Foreign Ministry, August 3, 1961; cable, Consular Department of the Foreign Ministry to the Chinese Embassy in North Korea, August 9, 1961, CFMA 118-01026-07, 116, 118-119.

109. Cable, Jilin Provincial CCP Committee to Tonghua Prefectural CCP Committee and copied to the Foreign Ministry, November 25, 1961, CFMA 118-00948-02, 7-9.

110. Request for instructions, Foreign Ministry and Ministry of Public Security on illegal border crossings of Koreans into China, March 23, 1962, CFMA 118-01025-02, 1-3; outline of Gao Shikun's report on illegal border crossings of Korean residents to North Korea, May 10, 1962, CFMA 118-01028-04, 76-85.

111. Cable, Foreign Ministry and Ministry of Public Security to the Chinese Embassy in the DPRK, March 24, 1962, CFMA 118-01025-02, 4-6.

112. *Qingkuang fanyin* [Reflections on the Situation] 6, CFMA 118-01028-01, 98-100; instructions, CCP Central Committee on the handling of the migration of Koreans in the northeast to North Korea, August 8, 1963, CFMA 118-01784-01, 8-9.

113. *Chaoxian zhengqing* [North Korea's Political Situation], CFMA 106-01128-01, 1-10.

114. Although China had begun to pay attention to establishing friendly relations with the developing countries in Asia, Africa, and Latin America, in the early 1960s China still had few allies. It was only after the Sino–Soviet split that China's diplomatic priority was to establish a revolutionary camp among the Third World countries. See Zhou Wan [Jovan Cavoski], "Yu ZhongSu zhengduo disan shijie: 1958–1959 nian Tietuo de Yafei zhixing" [Fomenting Discord Among the Afro-Asian Countries: The Sino–Soviet Alliance and Tito's Trip to the Asian and African Countries, 1958-1959], in Shen Zhihua and Li Bin [Douglas Stiffler], eds., *Cuiruo de lianmeng: Lengzhan yu ZhongSu guanxi* [Fragile Alliance: The Cold War and Sino–Soviet Relations] (Beijing: Shehui kexue wenxian chubanshe, 2010), 266-299.

115. Instructions, CCP Central Committee on the handling of the migration of Koreans in the northeast to North Korea, August 8, 1963, CFMA 118-01784-01, 8-9.

116. Records of conversations between Mao Zedong and the *Rodong sinmun* [Workers' Newspaper] delegation of North Korea, April 26, 1963.

117. For a detailed study of the Sino–Korean border issue during this period, see Zhihua Shen and Yafeng Xia, "Contested Border: A Historical Investigation into the Sino–Korean Border Issue, 1950-1964," *Asian Perspective* 37, no. 1 (January–March 2013): 1-30.

118. Bulletin on the negotiations between the Chinese Embassy in North Korea and the North Korean Foreign Ministry in 1962, CFMA 106-00644-03, 65, 67, 70-71; a record of major events in Sino-North Korean relations, 1961-1962, CFMA 106-00644-01, 19; Zhonggong Zhongyang Wenxian Yanjiushi, *Zhou Enlai nianpu*, 2:468.

119. Provincial Foreign Affairs Office research on historical materials on the Sino–Mongolian and Sino–Korean borders, April 19, 1962, Jiangsu Provincial Archives 3124-01399 (changqi), 5-22.

120. Minutes of Deng Xiaoping's conversation with Han Ik-su, April 30, 1962, CFMA 106-01380-18, 61-66.

121. Zhonggong Zhongyang Wenxian Yanjiushi, *Zhou Enlai nianpu*, 2:481.

122. Memorandum of the conversation between Zhou Enlai and the North Korean Supreme People's Assembly Delegation, June 28, 1962, CFMA 106-01379-03, 35-44; Zhonggong Zhongyang Wenxian Yanjiushi, *Zhou Enlai nianpu*, 2:487.

123. A record of major events in Sino–North Korean relations from 1961 to 1962, CFMA 106-00644-01, 31-33; Zhonggong Zhongyang Wenxian Yanjiushi, *Zhou Enlai nianpu*, 2:502; Liu Shufa, ed., *Chen Yi nianpu* [A Chronology of Chen Yi] (Beijing: Renmin chubanshe, 1995), 2:938.

124. Bulletin, Ministry of Foreign Affairs' dealings with the North Korean Embassy in 1962, CFMA 106-00644-02, 61-63.

125. Memorandum of the conversation among Liu Shaoqi, Zhou Enlai, and Pak Sŏng-ch'ŏl, March 20, 1964, CFMA 109-03909-07, 124-129.

126. M. Taylor Fravel, *Strong Borders, Secure Nation: Cooperation and Conflict in China's Territorial Disputes* (Princeton, NJ: Princeton University Press, 2008), 113.

127. Memorandum of the conversation among Richard Nixon, Henry Kissinger, Zhou Enlai et al., February 23, 1972, 2:00–6:00 P.M., in National Security Archive, "Nixon's Trip to China" (December 11, 2003). http://nsarchive.gwu .edu/NSAEBB/NSAEBB106.

128. Interview with Chen Xiaolu, November 27, 2013, Beijing.

129. Minutes of a conversation between Yao Guang, director general of the Second Asian Department of the Foreign Ministry, and Pak Se-Ch'ang, North Korean ambassador to China, August 21, 1964, CFMA 106-01434-07, 56-58.

130. Minutes of talks between the Chinese and Korean delegations on the Sino–Korean border issue, October 3, 1962, in Jilinsheng geming weiyuanhui waishiwei bangongshi [Foreign Affairs Office, Jilin Provincial Revolutionary Committee], ed., *Collection of Sino–Korean, Sino–Soviet, and Sino–Mongolian Treaties, Agreements, and Protocols,* trans. Northeast Asian History Foundation, internal material, no. 3 (Seoul: Dongbuga Yeoksa Jaedan, 2007), 14-16.

131. Guowuyuan Bangongting Dashiji Bianxiezu [Editorial Committee on the Chronology of the General Office of the State Council], *Zhonghua renmin gongheguo zhongyang renmin zhengfu dashiji* [A Record of Major Events in the Central Government of the People's Republic of China] (1991), 8:169.

132. An Longzhen, *Yanbian Chaoxianzu zizhizhou zhouzhi,* 497; Hongweibing Yanjishi hongse zaofan dajun [Yanji City Red Guard Rebellion Red Army] et al., "On the Treasonable Acts by Zhu Dehai, the Biggest Capitalist Roader in the Yanbian Commission of the CCP," July 24, 1967 (fourth batch of material), 1; "The Resolution by the CCP Yanbian Autonomous Prefecture on the Rehabilitation of Comrade Zhou Dehai," 7, cited in Yi Chong-sŏk, *Pukhan-Chungguk kwan'gye, 1945–2000* [The Sino-North Korean Relationship, 1945-2000] (Seoul: Chungsim, 2000), 233.

133. Zhonghua Renmin Gongheguo Waijiaobu Tiaoyue Falüsi, *Zhonghua renmin gongheguo bianjie shiwu tiaoyue ji: Zhong Chao juan,* 258-261.

134. It has been reported that Zhu Dehai, the chief administrator of the Yanbian Korean Autonomous Prefecture at the time, stated at the March 1963 Standing Committee meeting of the CCP Yanbian Committee: "When I was young, I knew that Changbai Mountain belonged to North Korea. If we did not give them a portion of Changbai Mountain, the North Korean people would curse Kim Il-sung." See Hongweibing Yanjishi hongse zaofan dajun et al., "On the Treasonable Acts by Zhu Dehai," 1.

135. Interview with He Zhangming, November 29, 2013.

136. Kim Il-sung, *Jin Richeng huiyilu: Yu shiji tongxing* [Memoirs of Kim Il-sung: With the Century] (Pingrang: Waiwen chubanshe, 1998), 8:254.

137. Yang Zhaoquan, *Jin Richeng zhuan* [A Biography of Kim Il-sung] (Hong Kong: Yazhou chubanshe, 2010), 1:366–367.

138. Minutes of a conversation between Mao Zedong and the visiting North Korean party and government delegation, October 7, 1964.

139. The slogan "China Is the Center of the World Revolution" was popular in China during the Cultural Revolution.

140. In 1959, China's foreign economic aid totaled 2 billion renminbi, with North Korea and Vietnam each receiving 800 million renminbi. The remaining 400 million renminbi went to Mongolia, Albania, and other small, poor countries. Zhonggong Zhongyang Wenxian Yanjiushi, *Zhou Enlai nianpu*, 2:52.

141. CFMA 204-00003-01, 1-3.

142. Minutes of Mao Zedong's conversation with the North Korean government delegation, December 6, 1958.

143. Li and Xia, *Mao and the Sino–Soviet Split, 1959–1973*, chap. 2.

144. CFMA 109-03158-03, 8-17; 109-03158-04, 18-23; 109-03158-02, 1-6; 109-03158-05, 25-30.

145. Minutes, Mao Zedong's conversation with the delegation from *Rodong sinmun*, April 26, 1963.

146. Li Danhui and Shen Zhihua interview with Zhu Liang, January 2010, Beijing. Zhu Liang was the director of the CCP Central Committee International Liaison Department from 1985 to 1993.

147. Jilin Provincial Archives 1/19-1/243, 2-20, 72.

148. Minutes, Mao Zedong's talks with Kim Il-sung, February 27, 1964.

149. Bo Yibo, *Ruogan zhongda juece yu shijian de huigu* [Recollections on Certain Major Policy Decisions and Events] (Beijing: Zhongyang dangxiao chubanshe, 1991), 2:1200; Zhonggong Zhongyang Wenxian Yanjiushi, *Zhou Enlai nianpu*, 2:643. For detailed studies on the Third Front, see Barry Naughton, "The Third Front: Defence Industrialization in the Chinese Interior," *China Quarterly* 115 (September 1988): 351–386; Lorenz Lüthi, "The Vietnam War and China's Third-Line Defense Planning Before the Cultural Revolution, 1964–1966," *Journal of Cold War Studies* 10, no. 1 (Winter 2008): 6–51.

150. Jin Chongji, ed., *Zhou Enlai zhuan* [A Biography of Zhou Enlai] (Beijing: Renmin chubanshe and Zhongyang wenxian chubanshe, 1998), 4:1769.

151. Wang Zhongchun, "ZhongMei guanxi zhengchanghua jinchengzhong de Sulian yinsu (1969–1979)" [Soviet Factors in Sino–American Normalization, 1969-1979], in Gong Li, William C. Kirby, and Robert S. Ross, eds., *Cong jiedong zuoxiang jianjiao: ZhongMei guanxi zhengchanghua jincheng zai tantao, 1969–1979* [From the Thaw to Normalization: Sino–American Relations, 1969-1979] (Beijing: Zhongyang wenxian chubanshe, 2004), 195.

152. CFMA 106-00767-01, 1-13.

153. CFMA 204-01267-05, 24-27.

154. CFMA 106-00719-09, 4-5.

155. CFMA 106-00719-09, 16, 18-21.

156. Li Danhui and Shen Zhihua interview with Zhu Liang, January 2010; CFMA 106-01128-03, 152.

157. CFMA 106-01129-09, 93-96.

158. Kim Il-sung, *Works* (Pyongyang: Foreign Languages Publishing House, 1984), 16:140-143.

159. "Report, Embassy of Hungary in North Korea to the Hungarian Foreign Ministry, April 5, 1962," *Cold War International History Project Bulletin* 14-15 (Winter 2003-Spring 2004): 124.

160. CFMA 106-00718-01, 39-44.

161. CFMA 106-00720-08, 14-15.

162. Wu Lengxi, *Shinian lunzhan: 1956–1966 Zhong Su guanxi huiyilu* [Ten Years of Polemics: Recollections of Sino–Soviet Relations, 1956–1966] (Beijing: Zhongyang wenxian chubanshe, 1999), 2:571-573; Mao Zedong's conversations with Kim Il-sung, May 29 and 30, 1963.

163. CFMA 204-01267-05, 7-10.

164. CFMA 106-01129-06, 71-81.

165. Jiangsu Provincial Archives 3124-0177 (changqi), 92-113.

166. CFMA 203-00566-02, 139-140.

167. CFMA 203-00566-02, 137-142.

168. CFMA 117-01164-01, 1-13.

169. CFMA 106-01435-02, 24-31.

170. CFMA 106-014334-03, 28-34.

171. "Note About a Conversation with the Ambassador of Czechoslovakia to the DPRK, Comrade Moravec," January 7, 1963, Wilson Center Digital Archive. http://digitalarchive.wilsoncenter.org/document/110521. Translation modified.

172. German Democratic Republic Foreign Ministry, Extra-European Department, Korea Section, "The Influence of the Chinese Communist Party on the Politics of the KWP," August 4, 1963; German Democratic Republic Embassy in the Democratic People's Republic of Korea, "Your Information on the Influence of the Chinese Communist Party on the Politics of the KWP," May 28, 1963, German Democratic Republic Ministry for Foreign Affairs A 7174.

VI. The Lowest Ebb, 1966–1969

1. Donald S. Zagoria, "North Korea: Between Moscow and Beijing," in *North Korea Today: Strategic and Domestic Issues*, ed. Robert A. Scalapino and Jun-Yop Kim (Berkeley: Institute for East Asian Studies, University of California, 1983), 357.

2. Chin-Wee Chung, "North Korea's Relations with China," in *The Foreign Relations of North Korea: New Perspectives*, ed. Jae Kyu Park, Byung Chul Koh, and Tae-Hwan Kwak (Boulder: Westview, 1987), 176–177.

3. Bernd Schaefer, "North Korean 'Adventurism' and China's Long Shadow, 1966-1972," *Cold War International History Project Working Paper* 44 (October 2004): 2–3. Also see Nobuo Shimotomai, "Kim Il-sung's Balancing Act Between Moscow and Beijing, 1956–1972," in *The Cold War in East Asia, 1945–1991*, ed. Tsuyoshi Hasegawa (Stanford, CA: Stanford University Press, 2011), 122–151.

4. Dong Ji, "Wenhua dageming qianqi ZhongChao guanxi de lishi kaocha, 1966–1970" [A Historical Investigation into Sino–North Korean Relations During the Early Phase of the Cultural Revolution, 1966–1970], *Lengzhan guojishi yanjiu* [Cold War International History Studies] 2 (2014): 78–97.

5. See Cheng Xiaohe, "The Evolution of the Lips and Teeth Relationship: China–North Korea Relations in the 1960s," in *China and North Korea: Strategic and Policy Perspectives from a Changing China*, ed. Carla Freeman (New York: Palgrave Macmillan, 2015), 129; Cheng Xiaohe, "The Evolution of Sino-North Korean Relations in the 1960s," *Asian Perspective* 34, no. 2 (2010): 173–199.

6. Schaefer, "North Korean 'Adventurism' and China's Long Shadow," 5–6.

7. Central Intelligence Agency, *China's Growing Isolation in the Communist Movement*, Current Intelligence Weekly Special Report, August 5, 1966, Digital National Security Archive, U.S. Intelligence and China: Collection, Analysis, and Covert Action, CI01760.

8. Report on the issue of fixing farm output quotas for cooperative brigades implemented in certain areas of North Korea, July 17, 1964, Chinese Foreign Ministry Archives (CFMA) 106-01132-05, 152–154; report on the issue of distributing the means of production in Kangwŏn province, July 19, 1964, CFMA 106-00760-02, 24–27.

9. Report, Embassy of Hungary in North Korea to the Hungarian Foreign Ministry, May 22, 1965, Magyar Országos Levéltár [Hungarian National Archives, Budapest], trans. Balázs Szalontai, XIX-J-1-j Korea, 1965, 73. doboz, IV-50, 001822/1/1965.

10. Central Intelligence Agency, *The Sino–Soviet Struggle in the World Communist Movement Since Khrushchev's Fall*, part 1, September 1967, Intelligence Report ESAU 34, 36–37. https://archive.org/stream/ESAU-CIA/The%20Sino-Soviet %20Struggle%20in%20the%20World%20Communist%20Movement%20Since %20Khrushchev's%20Fall%20(Part%201)_djvu.txt.

11. Minutes, Mao Zedong and Kim Il-sung conversation, November 8, 1964.

12. *Rodong sinmun* [Workers' Newspaper], December 3, 1964.

13. For a detailed discussion of this issue, see Danhui Li and Yafeng Xia, *Mao and the Sino-Soviet Split, 1959–1973: A New History* (Lanham, MD: Lexington, 2018), chap. 5.

14. Central Intelligence Agency, *The Sino–Soviet Struggle*, part 1, 38.

15. Chin W. Chung, *P'yŏngyang Between Peking and Moscow: North Korea's Involvement in the Sino–Soviet Dispute, 1958–1975* (Tuscaloosa: University of Alabama Press, 1978), 113.

16. Russian State Archive of Contemporary History (RGANI), f. 5, op. 30, d. 479, l. 79.

17. S. L. Tikhvinskii et al., *Otnosheniia Sovetskogo Soiuza s naradnoi Koreei 1945–1980: Dokumenty i materialy* [USSR Relations with People's Korea, 1945-1980: Documents and Materials] (Moscow: Nauka, 1981), 240–245.

18. South Korean Diplomatic Archives D-0009-44, 4–5.

19. RGANI, f. 5, op. 61, d. 463, ll. 21–23.

20. See Donald S. Zagoria and Young Kun Kim, "North Korea and the Major Powers," in *The Two Koreas in East Asian Affairs*, ed. William J. Barnds (New York: New York University Press, 1976), 46.

21. Central Intelligence Agency, *Kim Il-sung's New Military Adventurism*, November 26, 1968, Intelligence Report ESAU 41, 3–4, 9. https://www.cia.gov/library /readingroom/docs/esau-39.pdf.

22. Central Intelligence Agency, *The Sino–Soviet Struggle in the World Communist Movement Since Khrushchev's Fall*, part 3, September 1967, Intelligence Report ESAU 36, 25–26, https://archive.org/stream/ESAU-CIA/The%20Sino-Soviet%20Struggle%20in%20the%20World%20Communist%20Movement%20Since%20Khrushchev's%20Fall%20(Part%203)_djvu.txt; record of conversation with the Minister of Foreign Affairs of the Democratic People's Republic of Korea (DPRK) Comrade Pak Sŏng-ch'ŏl, Archive of Foreign Policy of the Russian Federation, f. 0102, op. 22, p. 107, d. 4, ll. 1–5, cited in the Cold War International History Project Digital Archive.

23. Central Intelligence Agency, *China's Growing Isolation in the Communist Movement*, 4; Central Intelligence Agency, *The Sino–Soviet Struggle in the World Communist Movement Since Khrushchev's Fall*, part 2, September 1967, Intelligence Report ESAU 35, 106. https://archive.org/stream/ESAU-CIA.

24. Schaefer, "North Korean 'Adventurism' and China's Long Shadow," 9.

25. Central Intelligence Agency, *Kim Il-sung's New Military Adventurism*, 3; memorandum on Sino–Korean relations in 1966, Soviet Embassy in the DPRK, December 2, 1966, no. 312, in James F. Person, ed., "Limits of the 'Lips and Teeth' Alliance: New Evidence on Sino–DPRK Relations, 1955-1984," *North Korea International Documentation Project Document Reader* 2 (March 2009): 27.

26. Balázs Szalontai, "In the Shadow of Vietnam: A New Look at North Korea's Militant Strategy, 1962–1970," *Journal of Cold War Studies* 14, no. 4 (Fall 2012): 157; Szalontai, "Whose War Plan Was It? Sino–DPRK Relations and Kim Il-sung's Militant Strategy, 1965–1967," North Korea International Documentation Project, e-Dossier 20 (April 2016). https://www.wilsoncenter.org/publication/sino-dprk-relations-and-kim-il-sungs-militant-strategy-1965-1967.

27. Szalontai, "In the Shadow of Vietnam," 157.

28. See Merle Pribbenow, "North Korean Pilots in the Skies over Vietnam," North Korea International Documentation Project (December 1, 2011). https://www.wilsoncenter.org/publication/north-korean-pilots-the-skies-over-vietnam.

29. Central Intelligence Agency, *The Sino–Soviet Struggle*, part 2, 107.

30. Central Intelligence Agency, *The Sino–Soviet Struggle*, part 2, 111; Chung, *P'yongyang Between Peking and Moscow*, 132.

31. Schaefer, "North Korean 'Adventurism' and China's Long Shadow," 5–6.

32. Liu Jinzhi, Zhang Minqiu, and Zhang Xiaoming, eds., *Dangdai Zhong Han guanxi* [Contemporary China–Republic of Korea Relations] (Beijing: Zhongguo shehui kexue chubanshe, 1998), 43.

33. "Telegram from Pyongyang to Bucharest, no. 76.171, Top Secret, May 20, 1967," North Korea International Documentation Project, Romanian Documents.

34. Socialist Unity Party of Germany Central Committee, Department of International Relations, April 23, 1968, memorandum on the visit of the party and government delegation of the German Democratic Republic (GDR), led by Comrade Prof. Dr. Kurt Hager, with the general secretary of the Korean Workers' Party and prime minister of the DPRK, Comrade Kim Il-sung, on April 16, 1968, Ministerium für Auswärtige Angelegenheiten [Files of the Ministry for

Foreign Affairs, Berlin] C 159/75, cited in Schaefer, "North Korean 'Adventurism' and China's Long Shadow," 67.

35. Liu Jinzhi, Zhang Minqiu, and Zhang Xiaoming, *Dangdai Zhong Han guanxi*, 43. For instance, a search of the keywords "North Korea" and "Kim Il-sung" in *Renmin ribao* reveals more than 350 items in 1965, 96 items in 1966, 12 items in 1967, 22 items in 1968 (mainly on the *Pueblo* incident), 17 items in 1969, and more than 400 items in 1970, when Sino–North Korean relations began to improve.

36. "Telegram from Pyongyang to Bucharest, no. 76.171."

37. "Telegram from Pyongyang to Bucharest, no. 76.171."

38. *Renmin ribao*, September 10, 1966.

39. *Guoji gongyun cankao ziliao* [Reference Materials on the International Communist Movement], March 8, 1967, 20–21.

40. Beijing Shifan Xueyuan *Douzheng Shenghuo* Bianjibu [Beijing Teachers' College *Life of Struggle* Editorial Board], ed., *Wuchan jieji wenhua dageming ziliao huibian* [Collection of Documents on the Great Proletarian Cultural Revolution] (December 1966), 409.

41. Hongdaihui Sanzhong Linshi Geming Weiyuanhui Zongbu Jinggangshan Tongxunshe [The Provisional Revolutionary Committee of the Third Congress of the Red Guard Red Flag Headquarters of Jinggang Mountains News Agency], ed., *Qingfeng* [Green Mountain Peak] 30 (November 2, 1967).

42. Hongdaihui Sanzhong Linshi Geming Weiyuanhui Zongbu Jinggangshan Tongxunshe, ed., *Qingfeng* 29 (October 19, 1967).

43. Song Yongyi, ed., *Zhongguo wenhua dageming wenku* [Chinese Cultural Revolution Database] (Hong Kong: Chinese University Press, 2002).

44. Memorandum of the GDR party and government delegation and the North Korean party and government delegation, April 12, 1968, Foundation Archives of Parties and Mass Organizations of the German Democratic Republic in the Federal Archives, DY 30/11493.

45. Report on a conversation between N. G. Sudarikov and Kim Il-sung, December 14, 1968, RGANI, f. 5, op. 61, d. 463, ll. 48-62; report about changes in the views of the DPRK regarding the socialist bloc and the International Communist Movement, June 9, 1969, and report on a conversation between N. G. Sudarikov and Kim Il-sung, April 14, 1969, RGANI, f. 5, op. 61, d. 462, ll. 79–94, 95–101.

46. Report on a conversation between N. G. Sudarikov and Kim Il-sung, April 14, 1969, RGANI, f. 5, op. 61, d. 462, ll. 95–101.

47. "Report on the Official Friendship Visit to the DPRK by the Party and State Delegation of the GDR, Led by Com. Erich Honecker, 8-11 December 1977," *Cold War International History Project Bulletin* 14–15 (Winter 2003–Spring 2004): 31. In July 1973, Kim Il-sung repeated the following to a visiting Polish party delegation, "The PRC [People's Republic of China] applied pressure on the DPRK but we did not bend. They called us revisionists. Along the border the Chinese installed loudspeakers calling on our people to abandon the revisionist regime of Kim Il-sung." See "On the Visit of a PRP [People's Republic of Poland] Party and Parliamentary Delegation to the DPRK," GDR Embassy in Warsaw Information Report, document 22, in Person, "Limits of the 'Lips and Teeth' Alliance," 56.

48. Central Intelligence Agency, *The Sino–Soviet Struggle*, part 2, 115.
49. Central Intelligence Agency, *Kim Il-sung's New Military Adventurism*, 17.
50. Central Intelligence Agency, *Kim Il-sung's New Military Adventurism*, 17-18.
51. "Telegram from Pyongyang to Bucharest, no. 76.084, Top Secret, March 7, 1967," North Korea International Documentation Project, Romanian Documents.
52. Ma Jisen, *Waijiaobu wenge jishi* [The Cultural Revolution in the Foreign Ministry] (Hong Kong: Chinese University Press, 2003), 285.
53. *Guangdong wenge tongxun* [Newsletter of the Cultural Revolution in Guangdong], February 15, 1968, cited in Robert Scalapino and Chong-Sik Lee, *Communism in Korea* (Berkeley: University of California Press, 1972), 1:641.
54. Zhao Fengbin, *Wode rensheng zishu: Yige Chaoxianzu jiazu bianqian shilu* [An Account of My Life in My Own Words: A Record of Changes in a Korean Family] (Beijing: Minzu chubanshe, 2010); Hebei Provincial Archives 1057-2-8, 1-4; Wen Xingfu, "Yanbian pingfan sida yuan'an" [Redressing Four Important Unjust Cases in Yanbian], *Yanbian wenshi ziliao* [Yanbian Historical Accounts] 17 (2012): 236-272.
55. Schaefer, "North Korean 'Adventurism' and China's Long Shadow," 10.
56. On Albania's support of the Cultural Revolution, see Fan Chengzuo, *Wangshi rushi: Fan Chengzuo huiyilu* [The Past Is Like a Poem: Memoirs of Fan Chengzuo] (Nanjing: Nanjing chubanshe, 2008), 237; Fan Chengzuo, "Aerbaniya zhichi Zhongguo 'Wenhua dageming' shimo" [The Full Story of Albania's Support of the Chinese "Cultural Revolution"], *Zhonggong dangshi ziliao* [Materials on the History of the Chinese Communist Party] 4 (2004): 142-151; and Ana Lalaj, Christian F. Ostermann, and Ryan Gage, eds., " 'Albania Is Not Cuba': Sino–Albanian Summits and the Sino–Soviet Split," document no. 15, *Cold War International History Project Bulletin* 16 (Fall 2007-Winter 2008): 311-328.
57. Zhonggong Zhongyang Wenxian Yanjiushi [Chinese Communist Party Central Committee Literature Research Office], ed., *Zhou Enlai nianpu, 1949–1976* [A Chronology of Zhou Enlai, 1949-1976] (Beijing: Zhongyang wenxian chubanshe, 1997), 3:195-196.
58. Zhonggong Zhongyang Wenxian Yanjiushi, *Zhou Enlai nianpu, 1949–1976*, 3:196; Ma Jisen, *Waijiaobu wenge jishi*, 85-86.
59. Memorandum of conversations between Liu Shaoqi, Zhou Enlai, and Pak Sŏng-ch'ŏl, March 24, 1964, CFMA 1109-03909-07, 124-129.
60. Memorandum of a conversation between Zhou Enlai and the DPRK's ambassador to Beijing, April 28, 1964, CFMA 106-01434-03, 28-34.
61. Minutes of a conversation between Fang Yi and Kim Il-sung, September 5, 1964, CFMA 106-00767-01, 1-13.
62. Li Qiang to Zhou Enlai, December 20, 1965, CFMA 106-01477-02, 11-12; excerpts of minutes of a conversation between Kim Il-sung and Li Xiannian, December 26, 1965, CFMA 106-01477-04, 26-50.
63. CFMA 106-01230-02, 46-51; CFMA 106-01480-05, 46-49.
64. Lalaj, Ostermann, and Gage, "Albania Is Not Cuba," 320.

65. Bernd Schaefer, "Weathering the Sino–Soviet Conflict: The GDR and North Korea, 1949-1989," *Cold War International History Project Bulletin* 14–15 (Winter 2003–Spring 2004): 31.

66. Report on Sino–North Korean relations, April 25, 1969, RGANI, f. 5, op. 61, d. 466, ll. 96-99.

67. *Renmin ribao*, July 31, 1966; December 4, 1966, 5; November 27, 1967, 6; March 6, 1968, 4; January 25, 1969, 5; Weishengbu Guojisi [International Department, Ministry of Health], ed., *Weishengbu hezuo xieyi huibian, 1957–2001* [Collection of Health Cooperation Agreements, 1957-2001] (May 2002), 118-119. Unpublished.

68. "North Korean Foreign Trade," January 26, 1968, CIA Records Search Tool, document no. CIA-RDP85T00875R001500220012-5, National Archives and Records Administration, College Park, Maryland. We wish to thank Charles Kraus for sharing this document.

69. Shen Jueren, *Dangdai Zhongguo duiwai maoyi* [Contemporary China's Foreign Trade] (Beijing: Dangdai Zhongguo chubanshe, 1992), 1:262, 301–302; 2:371.

70. Comrade Jarck on current relations between the DPRK and the People's Republic of China, March 3, 1968, Political Archives of the German Foreign Ministry, Ministerium für Auswärtige Angelegenheiten [Files of the Ministry for Foreign Affairs, Berlin], G-A 344. Cited in Christian F. Ostermann and James F. Person, eds., *Crisis and Confrontation on the Korean Peninsula, 1968–1969: A Critical Oral History* (Washington, DC: Woodrow Wilson International Center for Scholars, 2011), 220. https://www.wilsoncenter.org/sites/default/files/NKIDP_Crisis_and_Confrontation_on_the_Korean_Peninsula_1968_1969.pdf.

71. Circular on guaranteeing the export of granulated sugar to North Korea, from the Ministry of Foreign Trade and the First Ministry of Light Industry, Hebei Provincial Archives 965-4-482, 28-30.

72. "Telegram from Pyongyang to Bucharest, no. 76.208, Top Secret, June 15, 1967," North Korea International Documentation Project, Romanian Documents.

73. "Haohua de Pingrang ditie shi Zhongguo zhantingle Beijing ditie yuanjiande" [China Had to Suspend Construction of the Subway in Beijing in Order to Help Build the Luxurious Pyongyang Subway], http://blog.sina.com.cn/s/blog_55d803000101d670.html [in Chinese].

74. "Telegram from Pyongyang to Bucharest, no. 76.208."

75. Byung Chul Koh, *The Foreign Policy of North Korea* (New York: Praeger, 1969), 102.

76. Comrade Jarck on current relations between the DPRK and the People's Republic of China, in Ostermann and Person, *Crisis and Confrontation on the Korean Peninsula*, 220.

77. During the nine-month period from May 1967 to January 1968, there were more than three hundred reported hostile acts, resulting in fifteen U.S. soldiers dead and sixty-five wounded. See Department of Defense, *Report of the 1971 Quadrennial Review of Military Compensation* (Washington, DC: Manpower and Reserve Affairs, March 17, 1972), 45. For recent studies on these issues, see Schaefer, "North Korean 'Adventurism' and China's Long Shadow"; and Mitchell

Lerner, " 'Mostly Propaganda in Nature': Kim Il-sung, the *Juche* Ideology, and the Second Korean War," *North Korea International Documentation Project Working Paper* 3 (December 2010).

78. *Renmin ribao*, January 29, 1968.

79. Comrade Jarck on current relations between the DPRK and the PRC, in Ostermann and Person, *Crisis and Confrontation on the Korean Peninsula*, 220.

80. "Telegram from Pyongyang to Bucharest, Top Secret, no. 76.054, Urgent," March 1, 1968, Wilson Center Digital Archive. http://digitalarchive.wilson center.org/document/113965.

81. "Telegram from Pyongyang to Bucharest, Top Secret, no. 76.069, Urgent," March 17, 1968," Wilson Center Digital Archive. http://digitalarchive.wilson center.org/document/113968.

82. See Lerner, "Mostly Propaganda in Nature," 5-10.

83. Report on Sino–Korean relations, April 25, 1969, RGANI, f. 5, op. 61, d. 466, ll. 96-99.

84. Report on the relations between the DPRK and the PRC from Chargé d'Affaires Apostol Apostolov in Pyongyang to the Foreign Ministry, July 29, 1969, Archives of the Bulgarian Foreign Ministry, Opis 20p, delo 17, no. 289. See also Schaefer, "North Korean 'Adventurism' and China's Long Shadow," 15.

85. Schaefer, "North Korean 'Adventurism' and China's Long Shadow," 7.

86. Archive of Foreign Policy of the Russian Federation, f. 0102, op. 23, p. 112, d. 24, ll. 5-12.

87. Report on relations between the DPRK and the PRC from Chargé d'Affaires Apostol Apostolov.

88. Interview with Kim Ch'ung-sik, February 17, 2010, and February 2011; Shaanxi Provincial Archives 196-1-340, 68-72, 87, 140–141.

89. Shaanxi Provincial Archives 196-1-340, 88–93, 24–25.

90. Schaefer, "North Korean 'Adventurism' and China's Long Shadow," 16.

91. Report on relations between the DPRK and the PRC by Chargé d'Affaires Apostol Apostolov.

92. Report on a conversation between N. G. Sudarikov and Kim Il-sung, March 17, 1969, RGANI, f. 5, op. 61, d. 463, ll. 120–129.

93. Memorandum on the conversation between Kim Il-sung and Todor Zhivkov, October 30, 1973, Wilson Center Digital Archive. http://digitalarchive .wilsoncenter.org/document/114533.

94. Memorandum of conversation between Erich Honecker and Kim Il-sung, May 31, 1984, in Person, "Limits of the 'Lips and Teeth' Alliance," 66.

95. On many occasions, Kim Il-sung spoke with Soviet leaders about his worries with regard to Chinese actions during the Cultural Revolution. See report on conversation between N. G. Sudarikov and Kim Il-sung, March 17, 1969; report on conversation between N. G. Sudarikov and Kim Il-sung, April 14, 1969; report on Sino–Korean relations, April 25, 1969; and *Domestic Situation and International Politics of the DPRK*, November 18, 1969, RGANI, f. 5, op. 61, d. 463, ll. 120-129; d. 462, ll. 95-101; d. 466, ll. 96-99, 246-264.

96. Zhengxie Yanbian Chaoxianzu Zizhizhou Weiyuanhui Wenshi Ziliao yu Xuexi Xuanchuan Weiyuanhui [Historical Data Committee and Propaganda Committee of the Chinese People's Political Consultative Conference of Yanbian Korean Autonomous Prefecture], *Nanwang de suiyue: Shanghai ernü zai Yanbian* [Unforgettable Years: Shanghai's Sons and Daughters in Yanbian] (Shenyang: Liaoning minzu chubanshe, 2007), 207–208. Interview with Lin Yonghai, October 16, 2011, in Shanghai. Lin, an educated youth from Shanghai who was living in Yanbian, later became deputy chairman of the Tumen Municipal Political Consultative Conference. Interview with Zhang Liankui, November 16, 2011. At the time of these incidents, Zhang was working for the Tumen Municipal Public Security Bureau.

97. Dangdai Zhongguo Congshu Bianjibu [Editorial Department of the Contemporary China Series], ed., *Dangdai Zhongguo waijiao* [Contemporary Chinese Diplomacy] (Beijing: Zhongguo shehui kexue chubanshe, 1988), 212.

98. All Chinese ambassadors, with the exception of Huang Hua in Egypt, were recalled to China to take part in the Cultural Revolution. See Ma Jisen, *Waijiaobu wenge jishi*, 289.

99. "Memorandum from the President's Assistant for National Security Affairs (Kissinger) to President Nixon, Washington, April 29, 1969," U.S. Department of State, Office of the Historian, *Foreign Relations of the United States, 1969–1976*, vol. 17, *China, 1969–1972* (Washington, DC: Government Printing Office, 2006), 29.

100. "Response to National Security Study Memorandum 14, Washington, August 8, 1969," U.S. Department of State, Office of the Historian, *Foreign Relations of the United States, 1969–1976*, 17:60.

101. S. Kondrashow, "Dangerous Adventure of Washington," *Izevestia*, January 28, 1968.

102. Zagoria, "North Korea: Between Moscow and Beijing," 358.

103. South Korean Diplomatic Archives, D-0009-44, 4-5.

104. Kim Hak-chun, *Pukhan 50-yŏnsa: Uri ka ttŏ anayhal pantchok ŭi uri yŏksa* [A Fifty-Year History of North Korea] (Seoul: Tonga Ch'ulp'ansa, 1995), 180; Yi Chong-sŏk, *Pukhan-Chungguk kwan'gye, 1945–2000* [The Sino-North Korean Relationship, 1945-2000] (Seoul: Chungsim, 2000), 120.

105. Chung, "North Korea's Relations with China," 179-180.

106. Zhonggong Zhongyang Wenxian Yanjiushi, *Zhou Enlai nianpu, 1949–1976*, 3:320; Zhonghua Renmin Gongheguo Waijiaobu Waijiaoshi Yanjiushi [Diplomatic History Research Office of the People's Republic of China Ministry of Foreign Affairs], *Zhou Enlai waijiao huodong dashiji, 1949–1975* [A Chronology of Zhou Enlai's Diplomatic Activities, 1949-1975] (Beijing: Shijie zhishi chubanshe, 1993), 539-540; Wang Taiping, ed., *Zhonghua renmin gongheguo waijiaoshi, 1970–1978* [A Diplomatic History of the People's Republic of China, 1970-1978] (Beijing: Shijie zhishi chubanshe, 1999), 36.

107. "On the Visit of a PRP Party and Parliamentary Delegation to the DPRK," in Person, "Limits of the 'Lips and Teeth' Alliance," 56.

108. Report on a conversation between Kim Il-sung and N. M. Shubnikov, September 19, 1969, RGANI, f. 5, op. 61, d. 434, ll. 35–37.

109. Wang Taiping, *Zhonghua renmin gongheguo waijiaoshi, 1970–1978*, 36-37; "Brief Summary of Conversation Between Comrades Zhou Enlai and Kang Sheng on 16 June 1970 with Myself (Kadri Hazbiu) and Cmrade [sic] Xhoxhi Robo," June 16, 1970, Wilson Center Digital Archive. http://digitalarchive.wilson center.org/document/117305.
110. Wang Taiping, *Zhonghua renmin gongheguo waijiaoshi, 1970–1978*, 37.
111. Records of Mao Zedong's conversation with Ch'oe Yong-gŏn, chairman of the Presidium of the Supreme People's Assembly of the DPRK, in Zhonghua Renmin Gongheguo Waijiaobu [People's Republic of China Ministry of Foreign Affairs], ed., *Mao Zedong jiejian waibin tanhua jilu huibian* [Collection of Records of Mao Zedong's Conversations with Foreign Guests], 13:189-194. Unpublished.

VII. China's Last Ally, 1970–1976

1. William C. Kirby, Robert Ross, and Gong Li, eds., *Normalization of U.S.– China Relations: An International History* (Cambridge, MA: Harvard University Asia Center, 2005); Kazuhiko Togo, "Japan's Foreign Policy Under Détente: Relations with China and the Soviet Union, 1971-1973," in *The Cold War in East Asia, 1945–1991*, ed. Tsuyoshi Hasegawa (Stanford, CA: Stanford University Press, 2011), 180–212; Yafeng Xia, "Vietnam for Taiwan? A Reappraisal of Nixon-Zhou Enlai Negotiations on [sic] Shanghai Communiqué," *American Review of China Studies* 3, no. 1 (Spring 2002): 35–55; Yafeng Xia, "The Taiwan Issue in Sino–American Rapprochement Negotiations," in *Taiwan in the 21st Century*, ed. Xiaobing Li and Zuohong Pan (Lanham, MD: University Press of America, 2003), 281–317.
2. Bernd Schaefer and Gregg Brazinsky study this issue from the perspective of North and South Korean relations. See Bernd Schaefer, "Overconfidence Shattered: North Korean Unification Policy, 1971–1975," *North Korea International Documentation Project Working Paper* 2 (December 2010); Gregg Brazinsky, "Korea's Great Divergence: North and South Korea between 1972 and 1987," in Hasegawa, *The Cold War in East Asia*, 241–264.
3. Chris Tudda, *A Cold War Turning Point: Nixon and China, 1969–1972* (Baton Rouge: Louisiana State University Press, 2012).
4. Gregg Brazinsky, "Between Ideology and Strategy: China's Security Policy Toward the Korean Peninsula Since Rapprochement," in *Trilateralism and Beyond: Great Power Politics and the Korean Security Dilemma During and After the Cold War*, ed. Robert Wampler (Kent, OH: Kent State University Press, 2011), 166–171.
5. Li Danhui, "ZhongMei huanhe yu yuanYue kangMei: Zhongguo waijiao zhanlüe tiaozheng zhong de Yuenan yinsu" [The Sino–American Rapprochement and the War to Aid Vietnam and Resist America: The Vietnam Factor in China's Diplomatic Strategic Adjustment], *Dangde wenxian* [Party Literature] 3 (2002): 67-77; Li Danhui, "Vietnam and Chinese Policy Toward the United States," in Kirby, Ross, and Gong, *Normalization of U.S.–China Relations*, 175-208.

6. Henry Kissinger, *The White House Years* (Boston, MA: Little, Brown, 1979), 183; Henry Kissinger, *On China* (New York: Penguin Press, 2011), 219.

7. Mao Zedong had first asked the four marshals to study international issues on February 19, 1969. On the afternoon of March 1, 1969, the marshals held their first meeting in the Zhongnanhai leadership compound. See Chen Yi Zhuan Bianxiezu [Chen Yi Biography Editorial Committee], *Chen Yi zhuan* [A Biography of Chen Yi] (Beijing: Dangdai Zhongguo chubanshe, 1997), 614; Pang Xianzhi and Feng Hui, eds., *Mao Zedong nianpu, 1949–1976* [A Chronology of Mao Zedong, 1949-1976] (Beijing: Zhongyang wenxian chubanshe, 2013), 6:229–230.

8. Xiong Xianghui, *Wo de qingbao yu waijiao shengya* [My Careers in Intelligence and Diplomacy], 2nd. ed. (Beijing: Zhonggong dangshi chubanshe, 2006), 178–179.

9. Xiong Xianghui, *Wo de qingbao yu waijiao shengya*, 198–200.

10. For a discussion of the war scare in Beijing in 1969, see Kuisong Yang, "The Sino–Soviet Border Clash of 1969: From Zhenbao Island to Sino–American Rapprochement," *Cold War History* 1, no. 1 (August 2000): 35–37; Yafeng Xia, *Negotiating with the Enemy: U.S.–China Talks During the Cold War, 1949–1972* (Bloomington: Indiana University Press, 2006), 138–139.

11. Gao Wenqian, *Wannian Zhou Enlai* [Zhou Enlai's Later Years] (Hong Kong: Mingjing chubanshe, 2003), 419–420; Zhonggong Zhongyang Wenxian Yan-jiushi [Chinese Communist Party Central Committee Party Literature Research Office], ed., *Zhou Enlai nianpu, 1949–1976* [A Chronology of Zhou Enlai, 1949–1976] (Beijing: Zhongyang wenxian chubanshe, 1997), 3:357, 360.

12. Zhonggong Zhongyang Wenxian Yanjiushi, *Zhou Enlai nianpu, 1949–1976*, 3:400.

13. Yi Chong-sŏk, *Pukhan-Chungguk kwan'gye, 1945–2000* [The Sino–North Korean Relationship, 1945–2000] (Seoul: Chungsim, 2000), 252–253.

14. Xia, *Negotiating with the Enemy*, 136–159.

15. Xia, *Negotiating with the Enemy*, 167–173; Kissinger, *On China*, 239–240.

16. "Memorandum of Conversation (Between Kissinger and Zhou Enlai), Beijing, July 9, 1971," in U.S. Department of State, Office of the Historian, *Foreign Relations of the United States [FRUS], 1969–1976, Richard M. Nixon/Gerald R. Ford*, vol. 17, *China, 1969–1972* (Washington, DC: Government Printing Office, 2006), 388–389.

17. *FRUS*, 17:390–391.

18. National Security Decision Memorandum 48, March 20, 1970. https://fas.org/irp/offdocs/nsdm-nixon/nsdm-48.pdf.

19. "Memorandum for Kissinger," August 6, 1971, China, HAK Memcons, box 1033, National Security Council (NSC) files, Nixon Presidential Materials Project (NPMP), National Archives (NA); "Memorandum for the President from Kissinger," July 14, 1971, miscellaneous memoranda relating to Kissinger trip to the People's Republic of China (PRC), July 1971, box 1033, NSC files, 13, 18; "Memorandum of Conversation: Kissinger and Chou En-lai [Zhou Enlai], July 11, 1971," in *FRUS*, 17:449–450.

20. Li Danhui, "Dakai ZhongMei guanxi jincheng zhong de Zhou Enlai" [Zhou Enlai in the Sino–American Rapprochement], *Lengzhan guojishi yanjiu* [Cold War International History Studies] 6 (Summer 2008): 158.

21. Hebei Provincial Archives 0.979-10-826, 14–16.

22. Fan Chengzuo, "Aerbaniya zhichi Zhongguo 'Wenhua dageming' shimo" [The Full Story of Albania's Support of the Chinese "Cultural Revolution"], *Zhonggong dangshi ziliao* [Materials on the History of the Chinese Communist Party] 4 (2004): 142–151. Fan was a senior Chinese diplomat who served as an Albanian-language interpreter for Mao Zedong and Zhou Enlai during the 1960s and 1970s. He was China's ambassador to Albania from 1986 to 1989.

23. Jon Halliday, ed., *The Artful Albanian: Memoirs of Enver Hoxha* (London: Chatto & Windus, 1986), 285.

24. Yi Chong-sŏk, *Pukhan-Chungguk kwan'gye*, 121; Chen Jian, *Mao's China and the Cold War* (Chapel Hill: University of North Carolina Press, 2001), 269; Schaefer, "Overconfidence Shattered," 6.

25. Wang Taiping, *Zhonghua renmin gongheguo waijiaoshi, 1970–1978* [Diplomatic History of the People's Republic of China, 1970–1978] (Beijing: Shijie zhishi chubanshe, 1999), 3:39-40.

26. Central Intelligence Agency, *China and the Lesser Dragons*, intelligence memorandum, July 24, 1972, CIA Records Search Tool (CREST), CIA-RDP85T00875 R001100140013-7, 1.

27. "Minutes of Conversation on the Occasion of the Party and Government Delegation on Behalf of the Romanian Socialist Republic to the Democratic People's Republic of Korea," June 10, 1971, in Archives of the Central Committee of the Romanian Communist Party 43/1971, cited in James Person, ed., "New Evidence on Inter-Korean Relations, 1971–1972," document 1, *North Korea International Documentation Project Document Reader* 3 (September 2009).

28. Wang Mingxing, "Gaoli lianbang gongheguo tongyi fang'an de tichu ji lishi yiyi" [The Proposal and Historical Significance of the Unification Scheme of the Koryo Federal Republic], *Hanguo yanjiu luncong* [Collected Papers on Korean Studies] (Beijing: Shijie zhishi chubanshe, 2003), 10:63–77; Wang Taiping, *Zhonghua renmin gongheguo waijiaosh, 1970–1978*, 3:40.

29. Kim Il-sung, "The Revolutionary Peoples of Asia Will Win in Their Common Struggle Against U.S. Imperialism," August 6, 1971, in Kim Il-sung, *Works* (Pyongyang: Foreign Languages Publishing House, 1986), 26:186, 192.

30. Lee Dongjun, *Mikan no heiwa: Bei-Chū wakai to Chōsen mondai no hen'yo, 1969–1975* [Incomplete Peace: Sino–American Rapprochement and the Transformation of the Korean Issue, 1969-1975] (Tokyo: Hōsei dagaiku Shuppankyoku, 2010), 156.

31. Central Intelligence Agency, *China and the Lesser Dragons*, 14.

32. "Embassy of the GDR [German Democratic Republic] in the DPRK [Democratic People's Republic of Korea], September 21, 1971, Assessment of the Visit by a Delegation of the KPA, Headed By the Member of the Political Committee of the Central Committee of the KWP and Chief of the KPA General Staff, Army General O Chin-u, in the PRC," in Politisches Archiv des Auswärtigen Amtes [Political Archive of the German Foreign Ministry] (PolAAA), Ministerium für Auswärtige Angelegenheiten [Files of the Ministry for Foreign Affairs, Berlin] (MfAA), C 944/76, North Korea International Documentation Project Archives; Bernd Schaefer, "North Korean 'Adventurism' and China's Long

Shadow, 1966–1972," *Cold War International History Project Working Paper* 44 (October 2004): 36.

33. Kissinger to Nixon, "Briefing Papers for the China Trip," February 8, 1972, folder 4, box 847, NSC files, NPMP.

34. Xia, *Negotiating with the Enemy*, 177–180.

35. "Memorandum from the President's Assistant for National Security Affairs (Kissinger) to President Nixon, November 1971," *FRUS*, document 164, 17:526.

36. "Memorandum of Conversation, Beijing, October 22, 1971," in U.S. Department of State, Office of the Historian, *Foreign Relations of the United States, 1969–1976*, vol. E-13, *Documents on China, 1969–1972* (Washington, DC: Government Printing Office, 2006), document 44, http://2001-2009.state.gov/r/pa/ho/frus/nixon/e13/72460 .htm; "Memorandum from the President's Assistant for National Security Affairs (Kissinger) to President Nixon, Washington, November 1971," *FRUS*, 17:546.

37. *FRUS*, 17:546.

38. "Memorandum from the President's Assistant for National Security Affairs (Kissinger) to President Nixon, Washington, November 1971," *FRUS*, 17:547; Kissinger, *On China*, 269-270.

39. Ch'oe Myŏng-hae, *Chungguk, Pukhan tongmaeng kwan'gye: Pulp'yŏnhan tonggŏ ŭi yŏksa* [Sino-North Korean Alliance Relations: The History of Inconvenient Cohabitation] (Seoul: Orŭm, 2009), 291-292.

40. *Renmin ribao* [People's Daily], November 17, 1971.

41. Kim Il-sung, "On Improving and Strengthening the Training of Party Cadres," speech to party cadre education instructors, December 2, 1971, in Kim Il-sung, *Works*, 26:431.

42. "Message from the President's Deputy Assistant for National Security Affairs (Haig) to the President's Assistant for National Security Affairs (Kissinger), Beijing, January 8, 1972," *FRUS*, 17:652.

43. *Yomiuri Shimbun*, January 10, 1972.

44. "GDR Embassy Pyongyang, Memorandum on a Conversation with the First Secretary of the Embassy of the Soviet Union, Comrade Kurbatov, on January 7, 1972, January 10, 1972," PolAAA, MfAA, C944/76, North Korea International Documentation Project Archives.

45. Schaefer, "North Korean 'Adventurism,' " 36–37.

46. "Memorandum of Conversation, Beijing, February 23, 1972," *FRUS*, 17:732–733.

47. "Joint Statement Following Discussions with Leaders of the People's Republic of China, Shanghai, February 27, 1972," *FRUS*, 17:813–814.

48. Zhou Enlai's remarks on the Shanghai Communiqué, March 3, 1972, Hebei Provincial Archives 1057-8-44, 194–217.

49. *Rodong sinmun* [Workers' Newspaper], March 4, 1972.

50. Wang Taiping, *Zhonghua renmin gongheguo waijiaoshi, 1970–1978*, 3:40–41.

51. "Note on a Conversation With the First Secretary of the USSR Embassy, Comrade Kurbatov, on 10 March 1972 in the GDR Embassy," March 13, 1972,

PolAAA, MfAA, C 1080/78, Wilson Center Digital Archive. http://digitalarchive
.wilsoncenter.org/document/110820.

52. Lee Dongjun, *Mikan no heiwa*, 170.

53. "North Korean Relations with Peking and Moscow: Developments During the
Past Year," October 1, 1973, CREST, CIA-RDP85 T00875R001100160072-0, 2.

54. "Note on a Conversation with Comrade Kurbatov, First Secretary of the
USSR Embassy, March 26, 1973, in the USSR Embassy," GDR Embassy to
DPRK, March 28, 1973, PolAAA, MfAA, C 295/78, North Korea International
Documentation Project Archives. Also see the political letter of the Soviet Embassy
in North Korea about the relations between North Korea and China, December 8, 1972, Russian State Archive of Contemporary History (RGANI), f. 5, o.
64, d. 422, ll. 230-239.

55. Lee Dongjun, *Mikan no heiwa*, 94.

56. Henry Kissinger to the president, "State Department Briefing Books for the
China Trip," February 14, 1972, NSC files, NPMP, folder 2, box 848.

57. Yi Chong-sŏk, *Pukhan-Chungguk kwan'gye*, 123.

58. National Security Estimate, "The Two Koreas," May 11, 1972, in Digital
National Security Archive (DNSA), *United States and the Two Koreas*, KO00127, 5–7.

59. "Memorandum from Richard H. Solomon of the National Security Council
Staff to the President's Assistant for National Security Affairs (Kissinger), Washington, June 9, 1972," *FRUS*, 17:907.

60. *FRUS*, 17:987–990.

61. Henry Kissinger to the president, "State Department Briefing Books for the
China Trip," February 14, 1972.

62. Charles K. Armstrong and John Barry Kotch, "Sino–American Negotiations on
Korea and Kissinger's UN Diplomacy," *Cold War History* 15, no. 1 (2015): 115.

63. "Memorandum from the President's Assistant for National Security Affairs
(Kissinger) to President Nixon, Washington, June 27, 1972," *FRUS*, vol. E-13, document 147. http://history.state.gov/historicaldocuments/frus1969-76ve13/comp1.

64. Chae-jin Lee, *China and Korea: Dynamic Relations* (Stanford, CA: Hoover
Institution, 1996), 103.

65. Choy Bong-yoon, *A History of the Korean Reunification Movement: Its Issues and
Prospects* (Peoria, IL: Research Committee on Korean Unification, Institute of
International Studies, Bradley University, 1984), 93–111.

66. Lee Dongjun, *Mikan no heiwa*, 182.

67. *Renmin ribao*, July 22, 1972.

68. "Memorandum of Conversation (Between Kissinger and Huang Hua), New
York, July 26, 1972," *FRUS*, 17:103–135.

69. Armstrong and Kotch, "Sino–American Negotiations on Korea," 118–119.

70. *Renmin ribao*, August 1, 1972; August 2, 1972.

71. "Memorandum of Conversation: Henry Kissinger and Huang Hua, August 4,
1972, 5:15–6:45 P.M.," DNSA, KT00538.

72. Zhonggong Zhongyang Wenxian Yanjiushi, *Zhou Enlai nianpu, 1949–1976*,
3:545–546; Zhou Enlai, "Guanyu guoji tongyi zhanxian" [On the International
United Front], August 24, 1972, Hebei Provincial Archives 1057-8-44, 53–64.

73. Report on a conversation between N. M. Shubnikov and Kim Tong-kyu, August 24, 1972, RGANI, f. 5, op. 64, d. 423, ll. 96-103.

74. "Memorandum of Conversation: Huang Hua and Henry Kissinger, New York, September 19, 1972, 6:17–7:45 P.M.," *FRUS*, document 253, 17:1075–1076.

75. *Renmin ribao*, September 22, 1972; September 25, 1972; Wang Taiping, *Zhonghua renmin gongheguo waijiaoshi, 1970–1978*, 3:41–42; Lee, *China and Korea*, 103.

76. Lee Dongjun, *Mikan no heiwa*, 197; Zhonggong Zhongyang Wenxian Yanjiushi, *Zhou Enlai nianpu, 1949–1976*, 3:545–546.

77. "Annex E: U.S. Relations with North Korea, NSSM [National Security Study Memorandum] 154—U.S. Policy Concerning the Korean Peninsula," April 3, 1973, record group 273, NA, 3.

78. Wang Taiping, *Zhonghua renmin gongheguo waijiaoshi, 1970–1978*, 3:42.

79. "Memorandum of Conversation, Beijing, February 18, 1973," in U.S. Department of State, Office of the Historian, *Foreign Relations of the United States, 1969–1976, Richard M. Nixon/Gerald R. Ford*, vol. 18, *China, 1973–1976* (Washington, DC: Government Printing Office, 2008), 139, 170.

80. "Call on USLO [U.S. Liaison Office] by North Korean Chargé in Peking," David Bruce to Kissinger, August 28, 1973, box 328, Director's Files of Winston Lord, record group 59, NA.

81. Lee Dongjun, *Mikan no heiwa*, 182.

82. Telegram 546 from Seoul, "Yi Hu-rak's View on South–North Dialogue," January 30, 1973, box 2429, Subject Numeric Files 1970–73, record group 59, NA.

83. Seuk-ryule Hong, "U.S.–China and Inter-Korean Relations in the Early 1970s," conference paper, East China Normal University, Shanghai, June 4, 2009, 11–13. For details on the kidnapping of Kim Dae-jung, see Don Oberdorfer, *The Two Koreas: A Contemporary History* (New York: Basic Books, 1997), 42–43.

84. The memorandum of conversation is in NSC Files, NPMP, NA, Kissinger Office Files, box 95, Country Files, Far East, China Exchanges, July 10–October 31, 1973, excerpted in *FRUS*, 18:322.

85. Zhang Tingyan, "Lianheguo taolun Chaoxian wenti" [The UN Discusses the Korean Issue], in *Fengyun jihui lianheguo* [Unpredictable Meetings at the United Nations], ed. Wan Jingzhang and Zhang Bing (Beijing: Xinhua chubanshe, 2008), 53–54; Zhonggong Zhongyang Wenxian Yanjiushi, *Zhou Enlai nianpu, 1949–1976*, 3:629.

86. Samuel S. Kim, *China, the United Nations, and World Order* (Princeton, NJ: Princeton University Press, 1979), 135–136; Wang Taiping, *Zhonghua renmin gongheguo waijiaoshi, 1970–1978*, 3:42–43.

87. Lee, *China and Korea*, 103–104; Wang Taiping, *Zhonghua renmin gongheguo waijiaoshi, 1970–1978*, 3:42–43.

88. Won Gon Park, "The United Nations Command in Korea: Past, Present, and Future," *Korean Journal of Defense Analysis* 21, no. 4 (December 2009): 485–499.

89. Henry Kissinger to the president, "State Department Briefing Books for the China Trip," February 14, 1972.

90. Lee Dongjun, *Mikan no heiwa*, 261.

91. "Termination of the UN Command in Korea," National Security Decision Memorandum 251, Washington, March 29, 1974. https://history.state.gov/his toricaldocuments/frus1969-76ve12/d253. Also "NSDM [National Security Decision Memorandum]: Dissolution of the UNC [United Nations Command]," March 29, 1974, box 376, Winston Lord Files, NA.

92. "Report for Peace and Unification of the Fatherland submitted by Hŏ Tam, Minister of Foreign Affairs, to the Supreme People's Assembly," *Rodong sinmun*, March 25 and March 26, 1974.

93. Narushige Michishita, *North Korea's Military–Diplomatic Campaigns, 1966–2008* (New York: Routledge, 2010), 58–60.

94. Michishita, *North Korea's Military–Diplomatic Campaigns*, 52–72; Lee Dongjun, *Mikan no heiwa*, 283.

95. "Memorandum of Conversation Between Anwar Sadat and Henry Kissinger, April 30, 1974," DNSA, Kissinger Transcripts, KT01125.

96. "Memorandum of Conversation Between Vasile Pungan and Henry Kissinger, August 26, 1974," DNSA, Kissinger Transcripts, KT01310.

97. In the mid-1970s, Japanese Prime Minister Miki Takeo actively promoted mediation and passionately worked for a solution to the Korean question via Great Power guarantees by the United States and China. Although Miki's efforts produced few results, these discussions demonstrate the nature and persistence of Japan's concerns about the Korean question. See Seung-young Kim, "Miki Takeo's Initiative on the Korean Question and U.S.–Japanese Diplomacy," *Journal of American–East Asian Relations* 20, no. 4 (December 2014): 377–405.

98. "The PRC and Termination of the UN Command in Korea," memorandum from Richard H. Solomon of the National Security Council staff to Secretary of State Kissinger, Washington, April 12, 1974, *FRUS*, 18:477–479.

99. Hong, "U.S.–China and Inter-Korean Relations in the Early 1970s," 14.

100. Lee Dongjun indicates it was a twenty-nine-nation lobbying effort. See Lee Dongjun, *Mikan no heiwa*, 298. But *Renmin ribao* reported that thirty-two nations, including China, wrote to the UN secretary-general on August 16 to demand inclusion on the agenda of the Twenty-Ninth Session of the UNGA a provisional resolution that "all foreign troops under the UN banner be withdrawn from South Korea." See *Renmin ribao*, August 19, 1974. On September 16, China and thirty-three other nations formally submitted a draft resolution to the UN. See *Renmin ribao*, September 18, 1974; December 1, 1974.

101. "Memorandum of Conversation between Kissinger and Chi'ao Kuan-hua [Qiao Guanhua], New York City, October 2, 1974," *FRUS*, 18:534–535.

102. Kissinger, *On China*, 292, 317.

103. *FRUS*, 18:562–645; Brent Scowcroft to the President, "Kissinger's Talks with Teng Hsiao-Ping [Deng Xiaoping] and Chiao Kuan-Hua [Qiao Guanhua] in Beijing, November 26, 1974, November 27, 1974," DNSA, China and the U.S., CH00324.

104. "Memorandum from Habib, Lord, and Solomon to Kissinger," July 3, 1976; Ford Library, National Security Adviser, NSC Staff for East Asia and Pacific Affairs, Convenience Files, Solomon Subject Files, box 39, PRCLO (3), May–July 1975, in *FRUS*, 18:703.

105. Lee Dongjun, *Mikan no heiwa*, 319.

106. Wang Taiping, *Zhonghua renmin gongheguo waijiaoshi, 1970–1978*, 3:43; Lee, *China and Korea*, 105.

107. On August 18, 1976, U.S. Army officers Arthur Bonifas and Mark Barrett were killed by North Korean soldiers while cutting down a poplar tree that partially blocked the view of the UN observers in the Joint Security Area. This led to increased tensions on the Korean Peninsula. Three days later, North Korea accepted responsibility and the crisis was over. For details, see Oberdorfer, *The Two Koreas*, 74-83.

108. "The Foreign Policy of China's Successor Leadership, June 1976," *FRUS*, 18:934.

109. Editorial note, *FRUS*, 18:929–930.

110. Schaefer, "Overconfidence Shattered," 6–7.

111. Zhongguo Renmin Jiefangjun Zongcanmoubu [People's Liberation Army General Staff], *Zhongguo renmin jiefangjun junshi gongzuo dashiji, 1949.10–1987.12* [A Record of Major Events in People's Liberation Army Military Affairs, October 1949-December 1987] (unpublished, December 1988), 496–497, 502, 511; telephone interview with Zi Zhongyun, September 20, 2015. Zi served as an English-language interpreter for those who participated in the project.

112. See Kuisong Yang and Yafeng Xia, "Vacillating Between Revolution and Détente: Mao's Changing Psyche and Policy Toward the U.S., 1969–1976," *Diplomatic History* 34, no. 2 (April 2010): 421. For a detailed analysis of Mao's theory of "three worlds," see Yafeng Xia, "Mao Zedong," in *Mental Maps in the Early Cold War Era, 1945–1968*, ed. Steven Casey and Jonathan Wright (Basingstoke: Palgrave Macmillan, 2011), 173–174.

113. *Renmin ribao*, April 9, 1975; "On the Visit of a DPRK Party and Government Delegation Headed by Kim Il-sung to the PR China from 18 to 26 April 1975," report from the GDR Foreign Ministry, PolAAA, MfAA, 300/78, North Korea International Documentation Project e-Dossier 7 (May 2012). https://www.wilsoncenter.org/sites/default/files/NKIDP_eDossier_7_Kim_Il_Sung_Beijing_1975.pdf.

114. Jeffrey A. Engel, ed., *The China Diary of George H. W. Bush: The Making of a Global President* (Princeton, NJ: Princeton University Press, 2008), 266.

115. Chen Jian, "Limits of the 'Lips and Teeth' Alliance," in *Uneasy Allies: Fifty Years of China–North Korea Relations*, Asian Program Special Report 115 (Washington, DC: Woodrow Wilson International Center, September 2003): 8. https://www.wilsoncenter.org/sites/default/files/asia_rpt115b.pdf.

116. Cited from GDR Foreign Ministry, "On Kim Il-sung's Visit to the PRC 18-26 April 1975," PolAAA, MfAA, C300/78, in Schaefer, "Overconfidence Shattered," 26.

117. For details on China's economic and trade relations with North Korea from 1970 to 1975, see Hebei Provincial Archives 940-11-43, 1-67; 940-11-86, 75-117; 940-11-140, 48-219; Gansu Provincial Archives 91-007-0022, 101-148.

118. For details on China military aid to North Korea, see Zhongguo Renmin Jiefangjun Zongcanmoubu, *Zhongguo renmin jiefangjun junshi gongzuo dashiji*, 497, 507-508, 510, 514, 520–521.

119. Adrian Buzo, *The Guerilla Dynasty: Politics and Leadership in North Korea* (London: I. B. Tauris, 1999), 98.

120. Charles K. Armstrong, *Tyranny of the Weak: North Korea and the World, 1950–1992* (Ithaca, NY: Cornell University Press, 2013), 178-179.

121. Excerpts from the collection Materials for Lectures About "Great Leader, Kim Il-sung," October 10, 1969, RGANI, f. 5, op. 61, d. 462, ll. 227-232.

122. Samuel S. Kim, "Pyongyang, the Third World and Global Politics," in *The Two Koreas in World Politics*, ed. Tae-Hwan Kwak, Wayne Patterson, and Edward A. Olsen (Seoul: Kyungnam University Press, 1983), 73. See also Armstrong, *Tyranny of the Weak*, 180.

123. Lee Dongjun, *Mikan no heiwa*, 311; Kim Hak-chun, *Pukhan 50-yŏnsa: Uri ka ttŏ anayhal pantchok ŭi uri yŏksa* [A Fifty-Year History of North Korea] (Seoul: Tonga Ch'ulp'ansa, 1995), 315-317; CIA staff notes, East Asia, September 8, 1975, CREST, CIA-RDP79T00865A001700150001-8, 6-8.

124. "On the Present Political and Economic Policies of the Democratic People's Republic of Korea and Some International Problems," in Kim Il-sung, *Works*, 27:24, 27.

125. Zhonggong Zhongyang Duiwai Lianluobu [International Liaison Department of the Chinese Communist Party Central Committee], ed., *Chaoxian laodongdang zhongyao yanlun, wenjian xuanji, 1972.10–1973.12* [Collection of Important Speeches and Documents of the Korean Workers' Party, October 1972-December 1973] (unpublished, 1975), 263-267.

126. Excerpts from the collection Materials for Lectures About "Great Leader, Kim Il-sung," October 10, 1969, RGANI, f. 5, op. 61, d. 462, ll. 227-232.

127. Zhonggong Zhongyang Duiwai Lianluobu [International Liaison Department of the Chinese Communist Party Central Committee], ed., *Chaoxian laodongdang zhongyao yanlun, wenjian xuanji, 1971.8–1972.9* [Collection of Important Speeches and Documents of the Korean Workers' Party, August 1971-September 1972] (unpublished, December 1972), 530-43; and *Rodong sinmun*, May 9, 1972.

128. Hwang Chang-yŏp, *Nanŭn yŏksa chillirŭl poatta* [I Witnessed the Historical Truth] (Seoul: Hanul, 1998), 179-80; Kim Ch'ang-hŭi, "Puk'anŭi t'ongch'iinyŏm 'kimilsŏng-kimjŏngilchuŭi' punsŏk" [An Analysis of North Korea's Governing Theory: "Kim Il-sung–Kim Jong-il–ism"], *Han'guk chŏngchi'i yŏn'gu* [Journal of Korean Politics] 22, no. 3 (2013): 193.

129. Zhonggong Zhongyang Duiwai Lianluobu [International Liaison Department of the Chinese Communist Party Central Committee], ed., *Chaoxian laodongdang zhongyao yanlun, wenjian xuanji, 1974* [Collection of Important Speeches and Documents of the Korean Workers' Party, 1974] (unpublished, 1976), 150-155.

130. Kim Il-sung, "Answers to Questions Raised by Australian Journalists," November 4, 1974, in Kim Il-sung, *Works*, 29:492.

131. Shen Yilin, ed., *Chaoxian zhuti sixiang ziliao xuanyi* [Selection of Translated Materials on North Korea's Juche] (Beijing: Renmin chubanshe, 1983), 284; Andrei Balkanskii, *Kim Ir Sen* [Kim Il-sung] (Moscow: Molodaia Gvardiia, 2011), 194-195.

132. Armstrong, *Tyranny of the Weak*, 193-194.

133. *Renmin ribao*, June 25, 1974; Byung Chul Koh, *The Foreign Policy Systems of North and South Korea* (Berkeley: University of California Press, 1984), 11-12. Although South Korea was able to establish observer mission status at the UN in 1949, it was not until July 1973 that North Korea was able to do so. As of July 1981, the DPRK had become a member of nine UN agencies and five intergovernmental organizations. See Tai Sung An, *North Korea: A Political Handbook* (Wilmington, DE: Scholarly Resources, 1983), 83.

134. GDR Embassy to DPRK, "Information About the Appraisal of the 10th CCP Party Congress in the DPRK," September 13, 1973. http://digitalarchive .wilsoncenter.org/document/116675.

135. Kim Il-sung, "The Peoples of the World Advancing Under the Uplifted Banner of Independence Will Certainly Win Their Revolutionary Cause," March 4, 1974, in Kim Il-sung, *Works*, 29:101. At an internal meeting of Soviet-Eastern European bloc diplomats, Comrade Janakiyev, second secretary of the Bulgarian Embassy in North Korea, said, "Kim Il-sung himself wanted to be recognized as the leader of world revolution." See GDR Embassy to DPRK, "Note on a Meeting in the Embassy of Czechoslovakia on 5 September 1973." http://digi talarchive.wilsoncenter.org/document/116674.

136. Kim Il-sung, "On Eliminating Dogmatism and Formalism and Establishing *Juche* in Ideological Work," speech to party propaganda and agitation workers, December 28, 1955, in Kim Il-sung, *Works*, 9:396.

137. Renata Keller, *Mexico's Cold War: Cuba, the United States, and the Legacy of the Mexican Revolution* (New York: Cambridge University Press, 2015), 226-227.

138. South Korean Foreign Ministry Archives, Seoul, D-06-0022-01, 2-16.

139. Central Committee, German Socialist Unity Party, "Memorandum of Conversation between Erich Honecker and Kim Il-sung," June 1, 1984, Foundation Archives of Parties and Mass Organizations of the German Democratic Republic in the Federal Archives, DY 30, 2460.

140. Balkanskii, *Kim Ir Sen*, 194-195.

141. *Renmin ribao*, October 14, 1980.

142. *Renmin ribao*, September 14, 1976; September 20, 1976.

143. Hong, "U.S.–China and Inter-Korean Relations in the Early 1970s," 9.

144. Thomas J. Christensen, *Worse Than a Monolith: Alliance Politics and Problems of Coercive Diplomacy in Asia* (Princeton, NJ: Princeton University Press, 2011).

Epilogue: China and North Korea in the Era of Deng Xiaoping

1. For a detailed analysis, see Yafeng Xia, "Deng Xiaoping," in *Mental Maps in the Late Cold War*, ed. Steven Casey and Jonathan Wright (New York: Palgrave Macmillan, 2015), 143–144.

2. Zhonggong Zhongyang Wenxian Yanjiushi [Chinese Communist Party Central Committee Party Literature Research Office], ed., *Deng Xiaoping wenxuan*,

1982–1992 [Selected Works of Deng Xiaoping, 1982–1992] (Beijing: Renmin chubanshe, 1995), 126–127, 289.

3. For details, see Xia, "Deng Xiaoping," 144–145.

4. On the occasion of Kim Il-sung's seventieth birthday, in April 1982, Deng Xiaoping and Hu Yaobang paid an unofficial visit to North Korea. During this visit, Kim Il-sung's successor, Kim Jong-il, was formally introduced to the Chinese leaders. Hu Yaobang invited Kim Jong-il to visit China, and, as a result, Kim Jong-il made an unofficial visit to China as a leading Korean Workers' Party official, in June 1983. During his visit, China formally endorsed Kim Jong-il as his father's successor. See Ilpyong J. Kim, "China in North Korean Foreign Policy," in *North Korean Foreign Relations in the Post–Cold War Era*, ed. Samuel S. Kim (New York: Oxford University Press, 1998), 102. On May 21, 1983, *Renmin ribao* [People's Daily] published a theoretical article by Kim Jong-il, and on July 8, 1983, it reported Kim Jong-il's unofficial visit as a leading North Korean official. Also see Donald S. Zagoria, "North Korea: Between Moscow and Beijing," in *North Korea Today: Strategic and Domestic Issues*, ed. Robert A. Scalapino and Jun-Yop Kim (Berkeley: Institute for East Asian Studies, University of California, 1983), 362; Yi Chong-sŏk, *Pukhan-Chungguk kwan'gye, 1945–2000* [The Sino-North Korean Relationship, 1945-2000] (Seoul: Chungsim, 2000), 252-253; Kim Hak-chun, *Pukhan 50-yŏnsa: Uri ka ttŏ anayhal pantchok ŭi uri yŏksa* [A Fifty-Year History of North Korea] (Seoul: Tonga Ch'ulp'ansa, 1995), 315-317. For a recent study on China's reaction to Kim Il-sung's succession plan, see John Delury, "The Problem of Feudalism: Sino–Korean Relations After Mao and from Kim to Kim," paper presented at the Association for Asian Studies annual conference, Washington, DC, March 24, 2018.

5. Zagoria, "North Korea: Between Moscow and Beijing," 367; Samuel S. Kim, "The Making of China's Korea Policy in the Era of Reform," in *The Making of Chinese Foreign and Security Policy in the Era of Reform, 1978–2000*, ed. David Lampton (Stanford, CA: Stanford University Press, 2001), 371-408; Gregg Brazinsky, "Korea's Great Divergence: North and South Korea Between 1972 and 1987," in *The Cold War in East Asia, 1945–1991*, ed. Tsuyoshi Hasegawa (Stanford, CA: Stanford University Press, 2011), 241-264.

6. Zhonglianbu Bangongting [General Office, Chinese Communist Party Central Committee International Liaison Department], ed., *Zhonglianbu laobu lingdao tan dang de duiwai gongzuo* [Retired Leaders of International Liaison Department Talk About Party's External Work] (unpublished, April 2004), 100–101.

7. Zhonglianbu Bangongting, *Zhonglianbu laobu lingdao tan dang de duiwai gongzuo*, 102–103.

8. *Nan Chaoxian dongtai* [Trends in South Korea] 26 (September 20, 1978): 2.

9. Memorandum of conversation between the president and People's Republic of China Vice Premier Deng Xiaoping, January 29, 1979, in North Korea International Documentation Project, *The Carter Chill: U.S.–ROK–DPRK Trilateral Relations, 1976–1979: A Critical Oral History Conference* (Washington, DC: Woodrow Wilson International Center for Scholars, 2013), 447. https://www

.wilsoncenter.org/sites/default/files/NKIDP_The_Carter_Chill_Briefing _Book.pdf.

10. Zhonggong Zhongyang Wenxian Yanjiushi [Chinese Communist Party Central Committee Party Literature Research Office], ed., *Deng Xiaoping nianpu, 1975–1997* [Chronology of Deng Xiaoping, 1975–1997] (Beijing: Zhongyang wenxian chubanshe, 2004), 1:468.

11. Zhonggong Zhongyang Wenxian Yanjiushi, *Deng Xiaoping nianpu, 1975–1997,* 1:508.

12. Memorandum of conversation between the vice president and the People's Republic of China Vice Premier Deng Xiaoping, August 28, 1979, in North Korea International Documentation Project, *The Carter Chill,* 663.

13. *Renmin ribao,* September 29, 1979.

14. Chin-Wee Chung, "North Korea's Relations with China," in *The Foreign Relations of North Korea: New Perspectives,* ed. Jae Kyu Park, Byung Chul Koh, and Tae-Hawn Kwak (Boulder, CO: Westview, 1987), 197.

15. *Chaoxian wenti ziliao* [References on the North Korean Issue] 7 (April 1979).

16. Jae Ho Chung, "South Korea–China Economic Relations: The Current Situation and its Implications," *Asian Survey* 28, no. 10 (October 1988): 1033.

17. Samuel S. Kim, *The Two Koreas and the Great Powers* (New York: Cambridge University Press, 2006), 56.

18. Zhang Tingyan, "Deng Xiaoping guanxin Chaoxian bandao jushi: Huiyi Deng Xiaoping er san shi" [Deng Xiaoping Cares About the Situation on the Korean Peninsula: Remembering Two or Three Things About Deng Xiaoping], *Dangshi bolan* [General Review of Chinese Communist Party History] 5 (2013): 27–28.

19. Li Xiannian Zhuan Bianxiezu, E Yu Bianqu Geming Shi Bianjibu [Editorial Board of Li Xiannian's Biography, and Editorial Board of the Revolutionary History of the Eyu Base Area], ed., *Li Xiannian nianpu* [Chronology of Li Xiannian] (Beijing: Zhongyang wenxian chubanshe, 2011), 6:201.

20. *Renmin ribao,* September 8, 1983; Zhang Tingyan, "Deng Xiaoping guanxin Chaoxian bandao jushi," 27–28.

21. Zhang Tingyan, "Deng Xiaoping guanxin Chaoxian bandao jushi," 27–28; Liu Yazhou, *Liu Yazhou wenji* [Collection of Liu Yazhou's Writings] (Beijing: Changjiang wenyi chubanshe, 2004), 2:317.

22. Zhonglianbu Bangongting, *Zhonglianbu laobu lingdao tan dang de duiwai gongzuo,* 105.

23. Tian Zongji and Ye Xinyu, ed., *Zhonghua renmin gongheguo shilu di sijuan: Gaige yu jubian—Kaichuang xiandaihua jianshe xin jumian, 1977–1992* [A True Account of the People's Republic of China, vol. 4, Reform and Great Changes—Creating a New Situation for the Construction of Modernization, 1977–1992] (Changchun: Jilin renmin chubanshe, 1994), 640; Kim Hak-chun, *Chaoxian wushiqinian shi* [Fifty-Seven Years of North Korean History], trans. Zhang Ying, Translated Series on China's Northeast Border (unpublished internal reference, 2005), 495; V. A. Shin, *Kitai i koreiskie gosudarstva vo vtoroi polovine XX stoletiia* [China and North Korea in the Second Half of the Twentieth Century] (Moscow: ID-vo MGU, 1998), 73–74.

24. South Korean Diplomatic Archives 21579/724.32US, 240; South Korean Diplomatic Archives 9388/722.2, 14–15, 43–44, 57, 62–63, 68–69; V. A. Shin, *Kitai i koreiskie gosudarstva vo vtoroi polovine XX stoletiia*, 74.

25. *Renmin ribao*, March 5, 1984; April 7, 1984.

26. South Korean Diplomatic Archives 9388/722.2, 65.

27. *Renmin ribao*, August 17, 1986. Also see Chung, "North Korea's Relations with China," 195.

28. *Rodong sinmun* [Workers' Newspaper], August 20, 1986.

29. South Korean Diplomatic Archives 9388/722.2, 89–91, 95–96.

30. Barry K. Gills, *Korea Versus Korea: A Case of Contested Legitimacy* (London: Routledge, 1996), 222.

31. Liu Yazhou, *Liu Yazhou wenji*, 2:310–311; Yan Jing, "Lishi de xuanze" [A Historical Choice], *Baogao wenxue* [Reportage Literature] 1 (2008): 72.

32. Yan Jing, *Chushi Hanguo* [Serving as an Envoy to the Republic of Korea] (Ji'nan: Shandong daxue chubanshe, 2004), 13–14.

33. Zhonglianbu Bangongting, *Zhonglianbu laobu lingdao tan dang de duiwai gongzuo*, 106.

34. Zhang Tingyan, "Deng Xiaoping guanxin Chaoxian bandao jushi," 27–28; Liu Yazhou, *Liu Yazhou wenji*, 2:287–288; Kim Hak-chun, *Chaoxian wushiqinian shi*, 527–528, 543.

35. Liu Yazhou, *Liu Yazhou wenji*, 2:282–284.

36. Yan Jing, "Lishi de xuanze," 70.

37. Jae Ho Chung, *Between Ally and Partner: Korea–China Relations and the United States* (New York: Columbia University Press, 2007), 44.

38. Zhonglianbu Bangongting, *Zhonglianbu laobu lingdao tan dang de duiwai gongzuo*, 106–107.

39. Zhonglianbu Bangongting, *Zhonglianbu laobu lingdao tan dang de duiwai gongzuo*, 180–189.

40. Liu Yazhou, *Liu Yazhou wenji*, 2:313–314, 318–326.

41. Zhonglianbu Bangongting, *Zhonglianbu laobu lingdao tan dang de duiwai gongzuo*, 194–196.

42. *Renmin ribao*, October 22, 1990.

43. Chung, *Between Ally and Partner*, 47; Liu Yazhou, *Liu Yazhou wenji*, 2:313–314. On November 30, 1990, Jeong Sang-gi, who was then deputy head of the Division of Northeast Asian Affairs (II) in the South Korean Foreign Ministry, was sent to the South Korean trade office in Beijing to be in charge of administrative affairs. In February 1992, the Chinese Foreign Ministry began to establish contacts with the South Korean trade office in Beijing. Interview with Jeong Sang-gi, Seoul National University, August 12, 2017.

44. *Renmin ribao*, December 14, 1991.

45. Chung, *Between Ally and Partner*, 70.

46. Yan Jing, "Lishi de xuanze," 72; Qian Qichen, *Waijiao shiji* [Ten Episodes in China's Diplomacy] (Beijing: Shijie zhishi chubanshe, 2003), 155. This book has been translated and published in English as Qian Qichen, *Ten Episodes in China's Diplomacy* (New York: Harper, 2006).

47. Qian Qichen, *Waijiao shiji*, 155–156; Yan Jing, "Lishi de xuanze," 73–74.

48. *Rodong sinmun*, October 1, 1990. Also see Kim, "China in North Korean Foreign Policy," 99–100.

49. Zhonglianbu Bangongting, *Zhonglianbu laobu lingdao tan dang de duiwai gongzuo*, 194–211.

50. Yan Jing, "Lishi de xuanze," 74.

51. Qian Qichan, *Waijiao shiji*, 158–159; Yan Jing, "Lishi de xuanze," 75.

52. Zhonglianbu Bangongting, *Zhonglianbu laobu lingdao tan dang de duiwai gongzuo*, 207.

53. *Asahi Shimbun*, October 8, 1991, cited in Shunji Hiraiwa, *Chosenminshushugijin-minkyowakoku to tyukajinminkyowakoku: "Shinshi no kankei" no kouzo to henyo* [The Democratic People's Republic of Korea and the People's Republic of China: The Structure and Transformation of the "Relationship Between Lips and Teeth"] (Yokohama: Seori Shobo, 2010), 199.

54. Interview by Shen Zhihua and Li Danhui with Jiang Zemin, who was general secretary of the Chinese Communist Party from 1989 to 2002 and president of China from 1993 to 2003. The interview took place in Beijing on September 24, 2009. During the interview, Jiang said, "Little Kim [Jong-il] is very cunning."

55. Unfortunately, the Chinese government and official media choose to ignore the reality of Sino–North Korean relations. At the Third Plenum of the Twelfth National People's Congress press conference on March 8, 2015, in response to a question, Chinese Foreign Minister Wang Yi claimed, "China and the DPRK are friendly neighbors. Chinese people keep faith and value ties of friendship. We treasure the Sino–DPRK traditional friendship, and are devoted to developing normal relations between our two countries." See Wang Yi, "Zhenshi ZhongChao chuantong youyi, zhili liangguo guanxi zhengchang fazhan" [Treasuring the Sino–DPRK Traditional Friendship, and Devoting Ourselves to Normal Development Between Our Two Countries], March 8, 2015. http://world.huanqiu.com/hot/2015-03/5853911.html [in Chinese]. This is the myth we intend to demolish in this book.

56. For details, see Jonathan D. Pollack, *No Exit: North Korea, Nuclear Weapons, and International Security* (New York: Routledge, 2011), 131-183.

Bibliography

Archival Sources

People's Republic of China

Chinese Foreign Ministry Archives, Beijing
Dalian Municipal Archives, Dalian, Liaoning
Fujian Provincial Archives, Fuzhou, Fujian
Gansu Provincial Archives, Lanzhou, Gansu
Guangdong Provincial Archives, Guangzhou, Guangdong
Guangxi Autonomous Region Archives, Nanning, Guangxi
Hebei Provincial Archives, Shijiazhuang, Hebei
Hubei Provincial Archives, Wuhan, Hubei
Ili Prefecture Archives, Yining, Xinjiang
Jiangsu Provincial Archives, Nanjing, Jiangsu
Jilin Provincial Archives, Changchun, Jilin
Shaanxi Provincial Archives, Xi'an, Shaanxi
Shanghai Municipal Archives, Shanghai
Shanxi Provincial Archives, Taiyuan, Shanxi
Sichuan Provincial Archives, Chengdu, Sichuan

Russia and Eastern Europe

AMVRB   Arhiv na Ministerstvoto na Vynshnite Raboti na Bylgaria [Archive of the Ministry of Foreign Affairs of Bulgaria]

APRF	Arkhiv Prezidenta Rossiiskoi Federatsii [Archive of the President of the Russian Federation]
ARAN	Archiv Rossiiskoi Academii Nauk [Russian Academy of Sciences Archives]
AQSH	Arkivi Qendor Shtetëror [Albanian Central State Archive]
AVPRF	Arkhiv Vneshnei Politiki Rossiiskoi Federatsii [Archive of Foreign Policy of the Russian Federation]
GARF	Gosudarstvennyi Arkhiv Rossiiskpi Federatsii [State Archive of the Russian Federation]
MfAA	Ministerium für Auswärtige Angelegenheiten [Files of the Ministry for Foreign Affairs, Berlin, Germany]
MOL	Magyar Országos Levéltár [Hungarian National Archives, Budapest, Hungary]
PolAAA	Politisches Archiv Auswärtiges Amt [Political Archive of the German Foreign Ministry]
RGANI	Rossiiskii Gosudarstvennyi Arkhiv Noveishei Istorii [Russian State Archive of Contemporary History]
RGASPI	Rossiiskii Gosudarstvennyi Arkhiv Sotsial'noi i Politicheskoi Istorii [Russian State Archive of Sociopolitical History]
SAPMO-BArch	Stiftung Archiv der Parteien und Masenorganisationen der DDR im Bundesarchiv [Archives of Parties and Mass Organizations of the German Democratic Republic in the Federal Archives]
TsAMORF	Tsentral'nyi Arkhiv Ministerstva Oborony Rossiiskoi Federatsii) [Central Archive of the Ministry of Defense, Russia]
TsKhSD	Tsentr Khraneniia Sovremennoi Dokumentatsii [Russian State Archive of Contemporary History]

South Korea

Diplomatic Archives, Republic of Korea Ministry of Foreign Affairs, Seoul

United States

CAESAR, POLO, and ESAU Papers, available at www.foia.cia.gov/collection/caesar -polo-and-esau-papers
Cold War International History Project, Washington, DC
National Archives II, College Park, Maryland
National Security Archive, Washington, DC
Nixon Presidential Materials Project, National Archives, College Park, Maryland
Wilson Center Digital Archive, available at http://digitalarchive.wilsoncenter.org

Other Sources

Newspapers and Journals

Chaoxian wenti ziliao [References on the North Korean Issue]
Jiefang ribao [Liberation Daily]
JinChaJi ribao [JinChaJi Daily]
Kulloja [Worker]
Nan Chaoxian dongtai [Trends in South Korea]
Neibu cankao [Internal Reference], Xinhua News Agency
Pravda [Truth]
Renmin ribao [People's Daily]
Rodong sinmun [Workers' Newspaper]

Interviews

Chai Chengwen, September 12, 2000, Beijing. Chai was chargé d'affaires and political counselor of the Chinese embassy in North Korea as well as chief Chinese liaison officer during the Korean armistice negotiations.

Chen Xiaolu, November 27, 2013, Beijing. Chen's father, Chen Yi, was Chinese foreign minister from 1958 to 1971.

He Zhangming, November 29, 2013, Beijing. He was at that time a counselor at the Chinese embassy in Pyongyang.

Jeong Sang-gi, August 12, 2017, Seoul. Jeong, deputy head of the Division of Northeast Asian Affairs (II) at the South Korean Foreign Ministry in the early 1990s, was sent to the South Korean Trade Office in Beijing to be in charge of administrative affairs.

Jiang Zemin, September 24, 2009, Beijing. Jiang was general secretary of the Chinese Communist Party from 1989 to 2002 and president of China from 1993 to 2003.

Kim Ch'ung-sik, February 17, 2010, and February 2011, Taiyuan. Kim was head of the Organization Department of the Pyongyang Municipal Committee of the Korean Workers' Party before fleeing to China in 1956.

Kim Kang, February 17, 2010, Taiyuan. Kim was deputy head of the Cultural Department of the Democratic People's Republic of Korea government before fleeing to China in 1956.

Ledovskii, Andrei M., July 31, 1996, Moscow. Ledovskii was Soviet consul general in Shenyang during the 1950s and one of the few Russian scholars who had easy access to the Archives of the President of the Russian Federation.

Lin Yonghai, October 16, 2011, Shanghai. Lin, an educated youth from Shanghai living in Yanbian, later became deputy chairman of the Tumen Municipal Political Consultative Conference.

Zhang Liankui, November 16, 2011, Beijing. Zhang worked for the Tumen Municipal Public Security Bureau.

Zhu Liang, January 2010, Beijing. Zhu was director of the International Liaison Department of the Chinese Communist Party Central Committee from 1985 to 1993.

Published and Unpublished Document Collections

Aimermakher, K. et al. *Doklad N. S. Khushcheva o kul'te lichnosti Stalina naXX s'ezde KPSS dokumenty* [Khrushchev's Report on Stalin's Personality Cult in the Documents of the 20th Congress of the CPSU]. Moscow: Rosspen, 2002.

Archive of Foreign Policy of the Russian Federation, ed. "Khronologiia osnovnykh sobytii kanuna i nachal'nogo perioda koreiskoi voiny, ianvar' 1949–oktiabr' 1950 gg." [A Chronology of the Basic Events on the Eve of and During the First Period of the Korean War, January 1949–October 1950]. Manuscript.

Beijing Shifan Xueyuan *Douzheng Shenghuo* Bianjibu [Beijing Teachers' College *Life of Struggle* Editorial Board], ed. *Wuchan jieji wenhua dageming ziliao huibian* [Collection of Documents on the Great Proletarian Cultural Revolution]. December 1966.

Fursenko, A. A. et al., eds. *Prezidium TsK KPSS 1954–1964, tom 1* [Communist Party of the Soviet Union Central Committee Presidium, 1954–1964, vol. 1], *Chernovye protokol'nye zapisi zasedanii stenogrammy* [Draft Protocols of Meetings, Stenographic Records, and Decrees]. Moscow: Rosspen, 2003.

Jilinsheng geming weiyuanhui waishiwei bangongshi [Foreign Affairs Office, Jilin Provincial Revolutionary Committee], ed. *Collection of Sino–Korean, Sino–Soviet, and Sino–Mongolian Treaties, Agreements, and Protocols.* Translated by Northeast Asian History Foundation. Internal material, no. 3. Seoul: Dongbuga Yeoksa Jaedan, 2007.

Ledovskii, Andrei M., R. A. Mirovshchkaia, and V. S. Miasnikov, eds. *Russko-kitaiskie otnoshenie v XX veke, Dokumenty i materialy, tom V, Sovetsko-kitaiskie otnoshenie, 1946–fevral'1950,* Kniga 2: *1949—fevral'1950 gg.* [Russian–Chinese Relations in the Twentieth Century: Documents and Materials, vol. 5: Soviet-Chinese Relations, 1946-1950; no. 2: 1949-February 1950]. Moscow: PIM, 2005.

Liu Jinzhi, ed. *ZhongChao ZhongHan guanxi wenjian ziliao huibian, 1919–1949* [Collection of Documents on China's Policies Toward North and South Korea, 1919–1949]. Beijing: Zhongguo shehui kexue chubanshe, 2000.

North Korea International Documentation Project. *The Carter Chill: U.S.–ROK–DPRK Trilateral Relations, 1976–1979—A Critical Oral History Conference.* Washington, DC: Woodrow Wilson International Center for Scholars, 2013. https://www .wilsoncenter.org/sites/default/files/NKIDP_The_Carter_Chill_Briefing_Book .pdf.

Ostermann, Christian F., and James F. Person, eds. *Crisis and Confrontation on the Korean Peninsula, 1968–1969: A Critical Oral History.* Washington, DC: Woodrow Wilson International Center for Scholars, 2011. https://www.wilsoncenter.org

/sites/default/files/NKIDP_Crisis_and_Confrontation_on_the_Korean_Penin
sula_1968_1969.pdf.

——, eds. *The Rise and Fall of Détente on the Korean Peninsula, 1970–1974.* Washington, DC: Woodrow Wilson Center for Scholars, 2011.

Ostermann, Christian F. et al., eds. *Stalin and the Cold War, 1945–1953: A Cold War International History Project Document Reader.* Prepared for the conference Stalin and the Cold War, 1945-1953, Yale University, September 23-26, 1999.

Person, James F., ed. "Limits of the 'Lips and Teeth' Alliance: New Evidence on Sino–DPRK Relations 1955–1984." *North Korea International Documentation Project Document Reader* 2 (March 2009).

——, ed. "New Evidence on Inter-Korean Relations, 1971–1972." *North Korea International Documentation Project Document Reader* 3 (September 2009).

Shen Zhihua, ed. *Chaoxian zhanzheng: Eguo dang'anguan de jiemi wenjian* [The Korean War: Declassified Documents from the Russian Archives]. 3 vols. Taipei: Zhongyang yanjiuyuan, Jindaishi yanjiusuo, 2003.

——, ed. *Eluosi jiemi dang'an xuanbian: ZhongSu guanxi: 1945–1991* [Selected Collection of Declassified Russian Archives: Sino–Soviet Relations: 1945-1991]. 12 vols. Shanghai: Dongfang chubanshe, 2015.

——, ed. *Guanyu Chaoxian zhanzheng de Eguo dang'an yuanwen fuyinjian* [Copies of Original Documents on the Korean War in the Russian Archives]. Shanghai: Center for Cold War International History Studies, East China Normal University. 17 vols. Unpublished, 2004.

Shen Zhihua and Li Danhui, eds. *ZhongSu guanxi: Eguo dang'an yuanwen fuyinjian huibian* [Sino–Soviet Relations: Collection of Copies of Original Documents in the Russian Archives]. 22 vols. Shanghai: Center for Cold War International History Studies, East China Normal University. Unpublished, 2004.

Tikhvinskii, S. L. et al. *Otnosheniia Sovetskogo Soiuza s narodnoi Koreei, 1945–1980: Dokumenty i materialy* [USSR Relations with People's Korea, 1945-1980: Documents and Materials]. Moscow: Nauka, 1981.

U.S. Department of State, Office of the Historian. *Foreign Relations of the United States, 1969–1976, Richard M. Nixon/Gerald R. Ford.* Vol. 17, *China, 1969–1972.* Washington, DC: Government Printing Office, 2006.

U.S. Department of State, Office of the Historian. *Foreign Relations of the United States, 1969–1976, Richard M. Nixon/Gerald R. Ford.* Vol. 18, *China, 1973–1976.* Washington, DC: Government Printing Office, 2008.

——. *Foreign Relations of the United States, 1969–1976.* Vol. E-13, *Documents on China, 1969–1972.* Washington, DC: Government Printing Office, 2006. http://history.state.gov/historicaldocuments/frus1969-76ve13/comp1.

Vartanov, V. N. *Voiia v Koree 1950–1953 gg.: Dokumenty i materialy* [Korean War Documents, 1950–1953]. Moscow: unpublished, 1997.

Volokhova, A. "Dokumenty, arkhivy: Peregovopy o peremirii v Koree (1951–1953 gg.) (po materialam Arkhiva vneshnei politiki Rossii)" [Documents, Archives: Truce Negotiations in Korea (1951–1953) (based on Materials from the Russian Archive on Foreign Policy)]. *Problemy Dal'nego Vostoka* [Problems of the Far East] 2 (2000): 96–110.

Volokitina, T. V. et al. *Moskva I Vostochnaia Evropa: Stanovlenie politicheskikh rezhimov sovetskogo tipa: 1949–1953: Ocherki istorii* [War in Korea 1949–1953: Documents and Materials]. Moscow: Rosspen, 2002.

Weishengbu Guojisi [International Department, Ministry of Health], ed. *Weishengbu hezuo xieyi huibian, 1957–2001* [Collection of Health Cooperation Agreements, 1957-2001]. Unpublished, May 2002.

Yanbian Chaoxianzu Zizhizhou Dang'anguan [Archives of the Yanbian Korean Autonomous Prefecture], ed. *Yanbian diwei zhuanshu zhongyao wenjian huibian* [A Compilation of Important Documents of the Yanbian Prefectural Party Committee and the Prefectural Commissioner's Office] 1. Unpublished, December 1986. Cited from Xu Longnan, "Yanbianji Chaoxian renmin jun tuiwu junren caifanglu" [Record of Interviews with Ex-servicemen of the Korean People's Army in Yanbian], *Lengzhan guojishi yanjiu* [Cold War International History Studies], edited by Li Danhui (Beijing: Shijie zhishi chubanshe, 2008), 7:265–287.

Zhonggong Zhongyang Duiwai Lianluobu [International Liaison Department of the Chinese Communist Party Central Committee], ed. *Chaoxian laodongdang zhongyao yanlun, wenjian xuanji, 1971.8–1972.9* [Collection of Important Speeches and Documents of the Korean Workers' Party, August 1971-September 1972]. Unpublished, December 1972.

———, ed. *Chaoxian laodongdang zhongyao yanlun, wenjian xuanji, 1972.10–1973.12* [Collection of Important Speeches and Documents of the Korean Workers' Party, October 1972-December 1973]. Unpublished, 1975.

———, ed. *Chaoxian laodongdang zhongyao yanlun, wenjian xuanji, 1974* [Collection of Important Speeches and Documents of the Korean Workers' Party, 1974]. Unpublished, 1976.

———, ed. *Jin Richeng wenji, 1945–1967* [Collection of Kim Il-sung's Works, 1945–1967]. Unpublished, 1982.

———, ed. *Mao Zedong yu waibin tanhua jilu huibian* [A Collection of Records of Mao Zedong's Conversations with Foreign Guests]. Various vols. Beijing: Unpublished internal edition, 1977. Authors' personal collection.

Zhonggong Zhongyang Wenxian Yanjiushi [Chinese Communist Party Central Committee Party Literature Research Office], ed. *Jianguo yilai zhongyao wenxian xuanbian* [Selected Important Documents Since the Founding of the State]. 20 vols. (1949-1965). Beijing: Zhongyang wenxian chubanshe, 1992–1998.

Zhongguo Renmin Jiefangjun Dongbei Junqu Silingbu [Military Command of the Northeast Military Region of the People's Liberation Army], ed. *Dongbei sannian jiefang zhanzheng junshi ziliao* [Military Materials on the Three-Year War of Liberation in the Northeast]. Unpublished, October 1949.

Zhongguo Renmin Jiefangjun Zhongnanqu Disi Yezhanjun Zhengzhibu [Political Department of the Fourth Field Army of the Central–South Military Region of the People's Liberation Army], ed. *Chaoxian shi Zhongguo qinmi de lingbang gonghuannan de zhanyou* [North Korea Is China's Close Neighbor and Comrade-in-Arms in Sharing Hardship). Unpublished, October 1950.

Zhongguo Renmin Jiefangjun Zongcanmoubu [People's Liberation Army General Staff]. *Zhongguo renmin jiefangjun junshi gongzuo dashiji, 1949.10–1987.12* [A Record of Major Events in People's Liberation Army Military Affairs, October 1949–December 1987]. Unpublished, December 1988.

Zhonghua Renmin Gongheguo Waijiaobu [People's Republic of China Ministry of Foreign Affairs], ed. *Mao Zedong jiejian waibin tanhua jilu huibian* [Collection of Records of Mao Zedong's Conversations with Foreign Guests]. Various vols. Unpublished.

Zhonghua Renmin Gongheguo Waijiaobu Tiaoyue Falüsi [Treaty and Law Department of the People's Republic of China Ministry of Foreign Affairs], ed. *Zhonghua renmin gongheguo bianjie shiwu tiaoyue ji: Zhong Chao juan* [Collection on Border Affairs of the People's Republic of China: Volume on China and Korea]. Beijing: Shijie zhishi chubanshe, 2004.

Zhongyang Dang'anguan [Central Archives]. *Zhonggong zhongyang wenjian xuanji* [Selection of Documents of the Central Committee of the Chinese Communist Party]. 18 vols. Beijing: Zhonggong zhongyang dangxiao chubanshe, 1989-1992.

Secondary Sources in Western Languages

Acheson, Dean. *Present at the Creation: My Years in the State Department.* New York: W. W. Norton, 1987.

Agov, Avram. "North Korea in the Socialist World: Integration and Divergence, 1945-1970." PhD diss., University of British Columbia, 2010.

An, Tai Sung. *North Korea: A Political Handbook.* Wilmington, DE: Scholarly Resources, 1983.

Armstrong, Charles K. " 'Fraternal Socialism': The International Reconstruction of Korea, 1953-62." *Cold War History* 5, no. 2 (May 2005): 161-187.

——. "*Juche* and North Korea's Global Aspirations." *North Korea International Documentation Project Working Paper* 1 (2009).

——. "Trends in the Study of North Korea." *Journal of Asian Studies* 70, no. 2 (May 2011): 357–371.

——. *Tyranny of the Weak: North Korea and the World, 1950–1992.* Ithaca, NY: Cornell University Press, 2013.

Armstrong, Charles K., and John Barry Kotch. "Sino–American Negotiations on Korea and Kissinger's UN Diplomacy." *Cold War History* 15, no. 1 (2015): 113-134.

Bajanov, Evgueni. "Assessing the Politics of the Korean War, 1949-51." *Cold War International History Project Bulletin* 6-7 (Winter 1995–1996): 54, 87-91.

Balkanskii, Andrei. *Kim Ir Sen* [Kim Il-sung]. Moscow: Molodaia Gvardiia, 2011.

Barnett, Michael N., and Jack S. Levy. "Domestic Sources of Alliances and Alignments: The Case of Egypt, 1962-73." *International Organization* 45, no. 3 (Summer 1991): 369-395.

Brazinsky, Gregg. "Between Ideology and Strategy: China's Security Policy Toward the Korean Peninsula Since Rapprochement." In *Trilateralism and Beyond: Great Power Politics and the Korean Security Dilemma During and After the Cold War,* edited by Robert A. Wampler, 163–188. Kent, OH: Kent State University Press, 2011.

———. "Korea's Great Divergence: North and South Korea Between 1972 and 1987." In *The Cold War in East Asia, 1945–1991*, edited by Tsuyoshi Hasegawa, 241–264. Stanford, CA: Stanford University Press, 2011.

Buzo, Adrian. *The Guerilla Dynasty: Politics and Leadership in North Korea*. London: I. B. Tauris, 1999.

Cha, Victor. *The Impossible State: North Korea, Past and Future*. New York: Ecco, 2012.

Chen, Jian. *China's Road to the Korean War: The Making of the Sino–American Confrontation*. New York: Columbia University Press, 1994.

———. "Limits of the 'Lips and Teeth' Alliance." In *Uneasy Allies: Fifty Years of China–North Korean Relations*. Asia Program Special Report 115 (September 2003): 4–10. https://www.wilsoncenter.org/sites/default/files/asia_rpt115b.pdf.

———. *Mao's China and the Cold War*. Chapel Hill: University of North Carolina Press, 2001.

———. "Reorienting the Cold War: The Implications of China's Early Cold War Experience, Taking Korea as a Central Test Case." In *The Cold War in East Asia, 1945–1991*, edited by Tsuyoshi Hasegawa, 81–97. Stanford, CA: Stanford University Press, 2011.

Cheng, Xiaohe. "The Evolution of the Lips and Teeth Relationship: China–North Korea Relations in the 1960s." In *Chinese and North Korea: Strategic and Policy Perspectives from a Changing China*, edited by Carla Freeman, 119–137. New York: Palgrave Macmillan, 2015.

Choy, Bong-yoon. *A History of the Korean Reunification Movement: Its Issues and Prospects*. Peoria, IL: Research Committee on Korean Unification, Institute of International Studies, Bradley University, 1984.

Christensen, Thomas J. *Worse than a Monolith: Alliance Politics and Problems of Coercive Diplomacy in Asia*. Princeton, NJ: Princeton University Press, 2011.

Christensen, Thomas J., and Jack Snyder. "Chain Gangs and Passed Bucks: Predicting Alliance Patterns in Multipolarity." *International Organization* 44, no. 2 (Spring 1990): 137–168.

Chung, Chin W. "North Korea's Relations with China." In *The Foreign Relations of North Korea: New Perspectives*, edited by Jae Kyu Park, Byung Chul Koh, and Tae-Hawn Kwak, 169–199. Boulder, CO: Westview, 1987.

———. *P'yŏngyang Between Peking and Moscow: North Korea's Involvement in the Sino–Soviet Dispute, 1958–1975*. Tuscaloosa: University of Alabama Press, 1978.

Chung, Jae Ho. *Between Ally and Partner: Korea-China Relations and the United States*. New York: Columbia University Press, 2007.

———. "South Korea–China Economic Relations: The Current Situation and its Implications." *Asian Survey* 28, no. 10 (October 1988): 1031–1048.

Cumings, Bruce. *Korea's Place in the Sun: A Modern History*. Updated ed. New York: W. W. Norton, 2005.

———. *The Origins of the Korean War*. Vol. 2, *The Roaring of the Cataract, 1947–1950*. Princeton, NJ: Princeton University Press, 1990.

David, Steven R. "Explaining Third World Alignment." *World Politics* 43, no. 2 (January 1991): 233-256.

Delury, John. "The Problem of Feudalism: Sino–Korean Relations After Mao and from Kim to Kim." Paper presented at the Association for Asian Studies annual conference, Washington, DC, March 24, 2018.

Engel, Jeffrey A., ed. *The China Diary of George H. W. Bush: The Making of a Global President*. Princeton, NJ: Princeton University Press, 2008.

Fravel, M. Taylor. *Strong Borders, Secure Nation: Cooperation and Conflict in China's Territorial Disputes*. Princeton, NJ: Princeton University Press, 2008.

Freeman, Carla, ed. *China and North Korea: Strategic and Policy Perspectives from a Changing China*. New York: Palgrave Macmillan, 2015.

Gills, Barry K. *Korea Versus Korea: A Case of Contested Legitimacy*. London: Routledge, 1996.

Goncharov, Sergei N., John W. Lewis, and Xue Litai. *Uncertain Partners: Stalin, Mao and the Korean War*. Stanford, CA: Stanford University Press, 1993.

Gvalia, Giorgi, David Siroky, Bidzina Lebanidze, and Zurab Iashvili. "Thinking Outside the Bloc: Explaining the Foreign Policies of Small States." *Security Studies* 22, no. 1 (January-March 2013): 98–131.

Haas, Mark L. *The Ideological Origins of Great Power Politics, 1789–1989*. Ithaca, NY: Cornell University Press, 2005.

Halliday, Jon, ed. *The Artful Albanian: Memoirs of Enver Hoxha*. London: Chatto & Windus, 1986.

Hong, Seuk-ryule. "U.S.–China and Inter-Korean Relations in the Early 1970s." Conference paper, East China Normal University, Shanghai, June 4, 2009.

Keller, Renata. *Mexico's Cold War: Cuba, the United States, and the Legacy of the Mexican Revolution*. New York: Cambridge University Press, 2015.

Kim, Deok. "Sino–Soviet Dispute and North Korea," *Korea Observer* 10, no. 1 (Spring 1979): 3-30.

Kim, Donggil. "Prelude to War? The Repatriation of Koreans from the Chinese PLA, 1949–50." *Cold War History* 12, no. 2 (May 2012): 227–242.

Kim, Ilpyong J. "China in North Korean Foreign Policy." In *North Korean Foreign Relations in the Post–Cold War Era*, edited by Samuel Kim, 94–113. New York: Oxford University Press, 1998.

Kim, Il-sung. *All for the Postwar Rehabilitation and Development of the National Economy*. Pyongyang: Foreign Languages Publishing House, 1961.

——. *Selected Works*. Pyongyang: Foreign Languages Publishing House, 1971. 8 vols.

——. *Works*. Pyongyang: Foreign Languages Publishing House, 1984-2009. 50 vols.

Kim, Samuel S. *China, the United Nations, and World Order*. Princeton, NJ: Princeton University Press, 1979.

——. "The Making of China's Korea Policy in the Era of Reform." In *The Making of Chinese Foreign and Security Policy in the Era of Reform, 1978–2000*, edited by David M. Lampton, 371–408. Stanford, CA: Stanford University Press, 2001.

——. "Pyongyang, the Third World and Global Politics." In *The Two Koreas in World Politics*, edited by Tae-Hwan Kwak, Wayne Patterson, and Edward A. Olsen, 59–86. Seoul: Kyungnam University Press, 1983.

——. *The Two Koreas and the Great Powers*. New York: Cambridge University Press, 2006.

Kim, Seung-young. "Miki Takeo's Initiative on the Korean Question and U.S.–Japanese Diplomacy." *Journal of American–East Asian Relations* 20, no. 4 (December 2014): 377–405.

Kirby, William C., Robert Ross, and Gong Li, eds. *Normalization of U.S.–China Relations: An International History.* Cambridge, MA: Harvard University Asia Center, 2005.

Kissinger, Henry. *On China.* New York: Penguin, 2011.

——. *The White House Years.* Boston: Little, Brown, 1979.

Koh, Byung Chul. *The Foreign Policy of North Korea.* New York: Praeger, 1969.

——. *The Foreign Policy Systems of North and South Korea.* Berkeley: University of California Press, 1984.

Kovalev, Ivan. "The Stalin–Mao Dialogue." *Far Eastern Affairs* (Moscow) 1 (1992): 100-113; and 2 (1992): 94-111.

Kwon, Heonik. "The Korean War and Sino-North Korean Friendship." *Asia Pacific Journal* 11, no. 4 (August 8, 2013): 1–19.

Lalaj, Ana, Christian F. Ostermann, and Ryan Gage, eds. " 'Albania Is Not Cuba': Sino–Albanian Summits and the Sino–Soviet Split." *Cold War International History Project Bulletin* 16 (Fall 2007-Winter 2008): 183–340.

Lankov, Andrei. *Crisis in North Korea: The Failure of De-Stalinization, 1956.* Honolulu: University of Hawai'i Press, 2004.

——. *From Stalin to Kim Il-sung: The Formation of North Korea, 1945–1960.* London: C. Hurst, 2002.

Ledovskii, A. M. "Stalin, Mao Tszedun i koreiskaii voina, 1950-1953 godov" [Stalin, Mao Zedong, and the Korean War, 1950-1953]. *Novaia i noveishaia istoriia* [Modern and Contemporary History] 5 (2005): 79–113.

Lee, Chae-Jin. *China and Korea: Dynamic Relations.* Stanford, CA: Hoover Institution, 1996.

Lee, Dongjun. "The Politics of Lips and Teeth: Reexamining the 1961 Sino-North Korean Alliance Treaty from the Chinese Perspective." *Korean Journal of Security Affairs* 16, no. 2 (December 2011): 86-107.

Lerner, Mitchell. " 'Mostly Propaganda in Nature': Kim Il-sung, the *Juche* Ideology and the Second Korean War." *North Korea International Documentation Project Working Paper* 3 (2011).

Li, Danhui. "Vietnam and Chinese Policy Toward the United States." In *Normalization of U.S.–China Relations: An International History,* edited by William C. Kirby, Robert Ross, and Gong Li, 175–208. Cambridge, MA: Harvard University Asia Center, 2005.

Li, Danhui, and Yafeng Xia. "Competing for Leadership: Split or Détente in the Sino–Soviet Bloc, 1969-1961." *International History Review* 30, no. 3 (September 2008): 545-574.

——. *Mao and the Sino–Soviet Split, 1959–1973: A New History.* Lanham, MD: Lexington, 2018.

Lüthi, Lorenz. "The Vietnam War and China's Third-Line Defense Planning Before the Cultural Revolution, 1964-1966." *Journal of Cold War Studies* 10, no. 1 (Winter 2008): 26-51.

MacFarquhar, Roderick, Timothy Cheek, and Eugene Wu, eds. *The Secret Speeches of Chairman Mao: From the Hundred Flowers to the Great Leap Forward.* Cambridge, MA: Council on East Asian Studies, Harvard University, 1989.

Mastny, Vojtech. *The Cold War and Soviet Insecurity: The Stalin Years.* New York: Oxford University Press, 1996.

Mearsheimer, John J. *The Tragedy of Great Power Politics.* New York: Norton, 2001.

Michishita, Narushige. *North Korea's Military-Diplomatic Campaigns, 1966–2008.* New York: Routledge, 2010.

Miller, Eric A., and Arkady Toritsyn. "Bringing the Leader Back In: Internal Threats and Alignment Theory in the Commonwealth of Independent States." *Security Studies* 14, no. 2 (April–June 2005): 325-363.

Morris-Suzuki, Tessa. *Exodus to North Korea: Shadows from Japan's Cold War.* Lanham, MD: Rowman & Littlefield, 2007.

Nakajima, Mineo. "The Sino–Soviet Confrontation: Its Roots in the International Background of the Korean War." *Australian Journal of Chinese Affairs* 1 (January 1979): 19-47.

Naughton, Barry. "The Third Front: Defence Industrialization in the Chinese Interior." *China Quarterly* 115 (September 1988): 351-386.

Oberdorfer, Don. *The Two Koreas: A Contemporary History.* New York: Basic Books, 1997.

Owen, John M. "When Do Ideologies Produce Alliances? The Holy Roman Empire, 1517-55." *International Studies Quarterly* 49, no. 1 (March 2005): 73-99.

Park, Won Gon. "The United Nations Command in Korea: Past, Present, and Future." *Korean Journal of Defense Analysis* 21, no. 4 (December 2009): 485–499.

Person, James F. "From Anti-Foreignism to Self-Reliance: The Evolution of North Korea's *Juche* Ideology, 1953–1963." Paper presented at the conference Northeast Asia in the Cold War: New Evidence and Perspectives, Hokkaido University, Summer 2008.

——. Introduction to "New Evidence on North Korea in 1956." *Cold War International History Project Bulletin* 16 (Fall 2007-Winter 2008): 447–454.

——. "New Evidence on the 1956 September Plenum of the Korean Workers' Party." Paper presented at the international workshop "The Cold War and the Two Koreas," Woodrow Wilson International Center for Scholars, April 19, 2016.

——. "North Korea in 1956: Reconsidering the August Plenum and the Sino-Soviet Joint Intervention," *Cold War History* (September 25, 2018), pp. 1–22. Available at https://doi.org/10.1080/14682745.2018.1509849.

——. " 'We Need Help from Outside': The North Korean Opposition Movement of 1956." *Cold War International History Project Working Paper* 52 (August 2006).

——, ed. "Limits of the 'Lips and Teeth' Alliance: New Evidence on Sino–DPRK Relations 1955–1984." *North Korea International Documentation Project Document Reader* 2 (March 2009).

Pochtarev, A. N. "Iz istorii Sovetsko-Koreiskikh otnoshenii v 1920–1950e dofy" [The History of Soviet–Korean Relations, 1920–1950]. *Novaia i noveishaia istoria* [Modern and Contemporary History] 5 (1999): 135–160.

Pollack, Jonathan D. *No Exit: North Korea, Nuclear Weapons, and International Security.* New York: Routledge, 2011.

Postwar Reconstruction and Development of the National Economy of the DPRK. Pyong-yang: Foreign Languages Publishing House, 1957.

Pribbenow, Merle. "North Korean Pilots in the Skies over Vietnam." *North Korea International Documentation Project* (December 1, 2011). https://www.wilsoncenter.org /publication/north-korean-pilots-the-skies-over-vietnam.

Radchenko, Sergey S. "The Soviet Union and the North Korean Seizure of the USS *Pueblo*: Evidence from the Russian Archives." *Cold War International History Project Working Paper* 47 (April 2005).

Rees, David. *Korea: The Limited War*. New York: St. Martin's, 1964.

Resnick, Evan N. "Strange Bedfellows: U.S. Bargaining Behavior with Allies of Convenience." *International Security* 35, no. 3 (Winter 2010/2011): 144-184.

Scalapino, Robert, and Chong-sik Lee. *Communism in Korea*. 2 vols. Berkeley: University of California Press, 1972.

Schaefer, Bernd. "North Korean 'Adventurism' and China's Long Shadow, 1966-1972." *Cold War International History Project Working Paper* 44 (October 2004).

——. "Overconfidence Shattered: North Korean Unification Policy, 1971-1975." *North Korea International Documentation Project Working Paper* 2 (December 2010).

——. "Weathering the Sino–Soviet Conflict: The GDR and North Korea, 1949-1989." *Cold War International History Project Bulletin* 14-15 (Winter 2003-Spring 2004): 25-38.

Schweller, Randall L. "Bandwagoning for Profit: Bringing the Revisionist State Back In." *International Security* 19, no. 1 (Summer 1994): 72-107.

Scobell, Andrew. *China and North Korea: From Comrades-in-Arms to Allies at Arm's Length*. Carlisle Barracks, PA: Strategic Studies Institute, U.S. Army War College, March 2004.

Shen, Zhihua. "Alliance of 'Tooth and Lips' or Marriage of Convenience? The Origins and Development of the Sino-North Korean Alliance, 1946-1958." Translated by Min Song. *U.S.–Korea Institute at SAIS Working Paper* 08–09 (December 2008).

——. "China and the Dispatch of the Soviet Air Force: The Formation of the Chinese–Soviet–Korean Alliance in the Early Stage of the Korean War." *Journal of Strategic Studies* 33, no. 2 (April 2010): 211-230.

——. *Mao, Stalin and the Korean War: Trilateral Communist Relations in the 1950s*. Translated by Neil Silver. London: Routledge, 2012.

——. "On the Eighty-Eighth Brigade and the Sino–Soviet–Korean Triangular Relationship: A Glimpse at the International Antifascist United Front During the War of Resistance Against Japan." *Journal of Modern Chinese History* 9, no. 1 (2015): 3-25.

——. "Sharing a Similar Fate: The Historical Process of the Korean Communists' Merger with the Chinese Communist Party (1919–1936)." *Journal of Modern Chinese History* 11, no. 1 (2017): 1–28.

Shen, Zhihua, and Yafeng Xia. "Chinese-North Korean Relations and China's Policy Toward Korean Cross-Border Migration, 1950-1962." *Journal of Cold War Studies* 16, no. 4 (Fall 2014): 133-158.

——. "Contested Border: A Historical Investigation into the Sino–Korean Border Issue, 1950-1964." *Asian Perspective* 37, no. 1 (January–March 2013): 1-30.

———. "Hidden Currents During the Honeymoon: Mao Zedong, Khrushchev and the 1957 Moscow Conference." *Journal of Cold War Studies* 11, no. 4 (Fall 2009): 74-117.

———. *Mao and the Sino–Soviet Partnership, 1945–1959: A New History.* Lanham, MD: Lexington, 2015.

———. "Mao Zedong's Erroneous Decision During the Korean War: China's Rejection of the UN Cease-Fire Resolution in Early 1951." *Asian Perspective* 35, no. 2 (April-June 2011): 187-209.

———. "New Evidence for China's Role in the Hungarian Crisis of October 1956: A Note." *International History Review* 31, no. 3 (September 2009): 558-575.

———. " 'Whirlwind' of China: Zhou Enlai's Shuttle Diplomacy in 1957 and Its Effect." *Cold War History* 10, no. 4 (November 2010): 513-535.

Shimotomai, Nobuo. "Kim Il-sung's Balancing Act between Moscow and Beijing, 1956-1972." In *The Cold War in East Asia, 1945–1991*, edited by Tsuyoshi Hasegawa, 122–151. Stanford, CA: Stanford University Press, 2011.

Shin, Sera. "Politicheskaya bor'ba v rukovodstve KNDR v 1953–1956 gg.: Prichiny i dynamika" [Political Struggle within the DPRK Leadership in 1953–1956: Reasons and Dynamics], *Problemy dal'nego Vostoka* [Problems of the Far East] 3 (2009): 119–135.

Shin, V. A. *Kitai i koreiskie gosudarstva vo vtoroi polovine XX stoletiia* [China and North Korea in the Second Half of the Twentieth Century]. Moscow: ID-vo MGU, 1998.

Smith, Hazel. *North Korea: Markets and Military Rule.* Cambridge: Cambridge University Press, 2015.

Snyder, Glenn H. *Alliance Politics.* Ithaca, NY: Cornell University Press, 1997.

Snyder, Scott. *China's Rise and the Two Koreas: Politics, Economics, Security.* Boulder, CO: Lynne Rienner, 2009.

Suh, Dae-Sook. *Kim Il-sung: The North Korean Leader.* New York: Columbia University Press, 1988.

Suh, Jae-Jung, ed. *Origins of North Korea's Juche: Colonialism, War, and Development.* Lanham, MD: Lexington, 2013.

Synn, Seung-kwon. "Kim Il-sung Between Moscow and Peking." *Korean Journal of International Studies* 5, no. 2-3 (Spring-Summer 1974): 7-16.

Szalontai, Balázs. "In the Shadow of Vietnam: A New Look at North Korea's Militant Strategy, 1962–1970." *Journal of Cold War Studies* 14, no. 4 (Fall 2012): 122–166.

———. *Kim Il-sung in the Khrushchev Era: Soviet–DPRK Relations and the Roots of North Korean Despotism, 1953–1964.* Stanford, CA: Stanford University Press, 2006.

———. "Whose War Plan Was It? Sino–DPRK Relations and Kim Il-sung's Military Strategy, 1965-1967." *North Korea International Documentation Project, e-Dossier* 20 (April 2016). https://www.wilsoncenter.org/publication/sino-dprk-relations-and-kim -il-sungs-militant-strategy-1965-1967.

———. " 'You Have No Political Line of Your Own': Kim Il-sung and the Soviets, 1953–1964." *Cold War International History Project Bulletin* 14-15 (Winter 2003-Spring 2004): 87-103.

Szalontai, Balázs, and Sergey Radchenko. "North Korea's Efforts to Acquire Nuclear Technology and Nuclear Weapons: Evidence from Russian and Hungarian Archives." *Cold War International History Project Working Paper* 53 (August 2006).

Tkachenko, V. P. *Koreiskii poluostrov i interresy Rossii* [The Korean Peninsula and Russian Interests]. Moscow: Izd. firma "Vostochnaia literatura," 2000.

Togo, Kazuhiko. "Japan's Foreign Policy Under Détente: Relations with China and the Soviet Union, 1971–1973." In *The Cold War in East Asia, 1945–1991*, edited by Tsuyoshi Hasegawa, 180–212. Stanford, CA: Stanford University Press, 2011.

Torkunov, A. V. *Zagadocnaia voina: Koreiskii konflikt 1950–1953 godov* [The Mysterious War: The Korean Conflict of 1950-1953]. Moscow: Rosspen, 2000.

Tsui, David. "Did the DPRK and the PRC Sign a Mutual Security Pact?" Paper presented at an international conference on the Cold War in Asia, Hong Kong, January 1996.

Tudda, Chris. *A Cold War Turning Point: Nixon and China, 1969–1972*. Baton Rouge: Louisiana State University Press, 2012.

Wada, Haruki. "Stalin and the Japanese Communist Party, 1945–1953: In the Light of New Russian Archival Documents." Paper presented at an international conference on the Cold War in Asia, Hong Kong, January 1996.

Walt, Stephen M. *The Origins of Alliances*. Ithaca, NY: Cornell University Press, 1987.

Waltz, Kenneth N. *Theory of International Politics*. New York: McGraw-Hill, 1979.

Weathersby, Kathryn. Introduction to "New Findings on the Korean War." *Cold War International History Project Bulletin* 3 (Fall 1993): 1, 14-15.

——. Introduction to "New Russian Documents on the Korean War." *Cold War International History Project Bulletin* 6–7 (Winter 1995–96): 30-36.

Westad, O. A. "The Sino–Soviet Alliance and the United States: Wars, Policies, and Perceptions, 1950–1961." Paper presented at an international conference on the Cold War in Asia, Hong Kong, January 1996.

Xia, Yafeng. "Deng Xiaoping." In *Mental Maps in the Late Cold War, 1968–91*, edited by Steven Casey and Jonathan Wright, 137–155. Basingstoke: Palgrave Macmillan, 2015.

——. "Mao Zedong." In *Mental Maps in the Early Cold War Era, 1945–1968*, edited by Steven Casey and Jonathan Wright, 160–179. Basingstoke: Palgrave Macmillan, 2011.

——. *Negotiating with the Enemy: U.S.–China Talks During the Cold War, 1949–1972*. Bloomington: Indiana University Press, 2006.

——. "The Taiwan Issue in Sino–American Rapprochement Negotiations." In *Taiwan in the 21st Century*, edited by Xiaobing Li and Zuohong Pan, 281–317. Lanham, MD: University Press of America, 2003.

——. "Vietnam for Taiwan? A Reappraisal of Nixon-Zhou Enlai Negotiations on [sic] Shanghai Communiqué." *American Review of China Studies* 3, no. 1 (Spring 2002): 35–55.

Yang, Kuisong. "The Sino–Soviet Border Clash of 1969: From Zhenbao Island to Sino–American Rapprochement." *Cold War History* 1, no. 1 (August 2000): 21–52.

Yang, Kuisong, and Yafeng Xia. "Vacillating Between Revolution and Détente: Mao's Changing Psyche and Policy Toward the U.S., 1969–1976." *Diplomatic History* 34, no. 2 (April 2010): 395–423.

Yiu, Mike Myung-Kun. "The Factors of North Korean Neutral Behavior in the Sino–Soviet Conflict." *International Behavioral Scientist* 4, no. 1 (March 1972): 1-10.

Zagoria, Donald S. "North Korea: Between Moscow and Beijing." *North Korea Today: Strategic and Domestic Issues*, edited by Robert A. Scalapino and Jun-yop Kim, 351–371. Berkeley: Institute of East Asian Studies, University of California, 1983.

Zagoria, Donald S., and Young Kun Kim. "North Korea and the Major Powers." In *The Two Koreas in East Asian Affairs*, edited by William J. Barnds, 19–46. New York: New York University Press, 1976.

Zubok, Vladislov, and Constantine Pleshakov. *Inside the Kremlin's Cold War: From Stalin to Khrushchev*. Cambridge, MA: Harvard University Press, 1996.

Secondary Sources in Chinese, Korean, and Japanese

Acheng [Shan Ruhong]. *Wo jianfu de shiming: Magong zhongyang zhengzhiju weiyuan Acheng huiyilu* [My Mission: Memoirs of Malayan Communist Party Central Committee Member Acheng]. Kuala Lumpur: Ershiyi shiji chubanshe, 2007.

An Longzhen. *Yanbian Chaoxianzu zizhizhou zhouzhi* [Gazetteer of Yanbian Korean Autonomous Prefecture]. Beijing: Zhonghua shuju, 1996.

Bazhanova, Natalia. *Kiroe sŏn Puk Han kyŭngje* [The North Korean Economy at a Crossroads]. Translated by Yang Chunyong. Seoul: Hanguk kyŏngjie sinmunsa, 1992.

Bo Yibo. *Ruogan zhongda juece yu shijian de huigu* [Recollections of Certain Major Policy Decisions and Events]. 2 vols. Beijing: Zhongyang dangxiao chubanshe, 1991.

Chai Chengwen and Zhao Yongtian. *Banmendian tanpan* [The Panmunjom Negotiations]. Beijing: Jiefangjun chubanshe, 1989.

Che Zhejiu. "Zhongguo Chaoxianzu de xingcheng jiqi bianhua" [The Formation and Changes in China's Korean Situation]. *Yanbian daxue xuebao* [Journal of Yanbian University] 3 (1998): 137–142.

Chen Yi Zhuan Bianxiezu [Chen Yi Biography Editorial Committee]. *Chen Yi zhuan* [A Biography of Chen Yi]. Beijing: Dangdai Zhongguo chubanshe, 1997.

Ch'oe Myŏng-hae. *Chungguk, Pukhan tongmaeng kwan'gye: Pulp'yŏnhan tonggŏ ŭi yŏksa* [Sino-North Korean Alliance Relations: The History of Inconvenient Cohabitation]. Seoul: Orŭm, 2009.

Collected Works of Kim Il-sung. Pyongyang: Korean Workers' Party Press, 1993.

Committee on Korean Central Yearbook, ed. *General Book of North Korea (1945–1968)*. Seoul: Institute Communist Circle Issue, 1968.

Dangdai Zhongguo Congshu Bianjibu [Editorial Department of the Contemporary China Series], ed. *Dangdai Zhongguo waijiao* [Contemporary Chinese Diplomacy]. Beijing: Zhongguo shehui kexue chubanshe, 1988.

Ding Xuesong and Yang Dehua. *Diyiwei nü dashi: Ding Xuesong huiyilu* [The First Female Ambassador: Memoirs of Ding Xuesong]. Nanjing: Jiangsu renmin chubanshe, 2000.

Ding Xuesong et al. "Huiyi dongbei jiefang zhanzheng qijian dongbeiju zhu BeiChaoxian banshichu" [Recollections of the Northeast Bureau Office in North Korea During the Chinese Civil War in the Northeast]. *Zhonggong dangshi ziliao* [Materials on the History of the Chinese Communist Party] 17 (1986): 297–310.

Dong Ji. "Wenhua dageming qianqi ZhongChao guanxi de lishi kaocha, 1966–1970" [A Historical Investigation into Sino–North Korean Relations During the Early Phase of the Cultural Revolution, 1966–1970]. *Lengzhan guojishi yanjiu* [Cold War International History Studies] 2 (2014): 78–97.

Fan Chengzuo. "Aerbaniya zhichi Zhongguo 'Wenhua dageming' shimo" [The Full Story of Albania's Support of the Chinese "Cultural Revolution"]. *Zhonggong dangshi ziliao* [Materials on the History of the Chinese Communist Party] 4 (2004): 142–151.

——. *Wangshi rushi: Fan Chengzuo huiyilu* [The Past Is Like a Poem: Memoirs of Fan Chengzuo]. Nanjing: Nanjing chubanshe, 2008.

Gang, In Deok, ed. *Pukhan chŏnsŏ* [A Complete Book of North Korea]. Vol. 1. Seoul: Research Center of the Far East Issue, 1974.

Gao Wenqian. *Wannian Zhou Enlai* [Zhou Enlai's Later Years]. Hong Kong: Mingjing chubanshe, 2003.

Guowuyuan Bangongting Dashiji Bianxiezu [Editorial Committee on the Chronology of the General Office of the State Council]. *Zhonghua renmin gongheguo zhongyang renmin zhengfu dashiji* [A Record of Major Events in the Central Government of the People's Republic of China]. Unpublished, 1991.

Han Zheshi, ed. *Changbai Chaoxian zizhixian zhi* [Gazetteer of Changbai Korean Autonomous County]. Beijing: Zhonghua shuju, 1993.

Hong Xuezhi. *KangMei yuanChao zhanzheng huiyi* [Recollections of the War to Resist America and to Aid Korea]. Beijing: Jiefangjun wenyi chubanshe, 1990.

Hwang Chang-yŏp. *Nanŭn yŏksa chillirŭl poatta* [I Witnessed the Historical Truth]. Seoul: Hanul, 1998.

Jilinsheng Shekeyuan [Jilin Province Academy of Social Sciences], ed. *ZhongChao guanxi tongshi* [A General History of Sino–Korean Relations]. 4 vols. Changchun: Jilin renmin chubanshe, 1996.

Jin Baizhu. "Examining the Motives for the Formation of the Sino–Korean Alliance: On the Process of the Formation of the Sino–Korean Alliance" [in Japanese]. *Chūgoku kenkyū geppō* [Chinese Studies Monthly] 64, no. 5 (May 2010): 1–14.

Jin Chongji, ed. *Liu Shaoqi zhuan* [A Biography of Liu Shaoqi]. Beijing: Zhonggong zhongyang wenxian chubanshe, 1998.

——, ed. *Zhou Enlai zhuan* [A Biography of Zhou Enlai]. 4 vols. Beijing: Zhongyang wenxian chubanshe, 1998.

Jin Jingyi. "Guanyu Zhongguo jundui zhong Chaoxianzu guanbing fanhui Chaoxian de lishi kaocha" [A Historical Investigation into the Return to Korea of Ethnic Korean Officers and Soldiers from the Chinese Army]. *Shixue jikan* [Collected Papers on Historical Studies] 3 (May 2007): 52–61.

Junshi Kexueyuan Junshi Lishi Yanjiubu [History Research Department of the Academy of Military Science], ed. *KangMei yuanChao zhanzhengshi* [A History of the War to Resist America and to Aid Korea]. 3 vols. Beijing: Junshi kexue chubanshe, 2000.

KangMei yuanChao zhanzheng houqin jingyan zongjie: Jiben jingyan [Summary of the Logistics Experience in the War to Resist America and to Aid Korea: Basic Experience]. Beijing: Jindun chubanshe, 1987.

KangMei yuanChao zhanzheng houqin jingyan zongjie: Zhuanye qinwu [Summary of the Logistics Experience in the War to Resist America and to Aid Korea: Professional Logistics Affairs]. Beijing: Jindun chubanshe, 1987.

KangMei yuanChao zhanzheng houqin jingyan zongjie: Ziliao xuanbian (Tielu yunshu lei) (Xiace) [Summary of the Logistics Experience in the War to Resist America and to Aid Korea: Collection of Materials (Railways and Transportation). Vol. 2]. Beijing: Jiefangjun chubanshe, 1988.

Kardelj, Edvard. *Kade'er huiyilu, 1944–1957* [Memoirs of Kardelj, 1944–1957]. Translated by Li Daijun et al. Beijing: Xinhua chubanshe, 1981.

Kim Ch'ang-hŭi. "Puk'anŭi t'ongch'iinyŏm 'kimilsŏng-kimjŏngilchuŭi' punsŏk" [An Analysis of North Korea's Governing Theory: "Kim Il-sung–Kim Jong-ilism"]. *Han'guk chŏngchi'i yŏn'gu* [Journal of Korean Politics] 22, no. 3 (2013): 187–211.

Kim Donggil. " 'Sanguo tong moulun' fenxi: Chaoxian zhanzheng qiyuan de zai sikao" [An Analysis of the "Theory of Conspiracy Among the Three States": Reconsidering the Origins of the Korean War]. *Dangdai Zhongguoshi yanjiu* [Contemporary China History Studies] 2 (2006): 112–121.

——. "Zhongguo renmin jiefangjun zhong de Chaoxian shi hui Chaoxian wenti" [Some New Insights on the Return of the Ethnic Korean Divisions in the PLA to North Korea]. *Lishi yanjiu* [History Research] 6 (2006): 103–114.

Kim Hak-chun. *Chaoxian wushiqinian shi* [Fifty-Seven Years of North Korean History]. Translated by Zhang Ying. Translated Series on China's Northeast Border. Unpublished internal reference, 2005.

——. *Pukhan 50-yŏnsa: Uri ka ttŏ anayhal pantchok ŭi uri yŏksa* [A Fifty-Year History of North Korea]. Seoul: Tonga Ch'ulp'ansa, 1995.

Kim Il-sung. *Jin Richeng huiyilu: Yu shiji tongxing* [Memoirs of Kim Il-sung: With the Century]. 8 vols. Pingrang: Waiwen chubanshe, 1998.

——. *Jin Richeng zhuzuo ji* [Works of Kim Il-sung]. Various vols. Pingrang: Waiwen chubanshe, 1971-1996.

Kim Nam-sik, and Sim Chi-yŏn. *Pak Hŏn-yŏng nosŏn pip'an* [The Criticism of Pak Hŏn-yŏng's Line]. Seoul: Segye, 1986.

Kim Yong-hyeon. "Studies on the Nationalization of North Korea's Military: Focusing on the Years from 1950 to 1960" [in Korean]. PhD diss., Graduate School of Dongkuk University, 2001.

——. "A Study of the Role of the Chinese People's Volunteer Army After the Korean War" [in Korean]. *Pukhan Yŏn'gu Hakhoe* [North Korean Studies Review] 10, no. 2 (2006): 148–162.

Lee Dongjun. *Mikan no heiwa: Bei-Chū wakai to Chōsen mondai no hen'yo, 1969–1975* [Incomplete Peace: Sino–U.S. Rapprochement and the Transformation of the Korean Issue, 1969–1975]. Tokyo: Hōsei dagaiku shuppankyoku, 2010.

Lei Yingfu. "KangMei yuanChao zhanzheng jige zhongda juece de huiyi (xu yi)" [Recollections about Several Important Policy Decisions During the War to Resist America and to Aid Korea (Part 3)]. *Dangde wenxian* [Party Literature] 5 (1994): 39–49.

Li Danhui. "Dakai ZhongMei guanxi jincheng zhong de Zhou Enlai" [Zhou Enlai in the Sino–American Rapprochement]. *Lengzhan guojishi yanjiu* [Cold War International History Studies] 6 (Summer 2008): 141–200.

——. "Dui 1962 nian Xinjiang I Ta shijian qiyin de lishi kaocha: Laizi Zhongguo Xinjiang de dang'an cailiao" [A Historical Investigation of the 1962 Ili and Tacheng Incidents in Xinjiang: Archival Materials from Xinjiang]. In *Beijing yu Mosike: Cong lianmeng zouxiang duikang* [Beijing and Moscow: From Alliance to Confrontation], edited by Li Danhui, 480–509. Guilin: Guangxi shifan daxue chubanshe, 2002.

——. "ZhongMei huanhe yu yuanYue kangMei: Zhongguo waijiao zhanlüe tiaozheng zhong de Yuenan yinsu" [The Sino–American Rapprochement and the War to Aid Vietnam and Resist America: The Vietnam Factor in China's Diplomatic Strategic Adjustment]. *Dangde wenxian* [Party Literature] 3 (2002): 67–77.

Li Haiwen. "Zhonggong zhongyang jiujing heshi jueding zhiyuanjun chuguo zuozhan?" [When Did the Chinese Communist Party Central Committee Make the Decision to Dispatch the Chinese People's Volunteers to Fight Abroad?]. *Dangde wenxian* [Party Literature] 5 (1993): 85–88, 94.

Li Qianyu. *Cong Wanlong dao A'erjier: Zhongguo yu liuci YaFei huiyi (1955–1965)* [From Bandung to Algiers: China and the Six Afro-Asian Conferences (1955–1965)]. Beijing: Shijie zhishi chubanshe, 2016.

Li Xiangshu. "Guanyu Wu Ting de kangRi geming huodong yanjiu" [A Study of Mu Chong's Anti-Japanese Revolutionary Activities]. Master's thesis, Institute of Modern History, Chinese Academy of Social Sciences, 2006.

Lin Yunhui. *Zhonghua renmin gongheguoshi. Di 4 juan. Wutuobang yundong: Cong dayuejin dao dajihuang, 1958–1961* [The History of the People's Republic of China. Vol. 4, The Utopian Movement: From the Great Leap Forward to the Great Famine, 1958-1961]. Hong Kong: Chinese University Press, 2008.

Liu Chongwen et al., eds. *Liu Shaoqi nianpu, 1898–1969* [A Chronology of Liu Shaoqi, 1898-1969]. 2 vols. Beijing: Zhongyang wenxian chubanshe, 1996.

Liu Jinzhi, Zhang Minqiu, and Zhang Xiaoming, eds. *Dangdai Zhong Han guanxi* [Contemporary China–Republic of Korea Relations]. Beijing: Zhongguo shehui kexue chubanshe, 1998.

Liu Ningyi. *Lishi huiyi* [Historical Recollections]. Beijing: Renmin ribao chubanshe, 1996.

Liu Shufa, ed. *Chen Yi nianpu* [A Chronology of Chen Yi]. 2 vols. Beijing: Renmin chubanshe, 1995.

Li Xiannian Zhuan Bianxiezu, E Yu Bianqu Geming Shi Bianjibu [Editorial Board of Li Xiannian's Biography, and Editorial Board of the Revolutionary History of the Eyu Base Area], ed. *Li Xiannian nianpu* [Chronology of Li Xiannian], vol. 6. Beijing: Zhongyang wenxian chubanshe, 2011.

Liu Yazhou. *Liu Yazhou wenji* [Collection of Liu Yazhou's Writings], vol. 2. Beijing: Changjiang wenyi chubanshe, 2004.

Ma Jisen. *Waijiaobu wenge jishi* [The Cultural Revolution in the Foreign Ministry]. Hong Kong: Chinese University Press, 2003.

Mao Zedong junshi wenji [Collection of Mao Zedong's Military Writings]. 6 vols. Beijing: Junshi kexue chubanshe and Zhongyang wenxian chubanshe, 1993.

Nam Hyŏn-uk. *Chungsoŭi taebugwŏnjo mit muyŏkhyŏnhwang, 1946–1978* [Chinese and Soviet Assistance to North Korea and the Status of Trade, 1946–1978]. Seoul: Korea Institute of National Unification. Unpublished, February 1979.

Nie Rongzhen. *Nie Rongzhen huiyilu* [Memoirs of Nie Rongzhen]. 2nd ed. Beijing: Jiefangjun chubanshe, 1983.

Niu Jun. *Lengzhan yu xin Zhongguo waijiao de yuanqi (1945–1955)* [The Cold War and the Genesis of New China's Diplomacy (1945–1955)]. Beijing: Shehui kexue wenxian chubanshe, 2012.

Pang Xianzhi and Feng Hui, eds. *Mao Zedong nianpu, 1949–1976* [A Chronology of Mao Zedong, 1949-1976]. 6 vols. Beijing: Zhongyang wenxian chubanshe, 2013.

Pang Xianzhi and Jin Chongji, eds. *Mao Zedong zhuan 1949–1976* [A Biography of Mao Zedong]. 2 vols. Beijing: Zhongyang wenxian chubanshe, 2003.

Park Jung-cheol. "A Study of Sino-North Korean Relations Regarding the Withdrawal of the Chinese People's Volunteer Army" [in Korean]. *Kunsasa yŏn'gu ch'ongsŏ* [Military History Studies Series] 5 (March 2008): 193–241.

Park Myong Rim. "The Outbreak and Origins of the Korean War" [in Korean]. PhD diss., Korea University, Seoul, August 1994.

Park Yeong-sil. "The Chinese People's Volunteers Army's Aid to and Withdrawal from North Korea after the Armistice" [in Korean]. *Chŏngsin munhwa yŏn'gu* [Korean Studies Quarterly] 29, no. 4 (2006): 265–291.

Peng Dehuai. *Peng Dehuai zishu* [An Account in Peng Dehuai's Own Words]. Unpublished internal reference.

Peng Dehuai Zhuanji Bianxiezu [Editorial Committee for the Peng Dehuai Biography], ed. *Peng Dehuai junshi wenxuan* [Selected Military Writings by Peng Dehuai]. Beijing: Zhongyang wenxian chubanshe, 1988.

Piao Jianyi and Ma Junwei, eds. *Zhongguo dui Chaoxian bandao de yanjiu* [Chinese Studies on the Korean Peninsula]. Beijing: Minzu chubanshe, 2006.

Pu Xuanling. *Dongbei KangRi yiyongjun* [The Anti-Japanese Volunteer Army in the Northeast]. Beijing: Zhongguo youyi chubanshe, 1998.

Qi Dexue. *Chaoxian zhanzheng juece neimu* [Inside Stories Behind the Decision Making During the Korean War]. Shenyang: Liaoning daxue chubanshe, 1991.

Qian Qichen. *Waijiao shiji* [Ten Episodes in China's Diplomacy]. Beijing: Shijie zhishi chubanshe, 2003.

Sakurai, Yoshiko. "The First Publication on the Truth of the Korean War: Former Senior Official (Yi Sang-jo) Exposes the Fabricated 'Kim Il-sung Myth' " [in Japanese]. *Bungei shunju* [Spring and Autumn of Literature and Art] 68, no. 5 (April 1990): 168–178.

Shen Jueren, ed. *Dangdai Zhongguo duiwai maoyi* [Contemporary China's Foreign Trade]. 2 vols. Beijing: Dangdai Zhongguo chubanshe, 1992.

Shen Yilin, ed. *Chaoxian zhuti sixiang ziliao xuanyi* [Selection of Translated Materials on North Korea's Juche]. Beijing: Renmin chubanshe, 1983.

Shen Zhihua. "1953 nian Chaoxian tingzhan: ZhongSu lingdaoren de zhengzhi kaolü" [The Korean Armistice in 1953: The Political Considerations of the Chinese and Soviet Leaders]. *Shijie shi* [World History] 2 (2001): 2-18.

——. "KangMei yuanChao zhanzheng juece zhong de Sulian yinsu" [The Soviet Factor in the War to Resist the U.S. and to Aid Korea]. *Dangdai Zhongguoshi yanjiu* [Contemporary China History Studies] 1 (2000): 28–39.

——. *Mao Zedong, Sidalin yu Chaoxian zhanzheng* [Mao Zedong, Stalin, and the Korean War]. Guangzhou: Guangdong renmin chubanshe, 2003.

——. *Mao Zedong, Sidalin yu Chaoxian zhanzheng* [Mao Zedong, Stalin, and the Korean War]. 3rd. ed. Guangzhou: Guangdong renmin chubanshe, 2013.

——. "Sidalin, Mao Zedong yu Chaoxian zhanzheng zai yi" [Reconsidering Stalin, Mao Zedong, and the Korean War]. *Shixue jikan* [Collected Papers of History Studies] 5 (2007): 51-65.

——, ed. *Sidalin yu Tietuo: Su Nan chongtu de qiyin jiqi jieguo* [Stalin and Tito: The Origins and Outcome of the Soviet–Yugoslav Conflict]. Guilin: Guangxi shifan daxue chubanshe, 2002.

——. "Sugong ershida fei Sidalinhua jiqi dui ZhongSu guanxi de yingxiang" [The Twentieth Congress of the Communist Party of the Soviet Union, De-Stalinization, and Its Effects on Sino–Soviet Relations]. In *Guoji lengzhanshi yanjiu* [Cold War International History Studies], edited by Li Danhui, 1:28–69. Shanghai: Huadong shifan daxue chubanshe, 2004.

——. "Tongming xianglian: Chaoxian gongchandang ren rongru Zhonggong de lishi guocheng (1919–1936)" [Sharing a Similar Fate: The Historical Process of the Merger of the Korean Communists with the Chinese Communist Party (1919–1936)]. *Shehui kexue zhanxian* [Social Science Front] 2 (2015): 68–85.

——. *Zhonghua renmin gongheguoshi. Di 3 juan. Sikao yu xuanze: Cong zhishifenxi huiyi dao fan youpai yundong, 1956–1957* [History of the People's Republic of China. Vol. 3, Pondering and Choosing: From the Conference on Intellectuals to the Anti-Rightist Campaign, 1956-1957]. Hong Kong: Chinese University Press, 2008.

——, ed. *ZhongSu guanxi shigang, 1917–1991* [History of Sino–Soviet Relations, 1917-1991]. Beijing: Xinhua chubanshe, 2007.

Shen Zhihua and Li Bin [Douglas Stiffler], eds. *Cuiruo de lianmeng: Lengzhan yu ZhongSu guanxi* [Fragile Alliance: The Cold War and Sino–Soviet Relations]. Beijing: Shehui kexue wenxian chubanshe, 2010.

Shi Lin, ed. *Dangdai Zhongguo de duiwai jingji hezuo* [Contemporary China's Economic Cooperation with Foreign Countries]. Beijing: Zhongguo shehui kexue chubanshe, 1989.

Shi Yuanhua, ed. *Zhongguo gongchandang yuanzhu Chaoxian duli yundong jishi, 1921–1945* [A History of the Chinese Communist Party's Assistance to the Korean Independence Movement, 1921-1945]. Beijing: Zhongguo shehui kexue chubanshe, 2000.

Shi Zhe. *Zai lishi juren shenbian: Shi Zhe huiyilu* [By the Side of the Great Man: Reminiscences of Shi Zhe]. Edited by Li Haiwen, based on Shi Zhe's oral account. 2nd rev. ed. Beijing: Zhongyang wenxian chubanshe, 1995.

Shijie Zhishi Chubanshe [World Knowledge Publisher], ed. *Guoji tiaoyue ji, 1945–1947* [Collection of International Treaties, 1945-1947]. Beijing: Shijie zhishi chubanshe, 1959.

——, ed. *Guoji tiaoyue ji, 1948–1949* [Collection of International Treaties, 1948-1949]. Beijing: Shijie zhishi chubanshe, 1959.

Song Yongyi, ed. *Zhongguo wenhua dageming wenku* [Chinese Cultural Revolution Database]. Hong Kong: Chinese University Press, 2002.

Tian Zongji and Ye Xinyu, ed. *Zhonghua renmin gongheguo shilu di sijuan: Gaige yu jubian—kaichuang xiandaihua jianshe xin jumian, 1977–1992* [A True Account of the People's Republic of China. Vol. 4, Reform and Great Changes—Creating a New Situation for Modernization Construction]. Changchun: Jilin renmin chubanshe, 1994.

Wang Mingxing. "Gaoli lianbang gongheguo tongyi fang'an de tichu ji lishi yiyi" [The Proposal and Historical Significance of the Unification Scheme of the Koryo Federal Republic." In *Hanguo yanjiu luncong* [Collected Papers on Korean Studies], 10:63–77. Beijing: Shijie zhishi chubanshe, 2003.

Wang Taiping, ed. *Zhonghua renmin gongheguo waijiaoshi, 1970–1978* [A Diplomatic History of the People's Republic of China, 1970-1978]. Beijing: Shijie zhishi chubanshe, 1999.

Wang Xiaoju. *Eguo dongbu yimin kaifa wenti yanjiu* [Studies on Immigration and Development in Russia's Far East]. Beijing: Zhongguo shehui kexue chubanshe, 2003.

Wang Yan, ed. *Peng Dehuai nianpu* [A Chronology of Peng Dehuai]. Beijing: Renmin chubanshe, 1998.

Wang Yazhi. "KangMei yuanChao zhanzheng zhong de Peng Dehuai, Nie Rongzhen" [Peng Dehuai and Nie Rongzhen During the War to Resist America and to Aid Korea]. *Junshi shilin* [Journal of Military History] 1 (1994): 9–15.

Wang Zhongchun. "ZhongMei guanxi zhengchanghua jinchengzhong de Sulian yinsu (1969–1979)" [Soviet Factors in the Sino–American Normalization, 1969-1979]. In *Cong jiedong zuoxiang jianjiao: ZhongMei guanxi zhengchanghua jincheng zai tantao, 1969–1979* [From the Thaw to Normalization: Sino–American Relations, 1969-1979], edited by Gong Li, William C. Kirby, and Robert S. Ross, 193–220. Beijing: Zhongyang wenxian chubanshe, 2004.

Wen Xingfu. "Yanbian pingfan sida yuan'an" [Redressing Four Important Unjust Cases in Yanbian]. *Yanbian wenshi ziliao* [Yanbian Historical Accounts] 17 (2012): 236-272.

Wu Dianyao and Song Lin. *Zhu Lizhi zhuan* [A Biography of Zhu Lizhi]. Beijing: Zhonggong dangshi chubanshe, 2007.

Wu Lengxi. *Shinian lunzhan: 1956–1966 Zhong Su guanxi huiyilu* [Ten Years of Polemics: Recollections of Sino–Soviet Relations, 1956-1966]. Beijing: Zhongyang wenxian chubanshe, 1999.

Wu Xiuquan. *Huiyi yu huainian* [Recollections and Remembrances]. Beijing: Zhonggong zhongyang dangxiao chubanshe, 1991.

Xiong Xianghui. *Wo de qingbao yu waijiao shengya* [My Careers in Intelligence and Diplomacy]. 2nd ed. Beijing: Zhonggong dangshi chubanshe, 2006.

Xu Longnan. "Yanbianji Chaoxian renminjun tuiwu junren caifanglu" [Record of Interviews with Ex-Servicemen of the Korean People's Army in Yanbian]. In

Lengzhan guojishi yanjiu [Cold War International History Studies], edited by Li Danhui, 7:265–287. Beijing: Shijie zhishi chubanshe, 2008.

Xu Yan. *Diyici jiaoliang: KangMei yuanChao zhanzheng de lishi huigu* [First Encounter: Recollections and Reflections on the War to Resist America and to Aid Korea]. Beijing: Zhongguo guangbo dianshi chubanshe, 1990.

Yan Jing. *Chushi Hanguo* [Serving as an Envoy to the Republic of Korea]. Ji'nan: Shandong daxue chubanshe, 2004.

——. "Lishi de xuanze" [A Historical Choice]. *Baogao wenxue* [Reportage Literature] 1 (2008): 67–75.

Yan Mingfu. "1957 nian xingshi yu Fuluxiluofu fangHua" [The Situation in 1957 and Voroshilov's Visit to China]. *Bainian chao* [Hundred-Year Tide] 2 (2009): 12–20.

——. "Huiyi liangci Mosike huiyi he Hu Qiaomu" [Recollections on the Two Moscow Conferences and Hu Qiaomu]. *Dangdai Zhongguoshi yanjiu* [Contemporary China History Studies] 3 (1997): 6–21.

Yan Mingfu and Zhu Ruizhen. "Mao Zedong dierci fang Su he 1957 nian Mosike huiyi (yi)" [Mao Zedong's Second Trip to the Soviet Union and the 1957 Moscow Conference, Part I]. *Zhonggong dangshi ziliao* [Materials on the History of the Chinese Communist Party] 4 (2005): 8–36.

Yang Feng'an and Wang Tiancheng. *Jiayu Chaoxian zhanzheng de ren* [The Man who Controlled the Korean War]. Beijing: Zhonggong zhongyang dangxiao chubanshe, 1993.

Yang Kuisong. "Sidalin wei shenme zhichi Chaoxian zhanzheng? Du Shen Zhihua 'Mao Zedong, Sidalin yu Chaoxian zhanzheng' " [Why Did Stalin Support the Korean War? On Reading Shen Zhihua's "Mao Zedong, Sidalin yu Chaoxian zhanzheng"]. *Ershiyi shiji* [Twenty-first Century] 81 (February 2004): 130–144.

Yang Shangkun. *Yang Shangkun riji* [Yang Shangkun's Diary]. 2 vols. Beijing: Zhongyang wenxian chubanshe, 2001.

Yang Zhaoquan. "Jianguo 60 nian woguo de Chaoxian-Hanguo shi he Zhong-Chao Zhong-Han guanxi yanjiu zongshu" [Survey of Studies on the History of North and South Korea, and the History of Sino-North Korean and Sino-South Korean Relations]. *Chaoxian-Hanguo lishi yanjiu* [Historical Studies on North and South Korea] 12 (2012): 434–479.

——. *Jin Richeng zhuan* [A Biography of Kim Il-sung]. 3 vols. Hong Kong: Yazhou chubanshe, 2010.

Yi Chong-sŏk. *Pukhan-Chungguk kwan'gye, 1945–2000* [The Sino-North Korean Relationship, 1945-2000]. Seoul: Chungsim, 2000.

Yi Sang-suk. "The Causes and Impact of the Withdrawal of the Chinese People's Volunteer Army from North Korea in 1958" [in Korean]. *Pukhan Yŏn'gu Hakhoe* [North Korean Studies Review] 13, no. 1 (2009): 83–107.

Zhang Mingyuan. "Fengxue zhanqin: Yi kangMei yuanChao zhanzheng de houqin baozhang" [War Logistics During Windy and Snowy Days: Recollections of Logistics Support During the Korean War]. *Dangdai Zhongguoshi yanjiu* [Contemporary China History Studies] 6 (2000): 25–35.

——. *Wo de huiyi* [My Recollections]. Beijing: Zhonggong dangshi chubanshe, 2004.

Zhang Tingyan. "Deng Xiaoping guanxin Chaoxian bandao jushi: Huiyi Deng Xiaoping er san shi" [Deng Xiaoping Cares About the Situation on the Korean Pennisula: Remembering Two or Three Things About Deng Xiaoping]. *Dangshi bolan* [General Review of Chinese Communist Party History] 5 (2013): 27–28.

——. "Lianheguo taolun Chaoxian wenti" [The UN Discusses the Korean Issue]. In *Fengyun jihui lianheguo* [Unpredictable Meetings at the United Nations], edited by Wan Jingzhang and Zhang Bing, 52–55. Beijing: Xinhua chubanshe, 2008.

Zhao Fengbin. *Wode rensheng zishu: Yige Chaoxianzu jiazu bianqian shilu* [An Account of My Life in My Own Words: A Record of Changes in a Korean Family]. Beijing: Minzu chubanshe, 2010.

Zheng Xinzhe. *Zai Ri Chaoxianren lishi jiqi xianzhuang yanjiu* [Studies on the History and Current Situation of Koreans in Japan]. Beijing: Zhongguo fangzheng chubanshe, 2007.

Zhengxie Yanbian Chaoxianzu Zizhizhou Weiyuanhui Wenshi Ziliao yu Xuexi Xuanchuan Weiyuanhui [Historical Data Committee and Propaganda Committee of the Chinese People's Political Consultative Conference of Yanbian Korean Autonomous Prefecture]. *Nanwang de suiyue: Shanghai ernü zai Yanbian* [Unforgettable Years: Shanghai's Sons and Daughters in Yanbian]. Shenyang: Liaoning minzu chubanshe, 2007.

Zhonggong Henanshengwei Dangshi Yanjiushi [Party History Office of the Henan Provincial Chinese Communist Party Committee], ed. *Jinian Zhu Lizhi wenji* [Collection of Papers in Memory of Zhu Lizhi]. Beijing: Zhonggong dangshi chubanshe, 2007.

Zhonggong Zhongyang Duiwai Lianluobu [Chinese Communist Party Central Committee International Liaison Department], ed. *Chaoxian laodongdang lijie zhongyang quanhui gaikuang* [Basic Facts on the Central Committees of the Congresses of the Korean Workers' Party]. Unpublished, 1981.

Zhonggong Zhongyang Wenxian Yanjiushi [Chinese Communist Party Central Committee Party Literature Research Office], ed. *Chen Yun wenji* [Collected Writings by Chen Yun]. 3 vols. Beijing: Zhongyang wenxian chubanshe, 2005.

——, ed. *Deng Xiaoping nianpu, 1975–1997* [Chronology of Deng Xiaoping, 1975–1997]. 2 vols. Beijing: Zhongyang wenxian chubanshe, 2004.

——, ed. *Deng Xiaoping wenxuan, 1982–1992* [Selected Works of Deng Xiaoping, 1982–1992]. Beijing: Renmin chubanshe, 1995.

——, ed. *Jianguo yilai Mao Zedong wengao* [Mao Zedong's Manuscripts Since the Founding of the State]. 13 vols. Beijing: Zhongyang wenxian chubanshe, 1987–1998.

——, ed. *Zhou Enlai nianpu, 1949–1976* [A Chronology of Zhou Enlai, 1949-1976]. 3 vols. Beijing: Zhongyang wenxian chubanshe, 1997.

Zhonggong Zhongyang Wenxian Yanjiushi and Zhongguo Renmin Jiefangjun Junshi Kexueyuan [Chinese Communist Party Central Committee Party Literature Research Office and Academy of Military Science of the People's Liberation Army], eds. *Jianguo yilai Mao Zedong junshi wengao* [Mao Zedong's Military Writings Since the Founding of the State]. 3 vols. Beijing: Zhongyang wenxian chubanshe, 2010.

———, eds. *Zhou Enlai junshi wenxuan* [Selected Military Writings by Zhou Enlai]. 4 vols. Beijing: Renmin chubanshe, 1997.

Zhonggong Zhongyang Wenxian Yanjiushi and Zhongyang Dang'anguan [Chinese Communist Party Central Committee Party Literature Research Office and Central Archives], eds. *Jianguo yilai Liu Shaoqi wengao* [Liu Shaoqi's Manuscripts Since the Founding of the State]. 7 vols. (1949-1955). Beijing: Zhonggong zhongyang wenxian chubanshe, 2005-2008.

Zhonggong Zhongyang Wenxian Yanjiushi and Zhongyang Dang'anguan [Chinese Communist Party Central Committee Party Literature Research Office and Central Archives], eds. *Jianguo yilai Zhou Enlai wengao* [Zhou Enlai's Manuscripts Since the Founding of the State]. 3 vols. (1949-1950). Beijing: Zhongyang wenxian chubanshe, 2008.

Zhonggong Zhongyang Zuzhibu [Chinese Communist Party Central Committee Central Organization Department], ed. *Zhongguo gongchandang zuzhishi ziliao, 1921-1997* [Materials on the Organizational History of the Chinese Communist Party, 1921-1997]. 19 vols. Beijing: Zhonggong dangshi chubanshe, 2000.

Zhongguo Chaoxianzu Lishi Zuji Bianji Weiyuanhui [Editorial Committee on the History of Koreans in China]. *Sheng li* [Victory]. Beijing: Minzu chubanshe, 1992.

Zhonghua Renmin Gongheguo Waijiaobu and Zhonggong Zhongyang Wenxian Yanjiushi [People's Republic of China Ministry of Foreign Affairs and Chinese Communist Party Central Committee Party Literature Research Office], eds. *Mao Zedong waijiao wenxuan* [Selected Diplomatic Papers of Mao Zedong]. Beijing: Zhongyang wenxian chubanshe and Shijie zhishi chubanshe, 1994.

Zhonghua Renmin Gongheguo Waijiaobu Waijiaoshi Yanjiushi [Diplomatic History Research Office of the People's Republic of China Ministry of Foreign Affairs]. *Zhou Enlai waijiao huodong dashiji, 1949-1975* [A Chronology of Zhou Enlai's Diplomatic Activities, 1949-1975]. Beijing: Shijie zhishi chubanshe, 1993.

Zhonglianbu Bangongting [General Office, Chinese Communist Party Central Committee International Liaison Department], ed. *Zhonglianbu laobu lingdao tan dang de duiwai gongzuo* [Retired Leaders of International Liaison Department Talk About Party External Work]. Unpublished, April 2004.

Zhou Enlai Junshi Huodong Jishi Bianxiezu [Editorial Committee of the Record of Zhou Enlai's Military Activities], ed. *Zhou Enlai junshi huodong jishi, 1918-1975* [A Record of Zhou Enlai's Military Activities, 1918-1975]. 2 vols. Beijing: Zhongyang wenxian chubanshe, 2000.

Zhou Wan [Jovan Cavoski]. "Yu ZhongSu zhengduo disan shijie: 1958-1959 nian Tietuo de Yafei zhixing" [Fomenting Discord among Afro-Asian Countries: The Sino–Soviet Alliance and Tito's Trip to Asian and African Countries, 1958-1959]. In *Cuiruo de lianmeng: Lengzhan yu ZhongSu guanxi* [Fragile Alliance: The Cold War and Sino–Soviet Relations], edited by Shen Zhihua and Li Bin [Douglas Stiffler], 266-299. Beijing: Shehui kexue wenxian chubanshe, 2010.

Index

Democratic People's Republic of Korea
(DPRK), 3; on China's reform and
opening, 232; Chinese Civil War and,
14; Cultural Department of, 8;
damages related to Korean War, 79;
debts of, 111; Five-Point Program
of 1973, 223; Ministry of Foreign
Affairs of, 99; political attitude
toward Soviet Union, 131; postwar
reconstruction of, 149; "Regulations
on Chinese and Korean Border
Transit" (China and DPRK), 152;
secret visit to Moscow, 13; State
Planning Commission of, 86; Supreme
People's Assembly of, 125, 203, 224–25,
268n38; working class, 225, 226; Zhou
Enlai visit to (1970), 199

Deng Xiaoping, 132, 165, 168, 223;
economic development and
modernization strategy of, 231; Hu
Yaobang, 235; Kim Jong-il meeting
in Beijing, 311n4; Mondale and, 234;
in Tiananmen Square, 221; on
unlikeliness of world war, 232

Department for Liaison with
Communist and Workers' Parties in
Socialist Countries, 94

de-Stalinization, 100

détente, 122, 139, 142, 145, 197, 203,
228, 229; Qiao Guanhua and, 218

developing countries, 289n114

Ding Xuesong, 20

"Directive Regarding the Establishment
of the Chinese People's Volunteer
Army" (Mao), 79

dissent, 8, 14, 42, 89, 95, 97, 98,
100–101, 102, 105

dogmatism, 84, 85, 140, 175, 178

Dong Ji, 172

Dongbeiya luntan (Forum on Northeast
Asia), 246n3

DPRK. *See* Democratic People's
Republic of Korea

East Asia, 14

east front, 43

Eastern European Communist parties,
109; fall of, 233

Eastern European countries, 81, 83

EC-121 crisis, 188, 192, 203

economic aid: China economic aid
linked with opposition to Soviet
Union, 185; to North Korea, 6, 10,
77, 79, 82; from Soviet Union, 80

*Economic Problems of Socialism in the
USSR* (Stalin), 132

Eighth Route Army, 16, 17; Yan'an
faction and, 53

factionalism, 96, 99, 100

famine, 141

Fang Yi, 185

Fedorenko, Nikolai, 93, 99

Feng Biao, 181

First Ministry of Light Industry, China,
187

First Party Conference (DPRK), 130

Five-Year Plan, 80, 97, 110, 129; China
Third Five-Year Plan, 167; Korea
First Five-Year Plan period
(1957–1961), 153, 154; Korea Second
Five-Year Plan, 138; launch of
Korean, 86; Mikoyan on First
Five-Year Plan, 111; problems due to,
138

flunkeyism, 241, 248n19

Ford, Gerald, 7, 219

foreign policy: of China, 10, 12; of
DPRK, 5, 172; of Khrushchev, 151;
North Korea foreign policy of
exporting revolution, 227; of Soviet
Union, 170

Indochina, 21–23, 26, 28, 197, 200, 204, 220

Indonesia, 21, 23, 25, 174

industrialization, 80

inner-party struggles, 98, 100

International Association of Socialist States, 253n33

International Communist Movement, 4, 85, 194; CCP in, 23; importance of unity in, 244; members of, 231; struggle over leading role in, 137; threat of revisionism to, 149

International Labor Day, 124

International Liaison Department (ILD), 123, 165, 169

internationalism, 21, 85, 243; Korean Revolution and, 226; revolutionary, 43; revolutionary internationalism, 252n24

Ita incident, 155, 166, 288n98

Ivanov, V. I., 86, 90, 95, 97, 98, 105, 109, 110

Jamaican Workers' Liberation League, 227

Japan: imperial rule, 88; militarism, 11, 15, 181, 193; Russo–Japanese War (1904), 15; War of Resistance Against (1937), 15, 16, 53, 189, 241

Japanese Communist Party (JCP), 21, 177; Asian Cominform and, 22

Japanese Occupation, 88

JCP. See Japanese Communist Party

Jenkins, Alfred, 214

Ji Pengfei, 159, 160, 161, 162

Jiandao Treaty of 1909, 162

Jiang Jieshi, 23, 160

Jiao Reyu, 179

Jilin province, 16, 155, 157

Jilin Provincial Foreign Affairs Office, 123

Jinjiang Hot Spring, 163

Joint Command of Transportation, 64

Joint Railroad Military Management Bureau, 61, 62, 63

Joint Railway Maintenance Command, 65, 66

Juche, 9, 89, 143, 224; China and, 5; Dae-Sook Suh on, 78; as "Kim Il-sung-ism," 225; opportunity to assert, 136; proposal, 77, 84, 85; *Rodong sinmun* on, 227; weakening, 11

Kaesŏng, 69, 113, 169

Kang Kŏn, 17, 18, 20

Kangwŏn-do, 174

Khrushchev, Nikita, 89, 94, 99, 106, 143; de-Stalinization speech by, 100; détente and, 145; fall of, 177; foreign policy of, 151; Mao on, 111; revisionism of, 165; visit to North Korea, 140, 146; Zhou Enlai and, 115–16

KIL. See Korean Independence League

Kim Ch'ang-man, 89, 91, 92, 117, 118, 133, 189

Kim Ch'ang-pong, 189

Kim Chŏng-nyong, 125

Kim Ch'ung-sik, 8, 97, 121, 122, 125

Kim Chun-kŭn, 121, 123

Kim Dae-jung, 215

Kim Il, 89, 112, 175, 186

Kim Il-sung, 4, 19, 49, 102, *199*; adventurism of, 40; antagonism against, 93; armistice negotiations, meeting with Mao, 68; armistice negotiations and, 70; aspiration to lead world revolution, 226, 228; Brezhnev secret meeting with, 177; CCP demand for Kim to correct mistakes, 103; cease-fire and, 74;

Korean Revolution, 18, 30, 84, 99, 226

Korean Volunteer Army, 16, 17, 18, 20

Korean War, 3, 4, 75; armistice negotiations, 67–71; damages, 79; Gao Gang on China volunteering troops for, 37–38; Mao and, 8, 15; origins of, 27, 32; Soviet Union assistance in, 44; Stalin concerns over Chinese entry, 39; U.S. entry, 35; U.S. escalation, 38

Korean Workers' Party (KWP), 93; "antiparty clique" in, 111; Asian Cominform and, 22; cadres fleeing to China, 120–21; Chinese belief in KWP revisionist policies, 173; *Kulloja* theoretical journal of, 7; not attending World Communist and Workers' Parties Conference, 193; Organization Department of Pyongyang Municipal Committee of, 8; after Polish and Hungarian crises, 109; Politburo of, 38, 41, 56, 59; *Rodong sinmum* (Workers' Newspaper), 1; Sino–Soviet interference in internal affairs of, 139; Standing Committee of, 55, 88, 95, 104; Third Party Congress of, 90–92. *See also* Central Committee (CC) of KWP

Kosygin, Aleksei, 146, 171; leadership of, 173, 194; visit to Korea, 175–76

Kotch, John, 211, 212

Kovács, József, 174

Kovalev, Ivan, 21, 253n33

Kozlov, Frol, 139

KPA. *See* Korean People's Army

Kulloja (theoretical journal of KWP), 7, 225

Kurdiukov, I. F., 87, 88

KWP. *See* Korean Workers' Party

Lankov, Andrei, 97

Ledovskii, Andrei, 66, 255n59

Lee, Chong-Sik, 130

Lee, Dong-jun, 148

Legal Workers' Conference, 170

Leninism, 85, 90, 139

Li Fuchun, 129

Li Jishen, 19

Li Kenong, 70

Li Sin-p'al, 109

Li Weihan, 26

Li Xiannian, 235

Li Yunchuan, 179

Lian Guan, 25

Liao River, 162, 164

Liaoning province, 155, 166

Lin Biao, 19, 28, 29, 30, 182

Liu Juying, 61, 66, 67

Liu Shaoqi, 23, 25, 26, 29, 30, 33, 38, 41, 114, 115, 161, 165, 169, 170, 185

Liu Yalou, 19, 20

Luo Ruiqing, 98, 121

Lushan Conference, 125, 135

Ma Xulun, 20

MacArthur, Douglas, 27

Malaysia, 25

Malenkov, Georgi, 74

Mali, 225

Manchuria, 15, 18, 19

Mao Zedong, 2, 34, 58–59, 78, 102, 194; apology for interference in North Korean affairs, 117, 126; armistice negotiations, meeting with Kim Il-sung, 68; armistice negotiations and, 72; on Asian Cominform, 22; censuring Kim Il-sung, 106; Chinese Civil War and, 20; death of, 227–28; "Directive Regarding the Establishment of the Chinese People's Volunteer Army," 79;

North Korean-Chinese Friendship Association, 120

Northeast Asia, 3

Northeast Border Defense Army, 38

Northeast China, 5, 10, 15, 16; Eighth Route Army in, 17; Korean Volunteer Army in, 18

Northeast Democratic United Army, 20

Northeast Logistics Command, 62

Northeast Military District Transportation Command, 61

Northeast Military Region, 35, 37

Northeast People's Government, Trade Representative Office of, 29

Northern Limit Line, 217

North-Korean-Chinese Military Command, 45–46, 47, 48, 53

North–South dialogue, 203, 205, 210, 214; Deng Xiaoping promotion of, 234

No. 88 Independent Infantry Brigade, 8, 16; also called Anti-Japanese United Army Training Brigade, 248n18; First Battalion of, 16

O Paek-ryong, 189

October Revolution, 112, 133, 143, 175

"On Eliminating Formalism and Dogmatism and Establishing *Juche* in Ideological Work" (Kim Il-sung, 1955), 84

"On Internationalism and Nationalism" (*Dongbei ribao*, 1948), 85

"On the Historical Experience of the Dictatorship of the Proletariat" (*Renmin ribao*, 1956), 100

164th Division, 28

166th Division, 28

Ongjin Peninsula, 30

oral histories, 7

Order No. 6 (1945), 17

Paektu Mountains (Paektusan), 161, 162, 163, 164

Pak Ch'ang-ok, 84, 86, 89, 92, 93, 95, 96, 126; rehabilitation of, 104

Pak Chŏng-ae, 17, 95, 100

Pak Hŏn-yŏng, 17, 41, 50, 55, 56, 57, 63, 69, 72, 88, 90, 91

Pak Hyo-sam, 16

Pak Il-u, 16, 18, 41, 45, 46, 47, 50, 53, 84, 88, 92, 104, 105, 111, 121, 125; Kim Il-sung meeting with, 47

Pak Kŭm-ch'ŏl, 125, 126, 160, 164

Pak Se-Ch'ang, 170, 185

Pak Sŏng-ch'ŏl, 146, 151, 157, 159, 161, 168, 177, 182, 185, 206

Pak Ŭi-wan, 63, 64, 93, 95

Pak Yŏng-bin, 84, 89, 93

Pakch'ŏn, 46

Pan Zili, 269n49

Pang Hak-se, 95, 117

Panmunjom, 70, 210

Paris Peace Accords, 217

Park Chung Hee, 203, 215, 228

Peiping (Beijing), 24

Peng Dehuai, 45, 49, 51–52, 57–58; command of, 53–54; criticism of Great Leap Forward, 274n10; dismissal and purge of, 97, 135; on lack of coordination between troops, 46; letter to Razuvayev, 55; military plan of, 59; railway transportation and, 60; rightist opportunist clique headed by, 136; on troops need for rest, 56

Peng Min, 62

People's Commune movement, 127, 128, 134, 136, 137, 155

People's Daily (*Renmin ribao*), 1

People's Liberation Army (PLA), 19, 20, 23; ethnic Korean soldiers in, 28–29;

fact-finding mission to North
Korea, 37
People's Republic of China (PRC), 2,
223, 235; founding of, 1, 25, 31. *See
also* China
People's Revolutionary Military
Commission of the Central People's
Government, 61
personality cults, 89, 90, 91, 92; of Kim
Il-sung, 92, 94, 97, 99, 100, 127, 150;
of Stalin, 85, 149
Philippines, 21, 22, 23, 25
PLA. *See* People's Liberation Army
Plan for the CPVA to Withdraw from
the DPRK, 118
Plan for the Recovery and
Development of the National
Economy for the First Season of
1951 (DPRK), 60
Podgorny, Nikolai, 192
Polish crisis, 105, 107; CCP role in, 108;
KWP after, 109
Ponomarev, Boris, 99, 100
Popa, N., 178, 179, 187
POW. *See* prisoners of war
Poznan, 93
Prath, Karoly, 140
PRC. *See* People's Republic of
China
prisoners of war (POW), 47, 70–71;
repatriation of, 73, 74
profiteering, 157
propaganda, 37, 90, 99, 134, 141, 168,
183, 225, 285n53; "Great Leader, Kim
Il-sung," 224; Korean Propaganda
Department, 84, 134; Moscow
propaganda campaign, 118
Protocol on the Sino–Korean Border,
161, 162, 164
public ownership, 127
Pueblo incident, 176, 188, 192, 203

purges, 87, 88, 89, 93, 94, 103, 105, 178;
of Eastern European nationalists, 85;
of Kim Tu-bong, 130; of Moscow
faction, 9, 92, 94, 100; of Peng
Dehuai, 67, 97, 135; of Yan'an
faction, 76, 78, 121
Pusan, 40, 56
Puzanov, A.M., 110, 116, 138
Pyongyang, 4, 38; Beijing supplying
weaponry to, 224; Chinese Embassy
in, 45, 46; economic aid to, 10, 77;
foreign policy of, 5, 172; Moscow
technical aid agreement with, 144;
Northeast Bureau of CCP office in,
18; Sino–Soviet delegation to, 9,
103–5; Soviet delegations to, 102;
Soviet Embassy in, 30
Pyongyang Municipal Committee, 8,
91, 94

Qiao Guanhua, 181, 206, 215, 228;
Kissinger and, 218–19, 220
Qiao Xiaoguang, 86, 87, 98, 110, 116,
136, 146, 150, 151, 156

Radchenko, Sergey, 114
Railway Engineering Corps, 60, 62, 64,
67
railway transportation: Changchun
Railway, 35; coordination among
railway agencies, 62; Gao Gang
and, 60–61, 62, 64–65; military
takeover of, 67; Peng Dehuai
and, 60; railway administrative
bureaus, 63
Rákosi, Mátyás, 104
Razuvayev, V. N., 50, 59, 69; on
armistice negotiations, 69, 70, 71;
Peng Dehuai's letter to, 55
rear-guard affairs, 50
Red Cross, 125

Red Guards, 128, 173, 178, 179, 182; accusations by, 173, 180, 182, 183, 184; Mao Zedong Thought Red Guard Shenyang Headquarters, 180; Zhejiang Red Guards, 183

"Regulations on Chinese and Korean Border Transit" (China and DPRK), 152

rehabilitation: of Ch'oe Ch'ang-ik and Pak Ch'ang-ok, 104; of Korea, 203, 211

Renmin ribao (People's Daily), 1, 97, 100, 112, 126; on North Korea, 245n2; "On the Historical Experience of the Dictatorship of the Proletariat," 100

repatriation, 70–74

Republic of Korea (ROK). *See* South Korea

Republic of Korea–United States Combined Forces Command, 217, 220

Resolution on Several Issues Regarding the People's Communes, 134

Reston, James, 203

reunification, 11, 31, 33, 34, 119, 145, 205, 207, 216, 223, 241; UNCURK supervision of, 209

revisionism, 143, 149, 152, 169, 181; China belief that KWP carrying out revisionist policies, 173, 180; of Khrushchev, 165; Kim Il-sung on, 168; military conflicts provoked by, 166

Revolutionary Action Movement, Mexico, 226

Rhee, Syngman, 27, 74

Ri Jae-phil, 214

Ri Jong-mok, 215

Rockefeller, David, 217

Rodong sinmun (Workers' Newspaper), 1, 55, 127, 135, 148, 151, 166, 175, 178,

203, 208, 225, 227, 237, 238, 239; on *Juche,* 227

Roh Tae-woo, 237

ROK (Republic of Korea). *See* South Korea

ROK–U.S. Combined Forces Command, 217

Romania, 81, 217, 224

Roshchin, N. V., 33, 35, 40, 41

Russian Far East, 287n88

Russo–Japanese War of 1904, 15

Sadat, Anwar, 217

Scalapino, Robert, 130

Schaefer, Bernd, 172, 173, 190, 221

Selected Works of Mao Zedong, 38

Seoul, 42, 54, 210, 211, 212, 213, 216, 228, 236, 237, 239; line of defense around, 35, 41, 55, 57

September affair (1956), 107, 118, 150

Seven-Year Plan (DPRK), 138, 139; prospects for, 148

Shanghai Communiqué, 207, 208

Shanghai Municipal CCP Committee, 180

Shanghai Municipal Revolutionary Committee, 191

Shen Junru, 19–20

Shen Tu, 236

Shenyang, 28, 45, 48, 52, 61, 64, 66, 67, 83, 168

Shepilov, Dmitri, 114

Shi Zhe, 34

Shimotomai, Nobuo, 84

Shtykov, Terentii, 28, 29, 32, 36–37, 38, 42, 47, 48; Kim Il-sung and, 41; praise for CPVA, 48–49

Shubnikov, N. M., 193, 213

Sichuan Provincial CCP Committee, 123, 124, 125

Sihanouk, Norodom, 184, 203

State Department Bureau of Intelligence and Research, 7

State Planning Commission, DPRK, 86

"Stevenson" formula, 216

Su Yu, 257n77

Suh, Dae-Sook, 78

Suh, Jae-Jung, 279n75

Sunch'ŏn, 46

Supreme People's Assembly of DPRK, 125, 160, 161, 203, 224–25

Supreme Soviet, 92

Suwŏn, 54, 59

Szalontai, Balázs, 130

Taiwan, 27, 28, 32, 33, 35, 73, 160, 193, 200, 202, 204, 235, 257n77

Tao Zhu, 180

tennis team (South Korea), 236

Thailand, 21, 22, 25, 227

Third World countries, North Korea contacts with, 224, 226, 227

Third World movement, 211

38th parallel, 8, 17, 18, 35–36, 41, 42, 43; CPVA foothold near, 68; KPA–CPVA forces crossing, 53, 54, 55; U.S.-U.N. forces pushing past, 14

Three-Year Plan (DPRK, 1954–1956), 80, 83, 129

Tiananmen Square, 122; incident, 233, 238; Kim Il-sung and Deng Xiaoping in, 221

Tibet, 27, 28, 33; uprising in, 135

Tito, Josip B., 85, 106, 140, 224, 253n33

Tŏkch'ŏn, 45, 144

Tsedenbal, Yumjaagiin, 145

Tudda, Chris, 196

Tumen River, 161, 162, 190, 191

Tumen-Namyang port, 19

U-2 spy plane, 139

ultra-leftists, 192

UN. See United Nations

UN General Assembly (UNGA), 207, 211, 212; Eleventh Session of, 105; Twenty-Eighth Session of, 215; Twenty-Seventh Session, 210; Twenty-Sixth Plenary Session of, 206

UNC. See United Nations Command

UNCURK. See United Nations Commission for the Unification and Rehabilitation of Korea

United Front Work Department, 24, 25, 26

United Nations (UN), 7; China diplomatic champions for North Korea at UN, 211; forces pushing past 38th parallel, 14; Inch'ŏn, UN forces in, 40; military means to force troops from Korean Peninsula, 59; most destructive phase of bombing by, 68; North Korea as possible member of, 273n125; PRC role in, 204; South Korea status at, 212; UN Security Council, 192; withdrawal from Korea of, 118–19

United Nations Command (UNC), 215; dissolution of, 216, 219, 220

United Nations Commission for the Unification and Rehabilitation of Korea (UNCURK), 203, 205, 207, 209–10, 217; dissolution of, 216; supervision of reunification by, 209

United States (U.S.), 2, 218, 230; anti-U.S. imperialist struggle, 164; attempt to disband Commission of Neutral Countries, 113; bombing by, 41, 60, 68; common enemy of China and North Korea, 4; entry into Korean War, 35; escalation of Korean War, 38; forces pushing past 38th parallel, 14; Inch'ŏn, U.S. forces

United States (U.S.) (*cont.*)
in, 40; internal conflicts among
capitalist class of, 57; Kissinger on
U.S. objectives on Korean Peninsula,
205; Korean Peninsula, U.S. troops
leaving, 30; Mao and, 5; North
Korea's failed efforts to establish
direct contacts with, 213; ongoing
bombing by, 41; operational control
of ROK forces by, 216; possible
withdrawal of army, 57–58; PRC
policy of confrontation with, 198;
silence on Shanghai Communiqué,
208; U-2 spy plane invading Soviet
airspace, 139; Vietnam, direct U.S.
military involvement in, 217;
withdrawal from South Korea, 118,
204
Ussuri River, 198

Vietnam, 11, 25, 26, 117, 228, 233; direct
U.S. military involvement in, 217;
Kim Il-sung trip to, 117; North
Vietnam, 81, 173, 174, 175, 176, 197,
201, 202, 204, 206; North
Vietnamese Air Force, 177; Soviet
aid, 177; U.S. imperialism in, 175;
war, 222
Voroshilov, K. E., 24

Waldheim, Kurt J., 212
Wang Peng, 187, 189
Wang Yi, 314*n*55
War of Resistance Against Japan, 16, 53,
189, 241
Warsaw channel, 200
women in agricultural DPRK
workforce, 134
Woodrow Wilson International Center
for Scholars, 7
Workers' Newspaper. *See Rodong sinmun*

World Communist and Workers' Parties
Conference, 112, 182, 193
World Federation of Trade Unions, 137;
Asian Liaison Bureau of, 26
World Health Organization, 214, 226
World War II, 3, 4, 16, 37, 144, 241;
decolonization after, 17
Wu Lengxi, 134
Wu Xueqian, 235

Xiao Hua, 19
Xie Pusheng, 145
Xinhua News Agency, 116, 180, 236
Xu Xiangqian, 198

Yalu River, 42, 52, 75, 96, 101, 129, 161
Yan'an, 17, 18, 20, 37
Yan'an faction, 6, 9, 16, 77, 88, 164,
265*n*1; cadres of, 37, 53, 78, 94,
278*n*53; Chinese troops and, 43;
CPVA contacts with, 75; Eighth
Route Army and, 53; fleeing to
China, 98, 121; purges of, 76,
88, 121
Yanbian, 18, 156, 162, 184, 191
Yanbian Korean Autonomous
Prefecture, 291*n*134
Yang Il-p'yŏng, 121
Yang Kuisong, 31
Yang Shangkun, 233
Yang Yong, 112
Yang Zhaoquan, 2
Yao Wenyuan, 180, 181
Ye Jianying, 198
Ye Jizhuang, 150
Ye Lin, 61, 62
Yi Chong-sŏk, 3
Yi Chu-yŏn, 41, 81, 127, 141, 150, 170,
186
Yi Hŭi-sang, 121, 123
Yi Khi-sang, 121

STUDIES OF THE WEATHERHEAD EAST ASIAN INSTITUTE, COLUMBIA UNIVERSITY

Selected Titles

(Complete list at: http://www.columbia.edu/weai.columbia.edu/publications/studies -weai/)

The Invention of Madness: State, Society, and the Insane in Modern China, by Emily Baum. University of Chicago Press, 2018.

Idly Scribbling Rhymers: Poetry, Print, and Community in Nineteenth-Century Japan, by Robert Tuck. Columbia University Press, 2018.

Forging the Golden Urn: The Qing Empire and the Politics of Reincarnation in Tibet, by Max Oidtmann. Columbia University Press, 2018.

The Battle for Fortune: State-Led Development, Personhood, and Power among Tibetans in China, by Charlene Makley. Cornell University Press, 2018.

Aesthetic Life: Beauty and Art in Modern Japan, by Miya Mizuta Lippit. Harvard University Asia Center, 2018.

China's War on Smuggling: Law, Economic Life, and the Making of the Modern State, 1842–1965, by Philip Thai. Columbia University Press, 2018.

Where the Party Rules: The Rank and File of China's Authoritarian State, by Daniel Koss. Cambridge University Press, 2018.

Resurrecting Nagasaki: Reconstruction and the Formation of Atomic Narratives, by Chad Diehl. Cornell University Press, 2018.

China's Philological Turn: Scholars, Textualism, and the Dao in the Eighteenth Century, by Ori Sela. Columbia University Press, 2018.

Making Time: Astronomical Time Measurement in Tokugawa Japan, by Yulia Frumer. University of Chicago Press, 2018.

Mobilizing Without the Masses: Control and Contention in China, by Diana Fu. Cambridge University Press, 2018.

Post-Fascist Japan: Political Culture in Kamakura after the Second World War, by Laura Hein. Bloomsbury, 2018.

China's Conservative Revolution: The Quest for a New Order, 1927–1949, by Brian Tsui. Cambridge University Press, 2018.

Promiscuous Media: Film and Visual Culture in Imperial Japan, 1926–1945, by Hikari Hori. Cornell University Press, 2018.

The End of Japanese Cinema: Industrial Genres, National Times, and Media Ecologies, by Alexander Zahlten. Duke University Press, 2017.

The Chinese Typewriter: A History, by Thomas S. Mullaney. The MIT Press, 2017.

Forgotten Disease: Illnesses Transformed in Chinese Medicine, by Hilary A. Smith. Stanford University Press, 2017.

Borrowing Together: Microfinance and Cultivating Social Ties, by Becky Yang Hsu. Cambridge University Press, 2017.

Food of Sinful Demons: Meat, Vegetarianism, and the Limits of Buddhism in Tibet, by Geoffrey Barstow. Columbia University Press, 2017.

Youth for Nation: Culture and Protest in Cold War South Korea, by Charles R. Kim. University of Hawaii Press, 2017.

Socialist Cosmopolitanism: The Chinese Literary Universe, 1945–1965, by Nicolai Volland. Columbia University Press, 2017.

Yokohama and the Silk Trade: How Eastern Japan Became the Primary Economic Region of Japan, 1843–1893, by Yasuhiro Makimura. Lexington Books, 2017.

The Social Life of Inkstones: Artisans and Scholars in Early Qing China, by Dorothy Ko. University of Washington Press, 2017.

Darwin, Dharma, and the Divine: Evolutionary Theory and Religion in Modern Japan, by G. Clinton Godart. University of Hawaii Press, 2017.

Dictators and Their Secret Police: Coercive Institutions and State Violence, by Sheena Chestnut Greitens. Cambridge University Press, 2016.

The Cultural Revolution on Trial: Mao and the Gang of Four, by Alexander C. Cook. Cambridge University Press, 2016.

Inheritance of Loss: China, Japan, and the Political Economy of Redemption After Empire, by Yukiko Koga. University of Chicago Press, 2016.

Homecomings: The Belated Return of Japan's Lost Soldiers, by Yoshikuni Igarashi. Columbia University Press, 2016.

Samurai to Soldier: Remaking Military Service in Nineteenth-Century Japan, by D. Colin Jaundrill. Cornell University Press, 2016.

The Red Guard Generation and Political Activism in China, by Guobin Yang. Columbia University Press, 2016.

Accidental Activists: Victim Movements and Government Accountability in Japan and South Korea, by Celeste L. Arrington. Cornell University Press, 2016.

Ming China and Vietnam: Negotiating Borders in Early Modern Asia, by Kathlene Baldanza. Cambridge University Press, 2016.

Ethnic Conflict and Protest in Tibet and Xinjiang: Unrest in China's West, coedited by Ben Hillman and Gray Tuttle. Columbia University Press, 2016.

One Hundred Million Philosophers: Science of Thought and the Culture of Democracy in Postwar Japan, by Adam Bronson. University of Hawaii Press, 2016.

Conflict and Commerce in Maritime East Asia: The Zheng Family and the Shaping of the Modern World, c. 1620–1720, by Xing Hang. Cambridge University Press, 2016.

Chinese Law in Imperial Eyes: Sovereignty, Justice, and Transcultural Politics, by Li Chen. Columbia University Press, 2016.

Imperial Genus: The Formation and Limits of the Human in Modern Korea and Japan, by Travis Workman. University of California Press, 2015.

Yasukuni Shrine: History, Memory, and Japan's Unending Postwar, by Akiko Takenaka. University of Hawaii Press, 2015.

The Age of Irreverence: A New History of Laughter in China, by Christopher Rea. University of California Press, 2015.

The Knowledge of Nature and the Nature of Knowledge in Early Modern Japan, by Federico Marcon. University of Chicago Press, 2015.

The Fascist Effect: Japan and Italy, 1915–1952, by Reto Hofmann. Cornell University Press, 2015.

Empires of Coal: Fueling China's Entry into the Modern World Order, 1860–1920, by Shellen Xiao Wu. Stanford University Press, 2015.

Milton Keynes UK
Ingram Content Group UK Ltd.
UKHW031309061024
449308UK00004B/78